Campion

FAITH AND ETHICS

The Theology of H. Richard Niebuhr

D1133578

hᴀʀᴘᴇʀ 🔥 ᴛᴏʀᴄʜʙᴏᴏᴋꜱ

*A reference-list of Harper Torchbooks, classified
by subjects, is printed at the end of this volume.*

FAITH AND ETHICS

The Theology of H. Richard Niebuhr

PAUL RAMSEY, *Editor*

Waldo Beach	Julian Hartt	Raymond P. Morris
Hans W. Frei	Robert S. Michaelsen	Liston Pope
James Gustafson	Carl Michalson	George Schrader

HARPER TORCHBOOKS
The Cloister Library
HARPER & ROW, PUBLISHERS
NEW YORK

CONTRIBUTORS

WALDO BEACH, *Professor of Christian Ethics and Director of Graduate Studies in Religion, Duke University; Editor* (with H. Richard Neibuhr), Christian Ethics: Sources of the Living Tradition (*Ronald Press*, 1955); *Author,* Conscience on Campus (*Association Press*, 1958).

HANS W. FREI, *Associate Professor of Religious Studies, Yale University.*

JAMES M. GUSTAFSON, *Professor of Christian Ethics, and Chairman of the Department of Religious Studies, Yale University; co-author, with H. Richard Niebuhr and D. D. Williams, of* The Advancement of Theological Education (*Harper*, 1957); *author of* Treasure in Earthen Vessels: The Church As A Human Community (*Harper*, 1961); "Introduction," *to* H. Richard Niebuhr, The Responsible Self (*Harper and Row*, 1963).

JULIAN HARTT, *Noah Porter Professor of Philosophical Theology and Director of Graduate Studies in the Department of Religious Studies, Yale University; author* (with J. A. C. Auer), Humanism and Theism (*Antioch Press*, 1951); *author,* Towards a Theology of Evangelism (*Abingdon-Cokesbury*, 1955) *and* The Lost Image of Man (*LSU Press*, 1963).

ROBERT S. MICHAELSEN, *Professor of Religion and Director of the School of Religion, State University of Iowa; author of* "The Protestant Ministry in America, 1850 to the Present" *in the* Ministry in Historical Perspectives (*ed. H. Richard Niebuhr and D. D. Williams, Harper*, 1956) *and* The Scholarly Study of Religion in College and University (*New Haven, Conn.: The Society for Religion in Higher Education*, 1964).

CARL MICHALSON, *Andrew V. Stout Professor of Systematic Theology, Drew University; Editor,* Christianity and the Existentialists (*Scribner's* 1956), *and author,* The Rationality of Faith (*Scribner's*, 1963).

RAYMOND P. MORRIS, *Librarian, Yale Divinity School.*

LISTON POPE, *Gilbert L. Stark Professor of Social Ethics in Yale University Divinity School; Dean of that School from 1949 to 1962; author of* Millhands and Preachers (*Yale University Press*, 1942), *and* The Kingdom Beyond Caste (*Friendship Press*, 1957).

PAUL RAMSEY, *Harrington Spear Paine Professor of Religion, Princeton University; Editor* (with a critical introduction) *of Jonathan Edwards'* Freedom of the Will (*Yale University Press*, 1957), *author,* Basic Christian Ethics (*Scribner's*, 1950), Christian Ethics and the Sit-In (*Association Press*, 1961), War and the Christian Conscience (*Duke University Press*, 1961), *and* Nine Modern Moralists (*Prentice-Hall*, 1962).

GEORGE SCHRADER, *Professor of Philosophy and Chairman of the Department of Philosophy, Yale University; Master of Branford College, Yale; member of the Editorial Board of Kant-Studien; author of numerous scholarly articles in the major philosophical journals.*

HELMUT RICHARD NIEBUHR, Sterling Professor of Theology and Christian Ethics, Yale University, was born at Wright City, Missouri, in 1894. He graduated from Elmhurst College in 1912 and later from the Eden Theological Seminary in 1915. He took an M.A. degree from Washington University in 1917. He continued his education, receiving a B.D. degree from Yale Divinity School and a year later, in 1924, a Ph.D. at Yale. Eden Theological Seminary and Chicago University conferred upon him the D.D. degree in 1954, and in 1956 he received a Litt.D. from Franklin and Marshall and a D.D. from Wesleyan University.

H. Richard Niebuhr was ordained a minister of the Evangelical and Reformed Church in 1916 and he held a pastorate at St. Louis, 1916-18. Later he was a professor at Eden Theological Seminary from 1919-22 and again from 1927-31. He served as President of Elmhurst College from 1924-27. In 1937 he became a member of the faculty of the Yale Divinity School. At Yale University he was from 1953 the Director of Graduate Studies in Religion, and Fellow of Silliman College. He directed the Study of Theological Education in the United States and Canada in 1954-55.

Mr. Niebuhr was married to Florence Mittendorff Niebuhr, and they have two children, Cynthia and Richard. He died on July 5, 1962.

CONTENTS

viii   *Contents*

FOREWORD

... True and substantial wisdom consists of three parts: the knowledge of God, of companions, and of the self; and . . . these three are so intimately related that they cannot be separated. . . . Theology has as its complex object God in his relations to the self with its companions, and the self with its companions in their relations to God. . . . The proper study of mankind is God and man-before-God in their interrelation. . . . The complex object of theological study always has the three aspects of God in relation to man, of men in relation to God, and of men-before-God in relation to each other.

This quotation from H. Richard Niebuhr's *The Purpose of the Church and its Ministry*[1] explains the choice of title for a volume of essays in Professor Niebuhr's honor, in which the contributors attempt to treat, constructively and critically, the main elements of his thought, writing and teaching. "Faith" and "ethics" are ever inseparable modes of reflection and action.

The quotation also provides a succinct summary of the community of continuing "trialogue" in which men come to know what they are doing in the world, and do and are what they know. Unlike the usual *Festschrift*, therefore, this volume was *not* planned to coincide with some seventieth birthday or some moment of retirement; but instead is presented at a time when Niebuhr's present literary achievements already demand critical appraisal and while he has still greater contributions to make to our common understanding. It itself is a contribution, in return, to an ongoing discussion, a humble attempt to stand within dialogue, a modest moment in the intellectual love of God and of our neighbors under God, and a joint grappling with "the Mystery behind the mystery of human existence in the fatefulness of its self-hood, of being this man among these men, in this time of all time, in the thus and so-ness of the strange actual world."[2] Coming from the press this book enters a larger universe of discourse, and seeks to engage others—both students of theology and thoughtful men and women within the Christian churches, and philosophers and anyone else who have reason and human passion in exercise—in precisely this same dialogue which constitutes their very mode of being in the world.

For Niebuhr, the enterprise of theology (or, to say the same thing, theological ethics) has always been "a pure science, disinterested as all pure science is disinterested, seeking to put aside all extraneous, private or personal interests while it concentrates on its objects for their own sake only."[3] Moreover, insofar as men, from their various perspectives in conversa-

---

[1] New York: Harper & Brothers, pp. 113, 125.
[2] *Ibid.*, p. 36.
[3] *Ibid.*, p. 109.

ix

tion with one another, come to know the "complex object of theology"—
insofar as they receive God's love of self and neighbor and the neighbor's
love of God and self, and increase the self's love of God and neighbor—
there ensues "a constant process of a radically monotheistic reformation"[4]
in both thought and life. "Radical monotheism," its nature and consequence, is but another way of stating the theme with which we have constantly been engaged in writing these chapters. This, indeed, might have
been chosen as the title of the volume, if it were not a bit too impressive,
and for the fact that Niebuhr may want to reserve it for his own later use.

The first chapter, by Liston Pope, gives a personal appreciation of Niebuhr as a person and as teacher, a tribute to his impact on generations of
students at Yale Divinity School and an appraisal of his contribution to
theological education both at Yale and in the nation at large. Then follow
two chapters by Hans W. Frei which, taken together, analyze the theology
of Richard Niebuhr against its background in idealism, historicism and
existentialism, and the thought of Kant, Schleiermacher, Troeltsch and
Royce, and in its relation to Barth, Bultmann and Tillich. They may well
be the most accurate and penetrating review of nineteenth- and twentieth-
century religious thought yet written in English. In any case, from a careful
study of these chapters, the reader will discover how true it is to say (in the
words of *The Christian Century*[5] concerning Niebuhr's recent study of
theological education) that, in the entirety of his writings, H. Richard
Niebuhr has "made a brand new whole of the best parts of contemporary
theological thinking." Niebuhr's own forms of theological statement have
not prevented his doing what he as a person inclines to do: rejoice in the
otherness of the other viewpoint. Hence, for example, he was from the
beginning appreciative of the theological revolution effected by Karl Barth,
and understood what that troublesome genius was at work accomplishing,
more than most thinkers in this country have yet acknowledged; and this
without ceasing to be constantly conversant with the nineteenth century
and with the particular history of religion in America.

In part two, entitled "Problems of Faith and Ethics," the chapters become more varied, both in subject matter and in the degree of direct concern with Niebuhr's writings. Some continue the exposition, by quotation,
explanation and analysis, of Niebuhr's position; and in the course of these
chapters the broad range of his concerns is set forth as fully as space allows.
Other chapters are independent theological essays written, it is believed,
in the spirit of Niebuhr. Of these, and other critical departures throughout
even the mainly expository chapters, it may be said that each of the authors
has been true "in his fashion" to the teacher who is before us.

The first four chapters of the second part supply an extended consideration of ethics as such; and they are for this reason placed here together in
the middle of the volume. James Gustafson writes of the perspectives upon
social ethics and policy-making which may be drawn from Niebuhr's
thought, or from allowing the full range of Christian conviction about
God to penetrate into actual decisions. Radical monotheism, we are told,
means that God presides over deliberations about wages as much as over

[4] *Ibid.*, p. 46.
[5] LXXIV, 17 (April 24, 1957), p. 509.

deliberations about the natural law. My own chapter deals with the theme of "transformation" or "conversion" in ethics; and, after an explanation of this motif itself, relates it to the problem of relativism or objectivism in moral theory. George Schrader undertakes the philosophical task of analyzing the nature and meaning of valuation in Niebuhr's thought, and its relation to various types of philosophical ethics and theories of value, past and present. This chapter makes evident that Niebuhr and contemporary theology are not bound within the "circle of faith," but aim to serve, with philosophy generally, in the fuller illumination of man's total being in the world. Waldo Beach provides a theological analysis of beliefs and practices in race relations in America. This chapter will be of interest to anyone who seeks a religious analysis of this problem that probes more deeply than well-meaning clichés and brings to bear upon the issue more features of the Christian understanding of God and man than simply the ideal of brotherhood. Or—and this is the special value of its inclusion within this volume—the reader will find here a "case study" in special application of the ethics of response to Creation, to Judgment and Governance, and to Redemption, which has been so large a part of Niebuhr's teaching of Christian ethics, never written out fully by him, and without which understanding of his thought would be incomplete.

Then follow two specifically theological chapters. The one by Julian Hartt on the situation of the believer raises the question of the nature and ontological reality of the believing individual and his God in the faith-relationship, and suggests the need for ontology beyond that provided by relational-theology. Carl Michalson writes movingly on the hiddenness of God and his real presence hidden in Christ, and forcefully makes the point that this aspect of what Niebuhr calls "the deity of God" needs emphasis especially in the present-day, as it is always essential to men who want to take care in all their worship and striving that it is God whom they adore. The volume concludes with the chapter by Robert S. Michaelsen on the kingdom of God, which brings into focus Niebuhr's outstanding interpretations, in several of his volumes and a number of articles, of the history of Christianity in America; and this leads to a consideration of the present task of the church, if we are to prove faithful to the God we know in dialogue not only with our contemporaries about his meaning for us but in "internal history" with our fathers before us.

We shall be satisfied, by the publication of this volume, to have provided a footnote to accompany H. Richard Niebuhr's projected future publications, and his previous books, several of which are now being reissued, as they find their way to an increasing number of readers both here and abroad; and doubly gratified if anything that is said or explained in this provisional report contributes to that future final accounting of the thought of Richard Niebuhr among his peers in the world-wide community of theological scholars.

The contributors to this volume owe a special debt of gratitude to Daniel D. Williams, Professor of Systematic Theology at Union Theological Seminary in New York, who twice read the manuscript and gave us extensive criticism and suggestions. These, and his constant encouragement and confidence in the importance of the project, were of great assistance to us; while any failure to attain his and our own standard in the matter rests with us.

The authors are also indebted for criticism and suggestions to a wider group of Professor Niebuhr's former students, whose aid has been solicited in the preparation of this volume. These include Claude Welch of Yale Divinity School; Albert Outler, Perkins School of Theology, S.M.U.; Clyde Holbrook, Chairman of the Department of Religion, Oberlin College; Paul Pfuetze, Department of Philosophy, University of Georgia; Roger Hazelton, Chairman, Department of Religion, Pomona College; Howard Hopkins, Dean of School of Humanities, Stetson University; Robert Cushman, School of Religion, Duke University; Kenneth Underwood, Wesleyan University; Joseph Matthews, Education Director, Christian Life Community, Austin Texas; William Kirkland, McCormick Theological Seminary, Chicago; Art McGill, Wesleyan University; and Van A. Harvey, Department of Religion, Princeton University.

The portrait of Richard Niebuhr used as frontispiece is by Alfred Eisenstaedt—Courtesy LIFE Magazine.

As one among the list of contributors, my name is set down as editor mainly for the convenience of librarians.

PAUL RAMSEY

Princeton University
Princeton, New Jersey
July, 1957

Note to the Torchbook Edition:

Raymond P. Morris, Librarian, Yale Divinity School, and Miss Jane E. McFarland, Reference Librarian, Yale Divinity School, have revised and extended the Bibliography of H. Richard Niebuhr's Writings for this edition.

PART ONE

H. RICHARD NIEBUHR AS CHRISTIAN THEOLOGIAN

1.

H. RICHARD NIEBUHR:

A PERSONAL APPRECIATION

LISTON POPE

FOR nearly twenty-five years I have had the privilege of close association with Richard Niebuhr, first as his student and for the last two decades as his colleague. This relationship has been one of the most stimulating and satisfying experiences conceivable for any academic man —or any human being. Yet I find it extremely difficult to write about him as teacher and person.

For one thing, this is not an obituary or eulogy. Niebuhr told me recently that he hopes and believes that his best years of work are still ahead of him, and he has projected several books that may reveal his thought in new dimensions. Presumably he will read these words, and it is certain that he will do so with unfeigned embarrassment, despite my efforts to be scrupulously honest and sincere. For one of Richard Niebuhr's most profound traits is his selflessness, his reticence to talk— and one surmises, even to think—very much about himself. Ideas are another matter: in that realm he is capable of defending his views as readily as changing them. But the arcanum of his personal life has been seldom exposed even to his closest friends.

This does not mean that Niebuhr is either cool or unapproachable in his relations with students and associates. To the contrary, he is probably the most sought-after man on the faculty of Yale Divinity School. About *your* problems—personal, vocational, or intellectual—he is warmly sympathetic and profoundly understanding, and he will spend hours in the effort to help a student decide whether he should enter the ministry, or to comfort a German father whose son has been seriously injured far from home. One of the secrets of Niebuhr's great influence and power as a teacher is the fact that he conveys to the minds of students, certainly

3

without deliberate intent and in a rather inexplicable way, the assurance that he would be available if they needed him for counsel or friendship. They respect and value this assurance, and generally save their most difficult problems for him.

As might be expected in a first-rate dialectician, Niebuhr is a curious blend of simplicity and complexity as a person. He can enjoy the antics of a dog or the silly story of a colleague, and he can wince at puns or even perpetuate them himself. But those who know him fairly well, including his students, are aware that his life has been etched in profound interior struggle, and that this life itself is a result of a simultaneous dependence on God and the rebellion of a human being against Him. This delicate balance of personal traits comes through in his teaching: his students expect everything that Niebuhr says to be profound, and sometimes they are a little shocked when he meets some ethical question with a simple moralism or confession of compromise, born of his rigorous honesty. A moment later he may be involved in thought so exalted and intricate that only the very ablest students have the faintest notion as to what he is talking about.

Most of Niebuhr's lectures might be described as vignettes or etchings rather than as full portraits. While he is a master at analysis of alternative theological theories or ethical positions, his classroom becomes most electric when he is developing a particular line of thought, and especially when he is presenting his own views—always without ostentation. He has continued through the years to devote much time in preparation for each lecture, even if he has addressed himself to that same problem a score of times in previous courses. His lectures therefore always have a quality of freshness and new relevance instead of treating a perennial problem in the dusty context or frayed metaphors of last year—or of a decade ago.

Further, despite the careful preparation, Niebuhr always speaks in class—and in the pulpit—as if he were working out the problem rather extemporaneously. This is probably true a good part of the time; certainly he has never been hemmed in by his notes. In contrast to one of his greatest teachers, there is very little movement of paper as he proceeds. This generation of teachers can have seen few better examples of man thinking as he teaches. Yet there is remarkable lucidity and coherence as his thought develops, and even the occasional lacunae are instructive to the class, as they indicate that a juncture of various intellectual roads has now been reached and that a careful choice must be made. There is nearly always a sense of suspense and then of climax in each lecture.

It is bad form to speak in print of a colleague's personal mannerisms, but in Niebuhr's case they are important. His gestures and general atmosphere of a man in travail are less eccentric than those of his distinguished brother but they are hardly less fascinating. (As boys they played different musical instruments in the Niebuhr family ensemble: Richard

played the flute and Reinhold played the trombone. It may be that the muscular patterns involved had nothing to do with later developments.) Niebuhr groans—but always when there is something to groan about, some hard path to take. He growls—and the intellectual object of his growl had better be wary. He achieves all sorts of extraordinary patterns in the relation of his head and his hands. More important, he can look wise as a serpent or beatific as a saint, though never harmless as a dove. All of this goes on without thespian intent: Richard Niebuhr on the podium is not acting but feeling—man feeling as he is thinking. The combination means that there is never a dull moment, though humor is seldom introduced deliberately.

Niebuhr expects a great deal of his students, just as he requires much of himself. He has prepared extensive bibliographies for most courses, and they are kept clean and up-to-date. His students are expected to read widely and thoughtfully, and to read the best material available for the successive sections of the course—and Niebuhr knows what is the best. Examinations are stiff, and term papers must show good quality. On occasion Niebuhr can be quite a martinet about having assignments come in on time; his theory of human nature holds that discipline is necessary to overcome the lassitude of the flesh and mind. By the same token, in many years he still reads the mountain of papers himself, though this means a diversion of several weeks from other work of his own. He would not regard it as a diversion, but as part of the discipline a teacher should accept if he possibly can. The size of his own classes—for many years they have been among the largest in the Divinity School, though none of them is specifically required—has meant that he had to seek assistance occasionally, but he has never forsaken the principle that a teacher ought to evaluate the work of his students personally. In doing so the teacher can also get a notion of the continuing effectiveness of his own work.

Niebuhr has been less successful than some of his colleagues in provoking discussion in his lecture courses, partly because of the magnificence of the lectures themselves. One student wrote recently to a classmate: "Nobody asks questions in Niebuhr's *Christian Ethics*. That would be like shouting in a cathedral." When I reported this comment to Niebuhr, he characteristically replied: "That is not the way theology ought to be taught." I have the feeling that he is becoming rather impatient with the new fashion of conservatism among many theological students, a fashion that sanctions authority and orthodoxy in the theological and social realm rather than challenges it. Niebuhr was a rebel against the too-simple theology of the Social Gospel, but he probably feels more at home with the concerns of that theology, and certainly with its spirit, than he does with many of the latter-day trends in theology and ethics. He is a little disappointed that students do not choose to challenge him more often. In his graduate seminars, of course, student participation is the chief method of procedure and discussion has a better chance.

It is the purpose of this introductory essay to discuss Richard Niebuhr as teacher and person, rather than to deal with his ideas and scholarly achievements. But the power of his teaching derives very largely from the originality and richness of his views. It is not possible at this time to explore adequately the sources of his originality, if it will ever be. It is clear that he came out of cultural and intellectual traditions—especially the work of Ernst Troeltsch—that afforded alternatives to the "liberal theology" and acclimatized Christianity of a generation ago. Since most of his students do not know of these alternatives, his teaching has immense impact, opening up perspectives of which they had never dreamed. Before coming to Yale to sit at Richard Niebuhr's feet, I had been taught in seminary that the theology of Augustine was essentially that of a modern liberal theologian. Niebuhr's interpretation of Augustine was astounding! It sent me to *The City of God* itself (which the seminary discussion had not done) if only to ascertain whether my new mentor knew his business (there was less reverence in seminaries in those days). In the light of Niebuhr's perspectives the significance of Augustine's thought took on entirely new dimensions. (If I may digress, I am still pretty much a "liberal" in theological outlook, and I regret that Augustine was not. But I would join with Niebuhr in being skeptical of such labels in the first place, including the term "neo-orthodox").

From whatever sources, Niebuhr's thought has profoundly affected and altered the theological thought of his time, and especially that of his students. It seems less extraordinary to students today than it did a quarter century ago, partly because many of them have been taught in college by Niebuhr's own students and have read his books, along with those of Tillich, Reinhold Niebuhr, Kierkegaard, and other dialectical and existentialist thinkers, before they ever come to seminary. One could almost wish for them the excitement of exposure to a theological revolution when it was new. But they still find it exciting enough.

It should not be suggested that Richard Niebuhr's thought has not changed during the last thirty years. As already indicated, he rethinks his positions continually. In a rare moment of self-disclosure he once surmised that if one had to choose a type of dwelling for habitation by the intellect, he would be compelled to choose a tent. Further, the richness of his thought and teaching comes not only from an imaginative mind but also from the mounting dividends of a life of scholarship. His views are continually being affected by what he reads, now in this direction, now in that. His shift from primary interest in sociological approaches to paramount concern for theological understanding represented a profound reorientation. He may startle his students and readers by another metamorphosis, perhaps starting another intellectual revolution. But he is no faddist; if his views change, they do so because his scholarship and further thought have led in a new direction. Whatever his own views may be, his scholarship has produced books that will stand on their own merits for generations.

Any portrait of Richard Niebuhr as teacher would be incomplete if it did not take into account his influence as theological educator beyond the confines of the particular schools in which he has taught. His books have been used in theological schools around the world, and in other types of schools, both undergraduate and graduate, as well. During his years at Yale he has exercised primary supervision of the the Ph.D. programs of approximately seventy-five students, most of whom have subsequently gone into teaching, about twenty of them at the seminary level. Since 1953 he has been Director of Graduate Studies in Religion at Yale, and has in that capacity had varying degrees of relationship to the sixty Ph.D's who have gone out since that time, most of them into teaching. By no means have all gone out to teach Niebuhr's views; he himself would deplore any such result. But nearly all have been profoundly affected by his thought, and ideas received originally from him have gone out into the world beyond all calculation.

More recently (1954-1956) Niebuhr has directed a survey of Protestant theological education in America, and the eventual impact of the findings is certain to very great. Though the resultant volumes[1] reflect important contributions by his collaborators, the survey as a whole bears Niebuhr's imprint at nearly every point. Rather than being primarily a collection of facts or set of recommendations (though both are included), the report shows a man thinking—thinking hard and deeply about the purpose of the church, the nature of the ministry, and the sort of theological education that is therefore to be desired. He is not thinking merely in an armchair, but in the context of life, the life of the Church, of ministers, of the seminaries, and of his own. Here again Niebuhr's gift for integrity, for making theology and life reckon with each other and come to reconciliation so far as may be, is the distinguishing feature of his work.

As a result of their study Niebuhr and his colleagues came to the conclusion that the greatest institutional need of the seminaries is that of better teachers. Niebuhr's own career is a shining example of dedication to that end. On occasion he has been tempted to leave the

[1] H. Richard Niebuhr, Daniel Day Williams, and James M. Gustafson, *The Purpose of The Church and Its Ministry*. New York: Harper & Brothers, 1956.
H. Richard Niebuhr and Daniel Day Williams. *The Ministry in Historical Perspectives*. New York: Harper & Brothers, 1956.
H. Richard Niebuhr, Daniel Day Williams, and James M. Gustafson. *The Advancement of Theological Education*. New York: Harper & Brothers, 1957.

teacher's role for other positions of influence and renown. His early per-
formances as president of Elmhurst College and dean of Eden Theological Seminary demonstrated his abilities as an educational administra-
tor, and he could easily have returned to the prestige popularly associated with being the head of an outstanding institution. He has chosen
to remain a teacher, to the greater profit of theology and of theological
education and, if one may presume on the divine majesty, to the greater
glory of God.

2.

NIEBUHR'S THEOLOGICAL
BACKGROUND

HANS W. FREI

1. NIEBUHR'S THEOLOGICAL CONCERNS

TO SET the thought of any contemporary, let alone that of a mind as subtle and complex as H. Richard Niebuhr's, into the proper historical and contemporary "context" is a delicate task. The delineation of the "context" often successfully obscures and even obliterates the very contribution of the individual thinker which it is supposed to illumine. Hence our endeavor to gain historical and contemporary perspective must remain tentative and incomplete. Some of the essential lines may be sketched in, but they cannot be fully drawn. We shall, after this introductory section, be largely concerned in the present chapter with the background in nineteenth- and twentieth-century theology which is necessary for the understanding of Niebuhr. It is in the next chapter that we will deal in detail with Niebuhr's own thought, his theological method, and his doctrine of God and Christology, in the light of the background to be presented in this chapter.

In a picture of Niebuhr's thought painted with the broadest of strokes, one would immediately be struck by his unique, effortless interweaving of theological and sociological analyses. This fusion represents not so much a deliberate synthesis or method as a completely natural *modus operandi* of the mind. It is therefore somewhat artificial to single out the theological background of Niebuhr's thought as though it were something in itself and even in isolation from other factors.[1] Nevertheless, an attempt at purely theological analysis of Niebuhr's

---

[1] On the fitness and mutual internality of relation between Niebuhr's theological analysis and his reflections on the ways of human beings in their communities, see chap. IV by James Gustafson.

thought is commended by the fact that certain theological themes, e.g., that of radically consistent monotheism, recur persistently in Niebuhr's writings and are at the very center of his concern as teacher and writer.

Again drawing with very broad strokes, we may say that Niebuhr's theological thought has received its major impetus from two traditions. The first of these is the particular Protestant tradition which is so closely tied to the growth of the Church after the Reformation in Switzerland, Scotland, England, and later in the United States. The most prominent characteristic of this movement is its concern to find and to be the obedient community of the sovereign God and of his Christ. Life in the Church is a life of faith, of repentance and self-denial in the light of God's purity. This life involves criticism of the Church, but it is criticism from within, similar to that of the prophets who identified their own destiny with that of the people whom they called upon to return to their ancient allegiance to God.

This particular Protestant tradition challenges not only the Church. It seeks to claim the world, not for itself but for Jesus Christ, to extend obedience to God through all temporal cultural communities, and to express in all things gratitude for the whole creation and for redemption from sin. The ethic of this tradition is one of responsibility before and response to the God of grace and covenant. The most important among many antecedents of such an ethic is seventeenth-century Puritanism.

The second tradition which has instructed Niebuhr profoundly is what we shall later describe as the academic tradition in nineteenth-century Protestant theology. For our present purpose this movement—largely a product of the German universities—is the more important of the two. We may identify it in preliminary fashion by three dominant characteristics. First, it was profoundly influenced by the philosophies of Kant and post-Kantian Romanticism and metaphysical Idealism. Secondly, the thinkers to be identified with this academic tradition have customarily had to wrestle with the meaning of historical thought for theological assertions. Thirdly, in theology proper, the thinkers who constitute this tradition have been for the most part deeply indebted to Schleiermacher and his new approach to the mutually involved problems of theological method and revelation in Jesus Christ. Even the reaction against this nineteenth-century tradition in our own century is to a large extent still to be identified with it. For Karl Barth and his early friends and followers in the 1920's wrestled with the very issues and currents of thought which we have just mentioned, even though they expressed them in a manner different from and often opposed to that of their nineteenth-century predecessors.

The first tradition noted in Niebuhr's thought, that of Puritan background, despite its practical, moral emphasis, is not at too great a distance from the nineteenth-century academic tradition. The dominant stream in Protestant theology since the end of the First World War has tended to bring them together. The impact of theological thinking since the third decade of our century,[2] especially that of the so-called "crisis theology," has been to emphasize the transcendence and freedom of God over all categories of reflection. In the interpretation both of the moral life and of the life of the mind, theologians have tried to recapture the Reformation's insistence upon the sovereign Lordship of the living God, especially the sovereignty of his grace. Also, the Existentialist's endeavor to unite ethical and theoretical categories has helped greatly toward a renewed understanding that the life of theoretical and practical reason, of reflection and external activity is all one, and that in every dimension we are saved not by works (or by taking thought) but by grace.

Niebuhr's thought has received sustained challenge and impetus from both traditions, as well as from the crisis theology which arose both as inheritor to and rebel against the academic tradition of the nineteenth century. Indeed, crisis theology has helped him bridge the gap between the tradition of the nineteenth century and that of Puritan background.[3] Not that these traditions have wholly determined the pattern of Niebuhr's theological development, but between them they have provided the initial setting for the problems with which he has dealt persistently in his writings.

In addition there are many individuals and groups whose writings have provided Niebuhr with conversations by which his mind has been shaped through the years. Foremost among these has been Ernst Troeltsch, far too great a figure to be identified simply with the liberal traditions in culture and theology within which he arose. There was also Frank C. Porter, whose self-conscious liberalism had deep roots in a biblical theology that has influenced Niebuhr. Men as diverse as Martin Buber, Josiah Royce, F. D. Maurice, S. Kierkegaard, and D. C. Macintosh have made permanent contributions to his reflections. There are many others. Yet, if one seeks to identify the dominant traditions which, as such, have influenced Niebuhr's theological outlook, the two that have been mentioned keep coming to mind.

[2] The book which, it is generally agreed, was most important in pointing in a new direction was the second edition of Karl Barth's *Der Roemerbrief*, published in 1922.

[3] It is the challenge of the latter tradition that one may see in *The Kingdom of God in America*, (Chicago: Willett, Clark & Co., 1937) and in Niebuhr's contribution to the symposium *The Church Against the World*. Cf. H. R. Niebuhr, "The Idea of Covenant and American Democracy," *Church History*, XXIII (June, 1954), 126-35.

To a large extent these two movements have come to focus in America and Germany, respectively, although it would of course be quite wrong to think of them as national traditions. But the presence of these tendencies in the two countries makes Niebuhr an effective interpreter to each other of two diverse cultural strains.[4] Indeed, Niebuhr's theological writing is a genuinely intercultural activity to a degree rarely achieved in present-day Protestant theology. For this reason his "ecumenical" contribution may be of great importance. But in our time an "ecumenical" conversation among Christians requires more than profound mediation between differing cultural traditions. It requires that such mediation take place within the context of that unifying community which is the Church.

When we raise the question, to what audience is Niebuhr addressing himself, and how does he consider himself to be related to his hearers and readers, our first answer has to be this: Niebuhr's books and essays always seem first and foremost intended to contribute toward the ongoing process of critical self-appraisal which is the task of church theology. He speaks as a churchman to other churchmen. Apparently, he addresses himself most of all to the cultured believer who wants the tools for a critique of his faith's reasoning and is concerned with consistent monotheism in his faith and action.[5]

[4] Thus, *The Kingdom of God in America* has been translated into German as *Der Gedanke des Gottesreichs im Amerikanischen Christentum* (New York: Church World Service, 1948). On the other hand, for Niebuhr's interpretations of German theological thinking see, *inter alia*, his introduction to his translation of Paul Tillich's *The Religious Situation* (New York: Henry Holt and Company, 1931); "Can German and American Christians Understand Each Other?" in *Christian Century*, XLVII (1930), 914-16; "Religious Realism in the Twentieth Century," in *Religious Realism*, ed. D. C. Macintosh (New York: The Macmillan Company, 1931), pp. 413-28; *The Meaning of Revelation* (New York: The Macmillan Company, 1941), pp. 23-33; *Christ and Culture* (New York: Harper & Brothers, 1951), pp. 91-100.

[5] One may see Niebuhr's increasing realization of the "churchly" nature of all proper theological thinking reflected in a host of articles written in the last eight years. The symposium *The Church Against the World*, by H. R. Niebuhr, Wilhelm Pauck, F. P. Miller (Chicago and New York: Willett, Clark and Company, 1935), was but an earnest of a future concern. Increasingly, Niebuhr has spoken of the catholic nature of Christian thinking as it takes place in a catholic communion. Cf. "The Disorder of Man in the Church of God," in *Man's Disorder and God's Design*, vol. I; *The Universal Church in God's Design* (New York: Harper & Brothers, 1949), pp. 78-88; "The Responsibility of the Church for Society," in *The Gospel, The Church and the World*, ed. K. S. Latourette (New York, London: Harper & Brothers, 1946), pp. 111-33; "The Hidden Church and the Churches in Sight," in *Religion in Life*, XV (1945-46), 106-17; "The Norm of the Church," in *Journal of Religious Thought*, IV (1946-47), 5-15; "The Doctrine of the Trinity and the Unity of the Church," in *Theology Today*, III (1946), 371-84; "The Gift of the Catholic Vision," in *Theology Today*, IV (1948), 507-21; and of course *Christ and Culture*. In a sense the increasingly "churchly" nature of his theology is the difference between Niebuhr's early work, *The Social Sources of Denominationalism* (New York: Henry Holt and Company, 1929), and his subsequent major writings.

But it is impossible to address persons in the Church as if they were not also members of other communities. Some of these communities are more and others less concrete; some are more and others less generalized.[6] Niebuhr addresses himself to the churchmen also as directly related to God in national, social and intellectual communities. Theology of culture, in Niebuhr's view, is the duty of every Christian thinker. But a theology of culture invariably speaks not only to Christians but to cultured half-believers and active "disbelievers." At least indirectly Niebuhr speaks to such listeners also. But in doing so, Niebuhr cannot speak from a common, neutral ground between them and himself that is presumably divorced from any and every faith in some sort of god. Characteristically, he refuses to acknowledge the absence of faith in any man, no matter to what cultural and intellectual communities he may belong. Perhaps his appeal to the cultured disbeliever or half-believer is all the greater and more basic because it is confessional and thus theologically indirect rather than directly apologetical. For Niebuhr can, as a result, interpret culture irenically and freely rather than with the defensiveness and mechanically foreordained results of interpretation that usually mark the Christian apologist's treatment of "secular" culture.

The problem of the Christian writer, for Niebuhr, is to address his readers so far as possible solely from the point of view of faith in that God who alone is absolute and is the enemy of all the gods we worship with our naturally polytheistic tendencies, including even (or rather especially) our religious tendencies. In sum, in seeking to relate himself confessionally rather than apologetically to his readers, the Christian writer points continuously to the ultimate object from the particular place which he, the writer, occupies in time and culture, hoping thereby to direct the reader's attention away from the writer and to the same object.[7]

This way of putting the matter of Christian communication might seem to imply that the object of faith and thought is static and passive. This, of course, is not the case. The very act of communicating in speech or writing presupposes a common context provided prior to and during the act, a common context into which we step. It may be more accurate to say that communication presupposes and takes place in the presence of and with reference to an act by a transcendent subject

---

This characteristic persists in his present work; and yet one must add that Niebuhr, always determinedly and radically monotheistic, is profoundly suspicious of the tendency of the Church to substitute adoration of itself for the worship of God. Cf. his recent strictures against this idolatrous tendency in his book, *The Purpose of the Church and Its Ministry* (New York: Harper & Brothers, 1956), pp. 41ff.

[6] Cf. "The Ego-Alter Dialectic and the Conscience," *Journal of Philosophy*, XLII (June 21, 1945), 352-59.

[7] Cf. *The Meaning of Revelation*, chaps. 1 and 2.

that brings us together.[8] Though communication is a personal process occurring between and among selves, it nevertheless takes place through the prevenient grace of God. In regard to this process of interpersonal communication, Niebuhr's thought has been deeply influenced by the "I-Thou" doctrine of Martin Buber,[9] and to some extent also by the writings of Josiah Royce and George H. Mead.

Niebuhr's religious and historical relativism accentuates the problem of communication for him. Neither individual nor community, it seems to him, can escape the uniqueness and the constrictions put upon them by their limited places in history. Again, neither individual nor community can escape the particular and unique relation within which they are bound to God, from which they must make those final decisions that take them beyond argument, and from within which they testify to others. Such uniqueness of relationship makes for complexity in interpersonal communication.

In the first place, preoccupation with such problems in religious communication—which are largely personal in nature—gives a definite bent to Niebuhr's theological interests and dispositions. It reinforces the epistemological or methodological (rather than ontological) tendency of his thinking. Pressed to its ultimate conclusion, this epistemological interest of Niebuhr's may present a theological parallel to present-day philosophical developments. It could result in a critique of theological language for the purpose of illuminating the obscure process of theological communication. There are signs that Niebuhr would find this task congenial.[10] One may venture to predict that it would involve him in work on one doctrine to which he has paid almost no attention in his writings thus far: the doctrine of the Holy Spirit.

Secondly, his profound concern with the problem of interpersonal communication has determined in part Niebuhr's cultural interests and therefore the audience which he has sought to address. He is in contact more generally with the social sciences and the humanities than with the natural sciences. He is more interested in the interpretation of history, in the ideologies of literature and of the social studies, than in cosmology.[11] One may say that he converses more directly with social

[8] Cf. *ibid.*, pp. 22, 39 ff.; for Niebuhr's application to theological education of this understanding of interpersonal communication in the presence of a common, transcendent subject, see *The Purpose of the Church and Its Ministry*, pp. 117 ff.

[9] Cf. *ibid.*, pp. 46, 164.

[10] Cf. one of Niebuhr's later essays in which he examines the problem involved in drawing analogies between two different contexts of meaning by means of a common term: "The Idea of the Covenant and American Democracy," *Church History*, XXIII (June, 1954), 126-35.

[11] Cf. Julian Hartt, "Theology of Culture," *Review of Metaphysics*, VI (1953), 501 ff. Niebuhr has suggested that our understanding of nature within the compass of revelation must proceed through categories whose form is historical: *The Meaning of Revelation*, pp. vii, 48 f.

scientists, with those concerned with history as a unique (and not merely "natural") process, with poets, painters, anthropologists and psychologists rather than with mathematicians, physicists and biologists. His philosophical interests lie more in ethics, philosophy of history and epistemology than in logic, cosmology, ontology or metaphysics. Yet his theology avoids the Ritschlian's anticosmological bias.[12]

Thirdly, Niebuhr's interest in the problem of communication has found expression in the Existentialism that permeates his thought[13] and has helped to bring together the two traditions that have challenged him. Existence is a personal relation of the self in the community of other selves. Its categories of reflection and decision are ethical rather than natural. Communication is thought and decision "within" rather than "about" existence. It is indirect, bound to the particularity of the standpoints of selves that cannot be merged in a common realm. Also, communication expresses the fact that reflection, decision and act are bound together in a relationship that defies precise description because it is never smooth or symmetrical. Paradoxically, the contact of reflection and decision runs the risk of their mutual annihilation. Really to reflect "within existence" and really to communicate means to accept this dilemma and to rely upon the significance of a similar dilemma and movement in the "other." The big question is therefore not *what* or even to whom I communicate but *how* I am related to the other in communication. In the same vein Kierkegaard (as Niebuhr notes) is concerned with the "subjectivity," the "how" rather than the "what" of Christian faith—with the task of becoming what one is as a Christian.[14] If the content of communication is not actually in this doctrine reduced to its form, one may at least say that it is assimilated to its form.

In Niebuhr's case, the Existentialist's awareness of his own and the reader's or hearer's "situation" has resulted in some of his most important contributions to theology and theological education.[15] In the

---

[12] Cf. *Christ and Culture*, p. 101. Niebuhr condemns Ritschlianism and "culture theology" generally for their exclusion of "nature" from the purview of redemption. "Culture theology" is wrong in seeing man's fundamental situation to be conflict with nature.

[13] Cf. below, pp. 18 f., 78 f.

[14] *Christ and Culture*, p. 242; cf. H. R. Niebuhr, "Sören Kierkegaard," in Carl Michalson, ed., *Christianity and the Existentialists* (New York: Charles Scribner's Sons, 1956), pp. 23-42, esp., pp. 40 ff.; cf. below, p. 78 f.

[15] Cf., for instance, Niebuhr's understanding of the relation between theory and practice, reflection and action, in the work of theological education. He insists that they are related neither pragmatically nor intellectualistically. "Reflection precedes, accompanies and follows action but this does not make it the source or end of action. Reflection as a necessary ingredient in all activity is neither prior nor subservient to other motions of the soul. Serving these, it is served by them in the service of God and neighbor or of the self." *The Purpose of the Church and Its Ministry*, p. 128.

manner of the Existentialist Niebuhr has related himself to his hearers
and readers in such a way as to convey in conceptual terms the actual
movement of his concrete thought as it reflects, in turn, the decisions,
acts and interpretations by which one responds to the prior action of
God in creation, judgment and adoption. This is of course far more
than an author's customary indication that he is proceeding from one
idea to the next. *The Meaning of Revelation,* for example, keeps the
reader in an actual intellectual motion reduplicating that of the book,
and just as real. Such a double process is existential communication.
In achieving this quality, Niebuhr's writings, together with Barth's
earlier works, seem to me to be unique in modern theology. In Niebuhr's case, we see among other things an achievement based on years
of participation in the educational process. As a result he is, for many
in the "interim" or "post-liberal" theological generation, now coming
of age, *the* theological instructor. He has literally given them a new
vocabulary, a new conceptual mold, rather than merely a system of
his own. He has taught them to think in new terms; yet, while communicating to them the quality of novelty and a new conviction, he has
also directed them to a renewed connection with the past.

The mode of communication and instruction of which we have
spoken demands close conformity of content and literary form, of conception and expression. Niebuhr's writings always combine a sense of
drama and reflection. They combine theoretical and practical thought,
ethics and methodology (or epistemology). Their power lies in the
synthesis of all these and other elements in the actual writing. Form
and content are so completely appropriate to one another that the
style is assimilated to and shaped by the thought. Consequently, one
may say of Niebuhr's work that, unlike the writing of many other
theologians, it is best understood in the actual reading rather than in a
commentator's description and interpretation.

2. THE ACADEMIC TRADITION IN NINETEENTH-CENTURY PROTESTANT THEOLOGY

Of the two traditions that have furnished major challenge to Niebuhr, the academic tradition of the nineteenth century is the more
important for understanding his theoretical construction in theology.
We must now turn, first, to the identification of its main characteristics
and then to a systematic consideration of some of its more specialized
features which have particular bearing on Niebuhr's work. If we say
that this tradition comes to us largely from the German universities,
we are not trying to nationalize theology; we are simply stating one of
those strange cultural facts that crop up now and then in intellectual
history, when certain ideas find temporary shelter more easily in one
group or culture than in another which at first glance might have
seemed more congenial to them. In any case, to the extent that theology

after 1800 had to confront issues presented by new currents in philosophy and by the method of historical investigation, it was largely German influence that set the patterns of development.

a. Philosophical Influences on Theology: Idealism
and Existentialism

On the philosophical side, the developing academic tradition was influenced profoundly by German Idealism, with its claim of the priority of spirit over matter. Those who followed in the footsteps of Kant tended to reduce the metaphysical implications of the spirit-matter distinction to the status of problems within the question of knowledge. Furthermore, they frequently inherited the rigid distinction Kant had drawn between the theoretical and practical functions and areas of competence of human reason. Kant's assertion of this dichotomy, in turn, had a great deal to do with the development of one of the cardinal principles in nineteenth-century theology, i.e., the sharp distinction between religion and those theological affirmations that arise from it. Schleiermacher in Germany and Coleridge in England, the latter in more direct dependence upon Kant than Schleiermacher, were fountainheads in developing this new understanding.

There can be no doubt that Kant's thought was the crucial dividing point for Protestant theology in the nineteenth century. His thought was like a prism, through which reflection upon all previous philosophy had to pass. All paths led to Kant. But precisely because we must stress the significance of Kant later in this essay,[16] it is well for us to remember a qualification at this point: the influence on theology of post-Kantian Romanticism and metaphysical Idealism in philosophy was equally pervasive, though in subtler form. Metaphysical Idealism, especially in the form that Hegel gave it, insinuated itself into the thought and conceptualization even of those who rejected the "system" as such. It was as a thought-form that metaphysical Idealism actually made a tremendous contribution both to those who followed and to many who disavowed it. If Kant presented theologians with a whole new configuration of problems and thus forced them to make a new beginning in their thought about the nature of theological knowledge and evidence, Hegel frequently provided them with their conception of the movement of human thought and especially with an understanding of the unique historical process. One tends to forget this profound influence of metaphysical Idealism as a result of the violent reaction against Hegel in the second half of the nineteenth century on the part of thinkers who, despite themselves, were still deeply indebted to the great philosopher.

If the tradition of Kant tended to reduce metaphysical problems to

---

[16] In connection with systematic problems in theology; cf. below, p. 32 f.

the status of epistemology, precisely the opposite was true of meta-physical Idealism, in which epistemology was but the concrete exempli-fication of logic, and logic, in turn, was a description of the movement both of the mind and of the universe at large. The search of the meta-physical Idealists—and to a large extent of Romantics such as Schleier-macher, so intimately related to Idealism—was for the objective and immanent ground of unity underlying the cleavage entailed in the subject-object distinction in thought, a search for the unity underlying mind (or idea) and thing. To think of God meant to the Idealists going beyond the symbolism of religion into the immediacy and conceptual unity of concrete exemplification and logical possibility. God is the *prius* of both, equally far from and near to both. He is not *a* being, and therefore not an extramental "other" confronting particularity or pos-sibility. Rather, he is their ground, logically and ontologically prior to their separation. In God alone is the confluence of the truth and reality underlying individual things and persons. The transcendence of God is therefore not that of a sublime person separated from limited creatures. It is rather the transcendence of the ground of being and possibility which, as such, can never be the "object" of particular knowledge but is the basis of all knowledge and the ground of all objective reality. He is eternally subject and as such alone the spiritual bond in which all finite contradictions are transcended and resolved.

Connected with metaphysical Idealism, as response is related to challenge, is the movement called Existentialism. Since we shall refer to it throughout these two chapters, we must indicate how we intend to use the term. Rather than to its latter-day manifestations, we refer, in the context of this description of the academic theological tradition, to the work and *Problematik* of Kierkegaard and to the astonishing "discussion" with him that began to take place in theology after the close of the First World War, first on the European continent and then in Britain and America.

It was one of Kierkegaard's passionate aims to be a thinker and not simply an exemplification of thought and thought currents. Hence, we find him pointing, throughout his writing, pseudonymous and other-wise, to the author as one wholly responsible for this thinking, and in similar fashion to that individual who may be the author's proper and understanding reader. Not that Kierkegaard saw the individual as a center or focus of universal obligation and ethical freedom, as Kant and Fichte had maintained. Rather, responsibility and decision—empty possibilities in "pure thought"—were seen as brought with the indi-vidual across the awful, mysterious and infinite gulf from nothingness to concrete existence. Thus, the individual is nothing but his decision in freedom and responsibility (a situation most men do their best to escape), and freedom and responsibility, in turn, have no significant status outside of that which they obtain, not first in the individual's thought but in the crucial moment when he decides that he is a responsible, free person. It is in this ethical moment that the individual, in the concrete unity of his existence and critical reflection upon it in his thought, becomes what he is—an individual, perchance a Christian individual or individual Christian. And this moment is one that is given over to endless and crucial repetition.

To set forth the unity of the thinker as a concrete individual was, we have said, one of Kierkegaard's chief purposes. It always appeared to him that the broken lines of thought were quite inadequate to the task of doing this directly. We are therefore in a sense pointing away from the *individual* Sören Kierkegaard when we go on to say that he was, among many other things, also a philosopher and a philosophical theologian. To say this is really to present a problem about him rather than a clue to understanding him. The problem is that of understanding the manner in which the philosopher in his philosophical thought can be at one with the thinker who in *all* his thought wants to be consistently the same, existing individual. In the present context we can only aggravate that problem, for it must be said at once that as a philosophical theologian and a philosopher Kierkegaard cannot be understood apart from academic theology and philosophy in Germany; especially must he be seen in his dependence upon Hegel. The form, indeed the content, of Hegelian logic and metaphysics supplied the tools for their very antithesis, as Kierkegaard worked it out. Truth for him is strictly subjectivity, in contrast, first, to an objectivity like that of mechanical orthodoxy which eliminates subjectivity, but more particularly in contrast to that Hegelian objectivity which claims to include subjectivity and to reconcile it with objectivity. The dialectic of the responsible thinker is confronted by an infinite contradiction between infinity and subjective existence which makes mediation or reconciliation, grasping the two in one concrete thought, impossible. The responsible thinker is also confronted by the fact that spirit, the most acute expression of what it is to be human, is approached only in the paradoxical movement of dialectic, i.e., in a movement in which thesis and antithesis rest on a prior, yet conceptually unattainable (indeed contradictory) unity. Thus, the clash of thesis and antithesis is actually a clash within the individual himself. Thereby the individual loses all "immediacy" of relation both to himself (and the world about him) and to the Infinite as it intrudes into his subjectivity. The acceptance of this loss of immediacy, this abiding in mediacy in the presence of God, neighbor and self is the prerequisite to the task of faith, i.e., of being a witness to the truth, of being a Christian, just as the same acceptance is the clue to the meaning of truth as subjectivity.

For Hegel the process of the mediation of all things in the comprehensiveness of ultimate unity, at once given and yet to be realized conceptually, was absolutely basic. In opposing Hegel, Kierkegaard also rejected the temper of the times, in which the acceptance of some sort of internal, direct or immediate relation between God, the self and the universe was a prevailing dogma. Words are inadequate to describe in brief compass the immense subtlety and variousness of the endeavors men were making to provide principles of mediation which would be true to this presence to each other of the individual, the universe and God. Their common quest was perhaps the one most crucial element that post-Kantian Romanticism and Idealism contributed directly to theology. Yet even in breaking with the temper of the times, Kierkegaard had to utilize, in so far as he assumed the philosopher's role, the very concepts he opposed. The Idealists had formulated his philosophical problem, especially that of immediacy and the principle of mediation. So tenacious and pervasive was this idealistic outlook that the very *Problematik* of those who opposed it was formed on its basis. Kierkegaard's response is only one example, perhaps the most radical, of an experience common to him, to Feuerbach and to Marx. Only in the second half of the nineteenth century, when questions of the meaning of historical events and historical thought became more and more acute for Protestant theologians, did the formulation of basic problems shift away from idealistic grounds; and even then strong unacknowledged currents of Hegelian influence may be detected among some of the most positivistic of historical theologians, in their concepts of historical causation, and of the manifestation of particular historical "essences," etc.[17]

Some of the common ground occupied by Idealists and Existentialists may best be exhibited in certain common, negative consequences which both imply for theology. Both deny that God is known to the finite mind as "*a* being" among others, even as the greatest and most sublime. They deny that the primary mode of noetic relation between the core of created being and the inner nature of God is that of analogy. Finally, they deny that the concepts of the human mind are positively related to realities which are given and other than thought, and of which there is one "most real." Instead, the Idealist and the Existentialist, each in his own way, affirm the "transcendence" of God. Both of these philosophical points of view were tortured attempts to deal with the basic philosophical problem of modernity, the isolation of idea or concept from sense perception, on the one hand, and from "real" objects, on the other. Preoccupation with epistemology and the degeneration of the metaphysics of realism have gone hand in hand. In this connection there is one crucial problem for theology which

17 Cf. below, p. 25 f.

the philosophical Idealist appears to approach with far greater basic consistency than does the theological Existentialist. To the Idealist the understanding of God cannot be that of a person, except as a purely symbolic expression of a higher conceptual unity of spirit or reason. The Existentialist, on the other hand, tends to deny with equal firmness the conceptual validity or attainability of God's personhood and yet to affirm precisely the same tenet on the grounds of a wholly different and unique confrontation by God in "faith." It seems that thereby he pushes to the forc once again the very preoccupation of nineteenth-century theology against which he set out to protest: the isolated concern with the nature of theological method or epistemology based on the claim to a unique religious knowledge or awareness different from the process by which we know other realities.

b. *The Impact of Historical Consciousness and Method on Theology*

We must now mention a second characteristic of the nineteenth-century tradition in theology: the influence upon it of the rise of historical thought and historiography. If one defined the historical method merely as the tracing of interconnected links in an unbroken development through time, the method could be applied to any subject matter—geology and biology as well as the study of society. While this was one way of understanding it, historians of the ninetcenth century never lost sight of the conviction that history, properly so called, is a particular mode of the self-understanding of man. Their ambition was to establish not only the propriety of the claim that history is a "science," but that it is a science of a particular kind—of the reflection of man upon mankind in its social intercourse as it develops uninterruptedly through time in its myriad forms of polity, culture and thought. History came to be regarded as *Geisteswissenschaft* par excellence. The peculiar mode of this reflection was variously interpreted. The Positivist, who saw in history the pure examination of facts ordered by inductive laws closely paralleling those of the physical sciences, was a relatively rare phenomenon among nineteenth-century historians, despite the prominence of a certain second-rate type of thinking that endeavored to demonstrate "scientifically" the thesis of universal progress. Idealists interpreted the historical mode of man's self-understanding as an indirect way of confirming the continuous, infinitely varied self-fulfillment of the human spirit. For the Realist history was rather the patient, literal and particularized tracing through time of the processes by which men and societies of the present have come to be what they are.

But no one questioned the tools, the method of implementing historical consciousness. The method was the presuppositionless scrutiny of original as well as supplementary sources. Whatever evidence was secured must be interpreted critically by means of judgments that estimate the probable nature of the happenings under investigation. Such judgments include the abstraction, relating and comparing of events and hypotheses in the giant network of their interactions. Particularly exciting in the historians' ferment of thought was the tension between two pairs of opposites in historical work. The first of these pairs was the tension between particularism and universalism in historical writing. To the particularist, historical understanding is properly the exhaustive description and understanding of individual and unique manifestations. The universalist, on the other hand, feels that the analogies which the historian is bound to draw between historical phenomena will force him beyond so narrow a framework. Even individual events are not seen in their proper perspective unless set forth in their widest interrelation. The implicit assumption of historical understanding, in this view, is that universal history may, indeed must be written, because both historical method and the interconnection of events are universal in scope.

The second tension of opposites in historical thought lay between the demand for factuality and objectivity of description, strict and unadorned, whether the subject matter be political, cultural, diplomatic or any other history, and the equally compelling demand for the exercise of historical imagination, empathy and critical interpretation precisely in the description of the historical data. The feeling arose that the good historian is neither he who simply ranges descriptive sequences after each other nor he who molds them according to a preconceived *Weltanschauung*. Rather, the good historian unites internally, by imaginative re-creation, the "facts" and the "feel" of the situation. The connection in his narrative and interpretation is supplied by a necessity intrinsic to the data, not artificially furnished to them, and yet he must view the data and their connections from his own singular vantage point in time and culture. History must therefore be rewritten in every generation, just as human nature is always a discovery and not a constant factor that may be estimated once for all regardless of its march through time. Nevertheless, the historian is indebted to the work of his predecessors whose critical opinions and approaches furnish him with indispensable guides, even if they are in the form of antitheses, to his own understanding. To the first-rate historian, therefore, historiography, the study of the writing of history and the history of this study, is an indispensable portion of his craft, just as he exemplifies in his own understanding the tension between both sets of opposite factors that we have mentioned. So each epoch or historical "unit" becomes to the historian its own exemplification of the mysterious, chronically indefinite and yet objectively apprehensible story in which men and culture form both the substance and the ultimate questions. The great historians and critical reflectors upon history—men such as Leopold von Ranke, Jacob Burckhardt, Wilhelm Dilthey, and Ernst Troeltsch—brought these tensions as well as their understanding of historiography into fruitful interaction in brilliant fashion. Modern historians have honored Thucydides for a similar accomplishment in antiquity. Vapid and superficial contemporary critics of this profounder understanding, influenced by psychological, sociological and theological views, have lumped together these complex developments and have announced triumphantly that nineteenth-century historians thought they could be "purely objective" and leave aside all problems of presupposition and interpretation in the study of history. Nothing could be further from the truth, except for the small group of positivists and progress thinkers. For all others, historical objectivity was a far richer and more imaginative matter. To focus on "what actually took place" (in the words of Ranke's famous dictum) meant to them the investment of the past at once with all the precision and empathy and imagination that the historian and his craft could supply.

Obviously the consequences of the rise of historical consciousness and method were startling for biblical studies.[18] But theology and the writing of the history of Christianity were also seriously affected. For because of the nature of his craft it was unlikely that the historian could regard the church as an isolated phenomenon in history whose development was propelled forward simply by the momentum of its founder's impact or by the logic implicit in the new currents he had introduced into history. Inevitably the person of Jesus was drawn into the context of the search for an historical explanation of Christian origins. But there was a difference. Customarily, historians were unable to withstand the temptation to explain the origins of the Church in terms of its environment, i.e., in eclectic descriptions of the commingling of Oriental mysteries, Hellenistic Judaism, Jewish apocalypticism, etc. This was, as we shall see, especially the path of the *religionsgeschichtliche Schule*. The most important "lives" of Jesus, however, were almost without exception "internal" rather than "external." They sought to understand his life and teachings, particularly his teaching on the Kingdom of God and the relation of his own mission and personal significance to that Kingdom, by reconstructing the unifying consciousness that lay back of and was expressed in his acts and teaching. Yet even though most writers rejected environmental approaches to Jesus and brought them into play instead in explaining the transition from Jesus to the early Church, the uniqueness of Jesus was for them nevertheless (it goes almost without

---

[18] For a useful summary and discussion of the present status of the problem of the Bible and historical criticism, see E. Dinkler, "Bibelautorität und Bibelkritik" in *Zeitschrift für Theologie und Kirche* (47 Jahrgang, 1950), pp. 70-93.

saying) purely historical in nature. No supernatural—or, better, super-historical—appeal was permissible in the reconstruction of events and ideas, although perhaps the consciousness of the Lord which lay behind the historical manifestations might be of a uniqueness which historical reflection could not encompass. But to the extent that historical understanding could grasp Jesus of Nazareth, the miracle of the man was confined to him as an historical event, precisely in the manner in which every historical event has its own uniqueness, a fact that is particularly evident if the leading character in the event is cast in heroic mold. Miracle is simply identical with event in history, and historical understanding goes on to insist that the uniqueness of an event is in no way a denial of its explicability through its interconnections with other events.

But if the spiritual uniqueness of events and their universal interconnection is the only form in which divine providence is manifested in history, it becomes very difficult to maintain that a unique divine revelation focused in Jesus Christ is the clue to all other history. Belief in transhistorical and in this sense unique or miraculous revelation is a puzzle to historical thought, which has an axiomatic assumption that historical data have a uniformity of their own—albeit not that of natural phenomena—which makes history a unified study capable of a uniform method. It is out of this general *Problematik* that such particular questions as the relation of faith to history have arisen in our day. Is it possible to combine faith in an ultimate Creator and Redeemer, who limits space and time beyond all conceiving, with the "open-ended" and in its way uniform historical universe which historical consciousness presents to us?

Moreover, Christian historians in particular have been forced to ask themselves if it is possible to make clear distinctions between original facts, their original interpretations and the historian's interpretation. This question has arisen with regard to the Virgin Birth, the resurrection stories and the *kerygma* of the early Church. Perhaps the interweaving of event and interpretation is always greatest when the original event is "idea" rather than simply "external" event, i.e., when the history under consideration is intellectual history. Certainly, this interweaving is an important factor in contemporary historical and theological understanding of the New Testament. Historical understanding here seems to be subject to something parallel to the Heisenberg principle of indeterminacy. The historian's place in time and culture influences his measurement not merely—and not so much—of original data and sources, but of the original ideational complexes and their movements. Thus, historical theologians have begun to learn that the history of ideas cannot simply be a matter of direct comparison of ideas through their common co-ordination in a realm of ideas equally and directly accessible to all minds regardless of their positions in time. The task of understanding the history of certain concepts such as "God" and "Salvation" seems to be the much more difficult one of relating images to each other by means of certain "master images." These "master images" seem to have a double focus: on the one hand, they point to an indirect or broken representation of the common ground between original and later interpretations (including the historian's own interpretation), a ground that does not as such appear; on the other hand, they point to the concrete particularity of experience in time and tradition, in which every particular interpretation of ideas is necessarily clothed. In the course of the study of the history of religions, particularly in the theological interpretation of Christian history, such reflections have led to the consideration of myth and religious symbols. Are myths such "master images"? If so, are they now to be dispensed with as relics of a prescientific past, whose truth content may be transliterated into other, more up-to-date categories of reflection? Or are they so concrete and yet pregnant with transcendent meaning that the modern interpreter loses the significance of the history they represent, indeed of all genuine historicity, unless he appropriates the mythical image with its content for his own normative understanding?

Finally, in exploring the meeting between historical consciousness and religious study, we must point to certain profound influences of Hegelianism. The conviction began to grow during the second third of the nineteenth century—often with the exaggerated fervor of a new discovery—that the truth as well as the only real understanding of ideas and of the cultural, social configurations in which they were embodied lay in their development (this was in the days just before Germans were made aware by Darwin that nature, too, had a "history"). It was understood—largely thanks to Hegel—that this development followed laws of its own, laws that have no "existence" and no independent status of their own, outside their history; they simply constitute the inner meaning of the process of development. The Hegelian D. F. Strauss was ready to assert that purely historical study of Christian dogma would of itself dissolve the belief in the objective truth and fixity of that dogma. It was likewise an Hegelian, F. C. Baur, who opposed him in the profound conviction that it was precisely the purely historical study of Christian origins and dogmatic development—rather than the affirmation of dogma as an objectively true fact of miraculous nature—which constituted the only intellectual justification of the Christian faith.[19] In their mutually contradictory views both nevertheless agreed on the historical nature of truth.

[19] Cf. Emanuel Hirsch, *Geschichte der neuern evangelischen Theologie im Zusammenhang mit den allgemeinen Bewegungen des europaeischen Denkens* (C. Bertelsmann Verlag, Guetersloh), vol. V (1954), pp. 512-27.

Granted—as it generally was—that the inner essence of any historical manifestation.lay in its development, this very concept turned out to be a confusing notion when severed from the superstructure of idealistic metaphysics. One might indeed conceive of history as a stage in the return of Idea or Spirit to itself through the process of its own self-objectification. But historians by and large rejected this ontology not only (and not so much) on philosophical grounds, but because they were convinced—perhaps to an unfair degree—that it forced history into a dogmatically rational and unempirical strait jacket. Yet even so, historians (often quite unconsciously) adopted the notion of an essence unbroken in its development as the subject immanent in all particular history—a direct inheritance from Hegelian ontology. It is this essence, whatever it may be in a particular case, that *has* a history without being a ready-made notion or ideal fact outside of its history. But without Hegelian ontology, "historical essence" was capable of more than one interpretation.

First of all, it could be argued that the essence of an historical manifestation is present in unique and normative fashion in the original form of that manifestation, and that other and later forms may be judged to represent accretions, distortions or returns to the original. This was the spirit of Adolf Harnack's famous and controversial *Das Wesen des Christentums*, written at the end of the nineteenth century. The norm and essence of Christianity lay, for Harnack, simply and logically enough in the original teachings of Jesus Christ. And even in this original one had to distinguish between its essence and the temporal, cultural forms in which it was embedded.

The most formidable book in opposition to Harnack's thesis was Alfred Loisy's *L'Évangile et L'Église*, a defense of tradition and its development which earned its distinguished author the malediction of the Vatican. For Loisy insisted that the essence of Christianity is pre-formed neither historically, as it was seen by Harnack, nor dogmatically, as it was seen by the dominant ultramontane party in the Church of Rome. He put forth the thesis that the historical development of Christianity is neither a story largely external to the original essence nor simply a mechanical exemplification of an essence already finished, except in details, at the outset. The essence of Christianity lies rather in an unbroken unity of development within the manifestation of a long succession of external forms. None of these manifestations, not even the teaching of the founder, is normative in isolation from the others. Here, then, is a second understanding of the meaning of historical essence.

Yet between these two opposite points of view there is a certain note of agreement which serves to distinguish both from still a third estimate of historical essence. If the essence and norm of Christianity lie either in some original form or in its development, some estimate must be made of the lines of unity or continuity constituting the essence. It, in turn, must be distinguished from the forms in which it is embedded. In other words, a certain distinction between the "essence" and its shape at any given time seems inevitable. Harnack freely acknowledged this fact when he indicated the "kernel" of the gospel within the "husk" of its temporal, cultural expression even in the teaching of Jesus Christ. Loisy was more circumspect, yet he seemed to make the same distinction—for example, in his claim that the essence of the faith develops with steady continuity within its temporary dogmatic expressions.[20] Consequently, in such a theory it is very difficult to tell just *what* develops—the essence or the form of expression. Furthermore, the relation or unity between them remains completely unspecified.

It is a long way from Hegel to the historical writers at the turn of the century who were working on Christian origins: men like Harnack, Loisy, Johannes Weiss, and Albert Schweitzer. I do not mean to imply that these men were directly influenced by Hegel. Far from it! Only that the ideas with which they worked were in the intellectual atmosphere all about them. Loisy's notion of development, for example, was influenced by Cardinal Newman's *An Essay on the Development of Christian Doctrine*, a book that shows no trace of direct Hegelian influence. Certainly Newman would have been horrified to know that he perhaps contributed materially to the growth of Catholic Modernism.[21] But it may well be maintained that the philosophical antecedents of the kind of historical thought we have presented point back unvaryingly to Hegel. On the other hand, Hegel, in contrast to men like Harnack and Loisy, had suggested definite relations between essence in history and its external forms of expression, as well as laws for their development. The cunning of reason, he said, utilizes and as it were hides and reveals itself in the empirical forms in which it is immanent. The antithetical and synthetic movements are reason's own, though the concrete unity between form and essence in history is of course realized fully only as the truth of history is seen more inclusively in its transcendence in the Spirit.

The question we are really asking in the present essay is whether the notion of historical essence is workable and significant apart from such metaphysical and dialectical assumptions. Without them, is not either chaos or static reality the fundamental subject in any assertion of an immanent movement for which we cannot stipulate a specific relation

---

[20] *The Gospel and the Church* (English trans.; New York: Charles Scribner's Sons, 1909), pp. 212 ff.

[21] Cf. Alec R. Vidler, *The Modernist Movement in the Roman Church, Its Origins and Outcome* (Cambridge: The University Press, 1934), pp. 53 ff., 92 ff.

between essence and external form? Considerations such as these distinguished a third group of nineteenth-century historians from those represented by Harnack and Loisy, respectively. Writers of the *religionsgeschichtliche Schule* believed that the assumption of a particular essence indwelling a particular history and giving it continuity was an artificiality that represented unrecognized remnants of idealistic metaphysics in historical thinking. One must, they believed, eliminate the distinction between essence and external form and see that the essence of an historical manifestation *is* its development and not something immanent in, yet distinguishable from it. Obviously even this reconception is not enough. One must go on to recognize that the distinction between manifestations that belong "within" and those "outside" specific historical phenomena stands and falls with the notion of particular historical essences. If, for example, we exclude the notion of historical essence from the history of religions, then the uniqueness of Christianity as a specific, unified genus within that history is gone. All one may see is the particular process of particular forms developing within a network of universal interconnections. Christianity becomes one continuing, shifting series of religio-cultural syncretisms in the context of others. It has—to use a term of Austin Farrer's—no "subjective focus," but is related to all the other syncretisms and their individual ingredients on a basis of partial identity and partial difference. The logical outcome of such a position is of course not merely the denial of the historical uniqueness (to say nothing of the "absoluteness") of Christianity, but the denial of any real identity, discernible to historical judgment, between Christianity in its origin and the Western cultural religion of our day which bears the same name. To a lesser but still important degree the same judgment must be made of the intermediate stages of this religion. It is this whole approach which is properly called historical relativism. It is the most common underlying understanding of history formulated by thinkers of the *religionsgeschichtliche Schule*. It may be connected—though it need not always be—with a sort of value judgment which negates all qualitative priorities between the truths and moral ideals of the various world religions, even while admitting their distinctions. The most distinguished representative of this general point of view was Ernst Troeltsch.[22]

The critical views of the *religionsgeschichtliche Schule* haunted many theologians at the turn of the century, particularly the so-called Liberals in Germany, with their Christocentricity and their antimetaphysical bias. Explicitly acknowledged or dimly seen, the outlook of the *religionsgeschichtliche Schule* came to be the most consistent historical point of view with which they thought they would have to come to terms. (At this point quite obviously Harnack was anything but liberal!) Ritschl,

[22] See below, pp. 53-64.

Wilhelm Herrmann and the early Karl Barth in his liberal days are examples of men who seem to have regarded it quite naturally as the proper understanding of history. While they would have to come to terms with it (and they certainly shared its antimetaphysical bias), they would at the same time have to distinguish—and rescue—a particular Christian understanding of history from it, namely, some apprehension of Christocentric revelation in history.

In the endeavor to do this they partially drew upon and partially developed two converging lines of thought. The first of these lines emerged from the conviction which had grown among some historical thinkers in the course of the nineteenth century that history represents primarily neither the events in time that have to be understood nor simply a certain ready-made method (criticism of original sources, reconstruction of events through abstraction, comparison of data, etc.). Rather, history is a thing prior to both, for it is a given complex or relation between events and interpreter from which one may not abstract. It is precisely the relation that is basic to all historical knowledge, yet it is itself in turn understood critically only in two forms or proliferations of reflection. One of these forms is abstractive, objective, and in this sense critical. The other form tends to be normative and valuing, and thus critical in a different manner. One has to be careful to make the distinction, for the form was not the same for all men, nor was the distinction drawn by all with equal sharpness. Some thinkers felt that the closer one came to intellectual history, the more nearly not only source criticism but even critical reconstruction of ideational events became merely preparatory work. Thereafter the historian's work really begins, although it is misleading to put the point chronologically. Rather, all along—but especially after critical reconstruction—another mode of intellectual activity comes into play: the proper *Nachdenken* of and *Einfuehlung* into the thought events being reconstructed, their proper contemplation and re-presentation. Thus, the relation between the original event and the interpreter becomes a personal-spiritual one in which loyalty to and contemplation of the subject is added to abstractive-critical understanding of the subject as an event in a time past outside the observer. And in this process subjectivity and objectivity in the understanding of history become something less than an absolute disjunction.

History, then, was taken to be neither event nor method alone, but an original relation between event and interpretation that underlies two modes of understanding in which history is reflectively grasped: the abstractive and the personal or re-presentative. We may construct the following, very rough rule of thumb: the more nearly idealistic an historian the more nearly he tends to believe history at its center to be intellectual, and thus holds the abstractive and personal types of reflection together as two manifestations of the same basic apprehension or relation. The more nearly an historian leans toward the *religionsgeschichtliche Schule* the more strongly he believes these two types of reflection to be dichotomously related, i.e., in the manner of a complete parallelism rather than interaction.

Most of the German theological Liberals tended to insist sharply on the dichotomy. Thus, Ritschl thought that faith grasps the uniqueness of Christ by an historical value judgment, which as it were draws him out of the uniformity of the series of historical events. In its own way this value judgment is supposed to possess an objectivity and historical character equal to that of abstractive historical judgments with which it neither interferes nor has anything to do. Ernst Troeltsch was undoubtedly right when he called this whole method the "overcoming of history through history." Wilhelm Herrmann disagreed with his master to some extent. It seemed to him that Ritschl had both oversimplified the historical problem of theology and provided too rationalistic a solution for it. Yet Herrmann himself suggested a kind of experiential or immediate apprehension of the "inner life" of Jesus Christ, quite apart from abstractive reflection, as the historical starting point for faith. His position in essence asserted once again the dichotomy between normative or theological-historical and abstractive-historical modes of judgment and reflection.

The first of the two converging lines of which we are speaking was thus the introduction of a distinction between abstractive and personal or valuing understanding in history. By means of a valuing understanding, theologians have sought to point to the nature of a unique revelation in history in the person of Jesus Christ. H. Richard Niebuhr is one of those who in our own time have given painstaking attention precisely to this distinction and its use in theological thought, especially in the consideration of historical revelation. In *The Meaning of Revelation* he represents abstractive, historical thought and valuing, normative historical thought as completely parallel to each other. As modes of apprehension they are quite different in kind. They aid and never contradict one another when properly used, but only valuing, personal or "internal" historical thought is directly appropriated by theological method in the inquiry after revelation. There appears to be in this book no underlying vision of the unity of historical thought from which both types of reflection spring.[23] Perhaps the distinction is so sharp in *The Meaning of Revelation* because Niebuhr here is not reflecting upon concrete historical matters but upon purely methodological questions. When he actually writes history his method seems to be rather different. One notes in *The Kingdom of God in America* the appropriation of sociological insights to theological categories instead of a sharp dichotomy between sociological and theological categories.

[23] Cf. *The Meaning of Revelation*, pp. 59-90.

A similar observation may be made about the concept of the ministry which emerges in the course of *The Purpose of the Church and of Its Ministry*. But above all in *Christ and Culture* Niebuhr's historical method appears to have little to do with the method he has described in *The Meaning of Revelation*. It seems much closer to a conception of history like that of Wilhelm Dilthey, for whom intellectual and cultural history was *Geisteswissenschaft*, whose central task is critical rethinking of and empathy into the subject's thought from the historian's own particular place in culture. In the accomplishment of this task, abstractive and purely "objective" thought is but the handmaid of a more profound and unitive relation between the events and their interpreter. This unitive relation is more directly expressed in the scope of critical yet loyal reflection upon the thought of men in past time than in a sharp dichotomy between scientific-external and normative, personal or valuing viewpoints. The scope of Niebuhr's historical critique and appreciation of individual theologians, particularly in the portraits he has drawn in *Christ and Culture*, is reminiscent of Dilthey's historical understanding much more than of the dualism of the Christocentric Liberals.

The task of the German Liberals was to assert the historical uniqueness and revelatory nature of Jesus Christ without contradicting the views of the *religionsgeschichtliche Schule* and others who asserted the complete uniformity of historical events. In the process of doing this, the first of two converging lines of thought was the introduction of a dichotomy between two types of reflection about history. The other line of thought fitted in with it nicely. For the dichotomy we have discussed echoes another and similar duality in regard to the nature of theological method. In the academic tradition of the nineteenth century, religious knowledge (in contrast to scientific and philosophical understanding) was generally looked upon as being similar to normative, valuing historical knowledge—i.e., as a unique mode of apprehension nontheoretic in nature and thus not theoretically binding. And in further resemblance to normative historical knowledge, religious knowledge was generally thought to involve valuation and probably dependence upon some form of experience. Also, religious awareness like historical knowledge rests upon a prior relationship immanent in the awareness. This relationship is God's self-revelation. With so many parallels between normative historical and religious awareness, it is not surprising that theologians generally tended to see the two as belonging together and directly related. Thus, the awkward problem of relating a present and experienceable revelatory relationship to an event inexorably past lost its harsh contours. History and faith, it was thought, belong together; they are immanent to each other or at least similar in apprehension.

In a sense, then, many theologians believed that the historical problem of Christianity could be treated as one expression of the basic systematic problem confronting nineteenth-century theology, i.e., the mutually involved questions of Christocentric revelation and theological method.

c. The Systematic Problem: Revelation and Religious Knowledge

It is to basic questions in systematic theology that we must now turn. We note immediately the crucial positions first of Kant and critical philosophy and thereafter of Schleiermacher, in challenging the thought of nineteenth-century theologians and their contemporary successors, including H. Richard Niebuhr.

Before the beginning of the nineteenth century, theology had relied, even in its most antiphilosophical bearing, on a philosophical vindication of metaphysical principles. For the most part, Protestant orthodoxy had been undergirded by the rationalism of Leibniz and Wolff. God was thought of as *a* being, immaterial and eternal, but otherwise analogous to individual substances in the natural world in that he contains within himself his own being or individuality. Just as individual beings are related in a purely external manner to other individuals (since nothing can enter into the substantiality of something else), so the relation of God to his creatures is an external and thus indirect relation: he touches them through the agency of other creatures. In knowing God, the finite mind apprehends a being other than the knower, a being that is not thought but being-other-than-thought.

Faith was regarded as an act of trust that focused in the mind's cognition of this external relation. This act, together with the mental cognition and assent involved in it, is a response to God's revelation. Since the mind, tarnished by sin, is incapable of apprehending the objective divine truth, Scripture provides supernatural, objective revelation to the mind of the person to whom faith is simultaneously given. But in principle supernatural revelation corresponds wholly to the external, cognitive relationship of the creatures with God that would obtain in an unblemished natural state of creation.[24]

Hume had already threatened this symmetrical edifice and the similar construct of "natural religion." Kant's denial of metaphysics was, however, the more shocking because it was that of a rationalist and not of a skeptical empiricist. Kant believed, with natural religion and rational orthodoxy, in the positive functions of man's rational capacity. But, unlike those he called dogmatists, he insisted on investigating reason's

[24] For a brilliant and detailed account of this point of view see Emanuel Hirsch, *Geschichte der neuern evangelischen Theologie im Zusammenhang mit den allgemeinen Bewegungen des europaeischen Denkens* (C. Bertelsmann Verlag, Guetersloh, 1951), vol. II.

nature, possibility and limitations. It seemed to him that theoretical reason must apply itself to supersensuous objects in order to complete its quest for rational fulfillment. But such objects are no more than regulative ideas that can never become objects of actual, concrete knowledge. This is the crisis of the metaphysics which had hitherto undergirded theology. Although concepts provide the forms and categories under which perceptual intuition takes place and rises to knowledge, ideas themselves cannot rise through the *sensa* to the apprehension of being, to the intellectual vision of pure reality. There are no objects-as-such that we can reach either by intuition or by abstraction. There are indeed things-in-themselves for Kant (although not for some of his followers), but the conditions of knowledge prevent our having any positive knowledge of these, to say nothing of "reality in its pure state." If, as rational orthodoxy has insisted, the relationship of God and man is external, it cannot be one of rational cognition. On the other hand, God is not known in the realm of phenomena where theoretical reason operates. As a result all positive relation between revelation and faith (as the eighteenth-century traditions had conceived them), on the one hand, and theoretical reason, on the other, is sundered.

In this unhappy situation three alternatives seemed to be open for those hardy souls still desirous of explicating their faith in God in terms positively related to the cultural thought of the day.

First, there were those who assumed that religion is a formal or *a priori* structure in terms of which certain particular experiences in history must be explained. There is no universal, objective religious substructure underneath particular religions. Nor does religion grasp a transcendent object demanding devotion on our part. Instead, religion is derived from the structure of mind and history, logically though not empirically prior to all its specific embodiments. The pure form as such cannot be intuited. It is the transcendental (in the Kantian sense of that term) ground of its positive combinations with culture and history.

Representatives of this type of thought include some distinguished names: Rudolf Otto, Ernst Troeltsch (in his philosophy of religion only!) and the contemporary Swedish theologians of the Lundensian school, such as Anders Nygren.

Secondly, there were some to whom the peculiar and indefinite place of the knowing mind in Kant's philosophy suggested the possibility of a new metaphysical departure, one in which the duality between consciousness and the object would be overcome. Spirit (or subject, mind, "consciousness in general") and its objects are related immediately or internally, both in being and in knowledge. We have already outlined briefly something of this outlook and the subtle pervasiveness particularly of Hegel's thought, even among those who rejected his metaphysics. In our day the thought of Paul Tillich is responsible for a vigorous resuscitation of the idealistic tradition in theology. Tillich's thought is extraordinarily complex and far-ranging, drawing as it does on movements that are on the surface as divergent as medieval Realism and nineteenth-century Existentialism. In his ontology, however, it is metaphysical Idealism that gives focus and unity to questions of "ultimate concern." Between kerygmatic theology and philosophy—the quest for being in its most concrete and in its most inclusive aspects— no synthesis is possible. But both are possible only because there is a structure or ground of structure that underlies and precedes the dualities of self and world, subject and object, essence and existence. "Being" itself is not *a* being any more than it is "universal essence." "God" is the term we apply to that which is properly nameless, being-itself, beyond finitude and infinity, the power of being. As such, God transcends every particular being infinitely and yet not in such a way as to destroy it. Finite being participates in the very power of being that transcends it.[25]

In a sense, the term "faith" is best suited to express the manner in which, according to Tillich, we may understand the qualification of our existence by the power of being which is not another being separate from our own, but is rather the Unconditional which transcends reality without destroying it or merging it with itself:

The ultimate power of being, the ground of reality, appears in a special moment, in a concrete situation, revealing the infinite depth and the eternal significance of the present. But this is possible only in terms of a paradox, i. e., by faith, for, in itself, the present is neither infinite nor eternal.[26]

"Belief-ful realism" is the expression Tillich formerly used in order to describe the indirectness and tension, the paradoxical act by which the finite and its creative yet limiting ground are present to each other. It was this kind of formulation that first led contemporary theologians in America, such as H. Richard Niebuhr, to find Tillich suggestive for their own thought about faith and its realistic critique of contemporary culture. In his translation of Tillich's *The Religious Situation*, Niebuhr quoted the following words of Tillich to indicate the latter's intention:

By the connection of *belief-ful* and *realism* the most fundamental of all dualisms is called into question and if it is justly called into question, it is also overcome. Faith is an attitude which transcends every conceivable and experienceable reality; realism is an attitude which rejects every transcending of reality. . . . In view of the antithesis of these attitudes it is natural that the mind should be inclined to evade the tension which results from their union. Evasion is possible in one of two directions, either in the direction

[25] Tillich, *Systematic Theology* (Chicago: University of Chicago Press, 1951), vol. I, p. 237.
[26] Tillich, *The Protestant Era* (Chicago: University of Chicago Press, 1948), p. 78.

of a beliefless realism or in the direction of idealism. . . . Faith and realism, just because of the tension between them, belong together. For in faith the unconditioned tension is present and no attitude which weakens this tension can be associated with it. Idealism weakens it, beliefless realism cancels it, belief-ful realism expresses it.[27]

Yet over against—or perhaps we must say above and beyond—this position in which infinite and finite are related in paradox or unconditioned tension, Tillich affirms another understanding of the finite-infinite relation. "Man is immediately aware of something unconditional which is the *prius* of the separation and interaction of subject and object, theoretically and practically."[28] In this sort of statement one recognizes without difficulty the ultimate quest for unity through a principle of mediation between finite and infinite for which romantic and idealistic philosophers searched. There is "an essential unity of the unconditional and the conditioned in the ontological awareness; while in the word 'existential,' separation and decision are indicated. And the latter are elements of faith."[29] On this unity in the ontological awareness depends the only nonsymbolic statement about God: "The statement that God is being-itself is a nonsymbolic statement. It does not point beyond itself."[30] To the extent that philosophy—in contrast to religious statements—must use abstract language and conceptualization, this basic assertion of God as being is bound in some sense to be the source of all analysis of concrete, symbolic statements about God.

Despite his endeavor to express correlation between these and other magnitudes, Tillich's critics and commentators have not found it easy to relate his realistic or existentialist view of faith to his quite evidently idealistic ontology, especially since Tillich avows the impossibility of an ultimate synthesis of philosophy and kerygmatic theology. In any case one may assert safely that the elements of his ontology are independent of the situation of faith and that to this extent the basic impetus to his thought lies in the tradition of metaphysical Idealism, as the following quotation amply illustrates:

The power of being, the unconditional is the *prius* of everything that has being. It precedes all contents logically and ontologically. It precedes every separation and makes every interaction possible, because it is the point of identity without which neither separation nor interaction can be thought. . . . The immediate awareness of the unconditional has not the character of faith but of self-evidence. Faith contains a contingent element and demands

[27] P. Tillich, *Religioese Verwirklichung*, pp. 67-68, quoted in translator's preface to *The Religious Situation*, pp. xii and xiv.

[28] Tillich, "The Two Types of the Philosophy of Religion," *Union Seminary Quarterly Review*, I, No. 4 (May, 1946), 10.

[29] *Ibid.*, p. 11.

[30] Tillich, *Systematic Theology*, vol. I p. 238

a risk . . . based on the fact that the unconditional element can become a matter of ultimate concern only if it appears in concrete embodiment.[31]

The third alternative to the skeptical conclusion left by Kant's *Critique of Pure Reason* is the most important for the purpose of this essay. We recall that Kant's assault had destroyed the bases of rational orthodoxy, i.e., the notion of revelation as a formal system of truth whose contents are deductively arrived at, and especially the assumption of the externality of the relation between God and the human mind. Schleiermacher affirmed these negative consequences wholeheartedly in his rejection of natural religion and rational orthodoxy. But even if Kant was thus a negative determinant of Schleiermacher's thought, he appears to have exercised little positive influence over him. Indeed, Schleiermacher's positive philosophical position as it is outlined in his lectures on *Dialektik* was precisely that which romantic philosophers and metaphysical Idealists held in common, i.e., he sought to develop a principle of mediation in which the epistemic and ontic gulf between finite and infinite would be transcended. But in this work, as in others, he finally came to the conclusion that philosophy and theology, despite their intimate relations, are ultimately technically independent of each other.

Schleiermacher's theological intention was fundamentally realistic in the sense that he rejected the notion that the mind is capable of concrete comprehension of the internal relation between the Absolute (the "transcendental ground") and finite mind or ideation. It is precisely at this point, in specifying the direct relation between God and the human creature, that one must pass from philosophy to theology. Schleiermacher did indeed suggest that such a relationship exists, but precisely because it is direct and concretely real it is conceptually impure. God is directly present to consciousness, but this presence is inseparable from the awareness of oneself as standing in this relationship. It is customary to interpret Schleiermacher's difficult notion of "feeling" or "immediate self-consciousness" psychologically, i.e., as an empirical awareness of oneself. While this is doubtless a correct interpretation of later thought, it is probably unfair to Schleiermacher. His *Dialektik* makes clear that feeling refers to the subject-self in itself as it passes to and fro between agency and reflection. Thus, "feeling" seems to be closer to a metaphysical than to a purely psychological concept.

One may say that in consciousness, as Schleiermacher saw it, awareness of God and awareness of oneself in relation to God are given together, i.e., they are present to each other directly or immediately While it is an exaggeration to speak of this divine-human relation as "noncognitive," one must suggest that it is more inclusive, intimate and

[31] "Two Types," pp. 11, 13.

direct a relation and also less theoretical than the word "cognitive" would indicate. Above all, the relation undercuts the externality between the mind and God which rational orthodoxy's understanding of revelation had stipulated.

To translate this relation into more strictly cognitive terms involves a basic distortion and makes the interpretation of Schleiermacher difficult and subject to almost contradictory variations. When one undertakes nevertheless to do so, it seems that Schleiermacher intended to assert that the presence of God to consciousness is not simply identical with the contents of self-consciousness. God-consciousness is identical with self-consciousness only as the latter is in a specifically qualified or determined state, i.e., as consciousness in which God is present; or, to state it the other way, God-consciousness is identical with awareness of oneself as absolutely dependent. The content of God-consciousness is given to experience.[32] To this extent one may call Schleiermacher a realist rather than a subjectivist. He did not identify the ideal and the real, nor did he conceptually identify consciousness and its determinant.

But as soon as one has identified him as a realist in the sense that God and faith are for him given together but never identified metaphysically, one has to add the other side of this rational argument, distorted though it be: Schleiermacher rejected out of hand the externality or duality upon which pre-Kantian natural religion and rational orthodoxy had insisted. In this rejection he paralleled the Idealists of his day. For religious experience (though not for cognitive understanding) he denied the duality of subject and object. The "object" is "given" immediately in my self-consciousness (so that "given" and "object" are fundamentally theoretical and therefore distorting terms). God is not "a being" "over against" me. Nor is my knowledge of God based on an original concept or idea prior to feeling or consciousness. In that case "God" would only be another word for the philosopher's "Absolute," or else my knowledge of God would be no more than an inference (*Rueckschluss*) from my awareness of myself as absolutely dependent. But, on the contrary, Schleiermacher maintained that this awareness *is* my relation with God. There is no need for an inference from its actuality to God. ". . . God is given to us in feeling in an original way."[33] The nonmetaphysical Realism of this theory of consciousness insists that in consciousness God and the self, God and faith are "originally" or immediately related, and not external to one another.

All special doctrines, which are the content of divine revelation as heretofore conceived, are "scientifically" dogmatic only in so far as they have been established inductively rather than deductively. Otherwise

[32] F. Schleiermacher, *The Christian Faith* (Edinburgh: T. & T. Clark, 1948), par. 13, p. 67.
[33] *Ibid.*, par. 4, p. 17.

they are mere speculation, in Schleiermacher's view. They must be
direct expressions of the modifications of the religious consciousness
(*frommes Bewusstsein*). As Schleiermacher put it, the contents of
dogma must be expressions of faith (*Glaubensaussagen*). Later critics
have protested that Schleiermacher should have examined the objective
rather than the subjective pole of Christian consciousness. Schleiermacher would have found this reproach puzzling. Everything he said
seems to turn on the conviction that these two poles are inextricable
and that genuinely significant theological statements can be made only
about theses that show forth the original unity of God-consciousness
and Christian self-consciousness.[34] One cannot go back of this unity, this
simultaneous givenness and togetherness of revelation and the faith of
the recipient.

If this is the crux of Schleiermacher's position on revelation, it follows
that every endeavor to know God in himself or in his "essence," regardless of his relation to us, is idle speculation. We must say that "all attributes which we ascribe to God are to be taken as denoting not something
special in God, but only something special in the manner in which the
feeling of absolute dependence is to be related to Him."[35] Schleiermacher's Realism is thus not only nonmetaphysical but critical, i.e., the
object of faith is given together with the content of faith in such manner
that every attribute of or quality in the object is qualified by its being
a content of consciousness. To distinguish between such qualities or
attributes and those in God apart from the relation to faith is impossible.

This relational or critical theology came to be deeply influential.
Schleiermacher's more conservative followers tried to combine it with
metaphysical assertions. The later Liberals, on the other hand, joined
Schleiermacher in his rejection of metaphysics in theology. Both groups
followed his realistic intention. Moreover, the main stream of theological
thought followed him in the complete and exclusive Christocentricity
of his theology. Schleiermacher's conviction that God is known only in
relation, and that the immanent contact point of this relation is consciousness, was balanced or supplemented by his insistence that the sole
content of the specifically Christian consciousness at any given time is
its awareness of salvation through Jesus Christ. Revelation is thus not
only a matter of a given, present relation but also of a given historical
relation (somehow united to the present relation) behind or beyond
which one cannot go for concrete contact with God.

By and large nineteenth-century theologians followed Schleiermacher
in conceiving of revelation, the self-giving of God through Jesus Christ
in history and within a unique medium of present apprehension, as a

---

[34] *Ibid.*, par. 30, pp. 125 ff.
[35] *Ibid.*, par. 50, pp. 194 ff. For the application of the same principle to Christology,
see *ibid.*, pars. 90-94, pp. 369-389.

fact to be presupposed in theology. Not only the past fact but—and it is this that deserves emphasis—its present apprehension must be presupposed. In this sense, the rejection of all "natural theology" is by no means an innovation of the crisis theologians of the twentieth century. Rather, it was a basic tenet of the main stream of nineteenth-century theology. One had, the nineteenth-century theologians thought, to investigate the nature, conditions and content of the revelatory relationship by an analysis of that datum itself. But the datum one could take for granted; indeed, for methodological purposes it *had* to be taken for granted. The basic constant in theology, then, was the medium in which the togetherness of God and man could be posited and assumed. This medium was variously taken to be history, man's valuing and moral-rational capacity, or "consciousness," which was usually spoken of as faith. Within this medium was subsumed the relationship of revelation in which God was thought to be present, his presence given indissolubly in the relation itself. For most of the later nineteenth-century theologians, especially those of liberal persuasion, the existence of the revelation relationship tended to follow almost self-evidently if one could clearly set forth its nature and immanent contact-point within the human creature.

Following the lead of Schleiermacher, the dominant traditions of academic theology in the nineteenth century affirmed an exclusively Christocentric revelation and a sort of nonmetaphysical Realism in theology, in which God was seen as the direct object of a nontheoretic apprehension by the human subject. In both these respects they deliberately rejected metaphysical Idealism. Nevertheless, we must point out once again the perverse persistence of idealistic influence that lay back of the almost unanimous conviction—which Schleiermacher shared—that revelation is in some sense immediate and not merely "historical" in character, and that as a relationship it is an indissoluble constant that cannot be derived from some prior situation. Even when the later nineteenth-century Liberals, especially Ritschl and his followers, protested vigorously against the intrusion of philosophical thought into theology, Idealism lurked in the background. No other philosophical thought-form was so generally available and fully worked out; and at least as a thought-form, philosophy refused to be denied a place in systematic theological reflection.

Karl Barth and his early friends and followers stated the issue about revelation in a manner quite different from that of most nineteenth-century theologians. They refused to take the fact of revelation for granted. Thus, the constant in theology was for them not a datum in which God and man are co-posited in a relationship from which neither of the related terms could be abstracted. Instead, Barth laid a new and heavy stress on the freedom of the living God, a freedom that is fulfilled and not abrogated in his condescending grace. Thus, revelation and grace are always God's sovereign acts, miraculous acts and not constants of a relational datum. But it is interesting to note, as H. U. von Balthasar and other commentators have done, that even Barth's early and vigorous postliberal expression of these completely unliberal convictions rested on a sense of the immediacy and relational constancy of the original divine-human contact in creation, prior to sin and to all experience. Thus, like Kierkegaard, the early Barth was forced to clothe his genuinely new convictions—and they did represent a real break within the academic tradition in theology—in purely and sharply paradoxical form because, like Kierkegaard, he had no other *philosophical* mode of expression for his theological convictions than Idealism.

Nevertheless, most theologians whom Schleiermacher had influenced thought that he had pointed them toward theological Realism. In one way or another, a large number of men were dependent upon him, including such diverse figures as von Hofmann and Frank (the Erlangen confessionals), Richard Rothe, the mediating tradition, Martin Kaehler and the Liberals—men like Kaftan, Haering, Ritschl and Herrmann. They all agreed that Schleiermacher's greatest merit had been the turn from deductive to inductive theology. The knowledge of God must begin with faith, and faith fundamentally modifies whatever noetic content is given to it. It is in some sense an experienced or intuited state or quality. All agreed that it is not an empty form, nor simply a theoretical qualification of the mind through an act of understanding, nor a "leap" of decision in the face of historical and contemporary evidence. Faith is an immanent and continuous state which is present in man only as qualified or determined by revelation. From this relationship one may not abstract, but through faith one may rely upon its actuality and continuity. The relation between faith and revelation is the starting point and constant factor for all theological analysis. This is the root conviction of the main stream of the German academic tradition in systematic theology.

3. REVELATION AND THEOLOGICAL METHOD IN THE THEOLOGY OF KARL BARTH

Just as H. Richard Niebuhr has been deeply influenced by the nineteenth-century academic tradition in theology, so has he been profoundly affected by its twentieth-century successor, mainly through the thought of Karl Barth, the chief catalytic agent in the theological thought of our century.

Karl Barth's thought is often construed as a reaction against Liberalism. It seems more proper to say that in the process of an internal theological revolution he came in conflict with Liberalism—his own and in particular that of Schleiermacher. In part the instrument he used to express his new attitude was the language of metaphysical Idealism.

This is especially noticeable in the second edition of *Der Roemerbrief*, with its dialectical method and its understanding of God as absolute origin (*Ursprung*) beyond "reality" (or "givenness") and truth, and beyond the duality of the two. But increasingly during the decade from 1920 to 1930 his mode of expression was determined by the most fundamental debate in which he saw himself engaged at the time—the debate with Schleiermacher.[36] After that time, apparently, he felt he had overcome Schleiermacher's challenge sufficiently to go on to other concerns.[37]

While Barth sees something of the "indifference point" or "mediating" philosophy of Romanticism and early nineteenth-century Idealism in Schleiermacher, he apparently interpreted him (during the 1920's) basically as a critical Realist in theology. At stake in the debate were the doctrine of revelation and the nature of theological method.

It is impossible to describe a demand for renewal as drastic as Barth's in a few sentences. Fundamental in his concern is the acknowledgment of the freedom and Lordship of God. These qualities God affirms in his condescending grace. They are not restricted by creation or grace. It is the greatest perversion, therefore, to tie God "relationally" to any preconceived method, supposedly the echo of a "symmetrical" relation between divine revelation and an independently gained concept of religion. Instead, one must insist that grace is sheer miracle which we can only "*ac*-knowledge."

The Word of God is no "object" in the ordinary sense of the word, i.e., it is not "object" to consciousness or object in the metaphysical sense. The Word of God is not "given in" but is the "other" of our immanent awareness or knowledge. Barth is not now and was not in the 1920's "antiphilosophical." He has always been aware that theology has no conception or language (content or form) other than that of philosophy.[38] But he has argued heatedly and consistently that the subject matter of philosophy is totally different from that of theology. The fundamental difference—and it is one to which neither nineteenth- nor eighteenth-century traditions paid heed—is that for the theologian the basic fact is that God has spoken (*Deus dixit*); whereas in philosophy (or in religion, for that matter) the universe or a self speaks. Revelation

---

[36] See especially the essays "Schleiermachers 'Weihnachtsfeier'" and "Schleiermacher" in *Die Theologie und die Kirche* (Munich: C. Kaiser, 1928); also *Die Christliche Dogmatik im Entwurf* (Munich: C. Kaiser, 1927).

[37] The change may be dated from the appearance of a book which was of extraordinary significance for Barth's development: *Fides Quaerens Intellectum: Anselms Beweis der Existenz Gottes im Zusammenhang seines theologischen Programms* (Munich: C. Kaiser, 1931); cf. also *Die Lehre vom Worte Gottes, Die Kirchliche Dogmatik*, I, 1 and 2 (Evangelische Buchhandlung Zollikon, Zurich, 1932 *et seq.*), hereafter cited as KD; also the essay "Schleiermacher," in *Die Protestantische Theologie im Neunzehnten Jahrhundert* (Zurich, 1947).

[38] Cf. Barth's essay "Schicksal und Idee in der Theologie," in *Zwischen den Zeiten*, VII (1929), 309-348.

is real therefore only in so far as it becomes, from any human point of view, altogether problematical. It is an impossible possibility actualized in the event or occasion of revelation alone. This crisis is God's action in Jesus Christ.[39]

One must therefore never speak of revelation as a "given" condition or as a constant relation. Rather, theology must seek to express in rational manner the miraculous nature of an occurrence at once completely to be relied upon and yet wholly new at all times. Revelation is always act, the act of one who, because he is not acted upon, is always subject in his act and never object. The only way to affirm this act is to seek for the clue not in the relationship itself but in the Being-in-act of him who is subject and guarantor of revelation, the Triune God.

Barth was endeavoring to overcome a method in theology which conceived of the content of revelation as contingent upon the form, the religious relation in which revelation becomes real to us. Instead, he turned to a stringent Realism, in which God, his reality and nature are to be understood as being the independent ground of all relation of God with creatures. This view, if it can be worked out, would at least not be exposed to the dangers of subjectivism to which Schleiermacher's Realism fell prey, in Barth's opinion. On the other hand, such a theological Realism must not turn into an abstract *scientia de Deo* in the manner of eighteenth-century natural religion and rational orthodoxy, with their externality of relation between God and man. Moreover, Barth had to reject the temptation to transcend the Realism of revelation in the direction of idealistic metaphysics, i.e., in the overcoming of history through ideal essence. The latter task made Barth insist that there be no division between ontology and Christology. All ontic statements are made on the basis of the historical revelation in Jesus Christ. The difficulty of this task was compounded by the fact that until the end of the 1920's he seems to have feared all ontic or "nondialectical" statements as signifying either abstract metaphysics or a return to "immanentism."

In 1927, in the first edition of *The Doctrine of the Word of God*, Barth attacked what he believed to be Schleiermacher's and the nineteenth-century tradition's conception of the content of theology. Barth denied that dogmatic theology examines the Christian communion with God itself (*die christliche Sache selbst*). Such a claim would turn theology into *kerygma*. Schleiermacher and the subsequent tradition were not sufficiently critical with regard to the content of theology. They claimed direct knowledge of the inmost center of God's act in communion with men.

But it seemed to Barth that Schleiermacher made the opposite error

[39] Cf. *The Epistle to the Romans* (English trans.; Oxford University Press, 1950), p. 10.

with regard to the object (as distinguished from the content) of theology. In this respect he was completely dualistic. For God is the object of theological knowledge only in so far as he is directly present in "Christian religious consciousness." Since the latter is a precognitive and immediate relationship, theology cannot have God for its object. Faith, or "Christian consciousness," alone is its norm and content.

It does not matter that later critics, operating on the same ground as Schleiermacher, accused him of subjectivism, and that they claimed in their own positive constructions to examine faith—however conceived—for its "God-relatedness" or "objective content." This is exactly what Schleiermacher had done. His critics are doing the same—even if they understand faith more "historically," "morally," "objectively," and less "aesthetically" than Schleiermacher. As a matter of fact Schleiermacher never confused God-consciousness with self-consciousness. He saw them in their immediate togetherness in immanent awareness. Schleiermacher and all his critics, according to Barth, share an understanding of faith as an immanent state in which God is present, a constant relation in which God is posited as objective constituent and determinant.

Now, Barth does not intend to deny faith as immanent state in which God is present. He does not intend to counterattack so directly against Schleiermacher. For to do this would mean that Barth would still share common ground with Schleiermacher's own presuppositions. The only difference between them would be that Barth would understand the "relation" or "experience" of revelation to be a totally negative instead of a positive magnitude. Barth was tempted to say just this in his use of the "dialectical" method which stressed the radically indirect, negative relation between grace and the sinner's faith. But he never developed this point of view systematically and increasingly overcame the temptation to do so. Despite his abstention, however, his counterthesis to Schleiermacher has usually been understood as a *direct* denial of all immanent faith and positive relation to God. This misunderstanding has been especially prevalent in the English-speaking world.

Apparently the misapprehension is mainly due to Emil Brunner, who explained Barth in this manner and for a long time was the chief source of information about Barth's thought in England and America. Brunner attributed to Barth an anthropology in which the humanity of "man" is regarded as a sort of unchangeable substance or subject which through sin is wholly destroyed and in Christ is completely re-created. Brunner himself insisted that there is in man—whom he apparently conceives in a substantive manner—a constant formal quality, identical with man's humanity, which remains constant in creation, sin and redeeming grace. This formal constant is the presupposition for the reception of redeeming grace and faith. It becomes the point of contact (*der Anknuepfungs-*

punkt) between grace and man. This quasi-substantial view of man Brunner does not question. He does not see—Barth's explicit warning to the contrary notwithstanding—that Barth cannot share with him a common basis even for disagreement. Barth's problem was that of *overcoming* (rather than either denying or affirming) a theological method whose basic tenet and constant factor is "relationality," "religion," "the condition of man" or any other anthropological datum. Instead, Barth endeavored to begin with an understanding of revelation as miraculous grace, i.e., with the subject rather than the object of revelation. This puts his subsequent anthropology into a perspective wholly different from Brunner's, no matter whether there is accidental agreement or disagreement between them on the status of the *imago Dei*. Barth explicitly proclaimed this basic difference between them, beyond the difference over thesis and counterthesis within theological anthropology. Brunner did not understand then, and apparently still does not comprehend, the depth of this divergence in method and principle, and the fact that he and Barth each presuppose one constant, Barth's being a doctrine of the Word of God, his own being anthropological. Under these circumstances it is not surprising that Brunner now thinks that Barth's anthropology has undergone a complete change since the days of their controversy. In actual fact Barth's thought went through a radical transformation some time before his *Streitschrift* against Brunner, a change that was marked by the publication of his book on Anselm of Canterbury.[40]

Now, the curious and unfortunate fact is that until recently British and American commentators, whether they agreed with Barth or with Brunner (and they usually found Brunner's position the more congenial) almost to a man understood the controversy from Brunner's perspective and so read Barth through Brunner's eyes. For them, also, the basic and constant factor was a certain anthropological continuity that persisted in the midst of its own changes. They understood Barth as a "radical Protestant" and theological irrationalist, when all he did was to refuse to make this particular datum his basis in theological principle and method. He was accused of insisting on the total effacing of the image of God in man through sin, on the obliteration of all spontaneous response in human faith (both before and after redeeming grace) and of a whole raft of similar assaults upon the humanity of man.[41]

---

[40] Cf. above, p. 41 n. For the controversy between Brunner and Barth, see E. Brunner, *Natur und Gnade, zum Gespraech mit Karl Barth* (2nd ed.; Tuebingen, 1935), especially pp. 7-9; E. Brunner, "Der neue Barth. Bemerkungen zu Karl Barths Lehre vom Menschen" in *Zeitschrift fuer Theologie und Kirche*, 48. Jahrgang, 1951, No. 1, pp. 89-100; K. Barth, "Nein! Antwort an Emil Brunner," in *Theologische Existenz Heute*, No. 14 (1934), 1-14.

[41] Cf. W. M. Horton, *Contemporary Continental Theology* (New York and London: Harper & Brothers, 1938), pp. 105 f., 111 ff.; John Baillie, *Our Knowledge of*

What has Barth actually suggested about theological method? We may set the stage for his "counterthesis" to Schleiermacher by suggesting what Barth finds to be Schleiermacher's central motif and the central thesis of theology since Schleiermacher: it is the transformation of dogmatics into *Glaubenslehre*, teachings about faith. The actual objects of faith are objects for theology only in so far as they are direct expressions of faith (*Glaubensaussagen*). "The thesis about the object of dogmatics is the expression of that Copernican revolution which one . . . customarily associates with Schleiermacher's name."[42] This revolution had prior roots. Indeed, in his later writings Barth came to stress its origins in Protestant Scholasticism rather than Schleiermacher. In 1927, however, he felt that the important point was Schleiermacher's "canonization" of the change, so that theology at its core became the "science of religious experience as it takes place in the church." Against this transformation in method Barth pits his "counterthesis":

> The significance and the possibility, the object of dogmatics is not the Christian faith but the Word of God. For the Word of God is not based on and contained in Christian faith, but Christian faith is based on and contained in the Word of God. These are two different things, no matter how much the opposing side may speak of the objective content of faith.[43]

This relation is neither reversible, symmetrical nor a "given" content in an immanent state in which subjective and objective poles are balanced with proper delicacy.

Barth denies that his reversal forces theology back to the point it occupied before Schleiermacher's inductive "correlation" method, i.e., to a deductive science of religion or revelation. He simply refuses to acknowledge that the basic alternatives in theological principles are induction or "practical science," on the one hand, and deduction or "theoretical study," on the other.

It is indeed true, says Barth, that theology properly directed toward

---

God (New York: Charles Scribner's Sons, 1939), pp. 17-34; Reinhold Niebuhr, *The Nature and Destiny of Man* (New York, 1941 and 1943), vol. 1, p. 269, vol. 2, p. 64. Even the otherwise excellent essay on Karl Barth by H. R. Mackintosh, still one of the best in English, is vitiated by this misunderstanding: Cf. Mackintosh, *Types of Modern Theology* (New York: Charles Scribner's Sons, 1937), p. 316. The best antidote to this interpretation is H. U. v. Balthasar, *Karl Barth: Darlegung und Deutung seiner Theologie* (Olten, Hegner-Bucherei, 1951). More recently a whole body of perceptive essays on Barth has appeared in British and American journals. Cf. *Theology Today*, XIII, 3 (October, 1956); Giovanni Miegge, "A Roman Catholic Interpretation of Karl Barth," *Scottish Journal of Theology*, 7 (1954), 59-72; T. F. Torrance, "Karl Barth," *The Expository Times*, LXVI, 7 (April, 1955), 205-9; R. E. Cushman, "Barth's Attack upon Cartesianism and the Future of Theology," *Journal of Religion*, 36 (October, 1956), 207-23.
[42] Barth, *Die Christliche Dogmatik*, p. 87.
[43] *Ibid.*, p. 87.

its proper object is possible only when God gives faith. But the meaning of faith has been profoundly misunderstood by the nineteenth-century tradition, conservative or liberal. Whether one understands it as cognition or as trust, *fiducia* (and Barth, in opposition to Schleiermacher and Wilhelm Herrmann, likes to stress its cognitive aspect), faith has a juridical reference in the thought of the Reformation. It is grounded solely in promise, God's promise, and his pledge of that promise. Surely the word of promise cannot be derived from *fiducia*. Instead, the latter is faith only as it is related to the prior, nondeducible promise. The same holds true for every other aspect of faith also. This is Barth's Realism in theological method: faith, in actuality and meaning, is dependent upon neither its form nor its content but upon its object. This object has total priority over faith which is, in form and content, defined by the object.

Faith can be refused, but it is necessarily and altogether relation (and relation of the creature to the Creator) to *that in which* he has faith. No matter whether the word faith indicates human disposition and action (*fides qua creditur*); or the confession stipulated in concepts and words (*fides quae creditor*); or finally the divine "deposit" through the other two (*fides as donum Dei*, as living presence of the Holy Spirit in man): in any case, *Deus dixit*, God has turned to man in a way . . . which makes possible as disposition and action nothing but faith, to which nothing but the confession of faith can answer, which can be apprehended only as the gift of the Holy Spirit. Faith can be refused, but where it takes place, faith is answer, effect of the Word . . . of God. This address is not merely the objective content or even the expression of faith, but rather faith has in this address . . . its originating ground.[44]

The Word of God is "God speaking, an act whose subject is God . . . alone." This act is not given as content of faith. Indeed, "faith believes this reality precisely as that which is not given to man, as God's own and remaining God's own."[45] As such, strictly as subject, the Word of God gives itself to faith.

Next, Barth must face the question: if this denial of the immanent or "correlation" method is not based on an abstract science about God, is it not perhaps complete dualism or agnosticism, the denial that God comes genuinely within the compass of faith's knowledge? Barth's first defense against this accusation is to suggest that the consequences so dreaded in his own position actually flow from the assumptions of his opponents. The kind of indissoluble relation between God and man that Schleiermacher stipulates for consciousness effectively precludes any genuine turning of God toward man and vice versa.

[44] *Ibid.*, p. 90.
[45] *Ibid.*, p. 95.

In Gargantuan, fate-like power, God (or what passes for God) here crushes man precisely at the point where community between the two, speaking and hearing, command and obedience, should take place. In just this connection Schleiermacher ought to be a warning of the consequences of not keeping God and man apart honestly, precisely if one wants to speak of community between them.[46]

But such a negative defense of his radical Realism in theological method was hardly sufficient. The problem pressed him hard during the decade from 1920 to 1930. Would his radical Realism with regard to the "object of faith" land him in a "science" that would merely reiterate the dogmatic content of the tradition without transliterating it into the conceptual forms of his own day's thinking? Would he, on the other hand, remain a purely critical theologian by his basic affirmation about the subject of revelation, so that he would make only negative, dialectical statements about God? In this latter case, he would indeed condemn theology to being *prolegomena* that could never get beyond method to the content of faith's knowledge[47]—the very sin of the nineteenth-century tradition, committed all over again by its bitterest opponent! Barth was well aware that he was risking both of these diametrically opposed dangers at the same time in his radical Realism. But it seemed to him that the acclimatization of theology to culture had now gone on so long that these possibilities had to be risked—and risked genuinely. Proper theology, Barth was fond of repeating after Overbeck during this decade, can be re-established only by taking desperate risks. It seems that, despite his vehement opposition to Schleiermacher, Barth had as a steady companion during this decade the fear that Schleiermacher and the tradition following him had stated the only alternative to skepticism or dead rational orthodoxy. Was his own alternative merely a wedding of these two fatal dangers?

Undoubtedly Barth was absolutely sincere when he said that one is never done with Schleiermacher. For, in a sense, Barth was still on Schleiermacher's ground throughout the decade of which we are speaking, especially in *Die Christliche Dogmatik* of 1927. Not only is the volume largely devoted to the question of method in its very eagerness to overcome that problem; but, more important, Barth at that time shared that portion of Schleiermacher's ground which had been staked out by Kant's first *Critique*. Like the consequent Realism of Schleiermacher, Barth's much more radical Realism in this volume is non-ontological. He tried, at that time, to speak of God as one who is related to his creation as absolute origin (*Ursprung*), a term which he apparently took over from the epistemological Idealism of Hermann

---

[46] *Ibid.*, p. 313.
[47] Barth, *The Word of God and the Word of Man* (transl. by Douglas Horton; Pilgrim Press, 1928), pp. 216-217.

Cohen. God is the presupposition of every question about him. The relationship of the creature to him in its pristine, now lost, purity is one of such immediacy and togetherness that the very endeavor to see God and man in the distinction of absolute superiority and inferiority over against each other is a fundamental distortion. In our present, unhappy state faith must be the acknowledgment of the line that has been drawn irremovably between God and the sinful creature, the alienation in which they now stand over against each other as "objects": and God is the "nonintuitable" (*unanschauliche*) other, the one who cannot become "object" for thought or experience. In our alienation we are related to him objectively, yet he cannot be object, both because this is not his nature and because we are in distorted relation to him. The endeavor of a theological ontology is objectification of God. In this situation faith becomes an enduring dwelling in contradiction, the acknowledgment that this paradox cannot be overcome and its terms merged into any immediacy of relationship.[48]

Barth, in other words, was speaking of God in terms which avoid any implication of knowledge of transphenomenal being, of being as it actually is. It was an endeavor simultaneously to avoid the eighteenth century's errors, to obey Kant's "limits of pure, theoretic reason," and to transcend what Troeltsch has called the agnosticism of the nineteenth century's theory of religious knowledge. God as pure subject, as unintuitable actuality, was Barth's positive suggestion. But in actual effect this suggestion is wholly negative unless some sort of analogy may be found for it in the life of man, especially as it culminates in crisis, i.e., in religion. We are aware—existentially—that we are being grasped in our being by that abyss which is at once our complete destruction, our origination and the impossible possibility and actuality of new life. The endeavor to convert this impossible possibility into a possible one, into a human possession, is "religion."

But in the actuality of God's unintuitable grace, religion is defeated. We are existentially aware that we are being grasped by God. Such existential knowledge is not direct knowledge of our own being. It is, instead, the crisis of apprehending that our real and hidden (also "unintuitable") being is being apprehended. In this as it were negative knowledge there is an analogy to the knowledge and being of God. Such acute accentuation of the dialectic between the positive actuality of grace and the negative condition of knowledge as parable of grace marked the transition from the first to the second edition of *Der Roemerbrief*.

Barth seemed to try (if we may coin an awkward phrase) to transcend epistemological or methodological anthropocentrism without bypassing the human situation, in a kind of transepistemology, parallel to that of

[48] *Der Roemerbrief* (7th impression of the new ed., Zurich, 1947), p. 14.

Neo-Kantianism in which the content of thought as well as its actual objects are based on their origination in the absolute productivity of thought itself. Barth's notion of creation appears, during the 1920's, to have been something like that, for to him creation and knowledge of God in turn paralleled one another. There is here, neither in the doctrine of creation nor in that of revelation, a joining of epistemology to ontology, of an *ordo cognoscendi* to an *ordo essendi* prior to and different from it. The two are, instead, related in a paradox of total difference and identity. In original creation man's being, his knowing, and his being known of God are immediately related in indissoluble identity. To this extent one may say that grace and nature are absolutely identical. On the other hand, in the indirectness and distance of faith in the midst of sin, our knowing and our being known of God stand related only in the tension of a completely negative analogy (if this is possible and conceivable). Moreover, such knowledge is qualitatively infinitely distant from God's being and perhaps even from man's own being. For one objectifies both God and man if one claims direct or positive knowledge of them. To this extent sin and natural knowledge (if not human nature itself) are identical.

In such a paradoxical situation, theological knowledge, "prolegomena" to dogmatics, the knowledge of the Word of God, can be nothing other than "acknowledgment" (*Anerkennung*), the faith that we are being known in the actuality of God's grace in revelation. Indeed, Barth insists that faith as a knowledge of "being known," and no more than this, must end in a logical *petitio principii*.

Such a conclusion did not satisfy Barth. But if he went further he would have to go beyond the *Problematik* posed for him by Schleiermacher and Kant, indeed by all major philosophy and theology since Descartes's "anthropocentrism." Must one really start, in search for knowledge of God, with the problems of the human self, whether in its theoretical or practical activity? Is the reasoning of faith caught in the paradoxical situation we have described, or can one apprehend God's actual being in the act of grace? Does God actually stand revealed in the eternal Word directed usward, made flesh of our flesh?

It was St. Anselm's *Proslogion* that helped Barth solve his dilemma. Here Barth finds faith completely girded for a rational task. No extrinsic, nonrational considerations intrude—a fact that appeals to him because he, too, wants to speak in and from faith, without sundering faith and reason as the nineteenth-century tradition had done. Barth's book on Anselm is absolutely indispensable for a knowledge of the revolution in his thought between the two editions of *The Doctrine of the Word of God*.[49]

[49] Barth, *Fides Quaerens Intellectum, Anselms Beweis der Existenz Gottes, im Zusammenhang seines theologischen Programms* (hereafter cited as FQI). Barth

Faith for Anselm, Barth claims, is not only the striving of the human will toward God, but its striving "into" God. Thus, it is a participation (although a creaturely, limited participation) in God's "mode of being," his aseity.[50] Faith is in its nature a call to cognitive understanding.[51] God cannot be believed in without becoming the originator of a true reflection. Faith is indeed experience and obedience but only in so far as it is also faith *in God*, i.e., right or correct belief.[52] This itself would earn Barth the malediction of all Liberals! Faith, he insists after Anselm, is relative to the "Word of Christ," and is reception, knowledge, affirmation of this Word.

While faith shares with unbelief an understanding of the objective *Credo* of the Church as a "logico-grammatically expressed configuration of meaning,"[53] the actual *res* which the symbolism signifies is present only in faith and not in unbelief. At this point *intelligere esse in re* is mysteriously added to *esse in intellectu*. The beginning and the goal of understanding within faith are therefore given. The quest is for the road between these two, between the subjective *credere* of the Church's objective Credo and the presence of the object of *credere* and *Credo* in the understanding. "When *fides quaerit intellectum* we are concerned with the course between the notation which has taken place and the affirmation which has also taken place."[54] In this important but limited sense, then, theology is quite capable of performing its task. When Barth affirms this much, not only for Anselm but for himself, theological knowledge turns for him from a critical, dialectical instrument to a positive descriptive means. Knowledge and object correspond to one another positively, even though God in his revelation is only the indirect object of reflection.

It is of course true that all theological theses are inadequate to their object. Our participation in God's aseity is creaturely, and there is no identity between the Credo and its *res*. "The Word of Christ spoken to us is, as such, not inadequate to its object, but every . . . reiteration of this Word on our part (is inadequate). . . . We have concepts only of objects that are not identical with God."[55] Nevertheless, the crucial point, in contrast to Barth's previous point of view, is that

---

himself has characterized this book as his most satisfying effort. He chose it rather than the controversy with Brunner to characterize the change in his thinking in the decade following 1928. Cf. Barth, "How my Mind has Changed," in *Christian Century*, LVI, nos. 37 and 38 (Sept. 13 and 20, 1939).

[50] FQI, p. 6.
[51] *Ibid.*, p. 8.
[52] *Ibid.*, p. 13.
[53] *Ibid.*, p. 17.
[54] *Ibid.*, p. 17-18.
[55] *Ibid.*, p. 22.

. . . just as everything which is not God, would be nothing without God, but through God is something, in ascending intensity *aliqua imitatio illius essentiae;* so also theses which are actually commensurable only with objects not identical with God, can be true theses, *per aliquam similitudinem aut imaginem (ut cum vultum alicuius consideramus in speculo),* when applied to God.[56]

The reality of the knowledge of God, Barth always contends, is based on God's self-revelation: hence, where the Word of God is given effectively to men, they, through this Word, know God. This fundamental reality is absolutely basic: the very question of its *possibility* can be raised only on the grounds of, or posterior to, its actuality.

Thus, one must say that this turn to a positive doctrine of analogy, and a positive ontology, is a profoundly, indeed exclusively, Christological and Christocentric transformation.[57] The logical and ontological possibility of the knowledge of God, of God's being, is the actual occurrence of the gift to us of that Word—which is none other than God himself. And this noetic actuality and possibility in turn is grounded in the identity of God with himself when he is God for us; i.e., the actuality and possibility of knowledge of God is based on the identity of God's immanent Triune being with that being as it is revealed to us in the incarnation of the Son of God.

This Christological change has, then, an ontological and an epistemological aspect. First, it is a change from Barth's previous "Actualism" in the doctrine of God. It remains true for him that God is always *Subject-in-act.* But now Barth affirms that in grace, in Jesus Christ, this God, who is subject and nothing else, gives himself as object to us. God remains mysterious, but in this mystery it is *He* that is revealed. He that is hidden reveals himself in hiddenness. He who becomes God for us is no one other and nothing less than God himself. The living God gives himself as object, thereby affirming and not denying his living freedom. This formulation is, compared to Barth's position during the 1920's, a turn from dialectic to analogy, from critical to positive theology, from epistemology and transepistemology to the priority of ontology over epistemology, from Idealism to Realism. Hence, it represents a breakthrough from the problems of Schleiermacher, Kant, and post-Kantian Idealism to a new position. Barth no longer has to insist that in his radical Realism the knowledge of God is simply *ac-knowledgment* of myself as being known: in knowledge, as in existence, Barth seems now to say, I am actually and meaningfully confronted by the

[56] *Ibid.,* p. 23.

[57] Barth's tenacious and persistent Christocentricity from his liberal days to his latest writings is the most important of several themes that make one wonder if he has broken completely with "Liberalism." For this exclusive Christocentricity in the content of revelation has been one of the chief hallmarks of the German liberal tradition, from Schleiermacher to Ritschl, Herrmann, and Bultmann.

One who is the Lord of grace. But this happens solely in Jesus Christ and to faith: it is no return to the speculation of the eighteenth century nor to the "religiosity" of the nineteenth century, Barth insists.

Secondly, the change from "Actualism" in the doctrine of God, has, as its epistemological consequence, the de-emphasis (though perhaps not complete rejection) of the dialectical method. It is not necessary now (since Barth thinks that he has drawn sufficient attention to the fact) to affirm that we cannot, of ourselves, predicate any qualities of God, that he is the unpredictable or unintuitable (*unanschauliche*) center between positive and negative attributions and judgments. We must rather affirm now the complementary fact: if in his subjecthood God genuinely confronts us as object, there must be a correspondence in predicable qualities between him and his creatures: it is of his own grace that this is so, through the historical miracle that he has wrought. It is not a similarity or correspondence that we can seek in a neutral and common "being" behind grace and revelation, to which God and creature alike are "positively" related. No: our reliance for this similarity is upon his own act in making himself similar to the creature, and yet remaining identical with himself in this act. Hence, there is not identity, but correspondence and congruity, radical congruity between Creator and creature, grace and nature, but on the basis of grace and revelation alone. Barth has turned to a doctrine of analogy. In turn, this epistemological doctrine has for him an epistemological and ontological aspect. Epistemologically it is the analogy between our words, concepts, intuitions and their object, God, through the self-giving of God in his Word. This is the *analogia fidei*.[58] Later, he adds to this a corresponding ontic dimension, an *analogia relationis* between God and man.[59]

In all this, one need hardly add, the customary understanding of analogy is turned about. In the relation of faith, it is God who is the analogue and man who is the analogate. In faith and to faith the creature and not the Creator stands in need of explanation, of clarification by analogy.

The radical Realism, the objectivity of this theology is just as great as it was during the time of debate with Schleiermacher. But in the earlier view, the knowledge of faith meets a barrier which Kant and Schleiermacher, and not God, seem to have erected: God is not "given" to consciousness, to intuition, and therefore he is not "object." For the Word of God, Barth told us at that time, "takes place, is spoken in *Diakrisis*, in the decision between revelation and hiddenness, as a *giving*, not as something having been given." If we speak of the Word of God, we are not speaking of an object, but "of the subject which, turned into

---

[58] Cf. KD, I, 1, 250 ff.; II, 1, 68-93, 252-67.
[59] KD, III, 2, 262 ff.

an object, is not what it is; of an object which can only be object for us in strict 'non-objectivity.' "[60] Therefore, we do not recognize this Word, "rather we are recognized in it."[61] This was dialectic, and its result was an apparently invincible dualism in the theory of knowledge.

The only difference between this and the later view is that Barth now says that the miracle—and it is nothing less—does take place in Jesus Christ: he is indeed subject and not object, yet as subject he becomes object for us. He is no *positum*, no constant static content of faith, no "given," yet he enables us to know him as object in the act and decision of faith. We are recognized, we can only acknowledge, and yet therein we know him and know him genuinely. Dualism is overcome, the strange transepistemological leaning of the German idealistic tradition is left behind, the debate with Schleiermacher is no longer the primary issue. Barth affirms the priority of ontic over epistemological judgments in theology, the priority of the method of analogy over that of dialectic. This is his final answer to the nonmetaphysical, critical Realism of Schleiermacher, to the "relational" revelation theology that followed him, and to his (Barth's) own earlier dualism with regard to faith's knowledge of God.

4. THE RELATION OF FAITH AND HISTORY IN THE THOUGHT OF ERNST TROELTSCH

In the preface to *The Meaning of Revelation*, H. Richard Niebuhr writes:[62]

Students of theology will recognize that Ernst Troeltsch and Karl Barth have . . . been my teachers. . . . These two leaders in twentieth century religious thought are frequently set in diametrical opposition to each other; I have tried to combine their main interests, for it appears to me that the critical thought of the former and the constructive work of the latter belong together.

Niebuhr does not elaborate on this passage in the course of the book. We must endeavor to draw out some of its implications. We have seen something of the thought involved in Barth's decisive turn from the critical theology of his dialectical period to the positive and constructive view that followed it. We may now therefore turn to the thought of Ernst Troeltsch. Niebuhr is right when he indicates that Troeltsch's general turn of thought was and remained critical. He was perhaps the most prominent among the men whose thought cut sharply across the lines of division in post-Kantian Protestant theology. His influence on H. Richard Niebuhr has been both strong and abiding.

All his life Troeltsch looked toward a synthesis in which formal

[60] *Die Christliche Dogmatik*, p. 96.
[61] *Ibid.*, p. 103.
[62] *The Meaning of Revelation*, p. x.

philosophy, the interpretation of culture and history, and theology would all cohere without undercutting one another's autonomy. He did not attain the goal of his vision, but he developed a breadth of interest and sympathy probably unmatched by any other theological contemporary. His awareness of the complexity of the relations between theology and the problems of historical interpretation made him abandon what appeared to him to be the narrow confines of professional theology.

Troeltsch desired to overcome what seemed to be the provincialism of theology since Schleiermacher. He sympathized with its exclusive Christocentricity, developed on the basis of a special or "agnostic" theory of knowledge. At the same time he saw that just this preoccupation was also the weakness of theology, inasmuch as its claim to uniqueness of insight sundered it from all theoretical and universally valid understanding, especially from philosophy and historical method. He felt that it was especially urgent to find the presuppositions in human thought common to both historical and theological methods. Otherwise it appeared likely to him that the growth of the application of historical method would eventually destroy the credibility of theological statements.

Since the middle of the nineteenth century, it seemed to Troeltsch, theology "has everywhere withdrawn from the demonstration of scientifically valid, general truths to personal, subjective, confessional-type convictions and their potential mediation for the tradition and mode of expression which dominates the Church."[63]

The "agnostic" theory of knowledge which is the basis of this position consists in the distinction between religion and theology, between theoretical, normative conception and the source and content of a special religious awareness. This "dogmatic agnosticism" which resigns from all binding rational cognition is the supposed guarantor of the independence of theology and at the same time enables theology to compromise with rational knowledge by abdicating "from all theoretico-scientific knowledge which would grasp the transcendent world genuinely in its actuality."[64]

But theology cannot avoid all contact with historical investigation. Theologians themselves have recognized this fact. Such contact is made at two points, Troeltsch thought; first of all in the transcendental presuppositions of all human thought; and secondly, in the objective particularity of positive events. The task of the philosophy of religion is not to construct a positive doctrine of God but to indicate the nature of an *a priori* religious form by transcendental deduction. Such a pro-

---

[63] Troeltsch, *Gesammelte Schriften* (J. C. B. Mohr [Paul Siebeck], Tuebingen, 1913-1923), vol. II, p. 199.
[64] *Ibid.*, vol. II, p. 201.

cedure would locate the religious *a priori* as an irreducible structure in the noumenal self. This means that there is no universal "positive" religion. As actual content the religious form is always embedded in historical particularity. Moreover, one may assume that in its own way historical method, like theology, rests upon an *a priori* structure.

But in addition to such contact of the two disciplines in virtue of purely methodological considerations, theology and historical method meet in the objective, particular events they treat from their divergent points of view. It is here that Troeltsch's greatest theological difficulties arose. Historical method is ultimately congruous with the human spirit's grasp of the infinite and universal spirit through the particular, i.e., through the intuition of each historical-spiritual occurrence. But it is very difficult to integrate either historical method or historical-spiritual intuition with the claim of Christian faith to "absolute validity," derived as it is from certain historical events for which absolute uniqueness is claimed. Troeltsch was more responsible than any other single individual for the fact that this problem, destined to occupy theologians to the present day, had to be faced, and he stated it with perhaps greater force and profundity than anyone else before or since his time. He always felt that historical method was "the starting point for the upheaval of the world of Christian ideas."[65] We must therefore examine in some detail Troeltsch's views on those problems of history and theology which we have already found to be so significant in the academic tradition of nineteenth-century Protestant theology.[66]

The historical method, Troeltsch tells us, has three components. The first is that of criticism which tells us that there are only probability judgments about historical events. Second, there is analogy by which we judge the nature of lesser known events from that of others, better known. The third principle is that of "correlation," "the mutual interaction of all phenomena of the spiritual-historical life." The art of the historian is fundamentally that of empathy (*Nachempfindung*) with the original content and "the discovery of the correlated, mutually conditioned changes" which make history one universal stream in which every event is involved in every other.[67] At every point in history there is something individual, and yet both in the "eventfulness" in which the particular is given as well as in our grasp of it there is an element of the organic connection of the particular with the stream of the whole, and of its mirroring of this totality. In Troeltsch's epistemology and ontology of history there is something reminiscent of Leibniz's

[65] *Ibid.*, vol. II, p. 730.

[66] Cf. above, pp. 21-32.

[67] Troeltsch, *op. cit.*, vol. II, p. 733; cf. also his article, *"Historiography,"* in J. Hastings (ed.), *Encyclopedia of Religion and Ethics* (New York: Charles Scribner's Sons, 1914), vol. VI, pp. 716-23.

monadology (as Troeltsch himself observed)[68] and of A. N. Whitehead's organismic philosophy, although Whitehead did not, of course,
influence him.

It seemed to Troeltsch that this way of looking at history was at
odds with the dominant position in dogmatic theology since Schleiermacher and also, of course, with the "miracle faith" of Protestant
orthodoxy. The practitioner of historical method insists that it is proper
to compare the data provided by "revelatory" events with others
supposedly not in so privileged a position. Particularly where the event
is in chronological proximity to "non-Christian" data—the very essence
of the Church's founding events must be subjected to comparative
analysis to show whether or not such data actually enter into the essential nature of Christianity. Moreover, historical method substitutes
historical probability judgments for the certainty judgments of faith.
Finally, historical method has no room for theories maintaining that
God is revealed directly in one series of events but at best only indirectly in all others. In essence such theories appeal to a miracle of
direct or special intervention by God in man's inner, spiritual life
through the events connected with Jesus and the founding of the
Church. For historical method such claims for inner miracle are not
one whit better than were the claims for external, natural miracle in
the face of the earlier growth of natural science. Yet it is precisely on
such claims to internal miracle and its foundation in the special, direct
presence of God through a noncognitive source of practical knowledge
that dogmatic theology has been based since the days of Schleiermacher!

When Christian theology appeals to history it never claims to do
so on a "scientific-philosophical"[69] basis. Thus, for example, Ritschl, who
was confronted by an increasingly skeptical and positivistic historical
method, surmounted "history through history" and isolated Jesus Christ
(and also St. Paul and Luther) from the proper historical contexts.
The unique religious significance of Jesus is guaranteed by the practical-
religious effects emanating from him[70]; they, in turn, are the basis for a
value judgment concerning the meaning of the events connected with
the life of Jesus.

But the whole tendency of historical method has been to overthrow
all belief in a unique "essence" or "value" that might form the internal
structure of one series of events and distinguish it from all others. The
notion of "essence," as we have seen,[71] had been very useful since the day
of Hegel in the interpretation of the Christian faith and Church.
According to this dialectic, Christian faith and the Church arose by a
logical, inner necessity from the historical fact of Jesus of Nazareth.

[68] *Ibid.*, vol. III, pp. 675 ff.
[69] *Ibid.*, vol. II, p. 207.
[70] *Ibid.*, vol. II, p. 205.
[71] See above, pp. 26-28.

The comprehension of the "essence of Christianity" was therefore a matter of relatively uncomplicated interpretation of an internal and consistent development. This dialectical view and the somewhat variant but related Ritschlian isolation of the revelatory event in history were opposed, it seemed to Troeltsch, by an outlook that stressed increasingly that there could be no such "essences" or isolated events since none could be demonstrated to have an "internal" structure or to be connected to other events by logical-essential bonds.

The genesis of Christian faith and Church must therefore be sought, according to the historical method, not in Jesus but in the general history of religions as it impinged on the early Church. This is particularly true in view of the fact that shortly after the time of Ritschl the gravest doubts began to envelop the historical, "factual" portrait of Jesus, to say nothing of his connection with the Church. So historical method—in particular the *religionsgeschichtliche Schule*—came to question the most vital links that dogmatic theology saw between history and faith[72] and to apply the same corroding process not only to the genesis but to the development of Christian history. Economic and sociological interpretations of Christian history were the customary instruments of this positivist "historism." Thus, Troeltsch affirmed the dominance of the view we have already examined,[73] that, like other historical phenomena, Christianity *is* its history and development and not a unique, self-identical idea or essence that is developed through its own history.

As Troeltsch remarked toward the end of his life, the difficulty of the "total conception and evaluation of Christianity within the history of religions"[74] remained the center and starting point of his academic work.[75] In *Die Absolutheit des Christentums und die Religionsgeschichte*[76] he had mentioned two mistaken but popular ways to establish "the ultimate validity of the Christian revelation in opposition to the relativities revealed by the study of history."[77] One is the claim to internal miracle, a direct relation between God and human awareness in which God is revealed directly, whereas he is known only indirectly in all other events as *causa remota*, "the ground of the interconnection of all things." The second method of claiming absolute validity for Christian faith uses the conception of evolution in theology that came into being as a result of Hegel's notion of dialectical development. Christianity is then "simply the perfected expression of religion as such." By contrast, Troeltsch insisted that even Christianity as such, to say

[72] See above, pp. 28-32.
[73] *Ibid.*, vol. II, p. 213.
[74] *Ibid.*, vol. II, p. 216.
[75] Troeltsch, *Christian Thought, Its History and Application* (Univ. of London Press, Ltd., 1923), p. 4.
[76] Second ed., 1912.
[77] Troeltsch, *Christian Thought*, p. 9.

nothing of the history of religions, knows no such monistic or mono-
lithic structure as this view implies. On the contrary,

. . . each process works itself out in its own way, bringing ever-new series
of transformations in its train, until its powers are exhausted, or until it
enters as component material into some new combination. Thus the universal law of history consists precisely in this, that the Divine Reason, or
the Divine Life, within history, manifests itself in always-new and always-
peculiar individualizations—and hence that its tendency is not towards unity
or universality at all, but rather towards the fulfilment of the highest potentialities of each separate department of life.[78]

In this situation, the fundamental way of gaining conviction of the
truth of Christianity is a personal one, direct intuition, confirmed *a
posteriori* "by its practical fruits, and by the light it sheds upon all the
problems of life."[79]

In the search for a more objective, factual basis for Christian conviction, Troeltsch thought when he wrote *Die Absolutheit des Christentums* that he had found it in the purely spiritual ideality of Christianity
which excludes all particular limitations, such as those of race and
nation, and in the living and direct manifestation of God in persons
rather than reasoning processes. Christianity, he thought, "possesses the
highest claim to universality of all the religions, for this its claim is
based upon the deepest foundations, the nature of God and man . . .
it is the loftiest and most spiritual revelation we know at all."[80]

Later, in 1923, Troeltsch thought that this was too easy a way to
combine historical particularity with supreme validity. His work on
The Social Teaching of the Christian Churches[81] had shown him the
individual and relative nature of Christianity and its components more
forcefully than ever: the Christianity of the West really has nothing
in common with its Oriental counterpart. Furthermore, he found that
Buddhism and Brahmanism are fully as spiritual and humane as
Christianity and therefore have on this basis the same claim to absolute
validity.

Hence, in 1923, the individualized aspects of Christianity over-
shadowed, in Troeltsch's thought, its universal validity. European history
has transformed Christianity just as it has, in turn, been transformed
by Christianity. The latter could not have become the religion of so
subtly developed a people unless it possessed "a mighty spiritual power
and truth."[82] This is its primary claim to absolute validity. We cannot

[78] *Ibid.*, p. 14.
[79] *Ibid.*, pp. 19-20.
[80] *Ibid.*, pp. 19-20.
[81] English translation by Olive Wyon (New York: The Macmillan Company,
1931), 2 vols.
[82] Troeltsch, *Christian Thought*, p. 26.

do without religion, and this is the only religion we can endure because it has become part of our very being through history.

The evidence for its validity lies in our inner experience of God through Christianity. Yet, "this experience is undoubtedly the criterion of its validity, but, be it noted, only of its validity *for us*."[83] We must not preclude the possibility that among other peoples and climes of highly developed culture, God may have revealed himself in a totally different manner. Only God himself can make a final pronouncement in such matters. He is the divine source and goal from and to which all great historical religions come and go. He is the infinite Spirit that indwells their finite spirits. But, so far as the finite mind can pierce the future's veil, they will remain distinct and their relative value impatient of objective determination.[84]

There is an intimate connection between this problem of universal validity and that of historical "essence." In an earlier essay on "The Essence of Christianity,"[85] Troeltsch elaborated on the subjective ingredient in this necessary concept in the philosophy of history. "Essence," the idea which historical method has made it so difficult to explicate, signifies an "ideal concept" which judges a train of past circumstances in view of its importance for the present and the future. To employ essences is to write history "with concern," for "importance" is no merely factual judgment. A subjective factor of personal commitment is absolutely necessary for the genuine realization of the meaning of "essence," just as it is in the determination of what constitutes "validity for us." This subjective factor, the unique position of the historical observer and interpreter with regard to historical material cannot be dissolved into the objective element of the concept of "essence." Their intertwining cannot be effected by theory, but only by the living act which here as everywhere "unites the objective and the subjective despite their theoretical inability to unite. . . ."[86] Their union makes up the essence of historical events. The relativity of history is therefore not simply that of events, objectively viewed, but also, as Niebuhr rightly interprets Troeltsch's intention, "the acceptance of the relativity . . . of the subject, the observer and interpreter."[87]

Troeltsch's vision is neither as consistent nor as rigorous as that of Karl Barth. He does not have Barth's resolute intention to break through the self-encased theological presuppositions of the nineteenth century, or through the maze of critical and methodological considerations to positive construction. But Troeltsch's vision is more remarkable in the depth of appreciation of the mysteries of history, perhaps also simpler

[83] *Ibid.*, p. 26.
[84] *Ibid.*, p. 33.
[85] Troeltsch, *Gesammelte Schriften*, vol. II, pp. 386-451, esp. 423-48.
[86] *Ibid.*, vol. II, p. 428.
[87] *Christ and Culture*, p. x.

in its final proportions. In one respect at least there is a real similarity between the thought of the two men. Both desired to break through the "relational" or "practical-mediating, agnostic" understanding of revelation in theology, the total separation between faith and normative understanding (or reason). But Barth's endeavor to do this by means of a theology based on the ontic and noetic priority of the Word of God to faith would have seemed empty transcendentalism to Troeltsch, perhaps even a throwback to the supernaturalism of eighteenth-century orthodoxy. On the other hand, Troeltsch's attempt to undergird (or was it to overcome?) theology by a formal *a priori* and his attempt to balance historical relativism and spiritual certainty in the understanding of particular historical data must seem to Karl Barth to be a pinnacle of the very error he has wanted to combat, the domestication of revelation by means of a rational scheme or by the claims of the autonomous richness of historical or spiritual insight. The diagnosis of the two thinkers with regard to the malady of "modern" theology was almost the same. Their prescriptions for cure were diametrically opposed one to the other.

Moreover, Troeltsch did not possess Barth's single-mindedness. In Barth's view, the formal priority of the Word of God makes the latter the sole source of derivation of every content in theology, be it history, anthropology, atonement, Christology or the doctrine of God. This priority of ontic fact over epistemology stands in contrast to Troeltsch's reasoning. Instead of Barth's understanding of radical unity in the source of revelation, Troeltsch sees a series of relationships between God and his creatures, each one direct and independent of the others, each with a form peculiar to itself. Their final unity is one of the unrevealed mysteries of God. The visions of God in historical consciousness and Christian faith (or religion) may not be the same. Each has a validity of its own. And one must say the same of each among the varieties of the visions of God in the multiformity of history.

On the whole it seems safe to say that Troeltsch looked for the direct impingement of God within history in the inmost "essence" of each culture. But in saying this one must recognize that the term "essence" includes a whole complex of empirical-historical, normative-philosophical and existential judgments, and also recognize that in so affirming God's revelation one is confined to judgments about God's actions which lay no claim to comparing truths within historical events on the basis of an absolute standard. To be sure, each action is that of the universal God, but for us its universality is grasped only as the intellectually opaque side of the Western civilization of which we are a part. But even this limited vision is better than the "present faith," the relational theology of the nineteenth-century tradition with its epistemological "agnosticism."

However, Troeltsch did not really want to deprecate "modern theology" *in toto*. At times it seems that he merely wanted to set limitations upon it and to undergird it with a philosophy of religion, as he thought Schleiermacher had desired to do. But even then it is evident that he saw no clear way to combining these two paths, and that he found the apprehension of the Spirit of God much more vividly shown forth in the spirit of culture than in that of theology.

Troeltsch saw the purpose of history hidden in divine spirituality which must never be confused with the finite spirits of men and cultures that are informed by it. It goes without saying that his was no simple faith in mechanical or organic process (or progress). For Troeltsch, as for Hegel, the spirit of God has its own cunning. But Troeltsch, in contrast to Hegel, found no dialectic by which we may trace the Spirit's movement in an inclusive historical pattern either by an immanent teleology within history or by reference to an extrinsic causal pattern or goal. In contrast to that kind of thought, Troeltsch's understanding was more nearly aesthetic: Purpose, though it is there in history, is hidden. The vision of the Spirit of God is intensive rather than extensive, revealing the adorableness that lies in diversity-in-unity or universality-in-particularity for their own sake.

From the standpoints of both theology and historical interpretation, all appropriation of cultural or historical data (other than those connected with the revelatory event in Jesus Christ) for theological purposes would result in theological rationalism and probably in the crudest kind of apologetic. Because he refused all such appropriations, Troeltsch's understanding of culture was peculiarly nonapologetic. Cultures were to him phenomena admirable in themselves and with their own direct relation to God. They must not be vulgarized by an apologetic, at best provincial and aggressively defensive, that would assimilate the mysterious diversity of culture to a preconceived theological framework. He would be as strongly opposed, on such grounds, to the usually "orthodox" interpreters of our day as he was to their liberal progenitors.

Troeltsch did not know how to synthesize his philosophy of religion with his understanding of theology and his interpretation of history, and he saw too profoundly to merge them prematurely. It was only as interpreter of history that he attained something of that vision which ought to be the beginning and the end for the theologian. Even then he did not dare affirm fully what he had seen. But if, as a result, Troeltsch fragmentized his conceptual scheme unnecessarily, he did not, at any rate, domesticate the vision of God after the fashion of that relational or "practical-mediating" tradition in theology which he viewed with a disapproval surprisingly generous as well as incisive.

Troeltsch bequeathed the problem of history to an influential group of contemporary theologians who have made it their central concern.

While Troeltsch was undoubtedly its foremost exponent at the beginning of this century, it had been implicit in the tradition of German Idealism from the very beginning. The historicist claims that in order to understand man one must see him in a context other than the static and thing-like context of nature (at least as traditionally conceived). One must grasp the fact that the human being gains his depth and freedom by encountering himself in the life of humanity within time. Indeed, man and his world are "historicized" together. Rudolf Bultmann and his followers have pursued this theme, first proclaimed by Troeltsch, with a seemingly relentless consistency. Thus Bultmann tells us that the nature myths and miracles of the New Testament actually have an anthropological or historical rather than a natural reference. Friedrich Gogarten, a theologian profoundly sympathetic to Bultmann's views, sets the case forth most boldly:

This change [i.e. the rise of the historical approach] means nothing more and nothing less than that by it the world has for man become his own world. It is his world now no longer in the sense that it is set before him with its form as a world . . . to which it is his task to adapt himself in accordance with its pre-established order. It now becomes his world in the totally different sense that it is for him to watch over it and to provide it with a form and order. . . . And by the same token man himself now becomes the fundamentally historical being. . . . This change in the relation of man to his world implies that all reality has now become historical for him. . . . And this means that metaphysical thinking has lost its position of dominance. History is now no longer, as it was for the medieval theology of history, "a process within a stationary world. . . . On the contrary, the world and the entire relation of man to it have now become part of history."[88]

It seems at first glance that here Troeltsch's views have not only been adopted but pushed to their logical conclusion. And yet closer examination shows that Troeltsch's was the more consistently "historicist" position. He insisted that history presented a problem which the theologian could neither retreat from nor outflank. Troeltsch rejected every endeavor to assert a trans-historical certitude or immediacy in the relation between God and the inner man. Likewise he rejected the related theory of a unique, miraculous occurrence within the supposedly special historical sequence connected with Jesus Christ and the theory of the later believer's supposedly special relation to this sequence. Finally, to cap the consistency of his historicism, he refused to split what one may roughly label the positivist, critical elements of historical event and apprehension from existential history. For example,

[88] Friedrich Gogarten, *Demythologizing and History* (London: SCM Press, Ltd., 1955) pp. 25 f.; cf. F. Gogarten, *Die Verkuendigung Jesu Christi* (Heidelberg: Verlag Lambert Schneider, 1948) pp. 451 ff.; also Bultmann's brilliant essay, "The Problem of Hermeneutics," in *Essays Philosophical and Theological* (London: SCM Press, Ltd., 1955) pp. 234-61.

there was for Troeltsch an inexorable pastness about historical events which demanded that they be reconstructed critically, even literally. And yet to do just this meant to him that one grasped the significance of events—in their pastness—with an intensity that brings them into a relation to present culture and selves by means of that empathy which is the basis of historical thought. Troeltsch believed that positive and existential elements are united in the actual process of historical thought, no matter how difficult it may be to grasp this unity in reflection about the theory of historical thought.

Despite their insistence on the radical historicizing of man and world, it is doubtful whether Bultmann and his followers have Troeltsch's consistency. In their view of the *kerygma*, the past that becomes the present Word of God is indeed a unique event (in contrast to Troeltsch's insistence that historical thought cannot conceive of God as shown forth directly in one event but only indirectly in all). But as a unique event it appears to lose its location in the past and to become mysteriously and directly transformed into the present of the responsible and obedient Christian self. Troeltsch would see in this transformation a denial of genuine historicity. Such tendencies on the part of Bultmann and his followers indicate that, all endeavors to the contrary, they cannot sustain the consistent unity of positive and existential history that Troeltsch maintained. In their theology (if not in their critical exegesis) they seem unable to avoid a split between *historisch* (critically reconstructive) and *geschichtlich* (existential- or eschatological-historical) understanding. And finally it is the latter alone which is significant as the historical framework for theological knowledge.

But does not this position really signify a retreat from historicity to the special kind of apprehension which then proceeds to find its appropriate content in a unique historical event, Jesus Christ? And have we not now returned to the "agnostic," "practical-mediating" theory of knowledge, the internal-historical miracle that Christocentric Liberalism had proclaimed? If, as seems likely, these questions have to be answered affirmatively, one must go on to say that it was precisely this point of view which Troeltsch combated from the historicist side and Barth from the side of a radical ontological or metahistorical realism that lays claim to the genuine historicity (in the widest possible sense of that term) of the transhistorical Word of God.

If history is indeed the basic problem for Christocentric theology,[89]

[89] All that we have said here indicates that history is indeed a basic if not *the* fundamental problem in the academic tradition in Protestant theology. This historicist conclusion seems no more than a proper deduction from the sharp separation between spirit and nature on which German Idealists had insisted from the very beginning. One is bound to raise the question if this narrow, though admittedly profound conception of theological *Problematik* is the only possible one for contemporary theology. It is an amazing fact that until Barth's most recent work, no major

the basic issue seems to lie far more really between Troeltsch and Barth than between Bultmann and Barth. Troeltsch and Barth seem to climax respectively the historical and the systematic *Problematik* of the academic tradition in Protestant theology. H. Richard Niebuhr grasped precisely this fact when he found his thought polarized between the work of these two men. Troeltsch has influenced him by his nonapologetic view of culture, by his willingness to abide in the mystery of man's destiny as reflected in cultural plurality, as well as by his use of sociological thought in historical analysis. But one must ask this question about Niebuhr's thought: Has he indeed united Troeltsch's and Barth's intentions, or has he followed Troeltsch in his interpretation of culture while remaining, in his understanding of systematic theological principles and the distinction of "inner" from "external" history, within the confines of the debate between Barth and Christocentric Liberalism? In any case, the result of Niebuhr's encounter with these two thinkers has been that one of his major tasks is to unite a doctrine of radical monotheism and Christocentric revelation with an understanding of our life as responsible persons in an endlessly varied cultural history.

---

theologian in this tradition has fully faced the claims of the Roman Catholic tradition (which is also that of many contemporary Anglicans, e.g., Austin Farrer and Lionel Thornton) that man stands uniquely in the context of nature as well as of history. Of the newer cosmological thinking, e.g., of A. N. Whitehead, not a trace is to be found in the theological tradition that we have discussed.

3.

THE THEOLOGY OF
H. RICHARD NIEBUHR

HANS W. FREI

1. NIEBUHR AND THE PROBLEM OF THEOLOGICAL METHOD

READERS of H. Richard Niebuhr's *Christ and Culture* are familiar with the typology he has developed for analyzing the manner in which men have related their confessions of faith in Jesus Christ to the life of their cultural communities which seemingly owe no allegiance to the Lord. At the extreme ends are those who deny any problem of relation, either affirming with the sectarians that the life of culture is anti-Christian or insisting that the Christian life is but the highest expression of life in culture. Between these two extremes stand three median views. The dualists see Christ and culture paradoxically related. The life in culture is opposed to Christ and vice versa, just as justice and divine grace are mutually exclusive. Yet both must be affirmed, the one as God's demand in the civil community, the other as God's gift in Christ. The synthesists declare that man's life is ordered toward both natural and supernatural ends, and since the supernatural God is also the orderer of nature, the two realms are related in an harmonious, hierarchical structure. Finally, the conversionists insist that, while the life in culture is mortally beset by sin, the Redeemer from sin is also the infinite Agent in ongoing creation. Therefore the life in Christ is not in complete contrast to, but a transformation of cultural life. While this transformation is completed only beyond time, yet even in this realm, life in Christ and life in culture are not to be contrasted as the redeemed and the unredeemed life.

In the terms of this typology, Niebuhr's own faith and theology are those of a "conversionist." He has said of the relation of natural and

65

revealed religion that they involve "neither mutually exclusive principles nor yet distinct stages in a continuous development but rather transformation or conversion, in which the latter is less the product than the transformer of the previous stage."[1] To Niebuhr, as to many other contemporary theologians, revelation is not a spiritual good possessed but an ever-novel event to be accepted gratefully. Therefore, no matter at what point on the road of life and grace he be, the Christian is never without both natural or cultural religion and Christian faith. Thus it becomes necessary to assume two starting points in all thought concerning the relation of God and man.

There is, first of all, such a thing as natural or cultural religion, the product of the kaleidoscopic historical forces in the midst of which we have grown up, as they have become part of our spiritual appropriation. Yet this natural faith is not as such open for analysis to the Christian thinker. For the latter cannot play a part which in effect would claim that we have not really met Jesus Christ in our history, that in a sense we are in a situation prior to or apart from Christ's incarnation, atonement and resurrection. So, while the factual beginning of reflection about God and man again and again takes place in the context of natural-cultural religion, yet in terms of interpreted history, i.e., in his theological knowledge, the Christian begins with the knowledge of natural religion only as it is seen through faith in Jesus Christ. In other words, there is such a thing as natural religion, but there is no such thing as a Christian natural theology.

One may see the reflection of this "double start" in all the problems on which Niebuhr has worked. We shall confine ourselves here to an examination of his theological method, doctrines of God and Christology. In examining them, we shall see that the twofold beginning of his method is also emphatically dialectical. It is a continuing conversation between concrete persons involved in making this double start— between selves in a community of other selves, which is the Church. And this community, in turn, and the persons in it are in conversation with other persons and communities.

But it is quite apparent that the restlessness which underlies Niebuhr's continuous dialectic and necessitates it is due to the fact that in and through all other relations man is fundamentally related to an ultimate "Other" who confronts him at once as the haunting enemy of his natural religion and as the bestower of grace. One may, I think, say that in all problems of natural religion and Christian faith Niebuhr's primary convictions are those of the primacy of God and man's absolute dependence upon him. It is not man's own self, or history, or the failure of his ability to transcend himself by virtue of which the problem of God arises for man. It is God himself that is man's foremost problem;

[1] *The Meaning of Revelation* (New York: The Macmillan Company, 1941), p. viii.

so that these other contexts in and through which God is related to men become problematical by virtue of the primary and absolute relation.

One may therefore say that Niebuhr's theology and ethics are radically monotheistic. Indeed, they are theocentric rather than Christocentric inasmuch as the problem of natural religion never disappears; for we always face God, not by any means apart from Jesus Christ, but as the One who is also Other than Jesus Christ, as the enemy of all our longings and values. But having said that we face God as enemy, it is only fair to add that foremost in the problem of God stands the question of grace or revelation, the question of how it is possible to have faith in this terrifying deity to whom we are related in utter hostility. Niebuhr conceives of this problem in a Christocentric and confessional manner. Whatever others may say, Christians are bound to say that the goodness or grace of God has been revealed in Jesus Christ. This confession is a result of what has happened to us in history, but of course not as a result of our historical achievement. It is therefore not subject to our election but to God's initiative. It is no apologetic statement that leans on a prior universal knowledge of religious truth by which one might evaluate positive religions in a comparative scale. The point of view of revelation theology is thus strictly confessional and nonapologetic.

This is the sum of the matter: Christian theology must begin today with revelation because it knows that men cannot think about God save as historic, communal beings and save as believers. It must ask what revelation means for Christians rather than what it ought to mean for all men, everywhere and at all times. And it can pursue its inquiry only by recalling the story of Christian life and by analyzing what Christians see from their limited point of view in history and faith.[2]

The conversionist's faith is that the new start which revelation made and makes in our lives and in our knowledge can, by God's grace and by it alone, coincide with every present start in culture and natural religion.[3]

We have suggested that after Schleiermacher it was increasingly taken for granted that the Christian faith is a unique, immanent, experienced state or relationship. For purposes of theological analysis the uniqueness of the "point of view of faith" lies more in its own nature than in that of the object of faith. The primary task of Protestant theology after Schleiermacher therefore has been that of understanding the empirical reality, "faith," both internally and by distinction from other ways of knowing. This is the problem of theological method which is still very much with us, despite other currents of thought since the rise of crisis theology. It is one of the most persistent questions among those to which H. Richard Niebuhr has devoted attention.

[2] *Ibid.*, p. 42.
[3] *Christ and Culture* (New York: Harper & Brothers, 1951), pp. 194 ff.

a. Faith, Value and Existence

In view of Niebuhr's confessional approach to theology and his insistence on the primacy of God and our dependence on him, it is not surprising that the problem of method is for him a problem of the internal understanding of faith rather than of its distinction from other methods; and that the problem is primarily a question of the proper form for that content which is involved in the knowledge of God. The questions that Niebuhr has asked in his search for theological method have been such as these: *How* does the problem of God arise for us? How are we related to that One in and through all our other relations? In their general, epistemological form these questions mean: How do we know God?

Whether or not he inherited the understanding from the tradition of the nineteenth century, Niebuhr is convinced that faith has its distinct point of view. Christian theology presupposes faith in the Triune God. Faith, in turn, is more than the undergirding context in which the knowledge of God takes place. Faith enters as a constitutive factor into that relation with God: on its epistemological side it is a special type of nontheoretic, historically grounded apprehension. Beyond that it is, of course, trust, obedience and responsibility. To a degree Niebuhr therefore agrees with the relational tradition in nineteenth-century theology which held that faith is a quality or datum which fundamentally modifies (for noetic purposes) the content given to it. One has to speak of God and faith together, and whatever one says about the one is in part at least a positive statement about the other. So Niebuhr quotes Luther's famous words from the Greater Catechism that "faith and God hold close together" in answer to the question, "What does it mean to have a god, or what is God?"[4]

It is apparent that faith, so conceived, is understood rather as an existent value relation to God than as a completely contingent, created fact. Niebuhr goes on to suggest that this viewpoint was one of the motivating forces of the empirical theology of the nineteenth century. He suggests that at least in part the intentions of Schleiermacher may be paraphrased in this fashion:

The being we talk about in Christianity is, whatever else he is, a value and absolute value, that is a being on whom the self feels wholly dependent for any worth as well as any existence it possesses. Now we cannot begin to speak about some being which has no value or which is dependent on us for its value. Schleiermacher refrained from making the apologetic statement that we are never bare of some sense of personal value-relation so that when we speak about something on which we are not absolutely dependent we

[4] *The Meaning of Revelation*, p. 23; cf. also, "The Nature and Existence of God," *Motive*, IV, No. 3 (December, 1943), 43.

necessarily speak of something that is partly dependent on us. He recognized the fact but confined himself to faith; it was not the business of theology to transcend its limits as a theology of faith. It had enough to do in this area; God and faith belong together.[5]

In similar fashion, Niebuhr speaks about Ritschl's "relational value-theology."[6] Indeed, the criticism he makes of the two nineteenth-century theologians is not that their value-theology method was wrong but that they departed from what properly constitutes the highest value, God, in order to make the highest value in the one case faith, in the other case man's worth as a spiritual and not merely natural creature. Both really abandoned the point of view of faith in God for faith in some other value. And so one must say that "it is necessary to begin where Schleiermacher and Ritschl began for the same reasons that prompted them and not to begin where they left off."[7] But their aberration was not necessarily the fault of the method. On the contrary, Niebuhr has been able to say that "the enduring contribution of empirical theology, from Schleiermacher to Macintosh, lies in its insistence on the fact that knowledge of God is available only in religious relation to him."[8]

To say that Niebuhr identifies faith, religious knowledge and valuation is doubtless to oversimplify matters. Yet there can be no doubt that he has used these terms to denote similar aspects of theological method:

Religious knowledge has been shown (i.e. by empirical theology) to be unique, and this uniqueness has been shown to be due to the fact that it is a type of value-knowledge or valuation— as, indeed, all knowledge probably is. The knowledge of God, it has been pointed out, is not equivalent to the knowledge of doctrine or of a First Cause or a Designer. And its dissimilarity to theological or metaphysical knowledge is due not only to its immediacy— which may be questioned—but to its character as knowledge of a being having value of a certain sort.[9]

As time went on, valuation as such receded in importance for Niebuhr as a clue to the method of faith. Nevertheless, he never abandoned the notion of a close affinity between value-thinking and theology. One has to bear in mind that in later years ethical values appeared to him as though within a new setting. This new context was the coming together of the selves to whom good and evil, value and disvalue appertain. More and more it is selves and not values that concern him. Theological analysis, like moral analysis, is the reflection of the mind upon the meeting of persons in which it has participated. Thus value-theory does not

[5] *The Meaning of Revelation*, p. 24.
[6] *Ibid.*, p. 25.
[7] *Ibid.*, p. 36.
[8] "Value-Theory and Theology," *The Nature of Religious Experience. Essays in Honor of Douglas Clyde Macintosh* (New York: Harper & Brothers, 1937), p. 112.
[9] *Ibid.*, p. 112.

disappear from his theology. In one sense it runs side by side with theology; in another sense it is taken up in a broader understanding. What Niebuhr said in "Value-Theory and Theology" and has continued to say frequently about valuation remains therefore as a clue to his theological principles, provided one remembers that his approach was increasingly transformed by a method that did not, however, contradict it. All of this is an awkward matter for the commentator, since he is forced to speak of Niebuhr's use of valuation in both past and present tenses.

Instead of abandoning value-theory as a clue to faith, Niebuhr has sought to clarify their relation. It has seemed to him that valuation is really a boon to the method of faith; but this is true only on the basis of certain carefully worked-out specifications about value. Niebuhr insists that value is always logically and existentially dependent upon "being" or "structure" or "process." In other words, while the Platonic and modern intuitional understanding of hypostatized values may be right in its opposition to subjective or emotional value-thought, it is in itself abstract, even undefinable.

What is fitting, useful, complementary to an existence can be determined only if disinterestedness, abstraction from desire, is practiced and the nature and tendency of the being in question are studied. Yet relational value-theory does not pretend that value has existence in itself, that independence from desire is equivalent to independence from the being for which the valuable has worth. It agrees with the subjective value theory insofar as the latter regards value as relative to being. . . . Its fundamental observation is this: that value is present wherever one existent being with capacities and potentialities confronts another existence that limits or completes or complements it.[10]

Fundamentally, of course, value-theory as a clue to theological method must acknowledge that value is related to that being whom we call God, and that valuation is a clue to the distinctive knowledge of that being. In this connection, Niebuhr was disturbed about the value-theologies that seem to us now to be the distinctive mark of the liberal position: ". . . there is one thing which all of these theories have in common: they assume that men have a knowledge of absolutely valid values which is not only independent of their knowledge of God but which is also in some way determinative of God."[11] This, precisely, is the inversion of the correct order of things, so that we see values as hypostatized abstractions. Our task is not to learn to "embody" these bloodless specimens, but to learn to think in such a way that being and value are not separated in the first place. They belong together.

[10] H. Richard Niebuhr, "The Center of Value," *Moral Principles of Action*, Ruth Nanda Anshen, ed. (Science of Culture Series, vol. VI; New York: Harper & Brothers, 1952), p. 165.
[11] "Value-Theory and Theology," p. 95.

Niebuhr said that being, structure or process takes precedence over value in the order of being, since value "arises in the relations of being to being."[12] But it was much more difficult for him, apparently, to make a similar judgment about precedence in the order of knowledge. He still speaks of a certain agreement between "relational value-theory" and Christian and Jewish theologies: "Its realism, that is, its solid founding of value on the nature of being, agrees with their conviction that the starting point of all inquiry lies in the recognition of *that which is*."[13] Again, he criticizes those who "assume that men have a knowledge of absolutely valid values which is not only independent of their knowledge of God but which is also in some way determinative of God." Among these thinkers he includes those who use valuation for strictly methodological or epistemological purposes, i.e., "who make values the criteria by means of which the experience of divine reality is distinguished from other experience."[14]

But, on the other hand, Niebuhr has emphasized that as a method for gaining knowledge of the object of religious worship, valuation is indispensable; and he has rejected metaphysical questions about God, questions about the being of God in himself, as beside the mark.[15] They

[12] "The Center of Value," p. 169.
[13] *Ibid.*, p. 173.
[14] "Value-Theory and Theology," p. 95.
[15] The term "metaphysics," is used here in a rather restricted sense. Post-Kantian understanding—which Niebuhr shares—is that traditional metaphysics has undertaken to make affirmations about ultimate Being and Truth on the basis of purely factual or logical judgments. Rightly or wrongly, this argument assumes that traditional metaphysics has effectively ignored or at least subordinated the significance of valuational and practical judgments for the understanding of ultimate Reality.
   Theologians who endorse this post-Kantian understanding of traditional metaphysics usually go on to contend that the purely factual or logical quest for Being-in-itself is fatally abstract and theologically sterile, because it can never lead to an understanding of God as living and as related concretely to living beings other than himself. Precisely this is Niebuhr's objection to metaphysics as he conceives it. It is abstract, in his view, and involves a failure to recognize the Deity of what can at best be known only as absolute and neutral Being. At worst it involves a failure to know God at all. As Niebuhr has put it: ". . . theology . . . considered as a pure science does not have as its object God in isolation. . . . The God who makes himself known and whom the church seeks to know is no isolated God. If the attribute of *aseity*, i.e., being by and for itself, is applicable to him at all it is not applicable to him as known by the Church. What is known and knowable in theology is God in relation to self and to neighbor, and self and neighbor in relation to God. This complex of related beings is the object of theology." (*The Purpose of the Church and its Ministry*, pp. 112 f.)
   It may be questioned whether Niebuhr has exhausted the possibilities of relating metaphysics and Christian faith. In general one may contrast two approaches to this issue. The first asserts that faith is the heart's or will's reinforcement of the mind's quest toward the understanding of being. In this sense faith is a purely practical aid and does not contribute any content to the mind's apprehension of being. The second viewpoint, which Niebuhr shares, asserts in contrast to the first that

are not only wrong but irrelevant and abstract since they do not express a knowledge of him which understands, "valuationally," his deity:

The idea of deity does not have the value of deity; it is no more worshipped than the idea of the beautiful is aesthetically valued or the idea of goodness morally preferred. Moreover, a being is found to have the value of deity not as a separate quality but by virtue of those characteristics which enable it to fulfill the need for deity. Hence the important question for religion is not the question, whether a god exists, but rather, what being or beings have the value of deity . . . it is a being which is sought, not value as such. . . . The question about the existence or non-existence of the gods is a false question. The true query of religion is, "Which among the available realities has the value of deity or has the potency of deity?" And this question turns into the other query, "Which reality has those characteristics which are the foundation of the value of deity, or which fulfill the human need for God?"[16]

The "quality of deity" by which we apprehend God as God, or by which we are related to him in his deity, consists not in a separate quality—presumably not in an attribute immanent in the divine structure which is apprehended as such—but in those characteristics through which he fulfills "the human need for God."

It is tempting to ask if this rejection of metaphysics is not really an affirmation of the very position Niebuhr attacks in the first place. If the perfections of God are known to us by virtue of their fulfillment of "the human need for God," then do we not assimilate our knowledge of God to certain prior, independent "felt needs," i.e., values, even if they are never hypostatized? When one defines value in terms of relationships

---

faith is the indispensable relationship with God within which alone knowledge of God arises. Therefore the knowledge of God is at the same time the knowledge of our relationship with God. That is to say, faith enters as a constituent factor into the knowledge of God; and thus there is no understanding of God apart from an understanding of faith in, or living relation or encounter with, him.

The theologian who dissents from Niebuhr at this point asserts that the metaphysician's rational images are fit means for the expression of faith in the living God of being and grace. To justify this assertion one must set forth some relation between metaphysics and Christian faith other than the two just stated. Such a third possibility depends in large measure on the following affirmations: 1. The understanding of the relation between Being-in-itself and finite being involves—in the very act—a direct apprehension of Being-in-itself. 2. This apprehension is meaningful for our knowledge because there exists a positive analogy between infinite and finite being. 3. Likewise there is an analogy between statements about being and those concerning the relations involved in faith. This issue of analogy, bearing as it does on being and faith, Niebuhr, with many modern opponents of traditional metaphysical reasoning in theology, has perhaps not taken into sufficient consideration. It has been most fully explored by those theologians who combine a substance metaphysics with a realistic epistemology, e.g., Austin Farrer, *Finite and Infinite* (Westminster: Dacre Press, 1943).

[16] "Value-Theory and Theology," p. 114.

between beings and also speaks of a unique, valuational religious knowledge, then the experience of religious need or value would (1) imply God as a "necessary postulate" and (2) "make values the criteria by means of which the experience of divine reality is distinguished from other experience."

It is apparent, whether or not these inferences are correct, that Niebuhr in his valuational method, though he affirmed the precedence of being over value in the order of being, could scarcely affirm the precedence of being over value in the order of knowledge. To the extent that the theological empiricist has affirmed just this precedence and has claimed scientific objectiviy for his religious method, Niebuhr considers him laboring under an illusion. The metaphysician labors under the same illusion. The result is that all sorts of uncriticized values, wholly extrinsic to the knowledge of God for his own sake, enter into the method and become the actual absolutes presupposed by the method, even if they are not recognized as such.

So far as religious knowledge is concerned, the issue for Niebuhr is not that of getting rid of the valuational method. For the endeavor to do so and to substitute for it a more "objective" approach merely results in the unwarranted intrusion of values gained from nonreligious experience into theology, where they are then employed as the absolute criteria of theology.[17] Valuation therefore is really inescapable in religious knowledge. It is not a matter of affirming valuational method together with some other method, such as empiricism, in the apprehension of divine being. Rather, value takes precedence, indeed apparently exclusive precedence, over any other method in the apprehension of being from within the religious life, even if in the order of reality being has precedence over value.

Two consequences seem to flow from this formulation for Niebuhr. In the first place, valuation must be conceived of not as an intermediary between God and man, but rather as the expression of a direct relation between God and creature. The second consequence is an implication of the first. No value or value relation which arises outside the relation of God and creature can be a clue to the religious relationship.

But the question is bound to arise whether one can be wholly consistent and speak of values originating solely within this God-creature relation. What does it mean that "a being is found to have the value of deity not as a separate quality but by virtue of those characteristics which enable it to fulfill the need for deity"? Only two alternatives appear possible. (1) We enter into the relationship with God as it were "equipped" with prior values to which the relationship has to conform. This alternative Niebuhr rejects. (2) The "needs" themselves are contingent upon and hence to be understood only through criteria estab-

[17] Cf. *ibid.*, p. 110.

lished within the framework of the divine-human relation. In that case the value of deity coincides with the value that is realized in the relationship. Now at this point there is a link between Niebuhr's method and the content of theological assertions. Since value is contingent upon being, quite evidently there must be a coincidence between the answer to "the need for deity," the quality of God's "Godness" and the valuation realized in the divine-human relation.

The coincidence in question is God's self-revelation. The knowledge of God is that he knows us, that we are being known. The valuation of this relationship is that of being valued by one who as God, and because he is God, is the being that can value us.

The religious need is satisfied only insofar as man is able to recognize himself as valued by something beyond himself. That has the value of deity for man which values him. . . . Religious experience includes an evaluation on the part of man, but primarily it expresses itself in the judgment, "This is the being which values me or judges me, by relation to which I have worth or possibility of worth," while reflexively it issues in the judgment, "This is the being of supreme intrinsic value, which corresponds to all my deepest needs." Such a value-experience is primitive and original. It deals with that absolute source of all value by relation to which all other things have their value. To analyze this experience by reference to values known and regarded as absolute prior to the experience is to lose sight of this fundamental character and so to falsify it to an extent.[18]

A curious phenomenon in this statement serves to point up how much Niebuhr's thought is involved in all the difficulties that nineteenth-century methodological thought bequeathed to the present generation in theology. On the one hand, the externality of mind and the "Other" in the process of religious knowledge is sharply accentuated: here as elsewhere Niebuhr emphasizes the sharp duality with which Barth wrestled so vigorously during his "dialectical" period. My knowledge of God is apparently not a genuine apprehension, but rather an acknowledgment and as such indirect: I recognize myself as being valued by something beyond myself. Or again, revelation refers us to something in our history which is our first certainty. "It is our 'cogito, ergo sum', though it must be stated in the opposite way as, 'I am being thought, therefore I am', or, 'I am being believed in, therefore I believe'."[19] This is the accentuation of a kind of negative epistemological relation between mind and object.

On the other hand, the relational, nonmetaphysical Realism of nineteenth-century theology under the influence of Schleiermacher sought to arrive at a point where the unrelatedness, the mutual externality between God and man (the heritage of Protestant orthodoxy), or between

---

[18] *Ibid.*, p. 115.
[19] *The Meaning of Revelation*, p. 140.

a present internal impact and a stubborn historical fact, is overcome. Valuation as activity and receptivity, as revelation, or as "intrinsic value" and response to needs, seems to be the point at which Niebuhr thought one might speak of such relatedness. As "feeling" was for Schleiermacher, so was religious value knowledge "primitive" or "original" for Niebuhr at the time he wrote "Value-Theory and Theology."[20]

All this implies that the valuations of deity and of the divine-human relationship are contingent upon and intelligible only through criteria established within that relation. But we must add a *caveat*. It is indeed true that we have no prior values to which the divine-human relation must conform. However, the idea of conversion, which has come to play an increasingly significant role in Niebuhr's thought since the days when he wrote "Value-Theory and Theology," suggests that such prior values as we bring to this relation may well play a positive role in it. But they do so through the enabling power of divine revelation and not by their own agency or that of the created beings to which they are related. So much is therefore certain: the proper interpretation of the Christian meaning of "prior" values is possible only on the basis of the divine-human relation from which one cannot abstract.

Thus far we have observed three facets in Niebuhr's thought about theological method. In the first place, it is valuational. Second, it is relational. In the third place, it is "revelational" or objective, i.e., it seeks to stress the independent nature, the initiative of God in man's relationship with him. But in a manner, the tension between relationalism and objectivity points to the dilemma in which both nineteenth-century theologians and crisis theologians have found themselves. If one cannot abstract from the divine-human relationship—if every attempt to do so lands us in the abstract *scientia de Deo* that prevailed before Schleiermacher—then every attempt to speak of God as "living," in the sense that he holds the initiative and has the freedom to grant or to withhold himself in regard to any relationship, is itself a tissue of abstractions. On the other hand, those who confine theological thought to relationalism will be criticized by men like Barth precisely on the ground that they begin from a subjective point of view which can never reach the proper beginning for theology, the free and sovereign grace of God. It is quite apparent that Niebuhr's theology stands squarely in the midst of this quandary.

Niebuhr's thought has steadily been of a kind that one may describe as "relational objectivity." While the knowledge of God is of a unique kind and available only in relation to him, nevertheless even in knowledge God confronts man in such a way that God holds the initiative. Even in knowledge God remains the absolute being and norm "over against" faith, the "Other" who confronts the self. Because it is difficult

[20] "Value-Theory and Theology," p. 115.

to express this situation in value-theory, there is something fairly restrictive about the latter as a guide to theological method. Niebuhr has never jettisoned valuational method, but since the writing of "Value-Theory and Theology," he has sought for more inclusive modes of thought in the search for theological method. Since he has not indicated in writing the reasons for this development, we may hazard some speculations.

In the first place, the increasing "Trinitarianism" of Niebuhr's theological method led him to see that God confronts us alike in nature and in history. In opposition to the point of view of Ritschl and others that would make the juxtaposition of spirit and history against nature the fundamental fact in a religious view, Niebuhr has insisted that the power confronting us in our natural creatureliness is the same as that confronting us in history in Jesus Christ.[21]

Value judgment usually tends to ignore the natural creation except in so far as it enhances the reality of value experience. There is a strong tendency even among metaphysically inclined liberal theologians (e.g., Edgar Sheffield Brightman) to base metaphysical affirmations on the argument that an explanation of the natural cosmos must account for the rise and persistence of values. Nature is thus subordinated to values and serves little other purpose than to explain their presence and enhancement, and value-experience is usually regarded as the crucial element in the total experience of the environment. In the nonmetaphysical value-theologies this subordination of nature to values becomes a mutual isolation of the two. Niebuhr soon came to realize that values, as we know and cherish them, meet tragic defeat at the hands of the mysterious reality which frequently uses nature as its instrument in this work, especially in death. Thus, if any reconciliation is to take place in history, it must be a reconciliation with the same being who judges and defeats our values when we confront him in nature. It is dubious that the valuational method by itself can indicate the meaning of confrontation by the Triune God who is the Author of nature as well as the God of history.[22]

Similar to this question about the limits of value-theory is a second which we have already suggested. It is doubtful that Niebuhr's valuational theology could by itself set forth the precedence of being over value in the order of knowledge. However, in revelation there is real coincidence of being and knowledge.[23] God *reveals*, i.e., he either imparts knowledge or prepares the creature for reasoning.[24] But what he imparts to the creature is nothing less than *himself*, confrontation with his own

[21] *Christ and Culture*, p. 114.
[22] Cf. "The Doctrine of the Trinity and the Unity of the Church," *Theology Today*, III (1946), 371-84.
[23] Cf. above, 73-74.
[24] *The Meaning of Revelation*, p. 109.

reality. If value-theory cannot grasp being as such but only the value-quality of being in the process of knowledge, it is not likely to indicate the being that is the concrete ground of being and knowing. The valuational method may indeed indicate that there is a supreme value that allows the importation of no prior value into the relationship of revelation. However, it is doubtful that by itself the valuational method can express the meaning of confrontation by him who is the Lord of all being and not only the Creator and Guarantor of values, human or otherwise. Even in history, where value-theory seems more easily applicable than in cosmology, we have to deal with a certain "givenness" in events that value-theory may be unable to grasp.

Niebuhr may well have come to believe increasingly that value-theory by itself is little better than metaphysics, with its abstraction from all value and relation, in explaining the unity of personal goodness with concrete being disclosed in revelation. Apparently some method more comprehensive and concrete than both was needed.

Third, even in "Value-Theory and Theology" Niebuhr, while affirming the uniqueness of the knowledge of God, tentatively rejected the notion that it is "immediate,"[25] i.e., presumably prior to and independent of its conceptual and historical embodiment. Our rational endeavor to express the meaning of revelation must therefore indicate that revelation is not an immediate, direct or even transhistorical relationship but rather a direct confrontation in the medium of history. The distance between God and the self remains. To express this state of affairs necessitates the use of "image" thinking, of analogy and parable.[26] By contrast, value-theory has generally eschewed such means. On the one hand, it is usually predicated on the belief that it is an expression of a direct or immediate utterance of faith. To this extent parable and analogy are not needed. On the other hand, theoretical expression, to the extent that it draws on theoretical, conceptual norms, is so far removed from the immediacy of faith that images, parables, and so forth, can do no possible good in overcoming the barrier between faith and reason.

Finally, between "Value-Theory and Theology" and *The Meaning of Revelation*, Niebuhr's theology became more Christocentric than it had been earlier (indeed, more so than it has been since the writing of *The Meaning of Revelation*). But it is difficult to see how one can comprehend through value-theory the nature of the time-process of history, which is an important aspect of any modern understanding of Christology. Value-theory, like Existentialism, points to the present need and present use of beings and values, though this fact is not always apparent in value-theory. Men usually conceive of eternity, implicitly or explicitly, by analogy to one of the experienced dimensions of time—past, present

[25] "Value-Theory and Theology," p. 112.
[26] Cf. *The Meaning of Revelation*, pp. 94-109; 109-31.

and future; and therefore their concepts of eternity are customarily determined by and expressed in terms of one of these dimensions to the exclusion of the others. Thus, the timeless good of objective or intuitional value-theory seems to be related to an "isness," a being that is at any given time conceived of as present. Even when "what ought to be" is related by way of contrast to "what is," the very grammatical mood and tense indicate not so much a potential future reality as the present focus of an eternal, timeless imperative. But about the event Jesus Christ there is something that is at once final and, in its finality, past. What has it to do with present revelation? Niebuhr was bound to reject, as Wilhelm Herrmann and others had done before him, all notions of revelation which turn it into a normative, theoretic truth, accidentally anchored in history through its temporal beginning in Jesus Christ. On the other hand, he was equally determined to deny, with most Christocentric Liberals and with Kierkegaard, all conceptions of revelation as the cumulative historical influence of past events. He was therefore faced with the dilemma of conceiving of an event at once inexorably past and yet direct and totally present in its impact. Barth once indicated that this was the same dilemma Schleiermacher faced in the endeavor to combine an historical and a psychological interpretation of the gospel. Barth suggests that Schleiermacher resolved the dilemma in a psychological fashion and left the historical past in a totally anomalous position.[27] Niebuhr has made a somewhat similar suggestion about the general tradition of nineteenth-century Protestant theology.[28] There is no apparent reason to believe that value-theory, even relational value-theory, could keep from following the path into the same situation so damaging to Christology.

Considerations such as these may go far toward explaining the change in Niebuhr's thought about theological method. The positive counterpart to his negative conclusions is that he turned from dominant reliance upon valuational theology toward Existentialism, which he combined with a strong emphasis on historical continuity.[29] In this conception he included both an understanding of value[30] and of time as the duration within selves in which past and future meet in the present.[31] Such an existential view is not in contrast to valuational theology. It includes the latter's positive contribution within a broader and more concrete view of personal being and its relations to other personal being.[32] Indeed, in Niebuhr's later writings these two kinds of understanding are more and more appropriated to each other.

In what sense, then, is Niebuhr an "Existentialist"? His thought is

[27] K. Barth, *Die Protestantische Theologie im Neunzehnten Jahrhundert*, pp. 414 ff.
[28] "The Doctrine of the Trinity and the Unity of the Church," pp. 377 f.
[29] Cf. *The Meaning of Revelation*, chap. 2; *Christ and Culture*, pp. 241-49.
[30] *The Meaning of Revelation*, pp. 65-68.
[31] *Ibid.*, pp. 68-71.
[32] In addition to Existentialism these views have been influenced by Josiah Royce.

deeply indebted to Kierkegaard, rather than to the more systematic twentieth-century thinkers who bear the "existentialist" label. He is indebted to Kierkegaard's concern to be a responsible agent whose activities and decisions, though they outrun reflection, must somehow be echoed in thought, despite the gulf that separates thinking and decision. He is, further, deeply sympathetic to Kierkegaard's wrestle with such problems as the understanding of untranscendable human subjectivity, the puzzling and also untranscendable relation between subject and subject, self and others, and the methodological—and yet very concrete —problem of becoming what one is. In the case of the Christian this latter issue of "becoming" means a final confrontation, in the process of becoming, by an "other" who is the infinite, paradoxically present now because in a time now inexorably past he was once a man among many others.[33]

Existentialism means to Niebuhr among other things concern with the problem of communication.[34] But this issue can come to the fore only when being is fundamentally regarded as personal being, whose essential characteristics are ingredient in its communication and in the process the latter involves. Thus the process of communicating, the communicated content, and the being that communicates are inseparable. The endeavor to separate them—even in order to rejoin them—makes for tragic misapprehension, abstractness, and for the failure of mind genuinely to meet mind. Niebuhr's approach appears to be a more concrete understanding of persons and reality than that of the relation of value to being, even in relational value-theory. The relational value theorist, by referring value always to being, seeks to escape both the raw, subjective and subhuman vulgarity of equating the good with the placating of experienced desires, as well as the abstractness of hypostatizing an intuited, objective essence of the good. Yet Niebuhr doubtless has realized that it is difficult to see in what manner the relational value-theorist's apprehension of the good really arises in connection with the relation of being with being. Value-knowledge, even relational value-knowledge as a unique type of apprehension, seems to refer to a practical-abstractive (in contrast to a theoretical-abstractive) quality, i.e., to a quality or predicable which, as such, is still not concrete, not identical with the totality of the being to which it refers. Value-knowledge does not, by itself, refer to the hinge by which that being passes from not-being to being and from not being its own self to being its own self. In so far as value-theory is relational, the moral quality appears to be a kind of copula linking two beings in a manner which is a practical parallel to the

---

[33] Cf. H. R. Niebuhr, "Sören Kierkegaard," *Christianity and the Existentialists,* Carl Michalson, ed. (New York: Charles Scribner's Sons, 1956), pp. 23-42; cf. also above, p. 20 f.

[34] Cf. above, p. 14 f.

logical linking of two terms by a common predicate-copula. While this method of conceiving values is not necessarily wrong in the eyes of an Existentialist, it needs a more concrete context. One must be able to see, with Kierkegaard, that the moral quality is really the *act* and not merely a predicate of individual being. As an act it is the self-setting-forth of the agent. Thus, a quality such as goodness is a mode of the agent's total being and not simply one aspect among several of a more inclusive subject or focus of reference. And hence goodness (or any other value) can never be a copula between two or more beings or terms related as though through a common term. It is rather a total qualification of an existent, it is a mode of the total being that confronts (or is in communication with) other existents whose modes of existence are discovered or even originated in the act of untranscendable subject-subject communication or confrontation.

Such confrontation or communication is, of course, not a transitive relation. One self-being or its communication does not directly pass over into others. Each self must, as it were, rely on an uncoerced and original reiteration of the communication, which is oneself, in the others. Thus, the self must also wait willingly, to be not only agent but patient; it must await the possibility of reiterating the communication that is the substance of other self-beings.

This concrete "given," this dialectical relation, or better, this communication between subject and subject in indissoluble togetherness and yet untranscendable mutual otherness, is in a real sense the beginning of religious knowledge for the Existentialist. From this "given" one may not abstract in such a way as to go beyond it to a supposedly more fundamental primordial situation. Only within the interpretation of this concrete relation do specialized value-theories, theories of historical understanding, and the like, properly take their place. But once this "given" situation is understood to be the basic and concrete context for religious knowledge, such specialized theories may arise within it with relative diversity and freedom.

In all of this existentialist thought, it seems to Niebuhr to go without saying, there is implied a rejection of the views that regard truth as neutral, as an objective essence or thing to which we would be only noetically, and not morally, responsibly related. At least by implication, then, we must deny that truth is an essence or a thing which we can grasp in a purely theoretical manner somehow in itself, without reference to its relation to us. All this is included in Niebuhr's Existentialism, an Existentialism which, like Kierkegaard's, seeks to avoid all ontological or metaphysical claims.[35]

Niebuhr has endeavored to cast Existentialism into an historical mold doubtless in order to overcome the hiatus between revelation as present

[35] Cf. above, p. 71 and n. 15.

impact and as unique and irreducible past event: for in the history of existing selves time is such that the living past endures in it, so that the self is not confined to an isolated present "moment" for its meaning. In this way it may be possible to explain that revelation means Jesus Christ, without spiritualizing away his historicity or overcoming it as the accidental clue to the supreme and universal value of deity.

Existentialism for Niebuhr does not mean antirationalism. The Existentialist seeks to express a relationship with an "other" through faith and decision to which rational reflection is related at once as preparation and as spontaneous consequence. The existential relationship of faith and decision takes place only where self and self confront one another. The being to whom we are basically existentially related is thus a person —the divine person. It is doubtful that value-theorists interpreting the value-relation between God and man could point so concretely to the unity of ultimate value and the divine being. Existentialists, on the other hand, *must* point to the concrete being *qua* being, to whom we are related, and not simply to his value. They have to do this even if they can accomplish it only negatively or indirectly (in order to avoid a distortion of the existential relationship in some "metaphysical abstraction.") So the human existent as an "irreducible self" confronts in God an equally "irreducible self." Thus Niebuhr says:

The most important fact about the whole approach to revelation to which we are committed by the acceptance of our existential situation, of the point of view of faith living in history, is that we must think and speak in terms of persons. In our history we deal with selves, not with concepts. Our universals here are not eternal objects ingredient in events but eternal persons active in particular occasions; our axioms in this participating knowledge are not self-evident convictions about the relations of such objects but certainties about fundamental, indestructible relations between persons. We need, therefore, to put our question in the following form, "What persons do we meet in the revelatory event and what convictions about personal relations become our established principles in its presence?"[36]

The being of God as grasped in the existential relationship is irreducibly personal. There is no other way of talking about him. Of "being" behind and other than personhood we know nothing. To speak of God's being is to speak of him as a person. This, at any rate, is what we must say from our limited point of view in faith.

This "irreducible selfhood" of God is what Niebuhr wants to indicate by the "objectivity" of the method of historical Existentialism which must for him be fully as objective as and much more concrete than theocentric value-theory. Now, for Niebuhr it is indeed true that God is "subject" and not "object." That is to say, he is the center of free, self-originating purposive activity, and he is always initiator and agent rather

[36] *The Meaning of Revelation*, p. 143.

than passive recipient in his relations with his creatures. He is not limited or conditioned by these relations, whereas every created being is always conditioned: each is an object or "thing" by virtue of this fact. Nevertheless, God is objectively present, i.e., he remains a self, confronting other selves as an "other," even though he conditions those whom he confronts. God is the ground of the self-other dialectic, but not by virtue of being beyond it or beyond subject-object duality. He is the ground of the dialectic because in creation and revelation he confronts us in an original self-other relationship in which he is also present through all dialectical relations among finite selves.

One may question whether it is possible to conceive of a pure "subject" being "objectively" present as "other," without having some doctrine of analogy. Niebuhr has never explicitly developed one. In any case, one may now readily perceive the sharp differences between Niebuhr and Tillich's thought. It would be impossible for Niebuhr to agree to a doctrine which suggests that "God is being-itself" is the only direct, proper and nonsymbolic statement we can make about God.[37] It would seem to Niebuhr that this cannot be asserted from any religious-relational point of view, and Niebuhr thinks that in theology we are restricted to such a point of view by the relativity of our existence, as well as by the initiative of God. It follows from Tillich's statement, of course, that one may speak of God's living, creating personal being only in a symbolic sense. For God is not "a being," but the power of being beyond the contrast of essence and existence. Niebuhr would find it impossible to transcend the duality and dialectic of self and other, subject and object, in this fashion. This dialectic is the very nature of our relation with other finite selves precisely because God in revelation confronts us as a self. Being and personhood in God cannot be separated; personhood cannot be understood simply by symbolic correlation with the former, as Tillich undertakes to interpret it.[38] Furthermore, Niebuhr would doubtless agree that all language about God is imaginative, symbolic and analogical; but he would probably object to the thought that a concept of being—beyond existence and essence—can be excepted from this rule. Niebuhr would in all probability question whether such a concept of being is really concrete and significant.

[37] Paul Tillich, *Systematic Theology* (Chicago: University of Chicago Press, 1951), vol. I, pp. 238 f.

[38] Cf. *Ibid.*, p. 244: "The basic ontological structure of self and world is transcended in the divine life without providing symbolic material. God cannot be called a self, because the concept 'self' implies separation from and contrast to everything which is not self . . . . Both self and world are rooted in the divine life, but they cannot become symbols for it. But the elements which constitute the basic ontological structure can become symbols because they speak of qualities of being which are valid in their proper sense when applied to all beings and which are valid in their symbolic sense when applied to being-itself."

The difference between Tillich and Niebuhr, in other words, lies in the metaphysical and idealistic thought of the former, as contrasted to the realistic, nonmetaphysical thought of the latter. Tillich belongs among those who seek a new ontological view from the wreckage that Kant had left of traditional metaphysics. Niebuhr, on the other hand, belongs among those who, following their understanding of Schleiermacher, think of theological knowledge as nonmetaphysical and realistic, and based on a unique religious relation. If Niebuhr revolts against this realistic tradition, he at least rebels "from within."

We are bound, however, to remember the complexity of Tillich's thought and the presence of at least one other strand in it than the idealistic, namely, "belief-ful Realism." As existential thinkers confronting culture and reflecting upon the place of faith in the social life, Tillich and Niebuhr have much in common. Were this an essay on the theology of culture, we could stress these similarities. However, in questions of theological method, in the doctrine of God and in Christology, they are quite far apart.

But the "objectivity" of God means more to Niebuhr than simply God's irreducible selfhood and untranscendable otherness on which he insists, in contrast to Tillich. Niebuhr always stresses the uniqueness of the divine person, and thus also the uniqueness of our relation with God, when compared with all other relations.[39] When we speak of the person of God, we must not speak of the principle of human personality, not even of the person of Jesus of Nazareth: "When we say revelation we point to something in the historical event more fundamental and more certain than Jesus or than self. Revelation means God, God who discloses himself to us through our history as our knower, our author, our judge and our only savior."[40] He is unique; his activity, essence, and perfections are unique.[41]

Again, however, there is no doctrine of analogy here by which to indicate the *differentia* of God's personhood. As a result it is a real question whether the concept can have concrete and positive content. At least it involves Niebuhr in a serious dilemma. He may, on the one hand, be forced into the same complete epistemological dualism with regard to the understanding of revelation that Barth held during the 1920's. What does it mean, in that case, to know the content of the Word of God, and to speak of the meaning of the divine person? It means less a concrete apprehension of the person than it does a negative

---

[39] Cf. *Christ and Culture*, pp. 238-41, 254-56; *The Meaning of Revelation*, pp. 54 ff., 147-91; "Value-Theory and Theology," pp. 101 ff., 110 ff.; "Towards a New Other-Worldliness," *Theology Today*, I (1944), 78-87, esp. 81, 86; "Evangelical and Protestant Ethics," *The Heritage of the Reformation*, E. J. F. Arndt, ed. (New York: Richard R. Smith, 1950), pp. 211-29, esp. 219-24.

[40] *The Meaning of Revelation*, pp. 151 f.

[41] *Ibid.*, pp. 183-91.

knowledge of ourselves as being known, being believed in, being valued. In Barth's words it means "*ac*-knowledgment" rather than knowledge.[42] Such a notion can tell us nothing about the content that is revealed, except by the most tenuous sort of inferential judgment. Furthermore, it can provide no positive indication about the process of the reception of revelation, i.e., about the relation of faith and the actual event in which it is received. Just this is the accusation Niebuhr had earlier leveled against dialectical theology.[43] Yet he seems, at least at times, to share the same view. This is indicated by the strong tendency toward dualism in his description of our apprehension of the moment of revelation[44]; and also in the lack of a positive description of the process of conversion. The latter seems to involve a knowledge of what we are to be converted from, but the *telos* remains strangely hidden,[45] except to the extent that we know that our present faith and thought are to be changed by our undergoing a permanent revolution.

If epistemological dualism is one horn in this dilemma about God's personhood, the other is the reduction of the notion of God's selfhood to anthropomorphism, to the purely relational notions of Liberalism. This is precisely what Niebuhr wants to avoid when he says that to speak of the person of God is not to speak of human personality or of Jesus' person. Yet Niebuhr's aversion to ontology or metaphysics—to any knowledge of God not given in relation with him—always limits him to reflection about being in terms of its relational qualities. Therefore the immanent or metaphysical attributes of God cannot of themselves be significant. They must either be expressed in terms of, or give way to, moral and relational attributes. Even the basic and most nearly completely metaphysical attribute of self-being (aseity)[46] is transformed by Niebuhr into the notion of power as it impinges upon us.[47] Does this not mean that, so far as meaningful knowledge of God on our part is concerned, he is reduced to his relation with or confrontation of us? Are we not then in the method of historical Existentialism in the same situation which we faced in the use of valuation method? It appeared then that, if the perfections of God are known by virtue of their value, their fulfillment of "the human need for God," it is at least likely that the knowledge of God is after all assimilated to certain prior and independent values[48] and is not the knowledge of being. It is possible that

---

[42] See above, p. 49.

[43] Cf. "Value-Theory and Theology," pp. 110 f., and "Religious Realism in the Twentieth Century," *Religious Realism*.

[44] Cf. *The Meaning of Revelation*, pp. 152 ff.

[45] *Ibid.*, pp. 175 ff.

[46] *Ibid.*, p. 183.

[47] *Ibid.*, pp. 185-87; cf. *The Purpose of the Church and of Its Ministry* (New York: Harper & Brothers, 1956), pp. 112 f.

[48] Above, pp. 71-72.

our understanding of God as objective person is also based on a prior and purely relational understanding of revelation, and that this understanding is, in turn, based on the prior necessities and conditions of existential, historical experience.

As we have seen, this problem is precisely the issue that sundered Barth from the nineteenth-century tradition and posed his central problems in the 1920's.[49] Is our knowledge of God contingent upon our notions of a relation which we must of necessity understand to be immanent? Is the object of faith to be equated with the content of faith? Is the constant factor of theology the revelatory or faith relation with its "objective" and "subjective" poles? In both valuational and existential methods Niebuhr insists on the objectivity of God as he is revealed. His emphasis on this point is so strong that one is inevitably reminded of Barth's revolt against Liberalism, of the dualism of his theological epistemology during the 1920's. Niebuhr's concrete religious concern that God alone is absolute, alone to be worshiped, and that he is the ultimate and basic question of our existence, point his thought in just this dualistic direction. Yet there is the other side of his thought which comes to mind in the examination of his notion of objectivity: both as a valuational thinker and as an Existentialist, Niebuhr remains relational in his thought. At this point he fully acknowledges his indebtedness to the nonmetaphysical, realistic thought of the nineteenth-century tradition.[50]

One of the questions which the inevitable tension between objectivity and relational thinking raises is whether the position of the "conversionist" is really a consistent one. Does it not rather represent an eschatological hope, and at present an oscillation between dualism and the liberal position?[51] In regard to the knowledge of God through revelation, at any rate, this appears to be the case. After describing the knowledge we have of external objects as knowledge in which the self alone is active, in which it must treat all behavior—whether of atoms or of thoughts—uniformly and in disinterested abstraction from all personal concerns, Niebuhr goes on to say that "in the knowledge of other selves both the relationship and the related terms are different."[52] Quite apparently the terms in this case are at least partially contingent upon the relation, for "the most important fact about the whole approach to revelation to which we are committed by the acceptance of our existential situation, of the point of view of faith living in history, is that we must think and speak in terms of persons."[53] While this is doubtless true of

[49] Above, p. 40 f.
[50] "Value-Theory and Theology," p. 111; *The Meaning of Revelation*, p. 23.
[51] Cf. "Towards a New Other-Worldliness," one of Niebuhr's most pessimistic theological essays in which the tendency toward dualism is less relieved by the opposite tendency than in most of his other writings.
[52] *The Meaning of Revelation*, p. 145.
[53] *Ibid.*, p. 143.

the subjective term of the relation, is it not dangerous to insist that revelation means a necessarily personal self-disclosure of the divine person—just because this is the necessity of our existential situation? In that case our situation prescribes the nature of revelation, and the meaning of the divine or objective "term" is not only realized in but completely bound to the relation. And in the background there always hovers the question: even if God, because of the exigency of our situation, discloses himself as person and can only be known as person, what right have we to assume that he really *is*, in his inmost being, person?

In similar fashion Niebuhr, in an extraordinarily interesting article on "The Nature and Existence of God," makes reality, being, objectivity and even existence so far as it is an object of faith—all implicates of the faith relation: "Now to have faith and to have a god is one and the same thing, as it is one and the same thing to have knowledge and an object of knowledge. When we believe that life is worth living by the same act we refer to some being which makes our life worth living."[54] As in most of his other writings, this emphasis on relationality is balanced by a tendency toward a sharp dualism when Niebuhr describes the conversion of the negative, hostile relation to God into one of reconciliation through Jesus Christ.[55]

Karl Barth's radical Realism challenged Niebuhr vigorously. But we recall that Barth took one last step to overcome his own epistemological dualism which he thought represented a vestige, albeit negative, of the relational outlook of Liberalism. He turned to an ontology which acknowledges the absolute ontic priority of the subject of revelation, insisting on its priority to revelation while asserting that in revelation the subject becomes genuine object for analogical knowledge. Thus, to know God is a more positive act than the acknowledgment that we are being known. But grace, and grace alone, is the presupposition, the possibility and the actualization of this *analogia fidei*.[56] Such a step

[54] "The Nature and Existence of God," *Motive*, IV (1943), 43. One item of great interest in this essay is Niebuhr's implied disagreement with those who understand the "method of faith" to be simply a modern equivalent of the argument from God's essence to his existence, and not a method *sui generis*. The method of arguing from essence to existence Niebuhr seems to regard as the rough equivalent of the procedure of philosophy of religion. The search for a prime existent, a first cause, is that of metaphysics. But the method of Protestant theology is distinct from both. Its question is, "How is faith in God possible?" It is subjectively different from the others because it is "personal, practical trust," rather than intellectual assent; objectively different by virtue of its reference to God's power in relation to creatures rather than to his essence or existence. It is this distinction of faith-method from the others, when applied not only to our knowledge of God but in a slightly different sense to our understanding of history, that Niebuhr means when he refers to his approach as following to some extent that of Kantian practical reason. Cf. "The Nature and Existence of God," p. 14; *The Meaning of Revelation*, p. viii.

[55] "The Nature and Existence of God," pp. 45 f.

[56] Cf. above, p. 51.

Niebuhr has found it impossible to take. At this point he feels the claims of the nineteenth century to be justified. Even though one risks, with the earlier Barth, a consistent dualism in theological epistemology, one cannot allow a speculative, empty ontology to separate God's objectivity, his freedom and Lordship and absolute priority in revelation, from his relationship with us. For the alternative would seem to Niebuhr to be a theological Realism so extreme that it would tend to force theology back to the dead hand of pre-Kantian rational orthodoxy. With this step one would lose not only the gains of the nineteenth century but the insights of the Reformation into the meaning of faith.

b. Relativism

We must now turn to one other striking and perennial aspect of Niebuhr's method. He has drawn attention, early and late, to his own relativism.[57] He has qualified the term in many a way; it appears variously as moral relativism, historical relativism, value relativity, and as religious, theological and theocentric relativism.

When we remember Niebuhr's emphasis on "conversion," it can be no surprise that religious, theocentric relativism seems to be the most important aspect of his thought on relativism. The significance of the other relativisms is interpreted by reference to it. In worship, ethics, and theology we must remember that it is the one sovereign and gracious Lord who confronts us in all things. Theocentric or religious relativism is inescapable not because there is no absolute, but because there is one exalted being who *is* absolute, who defeats and converts our natural polytheism and forces us to acknowledge that all values and beings, even our thoughts and confessions about him, are relative:

Just because faith knows of an absolute standpoint it can therefore accept the relativity of the believer's situation and knowledge. . . . To deal as we must with the relative values of persons, things and movements does not involve us in relativism, when we remember that all these realities which have many values in relation to each other also have a relation to God that must never be lost to view.[58]

Niebuhr stresses two aspects of relativism. The first is distinctly reminiscent of the relationality of his thought on method; it is a stress on the relations between finites and the finite-infinite relation. Thus, the value of a being is dependent on the context of its relation to another being. There is a certain value relativity which is due to the finiteness of all values that in turn are finite because they arise in the relations of finite

[57] Cf. "Moral Relativism and the Christian Ethic" (International Missionary Council Publication. New York, 1929); "Value-Theory and Theology," pp. 106 ff., 113; *The Meaning of Revelation,* p. vii and chap. 1; *Christ and Culture,* pp. x, 234-41; "The Center of Value," pp. 168 ff.

[58] *Christ and Culture,* pp. 239 f.

beings. These beings are all related to the one being who alone is infinite and thus possesses infinite value:

> For the polytheistic theologies of value, usually called philosophical . . . monotheistic faith substitutes, first a central value-theory and then the recognition of an infinite number of possible, relative value-systems. Its starting point, its dogmatic beginning, is with the transcendent One for whom alone there is an ultimate good and for whom, as the source and end of all things, whatever is, is good. . . . With this beginning the value-theory of monotheistic theology is enabled to proceed to the construction of many relative value systems, each of them tentative, experimental, objective. . . .[59]

Niebuhr calls this relation among finite values and beings "objective relativism," because the relation of equality among the finites is due to their common value relation to the one, objective, infinite reality whose being is never contingent upon the needs or desires of any other being.[60]

The other aspect of relativity is limitation: the limitation that enters into the standpoint and judgments of the finite subject and encompasses his relations with other subjects and their times. Such limitation is apparently more properly speaking what is meant by relativism, in contrast to the relationship that exists in relativity. Limitation is at once existential and personal, and yet social. Decisions have to be made on the basis of more than individual reflections, but in the last analysis they are inescapably subjective and individual. Decision takes place in a present "moment," and its relation to truth is not one of universal inclusiveness. Rather, decision is wedded to truth as it is for the person in the moment. Nevertheless, decisions are made in the presence of others—in the common limitation of common existence and destiny in which particular persons and societies, both present and past, participate.[61] Indeed, the social or historical Existentialism of our limited, relative situation is not only an external dialogue between self and other; it becomes internalized in the very constitution of the self.[62] So relativism means not only personal but historical and social relativism.

Once again it is religious or theocentric relativism that is primary. Other relativisms are to be understood in the light of their conversion to and interpretation by it. The limitations of the self and its societies are to be accepted both as the embodiment of creaturely finiteness and as opportunities for humility and repentance. In this connection it is important to recall that limitation is never to be understood simply as a universal principle, but existentially as "my" or "our" limitation. The relativity of the subject in history is therefore of greater importance than

[59] "The Center of Value," pp. 173 f.
[60] *Ibid.*, p. 174; "Value-Theory and Theology," pp. 112 ff.
[61] Cf. *Christ and Culture*, pp. 241-49.
[62] Cf. "The Ego-Alter Dialectic and the Conscience," *Journal of Philosophy*, XLII (1945), 352-59.

that of historical objects.[63] ". . . man . . . is not only in time but time is in man."[64] So one must begin to think from the point of view of the particular historical community of faith which is in the self, just as the self is in it.

Thus, one will not only be aided in the clarification of the relationship of God to history, but also one will avoid forcing the multiformity and proliferation of history and culture into universalistic conceptual schemes. If it is possible to avoid this latter particularly grievous error, one may be able to avoid also the defensiveness that is customarily found in connection with the framing of universalistic schemes. We do indeed apprehend the Absolute, but only from particular vantage points and through particular historical judgments. To understand this is to comprehend also that "we can proceed only by stating in simple, confessional form what has happened to us in our community, how we came to believe, how we reason about things and what we see from our point of view."[65] In other words, historical and religious relativism and confessional theology go together.

Niebuhr has suggested that Ernst Troeltsch has informed his own relativism in two ways. First, he learned from Troeltsch "to respect the multiformity and individuality of men and movements in Christian history, to be loath to force this rich variety into prefashioned, conceptual molds, and yet to seek *logos* in *mythos*, reason in history, essence in existence."[66] Secondly, Troeltsch has emphasized for him the relativity not only of historical objects, but that "of the historical subject, the observer and interpreter."[67]

To these two strands in Troeltsch's thought that have influenced Niebuhr we may add several others. One of these is closely linked to the first. Troeltsch, as will be recalled, had a profound respect for the independent and direct relationships between varying cultures and God. He thought that these relations were clouded in mystery and far removed from our temporal understanding. Consequently he refused rather scornfully to utilize history for purposes of Christian apologetics.[68] Niebuhr's confessional, nonapologetic theology, his completely nondefensive understanding of culture has undoubtedly been deeply influenced by Troeltsch.

Furthermore, Troeltsch's analysis of historical method may have given considerable impetus to Niebuhr's distinction between external and internal history. Troeltsch saw in scientific-historical method a grave threat not merely to miracle-trusting faith or a stringent orthodoxy, but to the

[63] *Christ and Culture*, p. x.
[64] *The Meaning of Revelation*, p. 13.
[65] *Ibid.*, p. 41.
[66] *Christ and Culture*, p. x.
[67] *Ibid.*, p. x.
[68] See above, pp. 60-61.

claims for the historical uniqueness of Jesus Christ by the later nine-teenth-century tradition.[69] Undoubtedly Niebuhr felt that the historical method of Christian faith could not challenge this point of view, (which Troeltsch shared with so many others in modernity) in regard to the objects of historical knowledge. It is unwarranted dogmatism to except the event "Jesus Christ" from the laws of analogy, interrelation and probability that govern our knowledge of historical events. Instead of disputing the correctness of this understanding of the object, Niebuhr suggested that side by side with the "external," scientific method there is an existential, participative or "internal" understanding of history. Niebuhr has suggested that this interpretation is parallel to the Kantian distinction between pure theoretical and practical reason, the basis for which is to be found not in the nature of the object but in the forms governing our understanding. Similar to Kant's two types of rational activity, these two historical methods are not in conflict; indeed, they may necessitate one another. On the other hand, they are not really in methodological contact, so that we may speak here of a parallelism rather than interactionism in historical epistemology.[70]

Whereas the data of external history are impersonal, internal history deals with selves. Niebuhr appeals to Martin Buber's by now classic distinction between I-It and I-Thou relations to illustrate the difference between the two types of historical approach. In external, impersonal history value, for example, means "valency or strength. The objective historian must measure the importance of an event or factor by the effect it has on other events or factors in the series." In internal history, on the other hand,

value means worth for selves. . . . The valuable here is that which bears on the destiny of selves; not what is strongest is most important but what is most relevant to the lives of "I's" and "Thou's." Value here means quality, not power; but the quality of valued things is one which only selves can apprehend.

Similar distinctions must be made between the external historian's quantitative and serial understanding of time and the internal historical time which is duration, "a dimension of our life and of our community's being."[71]

Revelation, the communication or apprehension of unique occasions which in turn sheds light on other occasions, can point at once to God and to history only if it refers to internal and not to external history. Otherwise, revelation becomes entangled once again in the specious claims to miraculous events in nature and naturalized history, in the face of whose inerrancy ordinary human reason is supposed to suspend its

[69] See above, p. 55 f.
[70] Cf. *The Meaning of Revelation*, pp. 81-90.
[71] *Ibid.*, pp. 64-69.

operations. The distinction between the two types of history, Niebuhr claims, does no such violence to the theoretical operations of the mind. But the understanding of internal history is a result of the inevitable search for God or gods on the part of selves who cannot live in community without living in faith:

> The standpoint of faith, of a self directed toward gods or God, and the standpoint of practical reason, of a self with values and with a destiny, are not incompatible; they are probably identical. To be a self is to have a god; to have a god is to have history, that is, events connected in a meaningful pattern; to have one god is to have one history. God and the history of selves in community belong together in inseparable union.[72]

Revelation and internal history, though not identical, do therefore belong together. It is here, in inner history, that the difficult concept called "revelation" receives something of an acid test of its authority and conceptual workability. But the very distinction as well as positive connection between revelation and inner history—as well as the consequent duality between outer and inner history—reintroduces once again the pattern with which Christian theology has always been familiar: there is a duality, a two-worldliness about Christian theology and ethics which is inescapable. We may reject the classical expression of this dualism as it is applied to the uniqueness of divine-human relation in Jesus Christ, that he is one person in two natures. But even if we do so, the concept of uniqueness of relation, of duality, of a miraculous penetration of the transhistorical into internal history will remain.

It is doubtful that Troeltsch would have expressed more than a severely limited agreement with Niebuhr's solution of relating scientific and theological historical methods by distinguishing between external and internal history. He did agree that there is a subjective aspect, an activity that selects and makes decisions, in our understanding of history. He agreed also that we are confined to particular and not universal histories when we want to understand the meaning of the absolute validity "for us" of historical events, such as Jesus Christ represents for Christians. On the other hand, Troeltsch was loath to distinguish thus sharply between scientific-historical and theological-historical methods. Even if there are surds left over in the interpretation, the two methods must be brought together. The alternative is reliance, pure and simple, upon the "agnostic and practical-mediating" theory which claims a unique but never binding or normative source of knowledge—purely nontheoretical—in connection with an historical event.[73] We have seen that Troeltsch thought this understanding, the common heritage of the nineteenth-century tradition, would eventually prove disastrous to theology.

[72] *Ibid.*, p. 80.
[73] See above, p. 54.

The divergence between Niebuhr and Troeltsch in this respect is so great that Niebuhr's frequent reference to Troeltsch's influence on his thinking is quite puzzling in the context of an examination of his theological principles. For there can be little doubt that Niebuhr does indeed consider theological method—whether in regard to history or otherwise—to be based on a unique type of knowledge that takes place in connection with a unique occasion, and that he considers that this occasion cannot be known in its uniqueness apart from an apprehension which is distinctly nontheoretical, valuational and existential. In other words, it is once again Niebuhr's "relational" view which is at the center of the problem. It is this view which Troeltsch rejects, whereas Niebuhr, in this regard, stands in the tradition of Schleiermacher and Ritschl, as he himself has acknowledged. If he does revolt against this tradition, it is with Barth's earlier thought rather than with Troeltsch. The latter would have sought to ground historical knowledge in a general, epistemologically oriented philosophy of culture. Barth, on the other hand, constantly seeks to indicate the objectivity of revelation and the dependence of history for meaning upon revelation. Niebuhr, surely, has followed a program more like Barth's than like that of Troeltsch.

We may test this assertion in three ways. First of all, we remind ourselves that religious relativism "corrects" historical relativism; in other words, it is not derived from historical relativism. It is a "start" in thought which does not itself begin with historical relativism and, as we have seen, it is in large measure a search for religious statements that are both objective and yet indicate the indissoluble relation between subject and object. This is relational objectivity in theological method.

Secondly, Niebuhr doubtless finds congenial Troeltsch's understanding of history as a universal process in which all events impinge on each other in uninterrupted flow.[74] But Niebuhr utilizes this notion, held by so many thinkers since the turn of the century, in a specialized manner. From the kind of organic, causal process that Troeltsch apparently had in mind, he turned to find continuity in a distinct concept of time—internal, personal and concrete time or duration. As we have seen, this notion of time is particularly helpful to him in solving the dilemma of understanding revelation at once as an authoritative past and as a normative present event. Whatever its genesis, this concept of time is developed by him in conjunction with the thought of Existentialism, as a way to aid our interpretation of the meaning of confrontation by the divine person. Once again, although Troeltsch's influence is present, Niebuhr's thought seems to be shaped by a more fundamental position. In this connection we must remember, too, that Troeltsch, unlike Niebuhr, refused all ultimate methodological distinc-

[74] See above, p. 55.

tion or separation between external and internal, scientific and subjective or valuing history.

Finally, we may recall Troeltsch's suggestion that the "agnostic" theory of knowledge goes hand in hand with faith in an "internal" miracle.[75] The claim for a special apprehension in history and internal participation, Troeltsch contended, is no better founded than the orthodox argument for cosmic miracle. He thought that the simple transfer of miracle from nature to spirit was the common core of the nineteenth-century Christian historical tradition. Niebuhr's Christology and doctrine of grace in *The Meaning of Revelation*,[76] and other writings of that period, indicate how close he is to the position Troeltsch rejected. This is not particularly observable in Niebuhr's understanding of religious knowledge, for unlike many of the nineteenth-century thinkers, he emphasizes the closeness of rational interpretation to both faith and history. However, our confrontation and conversion by Jesus Christ in internal history is a miracle, a unique event which does not find its sufficient explanation in the matrix of other events in which it arises for us in internal history. In fact, it is in the understanding of the abruptness of God's entry into our faith that the dualistic tendencies we have observed in Niebuhr become most clearly evident. There is no possible description of the way of this ingression into our history. He is simply there, the great surd, and the fact that faith in God's faithfulness is created through Christ's sufferings allows only our confession, but no real explication. It is "absurd." It is a miracle.[77]

We are far from suggesting that Troeltsch did not influence Niebuhr strongly. Rather, we are saying that in regard to theological principles and systematic or dogmatic theology his influence on Niebuhr is secondary when compared to the basic tension over theological method that Niebuhr confronted through his interest in the debate between the nineteenth-century tradition and dialectical theology. Had we looked at Niebuhr's contribution as a theological moralist, as a theologian of culture and as an historian of Christian thought and Christian movements, the story would have been different. In these areas, in the relation between thought about Christ and about culture, Troeltsch's influence on Niebuhr has doubtless been paramount.

But one more thing needs to be said: Troeltsch's relativism and Barth's early dualism were both results of desperate efforts to break through the anthropomorphism and self-encasement of the nineteenth-century liberal tradition. Both men wanted to overcome the "agnostic" or relational understanding of Christian faith, with its confinement of

[75] See above, p. 56.
[76] Cf. *The Meaning of Revelation*, pp. 73-90; 109-37; 156-91.
[77] *Christ and Culture*, p. 254; Cf. "The Nature and Existence of God," p. 46.

God to a narrow strip of the creature's experience and its isolation of the Christian faith from the life of reason and culture.[78] It seems that the critical mind of Troeltsch saw in culture the hidden majesty of the same God whom the constructive mind of Barth saw revealed in Jesus Christ. Niebuhr in his "double wrestle" with Christ and culture has learned from "the critical thought of the former and the constructive work of the latter,"[79] and has sought to combine their interests in the framework of a conversionist theology for which the creative *logos* is the very Redeemer who converts to himself and to the Creator who is at one with him, in infinity and time, the straying historical creatures who despite their tragic errors and contrary wills still portray the good toward which he has made them.

2. THE DOCTRINE OF GOD

Niebuhr's relational objectivity and his Existentialism are both instruments for the expression of one of his most persistent problems: the conversion of our hostile confrontation with God into a relationship in which we will be related to him in faith, hope and love. It is not surprising that one whose notion of relationality is existential should find our confrontation by God the most important single theological consideration.

Whatever else one may say about Niebuhr's methodology, without a doubt he desires it to be no more than the expression of a consistent monotheism. He has said again and again that our natural worship is polytheistic—whether the objects of our devotion are social realities, persons, the self or abstract essences. We cannot live without living for a cause, without worshiping a being to hallow life. But in all our polytheistic faiths we are in perplexity, ignorance, hostility or distrust related to the One beyond, or in and among the many. In our own way we may hope for or fear a monistic integration of our faiths. In totally different fashion such hopes and fears are but the echo of reality apprehended through our distrust and distortion.[80] Whether in trust or distrust, we live our lives in confrontation with God. We cannot do otherwise.

When we are confronted by God outside of Jesus Christ, he comes to us as power. "Power" here is not simply equivalent to "reality" or "existence," although there is involved in it an element of sheer "thereness." But the question about God's existence is purely secondary, for theological method perhaps even a wrong question. What one must

---

[78] Cf. above, pp. 59-61.

[79] *The Meaning of Revelation*, p. x.

[80] Cf. *The Church against the World* (Chicago and New York: Willett, Clark & Company, 1935), pp. 123-56; *The Meaning of Revelation*, pp. 76-80, 175-91; "The Nature and Existence of God," pp. 13-15, 43-46; "Evangelical and Protestant Ethics," pp. 222 f.; "The Center of Value," pp. 172 ff.

point to, rather, is that there is, for human existence, an inescapable confrontation by a final and ultimate power that lies across the path of our destiny like an irremovable and insuperable road block. Our question must be, who or what is this being?[81] At stake is the nature of our inescapable relation with this being, and this relation is determined by his nature.

In any natural sense of the word, this being is certainly not "good." For our good is perverted, and he neither is, nor will he guarantee, the absoluteness of the relative values we seek to adore as absolute. He will not allow men to use him as an instrumental value. He brings all such strivings actively to grief; he is the enemy of our natural worship. In fact, in this hostility we receive the first inkling of his unity. He is the common adversary of all values and creatures. They all die, just as surely as they have been brought forth. We learn to know God's unity in the common defeat that befalls all endeavors to bring into the thought of him "the idea of such special unity as we had in ourselves."[82] Apparently, then, his unity is an aspect of a more basic quality, an aspect of the power with which he confronts us, just as we have seen his reality to be an expression of his power.

The relation between this power which is God and the divine goodness has occupied Niebuhr's thought over a long period of time. In God's confrontation of us in natural religion, he does not manifest himself in the sort of wrath reminiscent of man. On the other hand, he is not shown forth simply as an amoral, impersonal final cause or barrier, although Niebuhr believes that we often conceive of God as fate. Instead, the nature of this being, as we discover it or him through our natural religion, is one of active hostility: his power is that of an enemy.[83] He defeats all things, and in the end nothing is eternal except himself.

Power thus is the primary concept of God in Niebuhr's view of natural religion, with unity as one aspect of power and hostility as its prime positive qualification. Jesus Christ is the transformer of this relation, although in a sense one may view his life and death also from the vantage point of natural religion. For in him is exhibited God's hostile power in its most extreme form: "Here we confront the slayer . . ."[84] in the "crucifixion, the betrayal of Jesus Christ, who was utterly loyal to Him."[85]

In a real sense, then, Niebuhr's theology is theocentric rather than Christocentric: his theological problem is not in the first instance one

---

[81] The very order in the title of "The Nature and Existence of God" implies this order in asking the question about God.

[82] *The Meaning of Revelation*, pp. 183-84.

[83] "The Nature and Existence of God," p. 45.

[84] *Ibid.*, p. 46.

[85] *Christ and Culture*, p. 254.

of relation to Jesus Christ. Rather, it arises out of the fact that we are face to face with the God who is the hostile power over all things. But one should speak of a tendency only. We are suggesting that in natural religion and Christian faith, Niebuhr's starting point is with God the Father rather than with the Son. And yet the task of Christian theology is to express the conversion of our faith and its *new* understanding of God's power, unity and goodness in the light of God's act in Jesus Christ. Thus Christology is directly involved in Niebuhr's theocentric theology.

What is radically new now is that we confront God as Father of the Son and as our Father. We understand him no less than before to be power, but whereas in our natural relation of distrust we saw utter and complete separation between his power and goodness, we now see them to be one. God reveals himself, his Deity.[86] Goodness and power both express the fullness of God's undivided Deity. How are we to conceive of this ongoing conversion of our value-thinking and power-thinking, and above all of our thought concerning their unity, i.e., the unity of Deity? This question about the nature of God is not abstract, but the concrete question of religious crisis and conversion. It is the focus of a good many other questions, of atonement and reconciliation, of grace and the Trinity.

Niebuhr has not written directly about the atonement. However, one may glean something of the direction of his thought if one remembers its relational objectivity. The change that takes place in atonement is of course first of all in the divine-human relationship itself, from which one may not abstract. But what is the element of "objectivity" in this change in relation? Does it mean that the change in relation transforms only the human being so that he now recognizes that the "hostility" he saw in God's power was actually all along a product of man's own perverse imagination? Or is there perhaps an element of mysterious novelty and tragic reconciliation that has to be brought into the very concept of Deity itself, of divine wrath and divine love? Niebuhr has not said, and his "relational" position will doubtless keep him from all bold metaphysical affirmations. Yet one may suspect that relatively easy solutions like those of the subjective theory of the atonement and even Gustaf Aulén's "classic" theory[87] are not of sufficient scope to answer Niebuhr's quest for an understanding of the majesty and inscrutable dominion of the divine love. For both these positions in effect simply affirm the continuity of the divine love in the process of reconciliation, and contend that it is the creature alone rather than the Creator that must be reconciled. Even though Aulén asserts the "para-

[86] Cf. *The Meaning of Revelation*, chap. 4; "The Doctrine of the Trinity and the Unity of the Church," p. 372.

[87] G. Aulén, *Christus Victor* (New York: The Macmillan Company, 1951).

dox" of the divine wrath, it is plainly there for him as simply and quite undialectically transcended in God's love.[88]

Niebuhr has within him far too much of the Calvinist's adoration of the sheer majesty of God to be thus easily satisfied. It is not only that he vigorously rejects all endeavors to make "love" the sole clue to the nature of God and to the thought and being of Jesus Christ.[89] In addition, and more important, he protests the widely prevalent and to his way of thinking deceptive tendencies that arise from "the substitution of Christology for theology, of the love of Jesus Christ for the love of God and of life in the community of Jesus Christ for life in the divine commonwealth."[90]

If the long story of the Trinitarian debate in Christendom is to be re-enacted in our present time, its outcome may result in somewhat different formulations from those of the past, but scarcely in a substantive change of the affirmation that God is One and that however the doctrine of the *Personae* is stated it must still be affirmed that the Father is not the Son and the Son is not the Father and the Spirit cannot be equated with either. Yet in many churchly pronouncements the faith of Christians is stated as if their one God were Jesus Christ; as if Christ's ministry of reconciliation to the Creator were of no importance. . . . Historically and theologically we are dealing here with devout yet aberrant forms of faith that are unable to illuminate the more profound problems of human existence, suffering, guilt and destiny or to answer questions about human history in its wholeness.[91]

We recognize from all this, first of all, that there is no easy solution for Niebuhr of the problems of reconciliation and atonement, as there appears to be in Aulén's and the subjective theory's recourse to the unity and continuity of divine love. At the very least Niebuhr would have to say that these solutions do not do justice to "Christ's ministry of reconciliation to the Creator," nor therefore "to the more profound problems of human existence." They tend to reduce all problems involving tragedy to purely Christocentric rather than genuinely Trinitarian modes of thought.

This leads us to a second observation, namely, that Niebuhr, quite apparently, tends to subsume the problem of atonement or reconciliation within that of the divine unity, i.e., of the unity of divine power and love. It is already apparent from the lengthy statement of Niebuhr's which we have just quoted that he frequently (though not always!) considers the question of unity in the framework of the doctrine of the Trinity.

Niebuhr once wrote that

[88] *Ibid.*, pp. 115, 153. By contrast see *Christ and Culture*, pp. 158 f.
[89] Cf. *Christ and Culture*, pp. 15-19.
[90] *The Purpose of the Church and Its Ministry*, p. 44.
[91] *Ibid.* p. 45.

the existential problem of God and of man's relation to him leads inevitably to the question about the deity of the Creator of Nature, that is of his goodness, to the question about the deity of Jesus Christ, that is of his power, and to the question about the deity of the Spirit, that is whether among all the spirits there is a Holy Spirit.[92]

We have seen before that, in contrast to the traditional scheme, Niebuhr's theology does not permit him to distinguish between metaphysical or immanent perfections and moral or relational attributes of God. The doctrine of the Trinity thus also is a matter of the self-manifestation of God to his creatures. What we have here, therefore, is an example of economic Trinitarianism. As a matter of fact it was this type of Trinitarianism which prevailed among those of the nineteenth-century tradition who did not relegate the doctrine to metaphysical unimportance.

The greatest difficulty in this position, as I see it, is that it does not allow us to grasp firmly the unity of the three Persons in the one Deity. Such unity is a necessary implication, perhaps, but it is not given with the relational directness, i.e., it is not of the religious nature of the individual persons or "relations." It is, instead, an intellectual implication. But just this merely rational inference Niebuhr would want to avoid. The unity must be as real, religiously, as the distinctions within the Godhead.

One may make the same criticism by observing that the position of economic Trinitarianism cannot observe the rule that "the external effects of the Trinity are undivided." Unless the eternal Son, the Father and the Spirit are present in natural creation, historical redemption and present spiritual sanctification, God is not grasped in his undividedness. Hence also our responses to this unity in manifoldness must be interrelated. We do not simply respond with our reason to the Creator and with faith to the Redeemer and by an internal principle to the Spirit. Niebuhr emphasizes just this point in contrasting the theological convictions of the conversionist with those of the dualist:

. . . the conversionist tends to develop a phase of creation neglected by the dualist. On the one hand he emphasizes the participation of the Word, the Son of God, in creation, not as this took place once upon a time but as it occurs in the immediate origin, the logical and momentary beginning of everything, in the mind and power of God. On the other hand he is concerned with the redemptive work of God in the incarnation of the Son, and not merely with redemption in his death, resurrection, and return to power . . . he seeks to hold together in one movement the various themes of creation and redemption, of incarnation and atonement.[93]

Nevertheless, it seems true that in Niebuhr's Trinitarian thought (per-

---

[92] "The Doctrine of the Trinity and the Unity of the Church," p. 372.
[93] *Christ and Culture*, pp. 192 f.

haps in contrast to his doctrine of the present work of Christ), the "natural man" is related in hostility to the Creator *in his power*, and not to Jesus Christ or to the eternal Word in his goodness or to the Spirit. Again, it appears that the response to God as the Creator is that of reason and not of faith which is given only to God-in-Christ. Both the divine activities and our responses to them seem to be divided:

> . . . in ancient and modern times . . . the question arises whether indeed there is any unambiguous evidence that the power or reality declared in the invisible things of creation is indeed personal, so that it can be addressed, and whether it or he is good. Facing these questions the Unitarianism of the Creator discovers that it is dependent not simply on reason but also on the faith of Jesus Christ and that the God it worships is after all not simply the God of nature but the Father of Jesus Christ.[94]

Again, if one begins with the goodness of God the Creator, the question of his existence or power is bound to arise:

> For such a monotheism of the Father, the recurring problem arises whether after all this God of kindness, benevolence and Christlike character really exists. Having begun with the rational knowledge of a first principle of nature, but having interpreted that first principle in terms of revelation, or having asserted that the one God is the Creator and then affirmed that the character of the Creator is what is discerned in the Son, this Unitarianism is either required to find in Jesus Christ a reconciler to the Creator or to ask whether the Christ-like God has any existence.[95]

The same situation obtains with regard to the religions of the Son and of the Spirit. Thus, for example, in the case of the religion of Jesus Christ: "Though it has had no doubt about the goodness of Christ, about his deity in terms of value, it has not been able to avoid the question of his power."[96] So the question of value and being which we had to face in methodology returns in the doctrine of the Trinity, and in this context also it is difficult to see their concrete unity. We must ask again if the notion of power, understood exclusively as a relational value concept, can really become a clue to being or existence. Though one can see in each case that the particular relational value (goodness, power and spirituality) is incomplete without the others, it is doubtful that Niebuhr indicates the concrete nature of their unity or their necessary reference to existence.

We saw reason to believe that, at least in the order of our knowledge, "value" is prior to "being" for Niebuhr. Moreover, it seemed possible that the valuational or existential relationship is the determinant of the divine "content" or nature as it stands revealed.[97] The question is therefore bound to arise, whether the distinctions in the Godhead to

[94] "The Doctrine of the Trinity and the Unity of the Church," p. 380.
[95] *Ibid.*, p. 381.
[96] *Ibid.*, p. 382.
[97] See above, pp. 71 f., 84 f.

which we are related are not really three values that arise prior to the revelation of the divine Self, and whether these values are then identified with the three divine *hypostaseis*. The crucial question is whether, in the order of knowledge as well as of being, the unique divine *hypostasis* in question is the clue to a particular value, or whether the reverse is true. In either case it is difficult, once more, to see how the unity of the three can be understood except as an abstract implication. But more than that, if value is prior to being in our knowledge, this understand of the necessary interrelation of power, goodness and spirituality is in danger of being a pantheon of ethical-philosophical construction, rather than a testimony to the nature of the specific divine Self who stands revealed before us. This position Niebuhr of course wants to avoid.[98] But it remains as a question in his theology.

Niebuhr has sought for an understanding of divine unity not only in the doctrine of the Trinity but in the doctrine of revelation.[99] As a conversionist, he must show forth the meaning of unity in the mutual relations of power and goodness which are so antagonistic to each other in natural religion. Above all, he must show how our notions of power, foremost in the relation of the natural distrust we bear toward God, are converted so as to be in unity with goodness.[100] God's personhood is known in his self-revelation in Jesus Christ. The unity of the Godhead is that of a person, and this personal unity we see more directly in the relation of revelation as an existential confrontation than we see it in the understanding of Trinitarian doctrine in which it is reflected:

> God who comes to man in Jesus Christ is one, as the deity of our religious imagination is one, but he demands the reformation of every particular idea of unity we have, and the making of a new beginning in our effort to understand his nature. The doctrine of the Trinity is no satisfactory or final formulation of this understanding, but it is more satisfactory than all the ancient and modern pantheons wherein we ascend beyond the many gods or values to someone who is limited by them.[101]

We may note that Niebuhr's doctrine of revelation, having been profoundly influenced by Existentialism, is not as closely identified with a

[98] Cf. *The Meaning of Revelation*, pp. 164-85.

[99] Cf. *Ibid.*, pp. 138-54; 183-91.

[100] In *The Meaning of Revelation*, the issue appears to be the unity of goodness and power (reality), as well as that of present, objective confrontation and revelation in a past event. In other words, there is little doctrine of the Spirit in this book. Apparently at the time he wrote it Niebuhr was something of a Binitarian. The Trinitarian method developed later. Instead of the doctrine of the Spirit we have the concept of "internal history" which mediates the past event to confrontation in the present. Perhaps Niebuhr at the time was still in the throes of reaction against the one-sided pneumatology of the liberal tradition to which he himself has drawn attention ("The Doctrine of the Trinity and the Unity of the Church," pp. 377 f.).

[101] *The Meaning of Revelation*, pp. 184-85.

doctrine of the Trinity (an inescapably intellectualist rather than existential expression) as in the case of Barth's theology. For Barth, revelation *as such* means the revelation not of personhood but of *this* particular person whose identity is that he is the one God as Father, Son and Spirit. Thus, all valuational and existential relations which are established by revelation are contingent upon the unique being-in-act that is revealed. And the meaning of "being" in this case is secondary to and contingent upon *this* particular being-in-act who defines all being and value, rather than being defined, comprehended or included by them. Only after we have affirmed the priority to all else of *this* person, God, can we speak of his relation to other realities. And the ground of such relations is not a comprehensive concept of being, which would include (no matter how analogously and negatively) God and the creature, but an analogy of relation: God as he is first of all related internally to himself, relates himself in the second place as the same One to us. Thus, to Barth Niebuhr's Trinitarianism would point simply in the direction of three abstract relations extrapolated from a complex of values and existential reflections.

Niebuhr, on the other hand, would have to say of Barth's Trinitarianism that its complete identification with revelation in Christ makes it not a Trinitarianism but simply "Christo-monism." Far from providing an interpretation of God's redemption of his fallen creature, it points rather to the annihilation of the creative process by redemptive grace. It tends therefore toward a sort of Christocentric Unitarianism.

The unity of God is to be sought for, in Niebuhr's theology, not only in connection with Trinitarianism but in the understanding of the self-revelation of God as person, a doctrine whose content may not be completely equated with the doctrine of the Trinity. Just as singleness of moral selfhood rather than value-integration is demanded as the focus of unity in the human being, so revelation signifies that divine personhood, rather than value integration, is the focus of divine unity. This is the understanding of revelation which Niebuhr holds in common with other existentialist theologians. Between God and man there is the common ground (or should we say "the analogy"? Niebuhr has never made this clear!) of personal relation, communication or confrontation, of personhood. Niebuhr could therefore never agree with those theologians who speak of "the principle of personality in God," rather than of God as person. When we ask what is the real nature of the God whom we confront as hostile power in our natural distrust of him, the real nature of him who reveals himself in converting us, the answer has to be basically and irreducibly that he is a person. He is that person who is altogether powerful in his goodness, and good in his exercise of power, and in whom the unity of these two is that of unitary personal activity.

The task of theology to a large extent is to express, by means of our traditions and present-day language, an understanding drawn from biblical exegesis. In this task we have to avoid, on the one hand, a simple literal reiteration of biblical language and, on the other hand, the reduction of the contents of the Bible to the literal meaning of the thought-forms we are bound to employ. Barth in his doctrine of the Word of God, Tillich in his method of correlation, Niebuhr in his existential and valuational understanding of revelation all seek to perform this task. What biblical exegesis means by "the living God" the theologian thus has to express—not alone exegetically but theologically. This is what Niebuhr seeks to do by the concept of personhood. But this concept is notoriously one of the most difficult in theology. By what right do we use it? What positive content can we find in it? We have said earlier that in regard to this notion Niebuhr vacillates between a dualism which can give no specific content except "confrontation" to the concept and a relationalism that makes the content of the idea anthropomorphic.[102] God is the one who gives faith to us and involves this faith in a permanent revolution. He reveals himself as our author and finisher, our Creator, Judge and Redeemer. In him we know ourselves to be known and to be valued.

But in all of this reflection it is doubtful that the mind rises to apprehend the uniqueness of the personal being who is distinct from all other personal beings because he is God. For God is person because he is (as personality by definition always is) self-originating, active and purposeful event. Personhood is defined by the uniqueness through which it can enter or not enter into certain given and specific relations with others. It is not defined simply by its relations, because no single relation, nor a sum or synthesis of relations, adds up to the unique singular subject-center which is a person. This is true of God and man. If man is recipient rather than the initial agent vis-a-vis God, this would simply tend to show, as Barth has suggested, that God alone is properly person, and that man is person in a derived sense, that it is he and not God who "participates in the principle of personhood" and that he becomes a person only by virtue of the creative act of God.

In other words, if the concept of "personhood" describes God as well as man, it is man who stands in need of analogical explanation, and not God—who is in himself fully the content of person: he is *this* particular person, the particular act of being and self-originating purposive event who is Father, Son and Holy Spirit. As this person, this concrete identity of being and meaning, he is the Creator of all contingent being and value and meaning. We cannot go behind the Triune God for a notion of being, meaning or value. For he is, as this person, pure act, pure aseity. In himself, in his being in this identity and aseity,

[102] Cf. above, p. 83 f.

he is pure love and pure freedom.[103] His personhood is therefore defined by and in himself—and not in the first place either in positive relation to or distinction from (negative relation to) the creature.

It is just this understanding, vital to any knowledge of the positive content of personhood, which one misses in Niebuhr's existentialist use of the principle of personhood. God's person is understood by virtue of his qualities in relation to or distinction from us. On this basis we cannot arrive at an answer to the question to which revelation is actually a reply: Who—not what—is God: *which* person is he? In the absence of all ontology, the understanding of personhood is caught between dualism and anthropomorphism.

In a sense, Niebuhr's relational objectivity stands between Barth and Tillich on the question of understanding God's personhood. To Barth, the notion of God's being is proper and not merely symbolic because it is completely identical with the specific act (or person) which God is in that he is Father, Son and Holy Spirit. Tillich, on the other hand, rejects such a combination of "half-abstract" and "half-concrete" notions.[104] God may be understood symbolically as living person because he is being in whom the tension of unity and diversity is posited and overcome.[105] But the notion of *being* in regard to God is prior to "life" and "personhood," and only on the basis of the former may the latter two concepts be applied to God.[106] To go beyond this would be the reduction of the concepts of being and personhood to anthropomorphism. Moreover, it would represent an unjustifiable transcendence of the situation of "correlation": "correlation means that biblical-existential and philosophical-ontological concepts must as it were be interpreted through each other and not merged into half-kerygmatic, half-philosophical notions which are neither concrete nor abstract."[106] Of such a merger Tillich would presumably accuse Barth.

Niebuhr rejects the ontology of both men. He seems to suggest that to speak of God as *this* particular person (as does Barth) is an abstraction which seeks to penetrate, quite mistakenly, the divine mystery and fails to account for the "givenness" of the divine-human relation. On the other hand, to separate the being of God from his personhood (as does Tillich) inevitably submerges the existential nature of this relation, even if one does insist on participation of creaturely life in the ground of being (in opposition to some who would have it that men meet God accidentally and as a complete stranger).[107]

The very purpose, Niebuhr would suggest, of the existential method

[103] Karl Barth, KD, II, 1, pp. 299 ff.
[104] Tillich, *Systematic Theology*, vol. I, p. 243.
[105] *Ibid.*, p. 242.
[106] *Ibid.*, pp. 235-39.
[107] "Two Types of Philosophy of Religion," in *Union Seminary Quarterly Review*, (May, 1946), p. 3.

in regard to the conception of God is that it combines our understanding of confrontation by an irreducibly personal "Other" (lacking in Tillich) with an actual encounter, a relation with this Other (lacking in Barth). He would agree with Barth that theological concepts, though analogical, do not yield merely symbolic notions about God's activity. But he would add that one understands concretely only in so far as one understands by reference to a concrete, existential setting.

Existential thought is of necessity critical, and in that capacity Niebuhr has important contributions to make to the evaluation of such systems as those of Barth and Tillich. His persistent question about the concreteness of their thought is highly relevant. On the other hand, the difficulties of the existential method in the task of positive reconstruction of doctrine are notorious. Furthermore, its emphasis on concrete encounter makes it almost impossible to reproduce the uniqueness of such a constructive statement in an abstractive, analytical commentary.

3. CHRISTOLOGY

Niebuhr concludes a section of *The Meaning of Revelation* on the methods of internal and external historical knowledge and their interrelations by saying that "in all this we have only repeated the paradox of Chalcedonian Christology and of the two-world ethics of Christianity."[108] Quite clearly he belongs among the large number of theologians who would agree with Daniel D. Williams that

there is a growing insistence in theology today that if we are to bring any clarity into Christology we have to show how we distinguish and relate historical facts, interpretation of the facts, and the role of faith in creating and judging the interpretation. . . . The creeds unite the divine and supernatural nature with the human and earthly existence. The conviction that such a union has taken place was bound to be supported in large part by reference to miracles and other supernatural signs. Christ shows who he is by the exercise of extraordinary powers. But for those who are now driven by the critical understanding of Christian origins to a new view of the problem, the terms have subtly shifted. It is not two "natures" which have to be related; but two "histories." There is the history of our human existence with its fate, its freedom, and its course of events. In this history stands the real person, Jesus of Nazareth, who is just as truly "historical" as any other. There is also the history of God's creative and redemptive dealing with men which has come to its climax in the history of Jesus. It is these two histories which we have to relate to each other. When we look for God's redemptive action it is not supernatural existence but personal meaning which concerns us. The emphasis on miracle gives way to that on personal faith.[109]

[108] *The Meaning of Revelation*, p. 90.
[109] Daniel D. Williams, *What Present-Day Theologians Are Thinking* (New York: Harper & Brothers, 1952), pp. 100, 102 f.

The reaction against nineteenth-century Liberalism has generally been marked by a renewed emphasis on God's self-revelation and on the freedom and prevenience of the living God in that act. The rejection of miracle has not been complete in modern theology (as Troeltsch observed), and belief in it was certainly given new impetus by the rise of post-liberal thinking. But the miraculous event was no longer apprehended in the external cosmos. Instead, such faith came to depend more and more on the sharp distinction between nature and scientific thinking, on the one hand, and history and the unique methods appropriate to understanding it, on the other. In the understanding of history itself the tendency—of which Niebuhr's thought is an example—became more and more to think of God's revelation in Jesus Christ as an event that represented a "surd" in our comprehension. This event is an ingression into the flow of time which causes a revamping of thought about the whole process. It cannot be understood simply by its causal antecedents and consequences, nor by any prior scheme of meaning that had been attached to these events: it is a miracle.

The miracle of God in Christ thus takes place in history, but apprehending this fact demands a particular method of understanding history. For Niebuhr, as we have seen, as for many others it calls for a careful methodological distinction between "external" and "internal" history. The more Christology has been assimilated to the post-liberal understanding of revelation the more securely the basic Chistological issues have tended to be methodological. *How* do we know Jesus Christ to be God's self-revelation? What is the relation between faith and the history in which Jesus Christ has been revealed? *How* can a past event be present redemption and revelation? Such have been the questions of post-liberal Christology. In a broad sense these were also the questions with which the rise of higher criticism challenged the theology of the nineteenth century. This methodological approach to Christology is a common bond between nineteenth- and twentieth-century theology.

Since in this sort of approach fact and interpretation of the fact are closely interwoven, one may ask whether the event and our apprehension or interpretation of it can really be distinguished. Certainly the Chalcedonian formula asserted the immutability and unconfusedness of both natures. It is questionable if the more idealistic methodological tendencies in Christology over the past century and a half can follow the intention of the tradition at this point.

If we find a modern echo of the traditional duality in Christology, it lies chiefly in the sharp distinction drawn between two types of apprehension of Jesus Christ. We see him first of all through the eyes of faith in the mind's response to the revelation of God. Here it is surprising to note the extent to which Jesus Christ is frequently reduced, in modern theology, to the "revelatory" or "existential" impact he makes, the response he evokes. Thus—as in the extreme case of Bultmann—the object is lost sight of and Christology becomes merely a particular perspective on the human historical situation. "Christocentric" interpretation of history, sacred or secular, sometimes takes the place of Christology in modern thought, as D. M. Baillie has observed.[110]

But, secondly, we apprehend the same Jesus Christ as an inescapable, irremovable figure of a specific and limited past, a figure that demands the same critical and loyal understanding as does any person past or present. What is perhaps most amazing about Christology in the formative stage of post-liberal theology (approximately between 1920 and 1940) is not so much historical skepticism about the life of Jesus as the unwillingness of theologians to utilize their apprehension of Jesus of Nazareth for their understanding of Christocentric revelation.

In this sense, then, whatever epistemological remnant was left of the metaphysical dualism in traditional Christology has tended to be obscured in post-liberal theology, in the refusal to relate in positive fashion historical and revelatory understandings of Jesus Christ.

Whatever may be their many differences, neither Barth, Bultmann nor Tillich could be classed as a monophysite. None would deny the full, historical humanity of the incarnate Lord. But the situation is quite different with regard to their suggestions about our *knowledge* of Jesus Christ: here a tendency toward a sort of methodological or epistemological monophysitism appears to prevail. It is not clearly evident that the Christ present in revelation, or the one who confronts us existentially is in any sense significant for our knowledge of Jesus of Nazareth, or vice versa.[111] As a human, historical figure he is simply "there," but neither his life nor his teaching seems to have much connection with his personhood or with the historical-revelatory person's connection with us. The historical figure of Jesus is not significantly illumined in "revelation." Rather, it is the meaning of the course of history that is illumined, and the application of critical-historical estimates of the historical witness in the Gospels is productive of only minimal positive theological results for the interpretation of revelation.

When he wrote *The Meaning of Revelation*, Niebuhr quite evidently belonged among those for whom the understanding of Christocentric revelation in history was the basic issue in Christology. In other words, for him, too, basic Christological discussion was transferred from metaphysical to methodological or epistemological bases, from the "two natures in one person" to two ways of understanding one historical event.

---

[110] *God Was in Christ* (New York: Charles Scribner's Sons, 1948), pp. 71 ff.

[111] The later volumes of Barth's *Die Kirchliche Dogmatik* should be excepted from this generalization, although it certainly holds true of his earlier thought, including his Christological statement in KD, I, 2.

In this methodological approach to Christology there is implicit a further characteristic which has frequently been typical of Protestant theology: a reduction of Christology to a doctrine of the work of Christ. We have said that Niebuhr has not developed a doctrine of atonement but that there are certain indications of one in his understanding of divine unity and grace, in his search to understand the unity of divine power and love. For Niebuhr the problem of divine love in our existential, historical situation and apprehension lies in the fact that divine power is apparently hostile toward us. In a sense, therefore, Christ's being and historical *thereness* are simply taken to be an answer to or explained by the need for a concrete historical focus of the unity of divine love and power. Does this not tend to reduce Christology to the work of Christ, to the overcoming in history of the hiatus between the power of alienation and forgiving love? If this is the case, it would in effect deny something that Niebuhr has been eager to uphold in his more recent writings: that theologians must seek to show forth the unity of Jesus Christ not only with the One Almighty God who is Redeemer but also with the self-same One who is Creator and whose eternal Son is the Agent in creation as well as in redemption. In other words, Christology that relies completely on an interpretation of the work of Christ implies not a truly Trinitarian but rather a purely Christocentric or even Christomonistic theology.

By contrast to such tendencies toward a purely methodological approach to Christology, and toward a reduction of Christology to the work of Christ, Niebuhr undertakes a short but careful statement of the content of his Christology in the brief section of *Christ and Culture* entitled "Toward a Definition of Christ."[112] He does this strictly from the point of view of a "moralist" but in a manner which immediately leaves behind the tendencies to avoid a consideration of the objective content of the doctrine of the Person of Christ.

Niebuhr begins by pointing to the many varying interpretations of Jesus Christ through which Christians are related to their Lord. Yet in all of them it is the same Jesus Christ of the New Testament who is the subject, a definite person "in our actual history, in history as we remember and live it, as it shapes our present faith and action . . . one and the same whether he appears as man of flesh and blood or as risen Lord.[113] To be sure, he may take on varying characteristics in differing epochs and for differing men, but the original portrait remains. To define his essence is indeed difficult, since "concepts and propositions" can hardly be adequate "to a principle which presents itself in the form of a person."[114] Also, whatever we may say about him is relative to our stand-

[112] *Christ and Culture*, pp. 11-29.
[113] *Ibid.*, p. 13.
[114] *Ibid.*, p. 14.

point. Yet, "if we cannot point to the heart and essence of this Christ, we can at least point to some of the phenomena in which his essence appears. Though every description is an interpretation, it can be an interpretation of the objective reality."[115] It is at once clear that Niebuhr is less dependent here on the relational aspects of his method than has been the case hitherto, and that he affirms much more boldly not simply the objectivity of a personal event but the knowability of something of its positive content. Hence, also, he can point at once to the unity and the distinctions in the person of Christ who is "one and the same whether he appears as man of flesh and blood or as risen Lord"— an affirmation so hard to make on purely methodological grounds.

As a moralist, Niebuhr defines Christ by his virtues, i.e., "the excellences of his character which on the one hand he exemplifies in his own life, and which on the other he communicates to his followers."[116] Religious Liberalism had stressed love as the dominant characteristic in the life and teachings of Jesus, connecting it with the same characteristic as the dominant attribute of God. In itself this insight is not wrong. What is wrong is its exaltation of love for love's sake:

> The virtue of love in Jesus' character and demand is the virtue of the *love of God and of the neighbor in God,* not the virtue of the love of love. The unity of this person lies in the simplicity and completeness of his direction toward God, whether the relation be one of love or of faith. Love, to be sure, is characterized by a certain extremism in Jesus, but its extremism is not that of a passion unmodified by any other passions; it is the extremism of devotion to the one God, uncompromised by the love of any other absolute good.[117]

How is one to relate this inordinate love of God to the love of the neighbor in Jesus' ethic? Niebuhr reminds the reader that it is only God who is to be loved with all the heart, soul, mind and strength. "The neighbor is put on the same level of value that the self occupies."[118]

No infinite or intrinsic value is ascribed to the human soul. Man's worth, like the worth of anything in Jesus' teaching, is his worth to God, and hence "the virtue of neighbor-love in Jesus' conduct and teaching can never be adequately described if it is in any way abstracted from the primary love of God. Christ loves the neighbor not as he loves himself but as God loves him."[119] In the following passage one may see something of the distinction and unity of the divine and the human in the virtues of Jesus Christ as Niebuhr thinks about them:

> His love of God and his love of the neighbor are two distinct virtues that

[115] *Ibid.,* p. 14.
[116] *Ibid.,* pp. 14-15.
[117] *Ibid.,* p. 16.
[118] *Ibid.,* p. 17.
[119] *Ibid.,* p. 18.

have no common quality but only a common source. Love of God is the adoration of the only true good; it is gratitude to the bestower of all gifts; it is joy and Holiness; it is "consent to Being." But the love of man is pitiful rather than adoring; it is giving and forgiving rather than grateful; it suffers for and in their viciousness and profaneness; it does not consent to accept them as they are, but calls them to repentance. The love of God is nonpossessive *Eros;* the love of man pure *Agape;* the love of God is passion; the love of man compassion. There is duality here, but not of like-minded interest in two great values, God and man. It is rather the duality of the Son of Man and Son of God, who loves God as man should love Him, and loves man as only God can love, with powerful pity for those who are foundering. There seems then to be no other adequate way to describe Jesus as having the virtue of love than to say that his love was that of the Son of God. It was not love but God that filled his soul.[120]

Niebuhr then applies the same analysis to the virtues in Jesus Christ which the post-liberal period has emphasized: the virtue of hope that eschatologists have stressed, his radical obedience emphasized by the Existentialists, and his other virtues such as faith and humility. Of one and all it must be said that Jesus practices and teaches them

in a manner that seems extreme and disproportionate to secular, cultural wisdom. But he practices none of them and requires none of them of his followers otherwise than in relation to God. Because these virtues are qualities of conduct on the part of men who always confront the Almighty and Holy One, therefore they seem extreme.[121]

In regard to the virtue of hope, it does not seem that Jesus' ethic depended on his hope for the consummation of history, or vice versa. "The heroic character of Jesus' hopefulness does not stand alone, it is mated with heroic love and heroic faith; and all these have their source in his relation to the God who is Now as well as Then. Not eschatology but Sonship to God is the key to Jesus' ethics."[122]

Similarly, it is the relation of Jesus' faith to God that makes this quality in turn radical. It is the "faith of a Son of God, too extreme for those who conceive themselves as sons of nature, or of men, or of blind chance."[123] His humility also is before God, not before men.

Thus any one of the virtues of Jesus may be taken as the key to the understanding of his character and teaching; but each is intelligible in its apparent radicalism only as a relation to God. It is better, of course, not to attempt to delineate him by describing one of his excellences but rather to take them all together. . . . It seems evident that the strangeness, the heroic stature, the extremism and sublimity of this person, considered morally, is due to that unique devotion to God and to that single-hearted

[120] *Ibid.,* pp. 18-19.
[121] *Ibid.,* p. 19.
[122] *Ibid.,* p. 22.
[123] *Ibid.,* p. 26.

trust in Him which can be symbolized by no other figure of speech so well as by the one which calls him Son of God.[124]

No matter at what virtue in him we look, we find the same mediatorial (but in no sense "intermediate") quality between God and man. "Because he loves the Father with the heroic perfection of human *eros*, therefore he loves men with the perfection of divine *agape*, since God is agape."[125] Again, his perfect trust in God who is faithful accounts for the trustworthiness with which he is faithful toward faithless men. In sum, it has to be said that the moral Sonship to God of Jesus Christ involves not two persons or beings but one; not an intermediate figure but

. . . a single person wholly directed as man toward God and wholly directed in his unity with the Father toward men. He is mediatorial, not median. He is not a center from which radiate love of God and of men . . . hope in divine and in human action. He exists rather as the focusing point in the continuous alternation of movements from God to man and man to God; and these movements are qualitatively as different as are *agape* and *eros*, authority and obedience, promise and hope, humiliation and glorification, faithfulness and trust.

Other approaches besides the moral one must be taken if Jesus Christ is to be described adequately. Yet as the history of the church and its theologies indicate, each such approach tends toward the same issue. The power and attraction Jesus Christ exercises over men never comes from him alone, but from him as Son of the Father. It comes from him in his Sonship in a double way, as man living to God and God living with men.[126]

Niebuhr seeks the clue to the "moral Sonship" of Jesus Christ in the character of Jesus Christ as it is manifest in his teaching and his acts, i.e., in the unity of his moral being. Such an approach avoids two extremes which have handicapped modern Christological thinking.

Ever since Wilhelm Wrede there have been some who have insisted that Jesus had no "messianic consciousness." Some form critics, in particular Rudolf Bultmann, have argued this cause. Some of them have done so rather joyfully, feeling that thereby they proclaimed the liberation of their affirmations of faith from any dependence on the changeable findings of objective critical research and discussion. Certainly in the long run Wrede's suggestion may be more painfully disturbing (and demand more drastic countermeasures) than the apparently more revolutionary suggestion of Albert Schweitzer who, rejecting Wrede's thesis, thought that Jesus did indeed consider himself the Messiah—but of course mistakenly, since his claim was based on a dogmatic hope that never came to fruition. Against Schweitzer's thesis liberal theologians

[124] *Ibid.*, p. 27.
[125] *Ibid.*, p. 28.
[126] *Ibid.*, p. 29.

could always maintain that eschatology was the purely accidental, *zeitgeschichtliche* trapping within which the pure and ever-valid "self-awareness of a unique relationship with God" lay hidden.

But this claim would meet annihilation at the hands of a school of thought which simply denies all "unique self-consciousness in relation to God" to Jesus Christ. To a tradition which has always understood personality in subjective or psychological terms as "self-consciousness" this denial would spell the death of every realistic endeavor to understand the unity of God and man in the personal existence of Jesus Christ.

The result of this denial of "awareness of a unique relation to God," combined with the other claims of form criticism, was simply that from then on a kind of positivistic historical assertion was made about Jesus Christ by theologians who wanted to combine skeptical tendencies in criticism with theologies of revelation. Thus, in an oddly de-idealized Hegelian fashion, Bultmann's Existentialism reduces Christology to the encounter that each generation experiences in its particular contemporaneity within the historical stream. Other than this "encounter" we can assert nothing clearly about Jesus Christ: all that a "contemporaneous decision" needs is the completely formal, positivistic claim that Jesus Christ did once exist in human particularity.

This sheer epistemological agnosticism with regard to Jesus of Nazareth is the necessary complement to the monophysitism of which we have spoken, for which the eternal revelatory act is in our history, illuminating the relation between faith and history, but giving no noetic content to the revelatory event as history. The result appears to be a complete merging of revelation and existential or "internal" history, in Bultmann's thinking. For Barth the tendency toward epistemological monophysitism and historical skepticism resulted in an uneasy balance in Christology. In his *Prolegomena*[127] it seemed that there was a tendency toward monophysitism (e.g., in the all too easy explanation of *anhypostasis* and *enhypostasis*) which is balanced by, but not easily harmonized with, what he later has to say concretely in his anthropology about Jesus the man, and in his doctrine of redemption about reconciliation accomplished through the gospel history and the words and deeds of Jesus.[128]

The results of Bultmann's and Barth's former thinking tend to go in opposing directions, as a consequence of their common epistemological monophysitism: in Bultmann's thought, the revelatory event is merged into the existential response made to it. For Barth the earlier tendency, at any rate, was for the historical nature and content of Jesus of Nazareth to diminish beside the objective reality of the eternal Word made flesh.

[127] KD, I, 2, p. 180.
[128] KD, III, 2; IV, I, 2.

Between these two poles, then, much Christological thought has taken place: on the one hand, there is the endeavor to utilize for theological purposes the purely inferential, historical judgment that Jesus' self-consciousness was uniquely related to the presence of God. On the other hand, those who deny this thesis insist that for theological purposes the mere fact of the Lord's human existence is sufficient. All else must be "faith" interpreting this event.

When we ask why the issue came to be posed in this manner, and what concept of the personhood of Jesus Christ is involved, we are forced once again—as in so much that affects modern theology—to turn back to Schleiermacher. To him the unique indwelling of the divine essence in Jesus is the completeness of his God-consciousness. In this regard Jesus was and is our *Urbild* to whom we, with our imperfect God-consciousness, are derivatively related within the Church. The "higher self-consciousness" which is faith is, for Schleiermacher, an immediate datum of self-awareness—which is not moral or noetic—and the immanence of the infinite within it is such that their unity must be thought of as organic rather than as "correlated."

It is probably fair to say that no matter how thinkers felt about the nature of faith, in matters Christological Schleiermacher's views generally prevailed. Indeed, in a sense even the more objective Ritschlian Christology actually presupposes Schleiermacher's understanding. Most interpreters regarded the relation of God and Christ (these terms being preferable to "Father" and "Son" during the nineteenth century) to be internal, organic or immediate. One must stress that this internal relation was not understood metaphysically as the consubstantiality of the Father and the Son. Rather, if not with Schleiermacher, then at least in his tradition, the relation involves the immediate presence of God in the self-awareness of Jesus of Nazareth. In his inmost *Erlebnis* as a man, in the unity of his personality as empirical self-consciousness, God-consciousness and self-consciousness, were completely unified.

The general intention which this suggestion represented came to be particularly dominant among historical New Testament scholars: even when they were Ritschlian in their fundamental principles, they edged close to this experimental tradition in Christology at one important point which we must now emphasize.

The link which connects theology and historical scholarship, especially in regard to the person of Jesus Christ, is delicate and tenuous. Now if, on historical grounds, one can infer a psychological point of unity between Jesus Christ and God, a unity in the inmost recesses of self-consciousness (which was generally equated with "personality"), then a big step has been taken toward the solution of the Christological problem.

In the first place, this inference can never be disproved directly by the historian. Secondly, on its basis one can then exegete the meaning of more directly evident phenomena, e.g., Jesus' use of the term "Son of Man." In the third place, such an assumption can be assayed as the actual and valid kernel within the accidental, historical trappings of Jesus' messianic conceptions. Thus, one can cross the fine line between exegesis and theology: within the historical form, one could say, there is a personal conviction to which the evidence points, but which it cannot touch one way or the other. This conviction of Jesus', while arrived at *inferentially* on historical grounds, is at the same time the *immediate* ground for a theological judgment about Christ.

While this personal union of God and Christ in Jesus' self-consciousness is not worked out in precise terms, it nevertheless forms the basis for Christological interpretations even on the part of Ritschlian historians such as A. Harnack and Johannes Weiss.[129] Among men more definitely in the tradition of Schleiermacher, Rudolf Otto is an example of the same tendency. The bridge between the exegesis of Jesus' "Christology" and properly theological Christology is the union of God and Jesus Christ in the personality of Jesus, a union understood in psychological categories. One could say, as a result of historical infer-

---

[129] Cf. Johannes Weiss, *Die Predigt Jesu vom Reiche Gottes* (2nd ed.; Goettingen: 1900), pp. 53-57, 152-78. Page 176: "Indem wir diese eigenartige Form seines Bewusstseins aus den Quellen erschlossen haben, stossen wir auf einen Punkt, der unserem weiteren Vordringen Halt gebietet. Wie fuer den Naturforscher die Thatsache des Lebens, fuer den Kunstkenner die kuenstlerische Inspiration, fuer den politischen Historiker die unbezwingliche Energie grosser Staatsmaenner u. Voelker letzte Daten bilden, die man nicht weiter erklaeren kann, sondern einfach hinnehmen muss—so steht der Religionsforscher vor diesem eigenartigen religioesen Bewusstsein Jesu als vor etwas schlechthin Gegebenem, das er anzuerkennen hat. Es ist nicht weiter zu analysieren oder zu verstehen, hoechstens kann man es, wenn auch in sehr unzureichender Weise 'nachempfinden,' man darf es aber auch nicht meistern oder weginterpretieren wollen."

Pp. 153-54: "Das Christentum ist nicht durch eine neue Lehre entstanden, sondern dadurch, dass ein Mann auftrat, der mit groesstem Ernst und unbeirrter Sicherheit davon ueberzeugt war, dass Gott ihn gesandt habe, um der Welt das Gericht und das Kommen des Heils anzusagen. . . . Diese felsenfeste Gewissheit weist zurueck auf religioese Erlebnisse, deren besondere Art fuer uns natuerlich im Dunkel liegt. Aber, dass sie vorhanden gewesen sind, muss dem Historiker ebenso gewiss sein, wie dass Jesus ueberhaupt existiert hat."

A. Harnack, *What Is Christianity* (trans. of 2nd German ed. by T. B. Saunders; New York: G. P. Putnam's Sons, 1902), p. 139: "Jesus is convinced that he knows God in a way in which no one ever knew Him before, and he knows that it is his vocation to communicate this knowledge of God to others by word and by deed—and with it the knowledge that men are God's children. In this consciousness he knows himself to be *the* Son called and instituted of God, to be the Son of God, and hence he can say: *My* God and *my* Father, and into this invocation he puts something which belongs to no one but himself. How he came to this consciousness of the unique character of his relation to God as a Son; how he came to the consciousness of his power, and to the consciousness of one obligation and one mission which this power carries with it, is his secret, and no psychology will ever fathom it."

ence and on immediate grounds of religious-Christian awareness, that
the union of God and Christ is given to the religious consciousness, most
especially to that of the Lord himself. Granted that in other respects,
especially in regard to his *zeitgeschichtliches* understanding, Jesus' knowledge was fallible, at this point historical testimony would agree with
theological testimony about his uniqueness and the unique focus of God
in him. The link between the two was the experiential notion of personality, historically indirectly manifest but its truth always a matter of faith
—safe from the turns of historical speculation.

One can easily understand how men like Otto were appalled at the
denial of Jesus' messianic self-consciousness by some scholars among the
ranks of form criticism. One can understand equally well how those who
agreed with the major conclusions of form criticism would eschew the
notion of personality as a help in linking historical-exegetical and
theological judgments. We seem at present poised uneasily between
these two extremes: messianic self-consciousness, on the one hand, no
link between historical exegesis and theological Christology, on the
other. Under these circumstances the major theological attempts from
within the tradition we have examined, in order to advance to a more
complete understanding of Christology, have largely circled about questions of the interrelations between faith and interpretation of fact in
history; and these questions of method have then been applied *a posteriori* to Christology.

In such a quandary, a moral approach to the problem such as that
developed by Niebuhr holds every promise of being useful. It would
shift the emphasis, in understanding the person of Jesus Christ, away
from psychological interpretation to a more concrete basis. (It would
also get beyond the ingrown *Problematik* of a constantly reiterated
methodological discussion.) To the psychologizing view the essential
core of the person is really a substratum disconnected from or at
best inferentially connected with his moral, historical acts. To find the
divine-human union there is to posit it remotely, in isolation from concrete qualities, where noetic, interpretive understanding has no access;
hence the unity may be grasped only by an act or state that has no noetic
content. How, then, can one have an explicit Christology? Moreover,
it seems impossible to relate the distinctness of the two natures to such
a notion of their unity which is emptied of all conceptual content. But
are we therefore bound to say that we must simply acknowledge the
sheer existence of the man Jesus of Nazareth and remain satisfied to
draw no conclusions about the content of this historical being for the
content of Christology?

It seems to me that in the avoidance of the two extremes outlined
and in the actual countersuggestion of an understanding of Jesus' personhood significant for Christology, we have the core of the real impor-

tance of Niebuhr's essay, "Toward a Definition of Christ." Niebuhr departs completely from the endeavor to understand the unity of the one Lord in two natures by the inference of a self-consciousness of a particular, psychologically messianic type. Hence, there is no need for him at any point to argue for or against the question of messianic self-consciousness. It is not involved in his notion of personal being and therefore need not play a central role in his understanding of Christology.

But, on the other hand, he avoids the complete divorce of historical exegesis from Christology, the epistemological monophysitism of the other extreme. He seeks to understand Jesus Christ as having his unity in his moral purpose, as being one in his moral being. The being of the person Jesus Christ is not—as it is for the psychologizing school—an ineffable state of awareness behind act and teachings; nor is the full personal being inaccessible to us—as it is for the theologians influenced by form criticism. The unity of the person of Jesus Christ is embedded in and immediately present to his teaching and practice. It is the focus of unity in the teaching and acts of the Lord. In one sense, no series of acts or moral virtues in teaching and active exemplification exhausts the significance of a person's being. Nevertheless, one can say that the being does not stand ineffably behind the series or the essence behind the phenomena, distinguished from them and only inferentially to be interpreted: rather, the being is concretely exhibited, embodied in the series of phenomena. Hence, the teaching and the acts of Jesus Christ, his moral virtues, are themselves the direct clue to his being. In them one may find, by an historical and at the same time theological exegesis, in faith, hope and love, the unique moral Sonship to God of one who is completely at one with men.

Thus the question of the messianic self-consciousness as a necessary bridge from exegesis to Christology becomes a secondary one. For in and to faith there is exhibited, historically, one who in each and all of his virtues shows forth a disproportionateness, a radical being-for-man as moral Son of God, and thereby shows forth the unity in history, in a person, of God and man.

In this view, it seems to me, Niebuhr meets the test that the tradition always imposes on the content of a Christology regardless of the merits of its method or approach (which should be secondary issues). A Christology must indicate the Lord's consubstantiality with the Father according to his Godhead; his consubstantiality with us according to his humanity; the union of the two distinct natures; and the abiding distinctness and unconfusedness of these two natures in the one, unitary person. Particularly on the last two questions, the newer extreme is monophysite in method. The older view, on the other hand, apparently sets forth a union in an ineffable, psychological manner which leaves unexplained or, worse, denies by implication the abiding distinction of the two natures. In Niebuhr's view the distinction is indicated in a "double movement—with men toward God, with God toward men."[130] But by pointing to Jesus Christ "as the focusing point in the continuing alternation of movements,"[131] it seems to me that Niebuhr so shows the twofoldness and distinction in the moral being of this person that in, with, and through the twofoldness the unity is directly expressed and grasped as the unitary personal being, the personhood of Jesus Christ.

Moreover, since the moral analysis seeks to apprehend the personal being directly rather than inferentially, as does the psychological analysis, it is far more congruent with metaphysical analysis. For the latter asks the question implied in the moral analysis: What is the nature of the being whose actions may be characterized as "moral" and whose moral acts are identical with his being? Hence, Niebuhr is right in saying that this portrait needs to be complemented, and that it may be complemented by historical and metaphysical portraits.[132] For him this is a startling admission. It indicates that such moral analysis cannot take place in isolation, as has been true of so much of the methodological analysis in theology and Christology in the past one hundred and fifty years. In this brief outline of Christology, Niebuhr takes a new and suggestive departure, and goes beyond the question of methodology to turn to actual theological content.

So far this is an isolated moment in his own technical theological writing (as distinguished from his work in theological ethics, theology of culture and theological history). Does it indicate a new and major concern on the part of one who has always shown himself ready to cast aside static molds? Whether or not it will prove to do so, it is in itself an important and fruitful new suggestion in modern theology. And it may well be one of the most important individual contributions Niebuhr has made to technical, systematic theology—in addition to the many significant contributions he has made in other theological fields. Since theology is judged not so much by its method as by the fruitfulness of a method when applied to particular contents or doctrines, this Christological suggestion, as the culmination of careful systematic theological thought and biblical exegesis, merits close attention.

[130] *Christ and Culture,* p. 28.
[131] *Ibid.,* p. 29.
[132] *Ibid.,* p. 14.

PART TWO

PROBLEMS OF
FAITH AND ETHICS

4.

CHRISTIAN ETHICS
AND SOCIAL POLICY

JAMES GUSTAFSON

THE relation of the Christian Church to its cultural and social environment has differed from time to time through the centuries. Each relationship has rested upon assumptions about the nature of Christian responsibility for society. Sometimes these assumptions have been given clear theological articulation, viz., Christ is against culture or Christ and the best of culture are one.[1] At other times social relations between the Church and society have existed without intellectual clarification of their intention or consequences. Critical reflection came only after the fact.[2]

H. Richard Niebuhr has given attention to the problem of the nature of Christian society throughout his career. In *The Social Sources of Denominationalism*[3] he focused on the social determination of religious life in America. In *The Kingdom of God in America*[4] he developed the significance of a persistent religious and ethical idea for the Christian movement. *The Meaning of Revelation*[5] was a theologian's effort to come to grips with historical and cultural relativism. *Christ and Culture* contained an important typology for understanding the theological

[1] See H. R. Niebuhr, *Christ and Culture* (New York: Harper & Brothers, 1951). This book is primarily a theological analysis of the problem, only secondarily a sociological one.

[2] Ernst Troeltsch, *The Social Teachings of the Christian Churches* (2 vols.; trans. by Olive Wyon; Glencoe, Ill.: The Free Press; New York: The Macmillan Company, 1949), remains the best combined sociological and theological analysis of the history of the church-and-world problem.

[3] New York: Henry Holt and Company, 1929.

[4] Chicago: Willett, Clark and Co., 1937.

[5] New York: The Macmillan Co., 1941.

problems of Christian faith in relation to its cultural setting, as well as a brief interpretation of Niebuhr's own position. *The Purpose of the Church and Its Ministry*[6] brought many of these earlier reflections to bear on three problems: the purpose of the Church, the conception of the ministry, and the idea of theological education. Many of Niebuhr's fugitive essays also have dealt with particular facets of a Christian social theory.

1. MOTIFS IN NIEBUHR'S ETHICS

Niebuhr's system of ethics is in the deepest sense a personal system. It is characterized by both a critical quality and a personal involvement that cannot be reduced to principles or propositions. These qualities are rooted in faith, which is a lived experience before it is a theological point of view. The unity of Niebuhr's ethics is grounded in the unity of the person. There is no ultimate separation of the religious and the moral, the individual and the social, the past and the present in ethics, partially because these things cannot be extracted from each other in the man who teaches ethics and reflects about the moral life. Until his theological ethics are systematically reduced by him to print and paper, no one can adequately or accurately deal with Niebuhr's ethics and its implications.

There are, however, fundamental motifs in his ethics that can be defined. The first of these is the relativism of life in faith. The only absolute is the One beyond the many, the God revealed to be both power and goodness, the sovereign Lord who is the Alpha and Omega of nature and history. The consequences for ethics of this theological principle are many. The plurality of factors in moral experience can be recognized and accepted. Principles of oughtness must be recognized as rooted in some ground of isness. The complexities of selfhood are to be seen alongside the complexities of the external situation in which the self is called to act. The relativism of faith enables one to participate with a great measure of freedom in the given constellation of facts, principles, persons, and social structures. This relativistic freedom is not devoid of conscience, but is rooted in belief in the ultimate justification of the actor and in belief in the consummation of history and nature in the Kingdom.

Further, Niebuhr does not have to absolutize any particular touchstone of truth in Christian and philosophical ethics, but can learn from many sources. The Christian moral life is for him not only a life of obligation, it is also life with a vision of the final purpose and fulfillment of the world. Yet the vision of God does not supersede the concrete demands made upon man in his time and place. Christian moral action is rooted in the love of Being, in the joy of the knowledge of the end for which God created the world. Yet obligations are imposed upon

[6] New York: Harper, 1956.

man for which man can arouse no lyrical enthusiasm.

The relativism of faith enables the ethicist to let other disciplines speak for themselves. The limitations set for other disciplines by their nontheism or naturalism do not rule them out of significance for ethical reflection. To be sure, psychology and sociology, physics and economics are subject to criticism by the thinker for whom all things have their being in God. Such critical limitation, however, does not remove the possibility that particular insight into the nature of human life might be forthcoming precisely because sociologists, for example, are not occupied with theological problems. Significant meaning and interpretation of life can be derived from disciplines which are not concerned with the ultimate meaning of life, or which even have a clearly inadequate view of life's meaning.[7]

A second motif in Niebuhr's ethics is an existentialist personalism. Moral life is for him deeply personal and interpersonal. Moral decisions are radically different in nature from mathematical problems or chemical experiments. Tragedy is involved in every moral action. One must deny one good in order to achieve another. Also, the moral actor has conflicting loyalties that cannot be rationalistically resolved. The reason of the moral decision is always the reason of the heart for the serious person. Those who are affected by decisions and actions are never statistics or symbols, they are fully human. Thus, man weeps with those who suffer as a consequence of his decisions and rejoices with those who are benefited. Moral existence is personal existence, and personal existence is social. Persons are related to each other not only through external and depersonalized institutions, but in the inner being of a common humanity. Niebuhr cannot make the sharp differentiation between individual and society that has characterized much social thought in the Church.

A third motif in Niebuhr's ethics is response. Moral action is responsive action. One responds in the light of the total context of action. Response is more than a subconscious reaction to an external factor. It is a self-conscious personal relationship to institutions, persons, facts, principles, and Being itself. The moral act must be fitting, but the determination of the fitting act is no simple task. The fitting response is not easily defined by one touchstone of truth or virtue. Indeed, the more inclusive our awareness of the universe of action the more difficult it is to determine a proper response. Complexity, however, does not negate the responsibility to decide and act. The moral life is a life of response to Being in its ultimate form and to God's action upon us through the agencies of finite beings.

The Christian interprets his responsive moral action as a place and time in which God is acting. This faith and belief give him a framework

[7] See H. R. Niebuhr, "Theology, Not Queen but Servant," *Journal of Religion,* XXXV (1955), 1-5.

of meaning in which he understands and acts. God has revealed himself as Creator, Governor, and Redeemer. This is our knowledge in the Christian community. Our response to the persons, institutions, principalities, and powers around us is illumined and guided by our knowledge in faith. In moral action we confront the goodness of God's creative action; here the judgment of God becomes specific and concrete for us; here the gracious mercy of God is made known in human experience. The realities to which every man responds in moral action have these additional qualities and meanings for Christians.

Throughout these three motifs runs a fourth: the sense of flux and process in experience. One acts at a particular stage of an ongoing process of life. The structures and concrete realities that formulate one's place of decision are a heritage from the past. They go on changing, and one cannot predict the total consequences of an action. Involved in this process is not only change through time, but also the inner relatedness of beings. To act at one point is to affect many other points; the world is one of relationships.

Of these four motifs the first, the relativism of life in faith, is perhaps central, and the others derivative from it. Unity is in God, the One beyond the many. All things are in relation to him, all things are relative to him. The moral life is therefore lived in a network of relationships. Niebuhr's ethics enables us to understand the moral life, but the system of understanding is itself finally personal.

2. TOWARD CHRISTIAN SOCIAL ETHICS

Our purpose here is to delineate an interpretation of Christian social ethics which takes seriously the motifs present in Professor Niebuhr's thought, but is neither an application nor an exegesis of his writing and teaching. I owe a great debt to Niebuhr and share a common interest with him; presumably the point of view I am now about to set forth will not be wholly foreign to his thought and spirit.

Social ethics must have more than one starting point; one of these is the Christian revelation and faith, a second is an analysis of the self, and a third is an understanding of social structures and processes. There is, therefore, more than one premise to the argument. Theology, philosophy, and the human studies come together in understanding the moral act, which is by nature a social act. Analysis includes structures, functions, relations, processes, and meanings. The problems change, and with them ethical reflection must change.

Ethical analysis is difficult because moral and theological ideas are rational reflections about experience, and yet they have enough autonomy to be causal factors in culture and society.[8] Ethical thought is both

---

[8] This is a fundamental theme in both Troeltsch's and Max Weber's sociology of religion. See Troeltsch, *op. cit.*, and Weber, *The Protestant Ethic and the Spirit of Capitalism* (trans. Talcott Parsons; London: G. Allen and Unwin, 1930).

socially determined and determining; or (more cautiously) both culturally conditioned and conditioning. One cannot understand the changing conceptions of Christian social ethics in American Christianity from one single point of view. For example, Horace Bushnell's homiletical theology lent itself to blessing prudent Protestant entrepreneurs, but with the increasing industrialization of Washington Gladden's generation theology was redefined to give critical perspective on society. Urbanization, industrialization, immigration, the efficient rationalization of business institutions, and theological and philosophical ideas all enter into the reformulation of a Christian social ethic. Walter Rauschenbusch was not only preoccupied with the significance of the idea of the Kingdom of God (which was more complex for him than many critics suppose), he sought to be pertinent to the patterns of social behavior and action that existed in his decades of activity. The transition from Rauschenbusch to Reinhold Niebuhr represented a profound change of theological focus, but it also reflected global political and economic change. Thus we see that redefinition of its social ethics is a constant activity of the Church. In a time of economic prosperity, high productivity, welfare capitalism, and welfare statism, new opportunities and temptations are presented that differ from those of a period of economic depression. Global responsibilities add complexity to a problem that is at once moral and political (in the sense of policy determination). Passing resolutions is a relatively ineffective means of social change. If the Church is called to accept responsibility for society and culture it must develop in thought and action the most pertinent and effective ways of fulfilling this vocation.[9]

There are seven points around which I shall delineate a contextual, relational Christian social ethics. These are the nature of ethics as a discipline, the function of moral principles in moral action, the nature of values, the significance of Christian revelation and faith for the moral life, the nature of Christian love, the moral significance of the Church, and the doctrine of God.

[9] It should be pointed out that the position here delineated will be congenial to persons of diverse intellectual antecedents. Its relational and contextual characteristics may sound familiar to students of process philosophy, particularly as found in the theology of Henry Nelson Wieman and some of his students. Others will see the influence of the social psychology of Charles Horton Cooley and George Herbert Mead. Theories of social interaction developed by Georg Simmel and refined by American sociologists also shed light on the concepts of this essay. The sociologies of meanings and of the understanding, formulated by Wilhelm Dilthey and developed further by Max Weber, are clearly pertinent. The fruitful social thought extant within Josiah Royce's idealistic metaphysics has affinities to motifs of this essay. The doctrine of the governing sovereignty of God, as found in Augustine, Calvin, Edwards, and Barth, is important.

The Nature of Ethics

One's definition of the discipline of ethics in a large measure determines what data are ethically relevant. Thus, one of the key points in a reformulation of Christian social ethics is the idea of the nature of ethical inquiry. Various points of view about ethics are current. Bentham's utilitarianism was a "science" of the moral life in that the system rested on his analysis of human nature. For Bentham this was empirically verified. Herbert Spencer believed that a new science of ethics would emerge out of the analysis and classification of human behavior. Westermarck also aspired to discover the essence of morality by analyzing cultural data. Others have focused their inquiry on the nature of the good or the right somewhat in abstraction from the social and moral behavior of men. G. E. Moore, W. D. Ross, and others have tended to mold ethics into a definition of terms apart from their relations to concrete human behavior. Among philosophical moralists there have also been those for whom the moral question is an existential one: "What ought I to do?" Nicolai Hartmann, for example, beginning with this question, developed a moral theory that included the self, the nature of obligation, the situation in which obligation was fulfilled, and the nature of values that had historical realization in the situation. One may center ethical inquiry on the social and personal experience of men, on the definition of the right and the good, or on the establishment of a categorical imperative. In any case the direction of one's definition determines to a large extent what aspects of human experience are considered to be moral in character.

On this point H. Richard Niebuhr has been of great assistance to his students. With him they have studied ethics more as a critical inquiry into the nature of the moral life than as a study of abstract norms and values. Moral action, in his view, includes the nature of the moral actor in his freedom and determination, the judgments he makes, and his relationships to other persons, communities, and institutions involved in his actions. Christian ethics is critical reflection on the moral actions of the Christian community and its members. Christian ethics becomes more analytical than prescriptive; its first task is to understand the Christian moral life rather than to define values and rules of conduct in order to apply them. The data are the moral experiences of members of the Christian community.

Such a view of Christian ethics can be distinguished from both imperative-centered and metaphysics-centered views. John Bennett, for example, has written that "Christian ethics is the name given to the attempt to think through the implications of Christian faith for the moral life."[10] The process of ethical reflection is quite different where

[10] John Bennett *et al.*, *Christian Values and Economic Life* (New York: Harper & Brothers, 1954), p. 202.

the primary focus of attention is on such "Christian faith" rather than on the actions of Christians. There is a tendency in the former approach to ethics to define essential imperatives of Christian faith and doctrine, and then to apply them to particular situations in the moral life. Certainly the human moral dilemma is always sharpened if there is a clear definition of the "ought" in categorical terms.[11] When one professes loyalty to the Christian faith and understands its moral meaning to be, for example, a mandate to self-sacrificing love, every action is a shadow of compromise and disobedience. Guilt and contrition are stimulated, for there is no ready realization of the means of action. Implications for certain situations can be drawn out in prescriptive middle axioms or, if the norm is stated as natural law, in relative natural law. A line can then be drawn between the domain of ethics and that of technical knowledge.[12] Ethics, being deductive from absolute principles, must stop where technical data begin.

The analytical and relational moral reflection represented by H. R. Niebuhr and others can be distinguished not only from imperative-centered approaches, but also from the tendency to equate ethics with ontology. To be sure, ethics has to do with Being, the being of God in his relations to men, and the being of men in relation to each other. In distinction from the emphasis of Tillich's *Love, Power, and Justice*,[13] however, the prior analysis for Niebuhr is practical or experiential rather than ontological. Ethics is concerned more with relations between men and men, powers and authorities, and the relation of all these to the Sovereign Lord, than with the definition of qualities of Being and their moral significance.

In contextual, relational social ethics the "indicative" takes priority over the "imperative."[14] Enlightenment on "What ought I to do?" comes from critical reflection on what is being done by God and man in crucial moral situations. Rather than focusing on the moral principle or precept given in Christian faith, natural law, or a categorical imperative, the ethicist studies moral agents, the situations in which they act, and the considerations taken into account in action. "What is the nature of moral decisions?" becomes a key question. Are they made by deductive application of general principles to particular situations? Or is moral

[11] On this point there is a striking continuity in the method of ethics between the social gospel and Reinhold Niebuhr's *An Interpretation of Christian Ethics* (New York: Harper & Brothers, 1935).

[12] See William Temple, *Christianity and Social Order* (New York: Penguin Books, 1942), for a sharp distinction between ethical principles and policy formation.

[13] London: Oxford University Press, 1954.

[14] See Paul Lehmann, "The Foundation and Pattern of Christian Behavior," in John Hutchison, ed., *Christian Faith and Social Action* (New York: Charles Scribner's Sons, 1953), pp. 93-116, for an essay written from a perspective similar to ours. See also, Albert T. Rasmussen, *Christian Social Ethics* (Englewood Cliffs, N. J.: Prentice-Hall, 1956), chap. 6.

action a response of a person (bringing to bear in his freedom the meanings that give him personal identity) in a situation of other persons, authorities, and powers? To be sure, moral principles are involved in moral action, but they are viewed as part of a complex pattern of given agents, principalities, and powers.

In our present analysis of Christian social ethics no sharp differentiation can be made between tehnical data of economics, sociology, and political science, on the one hand, and ethical data or moral principles, on the other. Ethics, as a study of moral action, involves the most adequate possible understanding of the self, society and culture, the heritage of moral principles and Christian life, and the technical data pertinent to particular decisions. Christian social ethics becomes principally the analysis of policy and social decisions by students who have internalized the meanings of Christian revelation in faith. The Christian ethicist empathetically takes the roles of persons who are in actual positions of social power and makes himself aware of as many of the factors involved in the determination of policy as he can understand. Every policy decision is both moral and technical; there is a confluence of Christian faith and economic and social facts in every decision. Out of such an analytical process there emerge descriptive generalizations which in turn illuminate the decision-making process in other situations.

b. The Function of Moral Principles

Among the various factors in a policy decision are moral principles. Social ethics must analyze the function of moral principles in social action. For most churchmen social action implies deliberate efforts to shape the course of events through centers of social power. It is intentional moral action. For many sociologists social action means all behavior that takes into account the behavior of others. For Talcott Parsons a social system is fundamentally a system of action; for Max Weber action is social if it has subjective meaning for the actor and takes cognizance of the actions of others.[15] "Social action" does not have voluntaristic moral connotations for the sociologists. It is a descriptive interpretation of data which include explicitly moral actions and other actions as well.

Christian social ethics must analyze social action in the sociological sense. The possibility of effective moral action in society depends upon careful analysis of the social process and system. The moralist must know the patterns of personal and institutional interrelationships within

---

[15] See T. Parsons and E. Shils, eds., *Toward a General Theory of Action* (Cambridge: Harvard University Press, 1952); T. Parsons, *The Social System* (Glencoe, Ill.: The Free Press, 1951). See also, M. Weber, *The Theory of Social and Economic Organization* (trans. T. Parsons and A. M. Henderson, ed. T. Parsons; New York: Oxford University Press, 1947), pp. 88-115.

which he seeks to develop purposive change. He must understand how personality, culture, and society are interrelated; how political structures and processes are of economic significance, and how economic structures and processes are of political significance. The juncture of moral principles and political, economic, and social processes is the decisions and actions of persons. The ethicist is concerned to understand what factors are considered in a social decision and action. He seeks to discern lacunae in the considerations. Are the agents aware of possible unintended consequences that might be forthcoming from a particular decision?[16] Are important relationships between factors being ignored? How are moral considerations expressed in a policy decision? How do beliefs about the right and the good become causally effective in the social system?

Social action in the intentional moral sense must be grounded in knowledge of how decisions are made in the centers of social power. Effective moral action depends upon astute and accurate analysis of the social system in general and of the problem situation in particular. Such analysis does not ignore the significance of a "belief system" of moral and religious ideas. It tends to find, however, that moral principles are socially effective when they are internalized in social actors. Socially effective morality is part of the structure of the actor's total personality. It colors his analysis of the problem and makes him sensitive to dimensions of meaning involved in the decision of which he would not otherwise be aware. Values and principles are articulated for and by persons within a general social milieu, and in a particular decision-making context. The significant effect of values and principles is in the concrete ordering of factors in a given situation.

Moral beliefs that are not institutionalized, or not at least deeply embedded in persons who exercise social power, have little effect upon social policy. Social actors respond to concrete powers and persons more than to abstract concepts of values. A decision-maker does not isolate the values of freedom, order, and love, and find an abstractly balanced relation between them before acting. His moral predicament is for him concrete and often existential; he is involved in a dialogue between facts and powers which can have a more or less right order and good consequence. Christian social ethicists often assume that decision-makers operate more rationalistically and abstractly than is the case. Morality is not added to facts; the analysis of which facts are pertinent to a decision stems from ultimately moral considerations. Morality will be socially

[16] See Robert Merton, "Manifest and Latent Functions," in *Social Theory and Social Structure* (Glencoe, Ill.: The Free Press, 1949), pp. 21-81; also B. Malinowski, *The Dynamics of Culture Change*, ed. P. M. Kaberry (New Haven: Yale University Press, 1945). "Latent functions" is a sociological concept comparable in meaning to the theologian's use of "contingencies of history."

effective if the decision-maker operates from subjective (in the existentialist sense) moral truths.

Just as some Christian social ethicists think in terms of the implications of abstract values and principles for society, so others fashion an
image of what the ideal society would be. Then they develop possible
means for achieving it.[17] In some instances the model of the good society, often supposed to be the "natural society," is so far removed from
the structures of our industrialized and efficient social order that no
significant centers of action appear to join the two. Ends and means
become distinguished to the extent that they are almost irrelevant to
each other.

Decision-makers operate primarily with proximate ends. They are
often more realistic about the "latent functions" of their actions than
are the artists of ideal societies. Ends enter into the determination of
means, and possible means determine the definition of ends. The structures of power within which they work determine to a large extent the
goals of policy. Christian ethics has a more cogent authority when it
speaks concretely within the range of possibilities. How does the Christian *telos* inform the ordering of present powers? What meanings of the
present powers can be exposed for the decision-maker by the Christian
ethicist?

Moral principles and definitions of ends are socially effective in so
far as they have personal reality for men who make responses in decisive
situations. They are part of persons who think in terms of political,
social, and economic forces. For example, in a labor dispute the opposing
parties do not agree on a definition of justice, or the good society, and
then deliberate about the economic consequences of such in the current dispute. If such an agreement were made, its ideological character
(in the Marxist sense) would be revealed quickly by the failure to
agree on what justice or the good society means in the particular context.
Conceptions of the good society and justice (ends and moral principles) are involved in such discussions, but they become economically
and socially effective as they are part of the pattern of meanings that
the bargainers bring to bear as persons. They illumine possible consequences of specific decisions. In most cases they are not self-consciously
articulated. To be sure, ethical inquiry brings implicit moral assumptions to awareness in its reflections on social action. Principles and ends,
however, have social efficacy as they are internalized in persons making
concrete responses in particular situations. Deliberate social action becomes effective when persons in positions of social power think about

[17] The English "Christendom Group" engages in such an effort. The personal
organic society that is cast up reminds one of the period of the guilds and pre-
technological rural life. See Maurice B. Reckitt, ed., *Prospect for Christendom*
(London: Faber and Faber, 1945).

social, economic, and political facts as men grounded in a heritage of moral principles. The strategy for deliberate social action that emerges for them from this point of view minimizes the importance of developing statements of policy norms. These often appear to men in positions of power to be arid and unrealistic. These men need to be brought into a community in which there is a conversation between Christian faith and meanings and policy problems. Christian moral principles become part of social action through persons in whom they are internalized[18] more than through some inherent efficacy of their own as given in public pronouncements or through the establishment of a "Christian" pressure group among other pressure groups.

c. The Nature of Values

H. Richard Niebuhr has noted that recent value theorists "usually employ a relational theory of value which defines good by reference to a being for which other beings are good," when they move from general reflections about the nature of the good to concrete ethical problems.[19] The "subjective value theorist" for whom the good centers in the desire of a self must admit that desires are for something. The "objective value theorist" for whom values have an independent essential existence must face the problem of how they are related to persons who hold them and act according to them. Greater clarity about the relational character of the right and the good enables the ethicist to be socially and morally realistic. (Moral realism here refers not only to an acceptance of the sinful nature of man, but also to a grasp of the greatest possible number of factors pertinent to a particular decision.)

Love, justice, order, and freedom are generally discussed as "values" in Christian social ethics.[20] In such an approach moral predicaments can become highly generalized and abstractly oversimplified, as in the discussion of conflicts between justice and freedom. Freedom and justice are parts of moral experience, occurring in common life, and not independent entities divorced from relations between persons, institutions, and nature. They are relationships between persons within social structures; philosophical and theological discussions of them must encompass their particular realities. By dealing with freedom, order, justice, and love abstractly one paves the way for deductive ethics. If

---

[18] This view has a certain analogy to the analysis of moral habits or virtues in Roman Catholic ethics. The defects of Catholic moral theology and of moral perfectionism can be avoided, however, if the radical nature of the Fall and the consequences of our finitude are taken seriously; and not only the subjective moral character of the agent but also the objective moral consequences of his action are stressed.

[19] "The Center of Value," in Ruth Anshen, ed., *Moral Principles of Action* (New York: Harper & Brothers, 1952), p. 162.

[20] See the Ethics and Economic Life Studies sponsored by the Federal Council of Churches, and published by Harper & Brothers, 1953-1955.

justice, for example, is defined as an equitable distribution of the good, one can hypothetically state what a generally just distribution of wealth might be in a given society. But the moralist with this point of view does not come to grips with the economic and social structures and processes involved. If one begins with the ordering of wealth among men, however, one must deal with more than a definition of justice; justice becomes a relationship among particular objects and subjects.

The values most commonly dealt with in social ethics are ingredients of human moral experience. They have value not in and of themselves, but as relations among persons and institutions. They are more relational than substantive, and are socially and personally meaningful when we understand what the terms are—who is the subject and what is the object—in these relations. Freedom in social life and action is freedom for persons in a network of given social, economic, and political processes and institutions. This is acknowledged even by persons who speak of freedom as the ultimate value. To focus attention on freedom as a relation in specific contexts emphasizes its concrete, dynamic, and complex character. Moral decisions are specific; they involve subjects and objects that have value for each other and for the Creator. One does not choose for one value and against another; one relates himself in moral action to persons, institutions, and things. The good and right are relations among persons and objects. Thus, the "values" of order, freedom, and justice are not socially significant without some understanding of the "technical aspects" of these relationships. Social ethics involves knowledge of economic, social, and political relations in which the technical is moral and the moral is technical.

d. The Moral Significance of Christian Revelation

Recent Christian social ethics has continued the emphasis of liberal theology on love as the significant Christian contribution to ethics. The "law of love" is a major theme in Reinhold Niebuhr's *An Interpretation of Christian Ethics*. John Bennett has more recently written that "the distinctive element in Christian ethics is the primacy of love, the self-giving love that is known fully to Christian faith in the Cross of Christ."[21] This emphasis does not mean that other aspects of Christian doctrine are ethically irrelevant. The doctrine of sin, for example, stands at the heart of Christian ethical inquiry. The central imperative, however, is the transcendent law of love. The Christian life ought to be one of self-giving, self-sacrificing love.

Excessive emphasis on the moral imperative to love, however, abstracts part of the gospel from its fullness. Love becomes more law than grace. By contrast, the biblical message discloses in addition to self-sacrificing love the sovereignty of God, his gracious and judging action

[21] Dudley Ward, ed., *Goals of Economic Life* (New York: Harper & Brothers, 1953), p. 421.

in human history, his demand for obedience, and the hope of his coming Kingdom.[22] Christian revelation as it illumines the nature of Being in God and creation is in its totality relevant to the moral life. The isolation of one imperative out of its context of faith and hope in the sovereign redeeming Lord limits the significance of the revelation for moral action. Paul Lehmann suggests that "the primary question is not 'What does God command?' The primary question is 'What does God do?' "[23] The Christian moral life is lived in response to God's actions in the situations in which the self exists. One confronts the creative, governing, and redeeming work of God in a concrete place. Christian life is lived in grace; the Christian and his community seek to be means of God's action, recognizing that God is sovereign in all action, and man is at best an unprofitable servant. Christian life is a life in faith; we trust in God's goodness and power to redeem us and our actions. In God's own time the actions of men can be used for the glory of his Kingdom. It is a life of hope; apart from hope in God we would not dare to respond to any demand, for we are acutely aware of our partiality and unfaithfulness as well as the contingencies of future events.

All dimensions of the Christian life in God, revealed to us in Jesus Christ, are morally relevant. Moral decisions are made by the whole man, illumined by Christian faith. Christians are obedient not so much to a moral imperative as to a Divine Reality. God in whom we trust discloses himself as power and love in Jesus Christ; he is the Lord of life and death. His action continues in human events; we are not our own, but live in and respond to the continuing power and goodness of God. Decisions in social policy are affected by Christian revelation, not only as we try to see what the loving act is; our very *reading of the situation* is itself colored by our faith and unfaith. The revelation illumines our understanding of the demands made upon us, and illumines the nature of our response to them. In relating Christian ethics to social policy we must talk about the life of man under God, and particularly his life in the Christian community. The whole of our being, existing in the measure of faith that is ours, makes moral decisions. The whole disclosure of God to man in Christian revelation and faith is involved in our moral actions. The Christian dealing with technical, social and economic questions responds not only as a businessman or politician, but as a man in Christ, whose understanding of all experience and being is illumined in part by his faith.[24]

[22] See H. R. Niebuhr, *Christ and Culture*, pp. 15-29. Niebuhr develops the dimensions of humility, obedience, hope, and faith in the ethic of Jesus without losing the importance of love.

[23] Lehmann, "The Foundation and Pattern of Christian Behavior," in John Hutchison, *op. cit.*, p. 100.

[24] See D. D. Williams, "The Kingdom of God and the Kingdoms of this World," in *God's Grace and Man's Hope* (New York: Harper & Brothers, 1949), pp. 83-106.

e. The Nature of Christian Love

In emphasizing the importance of other aspects of Christian revelation for ethics, one does not deny the importance of love. The moral significance of God's love, however, includes more than self-sacrificing love. The self-giving, self-sacrificing love manifest on the cross does not exhaust the content of love made known in Christ. Also, the cross is more a revelation of God's being than an example to be emulated. D. D. Williams suggests that "the good which the love of God intends is an order of mutuality."[25] Love is relational and social in character. The love of God is made known to us through the love of others in and out of the Church. Our relationships are through a common center, the gracious love of God in Christ. The Christian community is related to God and man in love.[26] The love of God for man is efficacious as we respond to it in love. The reconciliation in Christ of the estranged involves persons, communities, and institutions. Proffered forgiveness, given out of love, meets contrition and repentance, given out of love. Christian love is profoundly social in character.

The reconciling love of God made concrete in community is as pertinent to social ethics as the self-sacrificing love of the cross. God's loving action continues through the actions of his people, transforming relationships. Our Christian vocation is more to respond to the gracious actions of God in our relationships to one another than to emulate the self-sacrificing love of God revealed on the cross. We are called to relate ourselves and the powers we represent to each other so that both restraint of evil and the enhancement of good can issue. In our faith in the sovereign Lord, who is not far removed from the events of common life, we seek to relate powers and authorities in love. Yet God acts sovereignly in conflict and tension as well as in harmony and peace. Justice and love are not easily distinguishable if the restraints of opposing powers that come into being in social policy are understood to be in some measure the consequences of God's gracious action.

H. Richard Niebuhr has commented that it was not love but God that filled the soul of Jesus Christ.[27] We are called upon to obey not love, but God. If Christian life is defined exclusively as self-sacrificing love, every deliberate social action is a compromise of this absolute. If it is understood as loving and obedient response to God as we are concretely related to our neighbors in personal and institutional relations, every social action is understood to be in some measure a means of God's action. The Christian moral life is lived not only in obedience

---

[25] *Ibid.*, p. 79.
[26] See H. R. Niebuhr, *Christ and Culture*, pp. 17-19, and *The Purpose of the Church and Its Ministry* (New York: Harper & Brothers, 1956), pp. 34-39.
[27] *Christ and Culture*, p. 19.

to a command to love, but more fundamentally in obedience to a loving God. This response to God is concretely a response to technical and personal powers and principalities that are the given factors in the time of decision.

f. The Moral Significance of the Church

The possibility of Christian response presupposes a self living in faith, though also in unfaith. Contemporary Christian realism, exemplified by the writings of Reinhold Niebuhr, has stressed an understanding of man that illumines our capacities of self-deception in the name of righteousness. The impact of this realism on public policy has been great in certain places. This is due to the incisive and accurate analyses of problem situations that have been made in the light of Christian realism. The social ethic that has emerged, however, has been largely one of the restraint of evil. The religious situation against which Christian realism protested was one of hopefulness in the accomplishments of man being obedient to the teachings of Jesus. Reinhold Niebuhr and others have corrected some of the errors of the social gospel.

Observing realistic skepticism, it is still important to study the significance for the Christian of being in the church. Individuals—such as Reinhold Niebuhr—do internalize meanings of Christian revelation and respond to public policy issues in their light. The believer in faith responds to every demand in humility and repentance, for he knows his weakness and sin. Yet in his life in the Church he knows the power of God to forgive, for he has been forgiven by others. In his participation in a congregation of the people of God, meanings of Christian revelation become part of the structure of his selfhood. The self in Christ and the Church understands, interprets, and responds to situations in part through these meanings. To be sure, other communities have contributed to his fundamental orientation to life. For most of us, other communities are more determinative of our decisions than is our membership in the Church. Nevertheless, the Christian conscience and the totality of the self are marked by God's action through the Church.[28]

The self comes into being as a member of various communities. Through interaction with other persons the child internalizes the meanings of gestures, language, and other symbols.[29] Attitudes are formed as the value and meaning orientations of one's family, neighbor-

[28] H. R. Niebuhr has developed a thesis pertinent to this discussion. See "The Ego-Alter Dialectic and the Conscience," *Journal of Philosophy*, XLII (1945), 352-59. See also "The Story of Our Life," in *The Meaning of Revelation*, pp. 43-91.
[29] See the following for theories of how culture becomes internalized: G. H. Mead, *Mind, Self, and Society* (Chicago: University of Chicago Press, 1934); C. H. Cooley, *Human Nature and the Social Order* (New York: Charles Scribner's Sons, 1922); Josiah Royce, *The Problem of Christianity* (2 vols.; New York: The Macmillan Company, 1912.) Much recent research in social psychology deals with this problem.

hood, class, nation, and church are incorporated into the personality. The self develops a personal identity, a continuing structure whose content reflects its participation in various social groups. It governs its behavior in the light of "collective representations" of the communities to which it belongs.[30] A pattern of meanings becomes the core of the self; these meanings condition its responses and decisions in various situations of life. The Christian community functions as one community in which the self continually reshapes its being, just as the social class, family, age group, and others do. Cultivation of common life under the Lordship of Christ in a congregation affects the fundamental meaning orientations of each member. This occurs through the processes of interaction and communication, as well as in decision and commitment. The content is given by the common center of this community, the Lordship of God, revealed in Jesus Christ and the Scriptures.

If one approaches a study of the moral life only through individual isolated decisions, one is struck by the awesome unpredictability and freedom of moral man. To be sure, one's community does not give such a unity of meanings that response to every moral demand is habitually "Christian." To be human is to be more complex than white rats and Pavlov's dogs. The precise decision of the Christian dealing with technical social policy data cannot be predicted. Yet a continuity in selves exists which enables one to anticipate how persons will act and react on most occasions.[31] The self in decision and action understands the demands made upon it as a self with a personal history, a structure of meanings. The structure is dynamic; the decisions made in freedom become part of one's personal history and in turn affect later decisions.[32]

Thus, the congregation, where Christian community becomes personal, is of great significance in deliberate social action. In worship, preaching, education, and church meetings the members of the congregation (who are social actors every day) internalize some of the meanings of the central events in the history and memory of the church. Existence is interpreted in the light of God's self-disclosure in Christ. Deliberations center on the meaning of faith in God for the people. Members are quickened to their vocation to be servants of God in all

[30] See E. Durkheim, *The Elementary Forms of Religious Life* (trans. Swain; London: G. Allen and Unwin, n.d.) and *Sociology and Philosophy* (trans. D. F. Pocock; London: Cohen and West, 1953).

[31] The way in which one's theological orientation enters into the interpretation of the meaning of social phenomena can be seen by comparing Quaker economist Kenneth Boulding's analysis of bureaucratization and social power with Reinhold Niebuhr's interpretation of its meaning. See Boulding, *The Organizational Revolution* (New York: Harper & Brothers, 1953) with Niebuhr's appendix.

[32] In Mead's language, the actions of the "I" (the self in action and decision, in its unpredictability) become part of the "me" (the structure of the self that has come into being through social interaction and internalization of meanings).

their activities. Particular issues of social concern can be discussed so that laity and ministry alike come to a clearer understanding of what it means to be a Christian social agent. "Deliberate" and "natural" social action become somewhat merged without violating the need for self-consciousness inherent in the former. Selves participating in the Christian community act in other groups somewhat under the impact of God's grace made known to them in the Church.

The danger of assuming that there is an automatic transformation of mind and spirit by participating in a congregation is evident. Although we have no adequate studies of what laymen believe and how beliefs affect action, the general impression is that minimal participation in church life often does little for conscience or for the quality of action. Some growth in grace comes through receiving the historical means of grace, the sacraments and the preached Word of God. For the purpose of social action, however, it is important to develop groups of mutual criticism and supplementary knowledge within the Church. The labor leader, for example, ought to find some persons in the Church with whom he can clarify his own moral and vocational situation. Also, clarification of meaning and ideas often comes after the deed; it is important that action and reflection be part of one total, larger church life. The calling of the congregation is to be a community of interpretation in which the events of "secular" life are recast in the light of the gospel, and the meaning of the gospel is clarified in the light of "secular" events.

To call the Church to a deeper understanding of its own sources of strength and truth is not to withdraw it from the world. Rather, part of its vocation is to be a servant of the Kingdom. It becomes a more effective servant of the Kingdom as it develops self-knowledge and intensifies its efforts to be faithful to its Lord. Its members witness to God's gracious action when they respond obediently to him as laborers, teachers, professional men, and politicians. The Church in both its social and historical existence and its vocation to become a royal priesthood is a crucial center for a strategy of Christian social action.

g. Faith in the Living God

Christian social ethics rest finally in faith in the sovereign God who acts, not only through the Church, but in the events of political, economic, and social life. One never clearly discerns the signs of his actions in the decisions that confront the moral actor. Yet in faithful knowledge of God's mercy and sovereignty, goodness and power, one dares to be a servant. Social and political events, like all history, are "images and shadows of Divine things." The judging and redeeming actions of God are never far removed from the events of men. The God who is far off is always the sovereign Lord of his creation. Though his ways are only seen through a glass darkly, yet we respond to him in the Church and out of the Church. Though we are faithful and unfaithful at once, both denying and affirming his sovereignty in all our actions, our final hope is in him. Life is in grace as well as in sin. Our calling is to respond to God's action wherever it is given for us to act.

For Christian social ethics, this means that God acts through "the technical" as well as "the moral." In fact the two cannot be separated. God, the One beyond the many, is as much the sovereign Lord of deliberations about guaranteed annual wages as he is of deliberations about natural law or categorical imperatives. Thus, the ethical and religious dimensions of human existence cannot be separated. The whole of life is lived in the knowledge that our being is a gift of grace to which we respond in thankfulness and obedience.[33] Christian social ethics must be ethics of faith in the living God.

3. SOME REMAINING QUESTIONS

Like every theory of Christian ethics, ours must undergo careful examination and criticism. Since one of its starting points is an analysis of moral and social behavior, it needs to be checked against human experience for partial validation. Human experience may appear to be a nontheological criterion of validity, and therefore an irrelevant one to some Christians. Such an assumption is explicitly rejected in this essay. Ethics is concerned with human behavior; the validity of an ethical theory in part depends upon its illumination of behavior. Ethical theory is informed by many sources; there is no theological ethics or anthropology that derives its total form and content from Christ, or from any other single doctrine. Indeed, a theological ethics is often to be accepted or rejected on the basis of its accuracy in predicting the course of human events. The prophetic tradition has always spoken to concrete issues and events. Contemporary prophets and those of old have been listened to if their understanding of specific situations was incisive and adequate.

Relational social ethics, centering its attention on decisions in a wide social context, needs validation by analytical study of the social-moral actions of people. A number of problems are involved in such studies. A principal one is that the analyst must be able to expose meanings and determinations of behavior, some of which are below the threshold of consciousness. He must conduct what Max Weber called a "mental experiment," asking whether a particular action could be accounted for without positing the existence of a particular meaning for the actor. In a more refined way the analyst must ask a question analogous to Weber's

---

[33] H. R. Niebuhr states his theory of the oneness of religious and moral existence in his development of "evangelical ethics" in E. J. F. Arndt, ed., *The Heritage of the Reformation* (New York: Richard R. Smith, 1950).

question about capitalism, i.e., can modern capitalism be accounted for without the behavioral consequences of the meaning of the Protestant this-worldly ascetic ethic? We must also find out if an extension of the pattern of meaning of activity, to include its relation to God, will affect social action. Other problems include the development of method and research techniques for conducting such a study. Few good studies of moral action exist at the present time. They must be developed, however, if we are to speak in any more than impressionistic terms about social-moral behavior.

Our theory of social ethics assumes that the present time and its given structures are the locus in which a person exercises his "deputy-ship" under God.[34] Several problems are involved in this assumption. One is the possible perversion of the ethics into culture-Protestantism. In comparison with Catholicism, Protestantism has little culture of its own. The perpetuation of a culture depends upon at least a relative absolutization of a particular ethos. This ethos enfolds itself in cultural systems, including philosophy, theology, art, music, literature, and ethics. Part of the ethos of Protestantism is that no culture can be absolutized; no philosophy can finally determine the definition of the meaning of faith, and no moral code can be equated with the moral law of nature. This "Protestant principle" is both the glory and the temptation of Protestant social ethics. Catholic ethics has a substantial body of traditional moral theology, grounded in a substantive view of the moral orders of creation. To be sure, this theology is flexible. Yet the Catholic has more to turn to than a minimal church culture centering on a critical principle. He has both a historical tradition and an ontology. Thus, his ground for standing against the secular culture is specific, concrete, and full of content. (It is surprising, however, how easily Catholic culture absorbs secular content.)

With a limited cultural tradition, the Protestant more easily identifies himself with the given structures. He accepts them as the place where he is to respond to God's action. One critical problem is the precise meaning of "acceptance" in particular situations. In order to act effectively within structures, do I implicitly assume that they are un-ambiguously good? Or, realizing that they stand between the Kingdom of God and the kingdom of evil, do I make my recognition of their demonic powers purely a matter of principle? (Some Protestant ethics tends to accept the structures as evil, and to recognize their created goodness purely as formal principle.) Naïvely to assume the goodness of the structures is to forget creation's fall. It is also to forget that I re-spond to the triune God; his judging as well as his redeeming action is known in the patterns of common life. Though Christ is Lord, he is Lord in faith and in hope. Christ's Lordship is never unambiguously

[34] See D. Bonhoeffer, *Ethics* (London: SCM Press, 1955), esp. pp. 194-209.

present in a given time and place, although it has a measure of social and historical actuality—we have a foretaste of that which is to come.

The Protestant has little distinctive culture; he lives as a Protestant in the given culture. He has patterns of meaning, however, that affect his interpretation of and action in his secular situation. His loyalty to God, understood in the tradition of Protestantism, is his point of stance. He dare not deny that what is given is given by God; yet he must say that, although the given is good, it is also fallen. Its full redemption is yet to come.

Other problems also are nascent in our position. Does a relational ethics become conservative in its effort to be relevant? That is, in responding in the concrete present and given, does one lose the possibility of a more radical criticism that commands more revolutionary action? At what point is it necessary to condemn the culture and the patterns of social relations as overwhelmingly demonic? A social realism demonstrates the strength of social and culture patterns. These seem to dictate the modes of effective action, and may lead to gradualism if not conservatism in social change. In the relatively prosperous and open society of the United States we may be able to afford gradualism. The problem is not purely a hypothetical one for us, for in the process of desegregation we are transforming social structures and culture patterns. We are, however, more certain of the rightness of radical action in desegregation than we are in fiscal policy. Issues may have to be graded with reference to the clarity of the mandate to engage in radical action. On certain issues action can be revolutionary because its rightness is clear. Yet we can never assume the absolute rightness for all people of any action; social change is costly for all involved. Good is destroyed as well as allowed to come into being in every social change.

Perhaps this ambiguity indicates the need for various patterns af action in various centers of social power, all in responsible obedience to God. For example, legal action as well as personal education is necessary in the desegregation process. Ameliorative programs for resettling Hungarian refugees must be developed while the United Nations and other forms of international power seek to deal with the problem of national self-determination. Relational ethics makes clear the complexity of involvement in good and evil, right and wrong, in any projected radical social change. It does not necessarily lead to conservative reinforcement of a social *status quo*. The power of structures inherited from the past is recognized, as is the necessity to preserve such good as we can in social change. We also recognize that new structures will present their own moral temptations for those who must act in and through them.

Does our social analysis tend to create a Christian ethics for the elite? The moralist may become enamored with the great centers of power and confine his attention to them alone. This is, however, a distortion of the social understanding involved. To be sure, Christian social ethics must realize that our culture and society are shaped more by power centers than by the general populace. The tendency of a modern economy is to rationalize the total pattern of social relations. We have "motivation research" to establish which appeals are most effective in getting us to buy things we do not need. The federal government through its taxation and fiscal policy is a major regulating mechanism for economic stability and economic growth. Policy is formed by the managers rather than the stockholders of large corporations. Trade-union leaders plan strategy rather than depend on "grass roots" developments. Such evidence indicates that a Christian social ethics that is irrelevant to persons in these key decision-making centers can have only limited effectiveness in transforming our culture.

Not all social power, however, is concentrated in a few hands. Administrative decisions affecting various levels of policy are made by subordinates in business and government. The two-party system enables the American public to have general responsibility for specific decisions about public policy made by legislators and government executives. Further, not all goals are national in scope. The lesser centers of power with limited ranges of social impact must also be reached by the Church. Every person has a sphere of responsibility in which decisions, with social consequences are made. For this reason any reduction of the sphere of Christian social action to the most powerful centers of society is unrealistic. To fail to see, however, that there are gradations of social influence due to the various concentrations of power in our society is equally unrealistic.

A final open question about both H. Richard Niebuhr's ethics and that of the present essay concerns the relation of ethics to ontology. Is it necessary to pursue questions about the assumptions concerning the nature of Being itself, in a relational and contextual social ethics? In our experience of a world of process, and of beings with internal relations to each other, are we participating in Being, and can we say that this experience gives us knowledge of Being? Further, can the patterns of value and meaning that the decision-maker brings to a situation be defended adequately in terms of their illuminative power? To what extent must we pursue the question of the existence of a purposive order given in Creation that seeks its own fulfillment? If such an order is accepted as a formal minimum for social policy, wherein lies our knowledge of it? To what extent can it be defined? If it can be defined, does the definition function as an imperative to act and as a pattern of action? These questions are tangential to the purpose of the present essay, and need not be answered to defend it. They must be kept in mind, however, in a further development of the social ethics suggested here.

5.

THE TRANSFORMATION
OF ETHICS

PAUL RAMSEY

IT HAS been said that, strictly speaking, the Bible contains no doctrine of man. Instead, it everywhere shows forth an understanding of man in the light of his relationship to God. In the same sense there is no biblical ethics, but only a viewing of the problems of morality in the light of God. This is pre-eminently true, also, of the thought and writings of H. Richard Niebuhr. In the ground bass and not simply in the grace notes this is the difference in emphasis between Richard and Reinhold Niebuhr, or between him and many another contemporary thinker who by contrast is more an anthropologist and an ethical or social analyst. ". . . The spirit of Evangelical ethics," Richard Niebuhr writes, "is not discernible in men; it exists only in the relations of men to God and of God to men. It is as erroneous to look for it in men or churches as it is fallacious to look for manifestations of magnetism in steel filings in the absence of a magnet." Of course, sin and other actualities of human existence are subjects for theological reflection. Indeed, "the negative counterpart of the realization that God is holy is the realization that men are all profane and that they fall short of his glory in everything they do."

But an ethics which starts with the realization of human ingloriousness, profaneness and sinfulness and in which men keep their eyes centered on the sin which stains all human acts will be profoundly different from the ethics of the glory of God. Evangelical ethics is God-centered, not sin-centered. When our fundamental orientation in life is that of persons who live *vis a vis* our own sinful selves rather than *vis a vis* God, the spirit of

Evangelical ethics takes flight no less surely than when we live in the contemplation of our own righteousness.[1]

The task of this chapter will be to explore the consequences of such "radical monotheism" for our understanding of man and morals.

It will be convenient to begin with Niebuhr's formulation of a theory of value and then trace his thought concerning the "transvaluation" or "transformation" of value under the impact of monotheistic and Christocentric faith. No doubt, for the Christian theologian there must be decisive reference to God in the formation no less than in the transformation of all thought about values. Nevertheless, these may be distinguished and a general theory of value formulated which may possibly commend itself to the consideration of philosophers who hold and are held by other faiths.

1. VALUE AND THE TRANSFORMATION OF VALUE

On the issue drawn between ethics and metaphysics, or between an ethical theology and theological ethics, by the currency in modern times of theories of abstract or "objective" values, Niebuhr ranges himself with those who affirm the primacy of "being" both in the way we know values and in the way value has its being. Unlike the Thomists, however, who define values (*verum, bonum, pulchrum*) as among the "transcendental" or universal attributes of being *as such* (no matter where or when), for Niebuhr value is an attribute of being-in-relation-to-being. In the midst of plural, interacting, becoming existences, "value is present wherever being confronts being." It is "a function of being in relation to being." Value may always be defined as "the *good-forness* of being for being in their reciprocity, their animosity, and their mutual aid," or as "what is fitting, useful, complementary to an existence." Apart from existences in interrelationship there are no values.

> . . . Value is present wherever one existent being with capacities and potentialities confronts another existence that limits or completes or complements it. Thus . . . value is present objectively for an observer in the fittingness or unfittingness of being to being. . . . Good is a term which not only can be but which . . . must be applied to that which meets the needs, which fits the capacity, which corresponds to the potentialities of an existent being.[2]

Other ethical terms are to be located in a similar fashion. "Right," for example, means "what is owed to another being."[3]

Such "relational value-theory" avoids *psychological* relativism, since "good-forness" and the required response vary not with desire but according to the conjunction of being with being. Niebuhr never uses

---

[1] "Evangelical and Protestant Ethics" in *The Heritage of the Reformation* (New York: R. R. Smith, 1950), p. 222.

[2] "The Center of Value" in *Moral Principles of Action*, ed. by Ruth Nanda Anshen (New York: Harper & Brothers, 1952), pp. 165, 169.

[3] *Ibid.*, p. 170.

the word "relative" in the psychological sense of relative to consciousness or desire, as if there were nothing either good or bad but thinking makes it so. The words "relational" and "relatedness" better represent Niebuhr's position than the words "relative" and "relativism" which he uses more frequently. Indeed, the technical philosophical designation "objective relativism" is not really adequate to describe the point of view of relational value-theory; and ought perhaps to be replaced by some such expression as "objective relatedness" or preferably "relational objectivism." Niebuhr's penchant for the word "relativism" is in part only a terminological matter of no great importance. However, it also shows the influence of the excessive contextualism of much modern social philosophy, idealistic and pragmatic, and the continued influence of Troeltsch's cultural or historical relativism upon Niebuhr's thought, which at many points is obviously breaking through the self-contradictory confines of these points of view. Relativism, and not as the term only, continues in play more than is warranted as one of the important themes in Niebuhr's writings, because of his belief that relativism of some sort is a direct implication of radical monotheism and of the "conversionist" motif in Christian ethics. The correctness of the latter opinion may and should be questioned. We shall return to these issues in the second part of this chapter.

If the "objective relativist" (or preferably the "relational objectivist" sets out to give a consistent and systematic account of what is right, his relational value-theory must have some "center of value":

. . . Relational value-theory . . . is evidently *dogmatically relativistic* since it is necessary to take one's standpoint with or in some being accepted as the *center of value*. . . . Every theory of value, so far as it is relational, is religious in character. Every such theory adopts as its explicit or implicit starting point some being or beings in relation to which also the rightness or wrongness of its relation to other beings is examined.[4]

Thus, the value-center for evolutionary ethics is life itself, and all questions within ethics are about the good-for-life. The question "What is life good for?" can be raised only by shifting to some being other than life as the center of value; as a consequence all ethical questions then become relative to this new center in being. Utilitarianism seems to have two centers of value—the individual and society—and questions in this ethics are conversant about both the good-for-the-individual and the good-for-society. Questions about what the individual is good for, or what society is good for, can be raised only by momentarily shifting to one of these centers of value as that relative to which all good-forness is to be defined, and which itself at the moment is not regarded as good for any being beyond itself. Thus, "the starting point of all [ethical]

[4] *Ibid.*, pp. 171, 172 (first italics mine).

inquiry lies in the recognition of *that which is;"*[5] and systems of ethics are distinguishable first of all according to the paramount being or beings in which they center, and by the prevailing ontic orientation discoverable within every value-system.

Theological ethics arises from the recognition that God is *he who is* and the only proper center of value. "Critical thought based on theocentric faith," Niebuhr writes, "objects only but strongly to the religious foundations of these relativisms," and it replaces one center by another.[6] But once this acknowledgment has been made, the procedure of ethical reflection remains the same: "Such faith no more begins by asking what God is good for than humanistic or vitalistic ethics begins with the inquiry what man or life is good for."[7] It asks rather what man is good for, what is the good for man and what are his responsibilities in the light of his being in relation to God.

When God's reign is thus acknowledged, man's understanding of his situation and his values begins to be changed. Something like this is true no matter what being has the value of God. The individualist who takes his standpoint with or in the being of society "may indeed discover that his values are included in the values of society, but the included values are not the same as those which he defined when he made his beginning with himself and sought to proceed from the values relative to personality to the values relative to society."[8] If this is true when one shifts from one finite center to another finite center of value, how much more thoroughgoing will be the impact of the shift from finite centers to the Infinite center of value. "The experience of the ground and source of all value leads to the criticism and reconstruction of the ethical system rather than to the support of one which has been accepted as absolute prior to the experience."[9]

[5] *Ibid.*, p. 173. Cf. "Value-Theory and Theology" in *The Nature of Religious Experience* (symposium in honor of D. C. Macintosh) (New York: Harper & Brothers, 1937), pp. 105-6: ". . . Every ethics rests at last upon a dogmatic basis." ". . . The dogmas of ethics are religious." Here, as in the above use of the expression "dogmatically relativistic," Niebuhr does not mean a dogmatic *conclusion*, but dogma in the exact sense of the word: a framework of interpretation or center in the midst of being from which all reasoning proceeds.

[6] *Ibid.*, p. 175.

[7] *Ibid.*, p. 174.

[8] "Value-Theory and Theology," p. 109.

[9] *Ibid.*, pp. 115-16. This chapter in the Macintosh *Festschrift*, published in 1937, clearly demonstrates that for many years the motif "Christ Transforming Culture" has governed Niebuhr's theological reflection, only to be developed climactically in *Christ and Culture*. It is the basis for his criticism of value-theology from Ritschl to Wieman and Macintosh on the ground that in this movement "values gained from nonreligious experience are employed as the absolute criteria of theology" (p. 110). He calls for the complete abandonment of this procedure of defining God by picking and choosing from among attributes we would like to assign him in order that he may the more readily subserve these same unaltered values. In a radically monotheist

A relational value-theory firmly grounded in related being fits into context with a number of other approaches which Niebuhr makes to an understanding of the nature of man, of the "good for" him and of his responsibility. Of all ethical notions none is more congenial to Niebuhr's main perspective upon man and morals than the concept of "responsibility." In brief, to be ethically responsible means to be a respond*ing* being in relation to other beings:

> To be responsible is to be a self in the presence of other selves, to whom one is bound and to whom one is able to answer freely; responsibility includes stewardship or trusteeship over things that belong to the common life of the selves.[10]

Responsibility as the response of being to being is made up of two components: *to whom* and *for what or whom* one is responsible. There is a corresponding double reference in *ir*responsibility: not responding to those *to* whom one owes response, and in answering giving a wrong account of the things or beings *for* which one is responsible. Responsibility is always *to* being, and responsibility *for* includes not only things but also beings who are selves. In man's ultimate relationship to being he knows himself to be responsible *to* God and responsible in some sense *for* everyone and everything that has being.

It may be noted at this point that there is a dynamic connection between these two aspects of responsibility running mainly in one direction: *to whom* we are responsible alters our understanding of the *for what* or *for whom* we are accountable. "What a man is responsible for depends in part at least on the being to whom he is accountable."[11] This fact is significant for the "transformation" of the ethics of responsibility in the light of God as the being to whom man is finally accountable.

Thus, the concept of "responsibility" shows most clearly the transition from Niebuhr's general theory of ethics to his concern for reviewing values and duties in the light of monotheistic faith. "The content of responsibility varies with the nature of the society to which men understand themselves to belong." This general truth about how *duty*

theology, God is seen to transform values rather than being transformed or known only by means of them: "A faith which finds in God the source and center of all value, which values personal existence only because it makes the enjoyment of God possible, and hopes for immortality only because it hopes for the vision of God, which founds its morality upon the sole value of God and the sacredness of his creatures because they are his creatures—such a faith must remain dissatisfied with an approach which, however disguisedly, makes him a means to an end, however noble the end in human esteem" (p. 103).

[10] "The Responsibility of the Church for Society" in *The Gospel, the Church and the World*, ed. by Kenneth Scott Latourette (The Interseminary Series, vol. 3; New York: Harper & Brothers, 1946), p. 114.

[11] *Ibid.*, pp. 115-16.

to affects the *scope* of responsibility provides the basis, in Niebuhr's view, for the theocentric "conversion" or "transformation" of responsibility; and this takes place both extensively and intensively:

> If a man responds to the demands of a universal God then the neighbors for whom he is responsible are not only the members of the nation to which he belongs but the members of the total society over which God presides. If one gives account to a God who tries the 'heart and reins', then one must answer for invisible as well as overt acts. . . . In the company of God and of immortal souls even family responsibility is greater and more inclusive than in the company of nations and of men who are regarded as purely temporal beings. When men know that they stand before an infinite judge and creator the content of their obligation becomes infinite.[12]

From thus describing the *theo*centric transformation of ethical responsibility, Niebuhr moves on by an almost imperceptible step (perhaps because the notion of the Triune God is the most radically monotheistic idea of God there is) to speak of how *Christo*centric faith affects the scope and nature of responsibility. He defines "the Being to whom" Christians and the Church are "answerable as *God-in-Christ* and *Christ-in-God*," or as "the redemptive principle in the absolute." This means immediately that "the content of responsibility is always mercy"; and that men must give account "for their treatment . . . of all the sick, imprisoned, hungry, thirsty men of the world—the neighbors, brothers and companions of an omnipresent being" Jesus Christ, to whom they are responsible. Here, again, the *to whom* both intensifies and also makes more extensive the *for what* or *whom* we are ethically responsible:

> Whatever is, is good in the world of this God-in-Christ. It may be perverted, sinful, broken; but it is not bad, for God-in-Christ has made it and maintains it. Such universal responsibility is incompatible with a spiritualism that limits the Church's concern to immaterial values, with a moralism that does not understand the value of the sinner and the sinful nation, with an individualism that makes mankind as a whole and its societies of less concern to God than single persons, and with any of these particularistic and polytheistic theories of value and responsibility which substitute for God-in-Christ some other deity as the source of valuable being.[13]

The above quotation also makes plain what may have been obscured in this brief sketch of Niebuhr's viewpoint: The response is not only *to* God. Instead, the extension and intensification of the scope of responsibility *for* is largely also a matter of response *to* every one of the creatures of God. The significance of such a theocentric transformation of ethical responsiveness can be seen by comparing the resulting view

[12] *Ibid.*, pp. 116, 117.
[13] *Ibid.*, pp. 119-20.

with those theologies which, having only a little god made to order from preconceived specifications about what is valuable enough to be called divine, as a consequence inculcate positive response to only part of what God has evidently made.

The motif of "conversion" in ethics has been succintly summarized by Niebuhr:

> . . . *Conversion is antithetical to substitution.* In the Christian life human *eros* is not supplanted by divine *agape* but the divine *agape* converts the human *eros* by directing it in gratitude toward God and toward the neighbor in God. The community of the family is not supplanted by a monastic society but the hearts of fathers and children and husbands and wives are turned toward each other in reconciliation because of the divine forgiveness. The gospel restores and converts and turns again; it does not destroy and rebuild by substituting one finite structure of life or thought for another.[14]

Nevertheless, human *eros*, or the best in man's spiritual aspiration, in no way remains untransformed. When wholly converted, *eros* becomes "nonpossessive *Eros*": loving God with pure adoration, gratitude, "consent to Being." Christlike love for God and man, therefore, does not mean a "like-minded interest in two great values, God and man." There is between love for God and love for neighbor "no common quality but only a common source." Love to God means "nonpossessive *Eros*"; love for neighbor, pure *agape*, compassion, "powerful pity."[15]

By analogy with the five main historical types of Christian attitudes toward culture suggested by Niebuhr in *Christ and Culture*, the following analysis might be made of the possible relationships between *agape* and *eros*: (1) *agape* "against" or in contradiction to *eros*, (2) the "identification" of *agape* and *eros*; (3) *agape* "above" and fulfilling *eros* in "hierarchical synthesis"; (4) *agape* and *eros* in paradox or continual tension and dialogue; (5) *agape* "transforming" *eros*. Adopting and elaborating the fifth, or conversionist, type of approach as the one most obviously implied by radical monotheism and the complete Lordship of Christ would put to rout the anti-Nygren Nygrenites of the present day—those theologians who first mistake Anders Nygren's *history* of the idea of Christian love for a *complete constructive* system of theological ethics and then sharpen excessively the dualism of the point of view they oppose, all to the end of raising a banner for the defense of ideal human *eros* untransformed, usually in "hierarchical synthesis" if not in "identification" with *agape*. As Niebuhr has said: "Conversion is antithetical to substitution" or the uprooting of *eros*. But conversion is also antithetical to identification or to any synthetic points of view in which human *eros* is fulfilled but remains untrans-

---

[14] "The Hidden Church and the Churches in Sight," *Religion in Life*, XV, No. 1 (Winter, 1945-46), pp. 115-16 (first italics mine).
[15] *Christ and Culture* (New York: Harper & Brothers, 1951), pp. 18-19.

formed. The transformation of human *eros* into *nonpossessive eros* means, of course, "the perfection of *eros*" toward God and invariably also *agape* toward man: Because Jesus "loves the Father with the perfection of human *eros*, therefore he loves man with the perfection of divine *agape* since God is *agape*."[16]

The same "conversionist" motif is restated in Niebuhr's discussion of the impact of "the deity of God" upon man's situation and values in *The Meaning of Revelation*. "The first change which the moral law undergoes with the revelation of God's person is in its *imperativeness*."[17] We know that the moral law is not what we demand or society demands but what God demands of us. In the second place, "the moral law is changed . . . by the revelation of God's self in that its *evermore extensive and intensive application* becomes necessary."[18] What this means has perhaps been sufficiently explained in connection with the transformation of moral responsibility. Niebuhr emphasizes that in being universalized and intensified the moral law is "reborn": "A *revolutionary transvaluation* occurs not in addition to the personal revelation [of God] but because of it."[19] Thirdly and finally, the transformation of the moral law under the impact of "the deity of God" reveals to us our *always already* sinful use of the moral law. ". . . A restoration is begun, for . . . we recognize that the moral law as we had entertained it, was always a corrupted thing . . ."[20] In particular, we see that we have made offensive and defensive use of the moral law "as interested men who served a creature rather than the creator." Revelation serves to "point the moral law at us, saying, 'Thou art the man'."[21] The "conversion" of morality means therefore not only enhanced, more extensive and intensive imperativeness, but also "the conversion of the imperative into an indicative" in which we see that it is we and not only our neighbors who serve idols even by moral goodness; into an indicative in which also we see the possibility of free love of God and of the neighbor in God replacing, as the greatest change, the love demanded by the law.[22] In sum, Niebuhr envisages as the significance of religion for ethics, not the "republication" by divine authority of the law of nature nor the giving of supplementary divine decrees, but "the beginning of a revolutionary understanding and application of the moral law rather than the giving of a new law."[23]

[16] *Ibid.*, p. 28.
[17] *The Meaning of Revelation* (New York: The Macmillan Company, 1946), p. 165 (italics mine).
[18] *Ibid.*, pp. 166-67 (italics mine).
[19] *Ibid.*, p. 168 (italics mine).
[20] *Loc. cit.*
[21] *Ibid.*, p. 169.
[22] Cf. *ibid.*, pp. 170-71.
[23] *Ibid.*, p. 172.

The end toward which the transformation of man and morals is directed in the ethics of Christocentric monotheism can be clearly seen in Niebuhr's consideration of "the virtues of Jesus Christ" in the section "Toward a Definition of Christ" in *Christ and Culture*[24] and in an unpublished paper on the theological virtues, "Reflections on Faith, Hope and Love." At these points in his writings, relational value-theory evidences to the maximum the impact of the "deity-value" of God as the center which man meets in the midst of being and in his ethical reflection and action. The distinctive character of "the virtues of Jesus Christ" and of the so-called theological virtues, faith, hope, and love, arises from being-in-relation-to-God and not from any quality they may or may not have in common with other virtues which have the same name but which prove to be attributes of being in relation to some other being.

The "theological virtues" are not, Niebuhr believes, "achievements or products of training" and "not habits somehow established in the constitution of the agent," which is the traditional philosophical understanding of the word "virtue." They "are given not as states of character but as relations to other beings and particularly as relations to God," "relations which depend for their duration on the constancy with which the objective good, to which the self is related in these ways, is given." In short, faith, hope, and love are "gifts" and "responses" —gifts of the presence to the self of the "deity-value" of God and "responses" to God the center of value, gifts from and responses to the valuation of the self from beyond itself:

The self does not think rightly or humbly of itself until God discloses himself in his majesty and graciousness and reveals the neighbor in his Christlikeness. Love is given in the gift of the lovely, the love-attracting; it is called forth by the gift of God himself as the supremely and wholly desirable good; by the gift of the neighbor, as one beloved by God, as lovely, and as loving the self. . . . Faith as trust is given with the self-disclosure to a person of God as the faithful One. . . . Faith as loyalty or faithfulness is given with the revelation of the supremely challenging cause, the cause of the Kingdom of God or the cause of Christ. Hope is given with the gift of a promise or with the gift of a future. . . . As responses [faith, hope, and love] are personal both on the side of the agent and on the side of the object, that is they are responses of a person to personal actions such as faithkeeping, love, promise.[25]

Faith, hope, and love, as attitudes or functions of being in relation to being, engage the *whole* being of man in relation to God, and this is what is meant by the interrelation of the theological virtues. These relational virtues "are as interconnected as are their bases in the

---

[24] Pp. 11-29.
[25] "Reflections on Faith, Hope and Love" (an unpublished paper).

creaturely constitution of the self as being devoted to value, as covenanting being and as being in time" (for "hope" engages a "being that has time in it"). As responses of man's total and concrete being to the self-disclosure of God, the responses or relational virtues are themselves aspects of one response. "Insofar as the unity of the self in Christian life needs to be defined, this can be done only" by reference to the complete presence of being with being in which man "responds faithfully, lovingly, hopefully to God-in-Christ and [the] companion-in-Christ."

Moreover, these relational virtues engaging the whole being of man in unified response cannot be adequately described as each a *donum superadditum*. Instead, they transform man's being and valuations to their roots. At the bottom and in the beginning of man's relationship to other beings and centers of value there were all along corresponding natural virtues of a relational sort. The theological virtues originate in the "conversion" and redirection of these relationships.

They seem . . . to represent the restoration and the perfection to its true activity of a personal capacity for response which has been perverted. The love of God and of the neighbor in God are not foreign to man's nature, or, better, to man in his natural situation; but in our fallen situation they are present as love of idol and love of the neighbor in relation to idols. Man does not exist without love of an objective good which is, in a momentary way at least, the object of his greatest concern. Nor does he seem to live without relation to the Ground of Being though in the fallen state this relation is one of hostility. The love of God is the restoration and perfection of a response which has always been present in misdirected and inverted form; this seems also to be true of love of the companion.[26]

The theological virtues are not a set of supernatural character traits supervening upon natural morality ("Christ *above* cultivated morality"). They are rather aspects of the ethics of redemption which engage the total being of man in a new relationship with God and with his companion in God. The redirective power of being in the presence of God reverberates throughout the whole and descends to every note in the scale ("Christ *transforming* natural or cultivated morality"). The theological virtues are directions in which man is undergoing transformation.

In defining the virtues of Jesus Christ in *Christ and Culture*, Niebuhr discusses love, hope, obedience, faith, and humility. Here he gains too easy a victory over contemporary Christian ethicists who have regarded love as the key to Jesus' ethics, by associating them with "religious liberalism" in this regard.[27] In the first place, in some of the writings

[26] *Loc. cit.*

[27] *Christ and Culture*, p. 15 and n. 13. In addition to the reasons given above for denying this association, the example of Karl Barth might be cited. He certainly cannot be accused of any lack of theological realism, or of shifting with liberalism to a stress on anthropology and man's subjective state of mind. Yet, speaking of "The Life of the Children of God," Barth sums up his views on theological ethics simply

of religious liberals—e.g., E. F. Scott, *The Ethical Teachings of Jesus*—
it is surprising how little attention is paid to love as the organizing
principle of Jesus' teachings. In the second place, Reinhold Niebuhr,
Anders Nygren, and others who today stress the perfection of love in
Jesus' life and teachings have not magnified this to the exclusion of all
other virtues. Instead, they have understood love only in vital relation
to and suffused by hope, obedience, faith, humility, and any other
virtue which it may yet appear necessary to take into account in describing Jesus' ethical practice and teachings and which *ensemble* were
a consequence of the directness and power of his relation to God.
Finally, it might be added—and this is something Niebuhr himself
knows well enough but some of his readers may not—that for the avoidance of the "moralism" of "the love of love" it helps not at all simply
to add on a cluster of other virtues besides love. Whether the ethics
of Jesus be analyzed in terms of a number of virtues including love side
by side with all the rest, or in terms of one only, love, whose nature is
clearly understood as inclusive of obedience, hope, faith, humility, and
all the rest, makes no great difference. The point is that in either case
these are relational virtues, and love is only a relation to God and the
neighbor in and under God, never a love for love itself.

In discussing each of the virtues of Christ, Niebuhr makes the same
point. These virtues, which men know in other forms in their ordinary
moral relationships, have all been transformed in the extreme in Jesus
Christ; and it is the "realization of God which makes all the virtues of
Jesus Christ radical."[28]

> Love . . . is characterized by a certain extremism in Jesus, but . . . it is
> the extremism of devotion to the one God, uncompromised by love of any
> other absolute good. This virtue in him is disproportionate only in the
> polytheistic-monotheistic sense, not in the sense that it is unaccompanied by
> other virtues perhaps equally great.
>
> [Hope, radical obedience, faith, humility also were] expressed in his
> conduct and teaching in a manner that seems extreme and disproportionate
> to secular, cultural wisdom. But he practices none of them and requires none
> of them of his followers otherwise than in relation to God. . . .
> . . . His hope was in God and for God . . . He hoped in the living God.
> The heroic character of Jesus' hopefulness does not stand alone; it is

---

by an extended commentary on the two love commandments which, he says, mean
respectively the love and praise of God; and he writes, "All things considered, the
Christian life . . . consists in these two concepts of love and praise. . . . Even faith
does not anticipate love. As we come to faith we begin to love. If we did not
begin to love, we would not have come to faith. . . . If we believe, the fact that we
do so means that every ground which is not that of our being in love to God in
Christ is cut away from under us." (*Church Dogmatics* [transl. G. T. Thomson and
Harold Knight; Edinburgh: T. & T. Clark, 1956], vol. 1, pt. 2, §18, p. 371.)
[28] *Ibid.*, p. 24.

mated with heroic love and heroic faith; and all these have their source in his relation to God . . .

. . . Obedience is radical when the whole man is involved, so that "he is not only *doing* something obediently but *is* essentially obedient." . . . Obedience was connected with a certain transcending of the mediate authority of the law, it . . . was addressed to the whole man, including every thought and motive as well as every overt deed, and . . . there was no escape from the responsibility of obedience.

He is indeed characterized by an extreme faith and by a radical humility. But faith and humility are not things in themselves; they are relations to persons—habits of behavior in the presence of others.[29]

Thus, each of the virtues is intelligible in its apparently radical and inordinate character only as a relation to God.[30] When the relation to God as the fundamental factor in Jesus' life is left out of account, his life and teachings seem too extreme. But when relation to the one God is placed in the center, one can begin to see why in his response he could love and hope and obey and trust and humble himself before the powerful fidelity of his Father no less than he did. And in so far as God-in-Christ and Christ-in-God have "the value of God" for men, as the One who ultimately values and judges them from beyond themselves, they can begin to see in him the very image of the being in response to whom they are being transformed, and to whom they are responsible for all.

2. CHRIST TRANSFORMING RELATIVISM OR CHRIST TRANSFORMING RELATIONALLY OBJECTIVE NORMS?

The title of this section is a *question*, and will remain so to the end. It is, however, a query which Richard Niebuhr and we who have studied with him or been influenced by him should constantly press.

We have now to suggest that a more adequate understanding of Niebuhr's thought is to be gained by emphasizing the objective element in his relativism. Also, in so far as the word "relativism" in anything like its ordinary meaning still may be regarded as appropriate, we shall point out that relativism has only been presupposed as a (perhaps thoughtless) conclusion within the present age; and indeed that such a general position cannot even be proposed by anyone as the truth about man's situation and truth-getting without cutting out the ground upon which it itself stands. But this interpretation, and apparently severe criticism, of Niebuhr's position can never become our main concern. If the exposition and rejection of Niebuhr's relativism were of principal importance, then we would be responsible for developing and enforcing an alternative point of view concerning the truth of ethical judgments. It is not necessary to undertake this here, since what must first be done is to give full and direct attention to the theme of the "conversion"

[29] *Ibid.*, pp. 16, 19, 21-22, 23, 25.
[30] *Ibid.*, p. 27.

of ethics which takes place whenever ethical reflection and decision come to be centered theologically in Christ. This is without any doubt Niebuhr's peerless contribution to Christian ethical analysis—the significance of which stands out all the more clearly because anyone who studies this theme as it is developed, for example, in *Christ and Culture* will see at once that it is simply *there* in Christian history and in the major documents of the Church's life. When this motif is isolated and carefully examined, it will become obvious that the problem of ethics is the problem of its conversion or redirection, not of its replacement. The transformist theme needs now to be distinguished from, or within, the context of Niebuhr's relativism, precisely because only so can the free lordship of Christ in encounter with every possible system of ethics be properly praised.

The reader's attention has been called to the fact that Niebuhr rejects subjective or psychological relativism in taking the point of view of "objective relativism." In one of his earliest and most well-rounded statements of this position, Niebuhr points out that it entails no prejudice whatever against the objectivity of value:

> Such a value-theory would recognize . . . the relativity of values without prejudice to their objectivity. The interpretation of values as relative to structure and organic needs, rather than to desire and consciousness, provides for such an objective relativism. The value of deity would appear, on the basis of such a theory, to be quite independent of human desire and the consciousness of need, but not independent of the human constitution and its actual need.[81]

What is denied is the view that "values are independent of structure and process." What is denied is not that values are objective but the "vitiating abstractionism" which separates, for example, truth and justice "from any being for whom they are valid" and teaches "that *they* ought to be rather than that *man* ought to be truthful and just. . . ."[32] In short, "objective relativism" excludes, on the one hand, subjectivism and, on the other hand, the ethical theories of Plato or Hartmann with their value-essences.

Only once in this statement of his case does Niebuhr mention "the relative standpoint of the observer,"[33] which is relativism of quite another kind and which does not enter at all into the exposition and defense of the relation of value to structure, process, actual need, being. For this reason I have suggested that Niebuhr's general theory of value be called "relational objectivism" and that the misleading word "relativism" be no longer used. Not only his early essay, published in 1937, but also the recent statement of relational value-theory in "The

[81] "Value-Theory and Theology," p. 113.
[32] *Ibid.*, p. 106.
[33] *Loc. cit.*

Center of Value," published in 1952, lends support to this suggestion.

Yet at many other points in his writings Niebuhr expresses beliefs for which the word "relativism" is to great extent warranted. This is particularly true of *The Meaning of Revelation*. The thematic presupposition of this book is "the religious as well as the historical bondage of theological reason,"[34] and in it Niebuhr proposes to draw out "the consequence of this understanding of theology's religious relativity as well as of its understanding of historical relativity."[35] The relativity entailed in the standpoint of the observer has special bearing upon the problem of man and morals. Yet the relativism of the historical and cultural point of view which a man occupies is nowhere established in this book, or elsewhere in Niebuhr's writings. It is simply assumed to have been established by some "prior science." The reader is asked to presuppose that a volume entitled "The Critique of Historical Reason" has already been written, and has clearly established itself in a consensus of "critical philosophers."

Theology . . . is concerned with the principle of relativity as this has been *demonstrated* by history and sociology rather than by physics, and if it is developing into a relativistic theology this is the result of . . . an attempt to adjust itself to a new self-knowledge.[36]

Critical idealists and realists knew themselves to be human selves with a specific psychological and logical equipment; their successors know themselves to be social human beings whose reason is not a common reason, alike in all human selves, but one which is qualified by inheritance from a particular society. They know that they are historical selves whose metaphysics, logic, ethics and theology, like their economics, politics and rhetoric are limited, moving and changing in time. . . . Our reason is not only in space-time but . . . space-time is in our reason.[37]

. . . Our historical relativism affirms the historicity of the subject even more than that of the object; man, it points out, is not only in time but time is in man . . . the time of a definite society with distinct language, economic and political relations, religious faith and social organization.[38]

. . . If reason is to operate at all it must be content to work as an historical reason.[39]

In all this there are dangers confronting human thought, Niebuhr admits, dangers such that "it is not strange that men today seek to avoid the problem by damning historical relativism itself as an aberration."[40] I propose at most to damn it as a relativism; and moreover as a rela-

---

[34] *Op. cit.*, p. 38.
[35] *Ibid.*, p. 37.
[36] *Ibid.*, pp. 7-8 (italics mine).
[37] *Ibid.*, pp. 9-10.
[38] *Ibid.*, p. 13.
[39] *Ibid.*, p. 16.
[40] *Ibid.*, p. 17.

tivism that has not and cannot establish for itself ground on which to stand.

We must proceed cautiously here, for Niebuhr himself believes that agnosticism need not be the conclusion drawn from historical relativism. He calls rather for "a new type of critical idealism which recognizes the social and historical character of the mind's categories and is 'belief-fully' realistic . . ."[41] Niebuhr urges that we distinguish between "universal views" and "views of the universal." A critique of historical reason must deny that man possesses "universal views"; but, Niebuhr believes, such critical idealism (or critical realism) may remain "belief-fully realistic" in the confidence that, despite "the social and historical character of the mind's categories," each of these gives a "view of the universal."

It is not evident that the man who is forced to confess that his view of things is conditioned by the standpoint he occupies must doubt the reality of what he sees. It is not apparent that one who knows that his concepts are not universal must also doubt that they are concepts of the universal, or that one who understands how all his experience is historically mediated must believe that nothing is mediated through history.[42]

Here Niebuhr appeals to his notion of dialogue (or triologue) in the verification and communication of knowledge of the universal. As the eye "cannot perceive the depth and distance and solidity of things save as it has a partner,"[43] so in viewing the universal (or within the community of the faithful who receive historical revelation and bear witness to the meaning of Christ) there is "the test of experience on the part of companions who look from the same standpoint in the same direction."[44]

Niebuhr's "relativism of the subject" does not lean as far as might appear in the direction of skepticism—nor, in my opinion, as far in the direction of relativism as seems at first to be the case. At first it may seem that only an irrational act of faith forestalls skepticism. The empirical sciences assume with "animal faith" that the sense impressions give us relative perspectives on the real world (or that each is a view of the universal), although there is no sense beyond the senses to tell us that this is true (i.e., there is no universal view). "Without this animal faith in a dependable external world we literally would not live as bodies, for if we were true skeptics we would be errant fools to eat food made up of sense-data only, to breathe an unsubstantial air with unreal lungs, to walk with unreal feet upon a non-existent earth toward imaginary goals."[45] In a similar fashion, there is no point of view be-

41 *Ibid.*, p. vii.
42 *Ibid.*, p. 18-19.
43 *Ibid.*, p. 58.
44 *Ibid.*, p. 21.
45 *Ibid.*, p. 79.

yond historically relative points of view which can inform us that our viewpoints give us concepts of the universal or that something objective is mediated through historical experience. Only by an act of faith, it seems, do we break through the confines of our historically conditioned categories and lay hold on the real.

The acceptance of the reality of what we see in psychologically and historically conditioned experience is always something of an act of faith; but such faith is inevitable and justifies itself or is justified by its fruits. A critical idealism is always accompanied, openly or disguisedly, by a critical realism which accepts on faith the independent reality of what is mediated. . . . So an historical relativism can and must proceed with faith in the midst of all its criticism of historical subjects and objects mediated through history.[46]

If this be the meaning of "belief-ful realism," if only an act of faith makes the difference between this position and skeptical relativism, then one might be forced to conclude that Niebuhr's objective relativism amounts to no more than skeptical relativism plus Hume's flair for playing the game of backgammon despite the inability of reason to justify the beliefs he invariably held while doing so.

But in interpreting Niebuhr one can lean just as far in the other direction, in the direction of objectivism. It is important to say whether the human mind or only an act of animal faith breaks through the charmed circle of the categories of historical reasoning and lays hold on reality. David Hume, even when at table with his friends, never believed *that the mind* could know anything; he *only believed*, with the animal faith requisite for backgammon, in the reality of friends, table, cards. The faith Niebuhr mentions is by contrast the faith that, in its views of the universal, the *mind* knows the real world. The belief of his "belief-ful realism" is actually the belief of a "critical realist." Amid relative historical perspectives, something of the universal is really grasped by reason. When Niebuhr writes that "we discern in all such formulations *elements* which are thoroughly relative to historical background,"[47] does he not—perhaps inadvertently—allow for the discernment of elements in knowledge which are not so thoroughly relative? Moreover, he states positively that "we need not doubt that the categorical imperative *contains* a universal meaning but Kant's formulations of it are historically relative and when we, in our later historical period, attempt to reformulate the Kantian thought we also do so as historically conditioned thinkers who cannot describe the universal save from a relative point of view."[48] Will not our attempts today to reformulate Kant's thought also "contain a universal meaning"?

[46] *Ibid.*, pp. 19-20.
[47] *Ibid.*, pp. 10-11 (italics mine).
[48] *Ibid.*, p. 11 (italics mine).

Indeed, the notion of "dialogue," which is so fundamental in Niebuhr's thinking, presupposes that each participant grasps something of the universal from his peculiar perspective and contributes this to, as well as receives correction from, the community of knowing minds. In fact, there is no impenetrable wall of separation between the point-of-viewing taken by one historical community and that of another. When describing the "religious relativism" of the Christian faith, Niebuhr is careful not to make this point of view impervious to other points of view: "To see ourselves as others see us, or to have others communicate to us what they see when they regard our lives from the outside, is to have a moral experience. Every external history of ourselves, communicated to us, becomes an event in inner history."[49] *To the extent* that such external accounts are communicated to us, has there not been actualized, through the dialogue of persons occupying different standpoints, a more inclusive community of interpretation? Here we see clearly the influence of Royce's idealism upon Niebuhr, and of the absolute community of interpretation which Royce believed to be presupposed in all human communication. Niebuhr as much as Royce accepts the *reality* of such an all-inclusive community. He simply denies that any finite perspective possesses such absolute comprehension of the truth. How much difference is there between Royce's "presupposition" or argument, that there must be such a universal community of interpretation even for error to be possible, and Niebuhr's when he writes the following?

The church's external history of itself may be described as an effort to see itself with the eyes of God. The simultaneous, unified knowledge from within and from without that we may ascribe to God is indeed impossible to men, but what is simultaneous in his case can in a measure be successive for us. The church cannot attain an inclusive, universal point of view but it can attempt to see the reflection of itself in the eyes of God.[50]

The crucial difference between Niebuhr's absolute monotheism and absolute idealism is not the reality of this last interpretation, which each presupposes, but the ultimate identity of the self in its wholeness with the Absolute. There is good reason, therefore, for interpreting Niebuhr in the direction away from relativism toward objectivism, and for denying that the word "relativism" adequately expresses what he means to say, as well as for replacing the term "objective relativism" with some such expression as "relational objectivism" (when the "relativity of the object" is at issue) or "perspectival objectivism" (when, as at present, the historical "relativity of the subject" has to be stressed).

"We are in history as the fish is in water," Niebuhr writes in one of

[49] *Ibid.*, p. 84-85.
[50] *Ibid.*, p. 88.

his unguarded relativistic moments.[51] But no fish wrote that such was its condition. No fish ever discoursed at length on the bondage of its reason to liquidity, or on the relativity of its point of viewing from the depths. "The Critique of Piscatory Reason" has not yet produced the thesis that fish are not only in water but water also in fish, wholly determining the categories of fish understanding. Indeed, we can set it down in advance that, were such a literary event to occur, the author would thereby have refuted himself by evidencing incontrovertibly that his own reason is not, to the whole extent of its being, bounded by liquidity.

The same fate overtakes "The Critique of Historical Reason," if indeed it is being written today. "Men who assert that all moral standards are relative," Richard Niebuhr wrote on one occasion, "still believe that it is right to speak the truth about the relativity of moral standards."[52] Likewise, men who assert that all moral standards are "objectively relative" still believe that it is right to speak the truth about objective relativism. Men who believe in the entire historicity of the subject still believe that *it is true* that human reason is only a historical reason, which means that in knowing this truth the reason was not wholly determined by the historical seasons. To be true, historical relativism must manifestly be false, or rather the truth of the theory would manifestly contradict what it says about the human mind. If true, this theory then itself would have truth not wholly "limited, moving and changing in time," and the capacity of the mind to know this would at least be something, something transcending the confines of the categories of historical reason. It may be that absolute idealism drew extravagant consequences from this argument against the earlier "critical idealism" of Kant. Nevertheless, the argument, that reason in knowing its historical limits has already in some sense transcended those limits, still holds true, even though, as Richard Kroner has pointed out,

It is not true that the acknowledgment of the limit allows me to penetrate into the realm beyond with limitless conquest. . . . Thus, philosophy in this definite sense transcends its own limits in knowing that it is limited. The land beyond its limits cannot be conquered, however; it can only be visited, as it were, and abandoned again with the consciousness that it always will be a foreign land, impenetrable and unfathomable as a whole.[53]

"Objective relativism" must have paid significant visits to the country where universal truth abides and brought back increased human discernment; or else at least some forms of absolutism would have equal truth when in season. As Niebuhr partly confesses in the preface to *The*

[51] *Ibid.*, p. 48.
[52] "Life is Worth Living," *Intercollegian and Far Horizons*, LVII, No. 1 (October, 1939), p. 4.
[53] *Culture and Faith* (Chicago: University of Chicago Press, 1951), p. 269.

Meaning of Revelation, he has indeed seized both horns of the dilemma[54] which knowledge confronts in facing up to the relativity of the historical standpoint of the observer; but it should be clear which horn he will have to let go as the discussion of the situation and problem of human knowledge proceeds. As precondition of his speaking the truth to us, even as precondition of the possibility of our significant disagreement with him, he can only mean "perspectival objectivism." This expression retains the full force of what he says about our "views of the universal" as distinct from "universal views" better than the oft-repeated use of the word "relativism."

However, the chief reason for Niebuhr's penchant for relativism is that he regards it as a direct consequence of radical monotheism and of the conversionist motif in Christian ethics. The faith of radical monotheism, he says, "makes relative all those values which polytheism makes absolute, and so puts an end to the strife of the gods." It is true that, as Niebuhr points out, faith in God does not relativize values in the way that self-love does. Since for monotheism "whatever is, is known to be good," this faith also upholds man's positive response to all being, so that "a new sacredness attaches to the relative goods."[55] Still, radical monotheism also subjects every value to radical scrutiny, making relative what polytheism absolutizes. Perhaps the best statement of the bearing of love for the one God upon relativism is to be found in the following paragraph in Niebuhr's essay on "The Center of Value":

. . . The value-theory of monotheistic theology is enabled to proceed to the construction of many relative value systems, each of them tentative, experimental, objective, as it considers the interaction of beings on beings, now from the point of view of man, now from the point of view of society, now from the point of view of life. But it is restrained from erecting any one of these into an absolute, or even from ordering it above the others, as when the human-centered value system is regarded as superior to a life-centered value system. A monotheistically centered value theory is not only compatible with such objective relativism in value analysis but requires it in view of its fundamental dogma that none is absolute save God and that the absolutizing of anything finite is ruinous to the finite itself.[56]

Now, we should not only note but proclaim the significant fact that Niebuhr says that all these "many relative value systems" are, among other things, "objective." Nevertheless, not all of what is said above follows necessarily from a serious effort to view morality in the light of God. To have "an absolute" in value-theory is not necessarily to substitute it idolatrously for *the* Absolute. And it is difficult to see why

---

[54] P. viii.

[55] "The Nature and Existence of God," *Motive,* IV (December, 1943), p. 46.

[56] *Op. cit.,* p. 174.

"ordering" one value system above another of necessity infringes the sovereignty of the one God, or why regarding one value as "superior" to another puts in question the "fundamental dogma that none is absolute save God." This may happen, but not inevitably. Monotheistic faith is incompatible only with idolatry, not with all ordering and rank among the (now subordinate) centers of value in various value-systems.

Consider the suggestion that a human-centered value-system may be regarded as superior to a life-centered value-system in theological ethics. Of course, if by "centered" is meant that we attribute the value of God to "man" or "life," this and every other idolatry monotheism purges away. But from this purging it by no means necessarily follows that all value-systems are absolutely leveled, or that the Christian living in the midst of these beings and values is reduced to viewing everything "now from the point of view of man, now from the point of view of society, now from the point of view of life" with considerable indifference to whether one of these relative centers may not be superior to another. It is true that in his total response to all the beings who are his companions in God, he will be sustained by a new sense of sacredness attaching to all relative goods. But neither does the limitation which monotheism places on all relative goods reduce the human-centered value-system, nor does the extension and intensification of the sense of the sacredness all beings have in God necessarily raise the life- or society-centered value-system, each to a qualitative parity with the other under God.

In his essay on "Value-Theory and Theology," Niebuhr found an ally in D. C. Macintosh in linking value with structure, being, or process, as against theories of abstract values or objective essences. The criticism of Macintosh's theology which Niebuhr succeeded in pressing home was his objection to making human values the starting point of the theological system or the antecedently-known criteria of the divine. Such procedure Niebuhr rightly rejected. But he did not seriously take issue with Macintosh's view that there is a certain "absoluteness of values relative to persons" or values "universally and permanently valid for persons."[57] This affirmation may still be true even when God is taken as the unconditioned starting point of a wholly disinterested theological science.

At the heart of Niebuhr's own theology, indeed, he acknowledges that a human-centered value-system may possibly be ordered in God's view above life- or society-centered systems. We stood once before at the heart of his theology when indicating how a redirecting influence and transforming power flows from man's responsible engagement with God as the center of value. This is only part of the meaning of God in

[57] *Op. cit.*, pp. 107-8.

human experience. Another, at least equally significant element consists in the "valuation" involved in what Niebuhr calls "deity-value" or deity-potency. "It is possible and necessary," he writes, "to interpret religion as an affair of *valuation* without assuming that such valuation must or can be made on the basis of a previous established standard of values."[58] It is not now a question of man's disinterested (but not uninterested) response to the Other whom he meets in the midst of being, but of this Other's action toward him through his sovereign call and divine judgment:

> The religious need is satisfied only in so far as man is able to recognize himself as valued by something beyond himself. That has the value of deity for man which values him. The valuation of which man becomes aware in religious experience is not first of all his evaluation of a being, but that being's evaluation of him. The latter evaluation does not need to be positive; on the contrary, in his experience of deity man frequently becomes aware of his disvalue, but he does not become aware of his unvalue.
> . . . The content of revelation is not the self-disclosure of an unknown being, but the unveiling of the value of a known being. What is revealed in revelation is not being as such, but rather its deity-value, not that it is, but that it "loves us," "judges us," that it makes life worth while.[59]

This same view of deity-value is restated in *The Meaning of Revelation*:

> Revelation means the moment in our history through which we know ourselves to be known from beginning to end, in which we are apprehended by the knower. . . . Revelation is the moment in which we find our judging selves to be judged not by ourselves or our neighbors but by one who knows the final secrets of the heart; revelation means the self-disclosure of the judge. Revelation means that we find ourselves to be valued rather than valuing and that all our values are transvaluated by the activity of a universal valuer. When a price is put upon our heads, which is not our price, when the unfairness of all the fair prices we have placed on things is shown up; when the great riches of God reduce our wealth to poverty, that is revelation. When we find out that we are no longer thinking of him, but that he first thought of us, that is revelation.[60]

Looking back upon the alternative idolatrous centers of relational value-theory it is possible now to say that what was sought in and through them all was not only value, or even some center in being in relation to which good-forness might be judged. What was sought was *reciprocal* being in relation to being. What was sought was being, power, purpose, judgment, deity-potency, and "deity-value" in the sense of an evaluation from beyond oneself (such as "the people" are endowed with

---

[58] *Ibid.*, p. 114.
[59] *Ibid.*, pp. 115, 116.
[60] *Op. cit.*, pp. 152-53.

capacity to make, when democracy is regarded as the source of ultimate judgment and redemption). What was sought was not only a center for our own relational value-judgments, but Being's relation to us in terms of which ultimate worthwhileness is given to us and purposed for us; not only a focus for our participation in being, but primarily the participation of Being in even our own existence.

In what Niebuhr calls "deity-value," value and being completely coalesce. In the need for God the question is not "whether a god exists, but rather what being or beings have the value of deity" and the potency of deity. ". . . It is a being which is sought, not value as such."[61] "We would not use the word God at all if all we meant were designated by the word good, but neither would we use it if we meant only power. To say that God and faith belong together is to maintain that no power could be apprehended as God save as its value were made manifest."[62] And elsewhere he writes that "Faith . . . always refers primarily to *character* and *power* rather than to existence. . . . Faith is an *active* thing, a committing of self to something, an anticipation. It is directed toward something that is also *active*, that has *power* or *is* power."[63] Thus, in the foregoing illustration, if "the people" has deity-*value* and deity-*potency* as in some forms of democratic faith, this refers both to the character *and* to the power of the people; "the people" is active, it has power or is power to give value and to sustain the meaning it gives to life.

Now, some sort of endorsement of the judgments of "a human-centered value-system" seems involved at the very core of what Niebuhr says about "value as valency" placed upon man from beyond himself by that being which has the valuation-potency of Deity. The infinite or sacred value of human selves cannot, it is true, provide the starting point of a system of theology, since "it cannot be true that the proposition about the infinite worth of persons is self-evident unless there be some infinite being to whom they are valuable." Nevertheless, Niebuhr writes, "*It is very true* that recognition of the infinite value of souls is a concomitant of revelation, but it could not be given were not something else given in that event—the infinite self for whom all souls are valuable."[64] Without claiming that in this perspective upon the universal *we* have completely vanquished the land where dwells the universal view of all things, is there not something *given* here which is entirely compatible with the view that the human-centered value-system is superior to the life-centered system even when human life has been displaced from *the* center? As a gift within man's God-relation-

[61] "Value-Theory and Theology," p. 114.
[62] *The Meaning of Revelation*, p. 188.
[63] "The Nature and Existence of God," p. 3 (italics mine).
[64] *The Meaning of Revelation*, p. 151 (italics mine).

ship, all idolatry is of course excluded—as well as any proposal to use the value of the self to establish the value of God, and any *self-interested* insistence on the value of one's own person as the elected center from which the rest of life may be exploited. But was Jesus any the less mindful of the sacredness of persons only in the eyes of God, or any the less regardful for the sacredness also bestowed on all their natural companions under God when he said of people in comparison to sparrows, "Are you not of much greater value than they?"

Finally, a careful inspection of Niebuhr's fundamentally conversionist outlook proves it to be harmonious with the objectivity of certain value-relationships and their possible ordering in some scale. It may be that in describing the transformation of man and his morals Niebuhr again "seizes both horns of every dilemma." His outlook, when properly grasped, however, may be interpreted more in the direction away from "Christ Transforming Relativism" toward "Christ Transforming Relationally Objective Norms." Perhaps this says more than he intends, and would alter the force of what he says at many points; but I would argue that it is quite in line with what he says in at least an equal number of other points. This is what he ought to say more definitely and clearly in all his writings.

"Transformation" does not mean the "republication" of the law of nature, and thus merely the provision of divine sanction for a moral law quite intact as it was already known to us. Nor does it mean *identification* with or mere *supplement* of such intact, untransformable moral principles. But neither does transformation mean *substitution*, the *replacement* of the moral law—whatever it is—by the demands existentially encountered in Christ. Morality (whatever its principles are found to be) should rather be subject to transformation in the light of these demands in Christ. If moral values are only relative, then the impact of Christocentric faith upon the moral life would mean "Christ transforming relativism." If, however, there are discoverable moral values and relationships, then this would mean "Christ transforming relationally objective norms." Nothing in the nature of radical monotheism or the conversionist-motif itself, but only a certain philosophical conception of human historical reason, seems to require that large concessions be made to relativism. What Niebuhr wrote concerning reason in general may also be said concerning man's capacity for moral judgments: "The pure reason does not need to be limited in order that room be made for faith, but [as one of the chief changes wrought by conversion] faith emancipates the pure reason from the necessity of defending and guarding the interests of selves, which are now found to be established and guarded, not by nature, but by the God of revelation whose garment nature is."[65] Man needs to be redeemed from sin and idolatry and all his values made responsive to God-in-Christ; he need not be delivered from his competence to make objective-enough value-judgments.

In *Christ and Culture*, Niebuhr again proclaims his "acceptance of the relativity not only of historical objects but, more, of the historical subject, the observer and interpreter." This is the lesson he learned (too well?) from Troeltsch, but Niebuhr distinguishes his own view from that of Troeltsch by reference to his effort "to understand this historical relativism in the light of theological and theo-centric relativism."[66] (This, it has been suggested above, were better called theological "relatedness," which is to go a long way toward the correction of relativism.) He speaks of "the reason which prevails in culture" and of "the understanding of right and wrong developed in the culture"[67] as one contender in the double-wrestle of Christian conscience with Christ and culture. Stated in this fashion, the ethics of natural or moral law seems to be a cultural work of man, indistinguishable from partial institutions like middle-class or workingmen's churches or like specific social policies once effective, such as the legislation of national prohibition. It cannot be too strongly emphasized that there would never have been any reason prevailing in culture if men of the past who placed a degree of confidence in reason had been persuaded theirs was only cultural or historical reason. Unless reason reaches beyond culture, culture prevails in reason and not reason in culture. Likewise, it cannot be too strongly emphasized that there would never have been any understanding of right and wrong developed in culture had men been of the opinion that all conceptions of right and wrong are moving and changing in time. Niebuhr defines culture as "the work of men's minds and hands"[68]; but men of the past who have championed right against wrong have ordinarily conceived their task as having in view what was most decidedly not the work of their own minds alone, and for all the flux of history they have believed it possible for two men to step twice in the same river.

Moreover, concerning the other contender in the wrestle of Christ with culture it is impossible to say anything "which is not also relative to the particular standpoint in church, history and culture of the one who undertakes to describe him." Thus, Christ also is subject to a religious and a historical relativism—so much so that the reader may occasionally wonder whether in the long run Christ transforms relativism or relativism transforms Christ.

[65] *Ibid.*, p. 175
[66] *Christ and Culture*, p. x.
[67] *Ibid.*, p. 11.
[68] *Ibid.*, p. 33.

With one horn of the dilemma firmly in his grasp Niebuhr then seizes the other; or to change the metaphor he gives back with one hand what he appears to have taken away with the other. Concerning views of right and wrong he says, as we have seen, that though each is a relative view, each may still be a view of the universal. Here reason breaks out from among the categories of historical reason and lays hold on the real. And concerning Christ he writes that "though every description is an interpretation, it can be an interpretation of the objective reality."[69] Here faith breaks through religious relativism and knows in whom it has believed. The Christ of Christianity is indeed one Lord seen from different perspectives, yet he is discernibly one. Humility before the one Lord requires us not to absolutize any one of five possible positions on the problem of the Christian's loyalty to the work of reason and culture. "Christ's answer to the problem of human culture is one thing," Niebuhr affirms at the outset, "Christian answers are another; yet his followers are assured that he uses their various works in accomplishing his own. . . . Christ as living Lord is answering the question in the totality of history and life in a fashion which transcends the wisdom of all his interpreters yet employs their partial insights and their necessary conflicts."[70]

To the end Niebuhr endeavors to stick by his resolution not to name *the* Christian answer: ". . . The giving of such an answer by any finite mind . . . would be an act of usurpation of the Lordship of Christ which at the same time would involve doing violence to the liberty of Christian men and to the unconcluded history of the church in culture. . . . We should need to assume, if we tried to give *the* Christian answer, that we are representatives of the head of the church, not members of its body . . ."[71] Yet Niebuhr necessarily has a *view of the universal* even when disclaiming the universal view, or when breaking the Christian answer into five different strategies in *Christ and Culture*. Just as of necessity Niebuhr must assert the more than historically relative truth of historical relativism itself, so he cannot avoid affirming that these five types *together* comprise the truth about Christian social ethics. In designating these five types and not five other or an indefinite number more types, he approximates, through the dialogue of these perspectives with one another concerning the meaning of Christ, the more Christian answer. He knows in whom Christians believe all the more from their historical discourse. Is this not better called a relational or perspectival objectivism than any sort of relativism? In appraising each position with fine sensitivity, Niebuhr plainly has in mind not just another relative perspective, but God-in-Christ beyond them all and discernible in part

[69] *Ibid.*, p. 14.
[70] *Ibid.*, p. 2.
[71] *Ibid.*, p. 232.

through them all. The way he is able to penetrate to the heart of each Christian perspective and comprehend them all together and evaluate them provides us with an example, not of the edification there is in the relativism believed to be required by radical monotheism, but an example of the illumination there is, *credo ut intelligam*, in knowing oneself as known by the Triune God.

The Trinity is not only the *arche* at work within Niebuhr's appraisals of all five types in their relatedness; it is also the *arche* at work in the transformation-motif itself. Therefore, it is not surprising to find evidence that Niebuhr's thought (despite his explicit disavowal) always tends toward conversionism as *the* most adequate Christian answer in the sense that it proves most responsive to the Triune God. The other Christian social outlooks which flank this one and help to sustain it seem discernibly less than responsive to all the meanings of this *arche*. They "belong" as possible types of Christian social witness which God-in-Christ also uses in working his will through the whole of the human story. Try as Niebuhr will, however, he cannot refrain from discriminating the flanks from the center of the line in recounting Christ's engagement with culture. In the light of this *arche*, the Triune God who is, Niebuhr cannot discover criticisms of the conversionist point of view as significant, theologically or culturally, as those he makes in the course of extremely sympathetic appraisals of other points of view.

Moreover, one cannot belong to all these positions, even though one may dimly see how they all belong. Though the fact is somewhat hidden from view in this volume by the inclusion of the fifth type along with the rest in the synoptic final chapter, which shows the author to be to a great extent a relativist, it is plain here and everywhere else in his writings that Niebuhr belongs to the type "Christ the Transformer of Culture." In articles and books conversionism has been his constant theme. Unavoidably he affirms this to be not only one view among many, but the view which most adequately expresses the meaning of God-in-Christ in relation to culture and morals and the community of mankind. Transformism gives us no instance of the edification to be found in religious relativism, but rather of the illumination, *credo ut intelligam*, which there is for moral reflection and the perpetual revolution that may be set going in the moral life from assuming (with firm conviction that herein faith has been grasped by the truth) such a perspective on the objective meaning of Christ for the whole of life.

The final issue is whether such an objective relatedness to the being of Christ, or such a view of his universal meaning, need deny the universal and permanent validity of certain ethical principles or hierarchy of values relative to the structure of man or to his mode of being in the world. Can there be no absolute or unchanging truths if man and his morals are subject to transformation in the light of the absoluteness of God-in-Christ?

To take a loaded illustration first: Surely, at all times and places and under whatever historical circumstances or conditions of personal relationships, rape is wrong, and the use of slaves as studs and the herding of women into barracks for the purpose of producing children by selected Nazi soldiers were horrible crimes. This can be said without that "vitiating abstractionism" which separates absolutes "from any being for whom they are valid." Men and women have the right to the free exercise of their sexual powers[72]—not that such freedom *ought to be* in the abstract in some world of essences, but that people ought to be free in this capacity. This we know, as Maritain might say, simply from reflecting upon the nature of man as man, no relative considerations of fact being taken into account. When legislatures determine the statutory "age of consent," and when juries and judges help to make law by their decisions of guilt or innocence before such statutes, of course they are in part exercising "cultural reason." The degree of responsible freedom and maturity assumed by (or too early forced upon) adolescent girls in our society today as compared to twenty-five or fifty years ago is a significant cultural change which should obviously be taken into account. This maturity means, in all probability, that eighteen is now too old for the age of consent in the state of California; and incidentally that the jury acted wisely and justly a few years ago in acquitting a celebrated movie actor of the charge of statutory rape, even though as the law now stands he may well have been technically guilty of the charge. But all this does not obviate the fact that a child still has a right to be treated as a child, and her "voluntary" consent at too early an age should still be regarded as forced upon her by the male. In seeking to determine some new age-figure or in tempering the application of old law, legislative or judicial reason simply asks, "When is a child still a child?" This may be partly a cultural question. However, the question would itself not be of importance to us were we incompetent to know something of the nature, meaning, and rights of human childhood and of mature human freedom in its sexual expression. The need for some new answer to the question posed by our contemporary cultural situation, or for answering it in particular cases that come before the courts, rests in part upon the moral certainty that a child has a right to be regarded as unfree and an adult person the right to be free in the exercise of sexual powers. (The foregoing does not raise the question of whether there are any norms for freedom in sexuality, such as monogamous marriage.)

Niebuhr himself gives a more significant illustration of an experienced

[72] Emil Brunner, *Justice and the Social Order* (New York: Harper & Brothers, 1945), pp. 60-61.

truth or value not independent of structure and process which neverthe-less seems to have permanent validity, and it is notable that he does so in immediate connection with submitting man's situation and values to radical transformation:

The Hellenic distinction between the temporal and the eternal was ac-cepted by the Christian movement, for it was evident that it corresponded to aspects of man's experience which the Hebrew scheme of two aeons left out of account. But the chief concern of Christian faith was to convert this Greek two-worldliness, so that the Greek might see through the revelation of God in Christ how personal were the other-worldly objects of the soul's contemplation, the form of the Good and the *logos*, and how graciously creative and redemptive they were.[73]

Here, simply by reflecting upon man as man in his being in the world, Niebuhr arrives at strikingly Augustinian conclusions which entail in part at least a "scale of being" and of value. "The temporal goods which satisfy a temporal being do not satisfy man or correspond to his nature," he writes. "That earth is not enough for him, his adventures, his crimes and glories on earth demonstrate. That an exclusively secular environ-ment does not correspond to his nature is indicated not only by the presence in him of personal freedom and conscience but by his hunger which earth cannot satisfy with all its goods."[74] In short, St. Augustine first and then Niebuhr himself are accepting the permanent validity and superiority of elements in the Greek approach to and interpretation of human experience, in contrast to one-dimensional world views; yet both writers see, through the revelation of God in Christ, how personal are the other-worldly objects of the soul's contemplation, the form of the good and the *logos*, and how graciously creative and redemptive is the eternal. Kierkegaard provides another great instance of the acceptance of the juncture of the eternal and the temporal in the structure of human nature (most vividly portrayed in *Purity of Heart*[75] and when-ever he considers "the lilies and the birds"), and yet at the same time the transformation of this understanding by the gospel in his *Christian Discourses*,[76] "The Anxieties of the Heathen," and "Joyful Notes in the Strife of Suffering," and in "The Lilies of the Field and the Birds of the Air: Three Godly Discourses."

The trouble with Greek-minded speculative philosophy and with the theory of natural law in ethics is not that truth has been discerned by them but that it is claimed they are autonomous, and are apt to be left so in "identification," "dualism," or "hierarchical synthesis" when

[73] "Toward a New Other-Worldliness, *Theology Today*, I, No. 1 (April, 1944), p. 79.
[74] *Ibid.*, p. 84.
[75] New York: Harper & Brothers, 1938.
[76] London: Oxford University Press, 1940.

brought under the aegis of Christ. Brunner's error is not that he speaks of "orders of creation" but that in *The Divine Imperative*[77] these orders were conceived of *primarily* as orders of "creation" and of "sin" refracting love, without being set in motion and commotion by the primacy of redemption. One cannot object to Brunner's reliance on man's sense of justice in *Justice and the Social Order*,[78] but only to the fact that he keeps the realm of justice unaltered and unalterably apart from the (consequently purely personal) dimension of love and grace. This same "dualism"—of Christ and Culture or Christ and Reason in Paradox—is repeated in the ethical sections of Brunner's *The Christian Doctrine of Creation and Redemption*.[79] The primacy of redemption in converting, transforming, invigorating, and redirecting natural reason would not deliver us from accepting the substantial validity of Brunner's tabulation of basic human rights[80]; but would ensure instead that the stress would fall no longer on *minimum* rights, but on maximizing the conditions for fullest human fulfillment on the part of all for whom Christ died. This would be to see how personal, how graciously creative and redemptive are those forms and principles we contemplate when considering only "nature and nature's God." Niebuhr's lectures on ethics, in which the Christian life is viewed as simultaneously responding to "creation," "judgment" or "governance," and "redemption," have always suggested to his students the indivisibility of these approaches, since God is he with whom we are always already engaged, and he is all these eventful acts toward us, wherever we are culturally and historically in our being in the world. In this there is promise of a dynamic ethics of redemption which does not simply build upon yet does not jettison the ethics of creation.[81a]

The relationship of Christianity and democracy provides another example of the Truth transforming truth. Without identifying Christ with liberal democracy, it may be affirmed that the growth of democracy in England in the seventeenth century was due in part to the "Christ transforming culture" motif in Puritan Protestantism. But were there not at work also principles concerning the good for man in society which have more than relative historical importance and which belong always to the good for man, even though, when account is taken of relative cultural factors, it may not be wise to attempt to realize them everywhere now? Certainly there were in the seventeenth century people who joined in transforming political life in the direction of democratic

---

[77] London: The Lutterworth Press, 1937, and Philadelphia: The Westminster Press.
[78] New York: Harper & Brothers, 1945.
[79] *Dogmatics* (Philadelphia: The Westminster Press, 1952), vol. II.
[80] *Justice and the Social Order*, chap. 9.
[81a] For illustration, see ch. VII below by Waldo Beach.

"covenant community," yet who were secular-minded enough to conclude that in the congregation, as well as elsewhere, "the odd man is the Holy Spirit." If there be any warrant for democracy on general principle, then the present dynamic relation of Christ to the ideal of liberal democracy is that of "Christ transforming relationally objective norms," although his relation to actual democratic cultures includes with this also a large measure of "Christ transforming the relativism" of many a historical peculiarity or variant moving and changing in time.

It is easy to see, and one should be wholly sympathetic with, the reasons why Niebuhr tends to think that both radical monotheism and an unrestricted conversionism make all other things relative. The transformation-motif so easily loses its dynamic and changes into one of the other types of Christian social outlook which defend some cultural achievement or some rational principle intact as it is. The criticism Niebuhr directs against certain of the other types might well apply to the interpretation of conversionism and moral law suggested here. Efforts to erect a hierarchical synthesis of Christ and culture or of Christ and the rational moral law into one system, he writes, tend "perhaps inevitably, to the absolutizing of what is relative, the reduction of the infinite to a finite form, and the materialization of the dynamic." In particular, the synthesist almost invariably formulates the moral law "in language and concepts of a reason that is always culturally conditioned," and indeed "no synthesist answer so far given in Christian history has avoided the equation of a cultural view of God's law in creation with that law itself."[81] Once having synthesized Christ with something evanescent, soon such a Christian "will be required to turn to the defense of that temporal foundation for the sake of the superstructure it carries when changes in culture threaten it."[82] Thus, a Christian, who began with a clear distinction between culture and Christ while loyal to both, soon becomes a "culture Christian."

The peril of transforming Christ into a cockpit from which to defend a culture that is withering away cannot, of course, be exaggerated. When the synthesist recognizes this danger "he is on the way to accepting another than the synthetic answer; he is saying then in effect that all culture is subject to continuous and infinite conversion." Yet Niebuhr errs slightly when he goes on to say that the conversionist, or the converted synthesist, will necessarily acknowledge in effect "that his own formulation of the elements of the synthesis, like its social achievement in the structure of church and society, is only provisional and uncertain."[83] Provisionally formulated, one might retort, but there is truth in the formula. Must *everything*, including reason's grasp of human

[81] *Christ and Culture*, p. 145.
[82] *Ibid.*, p. 146.
[83] Cf. *ibid.*, p. 102.

being, structure, and value, be "only provisional and uncertain" in order for conversion to be "continuous and infinite?" Must "Christ transforming relationally objective norms" be programmatically ruled out in order to preserve a fully dynamic conversionism and to avoid man's self-defensive holding on to some rigid cultural form? Niebuhr's own profound insight into man's self-defensiveness leads him to see that there is no help toward curing self-interestedness to be gained from limiting reason. This insight has only to be applied here for it to be sun-clear that men may quite as easily identify or synthesize Christ with such national legislation as prohibition or with the maintenance of early American social organization[84] (which no serious thinker would regard as directly grounded in the fundamental law) as for them to identify him for defensive purposes with any of the first principles of moral reasoning (if such there be).

Cultural or historical relativisms give no real assistance toward the avoidance of rigidities which might impede dynamic, continuous, and indefinite conversion of the moral life. The categories of historical reason are not less effective means for the self-defense of faithless men than are the truths or values in being which they may apprehend in their views of the universal. To see this clearly, let us suppose the case of a Christian ethicist who under the impact of a radically monotheistic faith and the regenerative Lordship of Christ allows his whole being to be transformed by the thought that God-in-Christ makes all else relative and nevertheless renews all. Imagine him a deep student of Dilthey and Troeltsch and the "sociology of knowledge." Will he not soon begin to find in these views support for the dynamic conversionist meaning he finds in Christ? From being intrinsically a conversionist he then soon becomes a synthesist, even though Christ be now synthesized with historical and other forms of relativism. These philosophies—for such they are, on all fours with every other philosophy with which Christian faith has ever been joined—seem to him quite plausibly to contain truth which it will be helpful for men to accept, or at least a point of view for them to adopt toward truth, before or while going on to the supervening perfections given in what happens to them, to their self-understanding and their understanding of the world in the light of Jesus Christ. Subtly there already has taken place here a confusion or even an "identification" between the subordination of the human heart and life to Christ and the subordination of the mind to this way of thinking (which, only by an illusion, seems to make the former easier). Then suppose that out of the depths there begins to take place a profound historical and cultural change. A Troeltsch, deeply troubled by certain tendencies in the German historical view of law, delivers in 1922 his address on "The

---

[84] *Loc. cit.*

Ideas of Natural Law and Humanity in World Politics."[85] And everywhere men are questing for certainties and remembering the asserted universal principles of their ancient ethical and political heritage. What happens to our Christian relativist? Why, having once synthesized Christ with something evanescent (historical relativism), soon such a Christian "will be required to turn to the defense of that temporal foundation for the sake of the superstructure it carries when changes in culture threaten it."[86] In this respect he becomes a "culture Christian." This is sufficient to show that, for preserving the dynamics of an ethics of redemption, there is no help from particular philosophies; and that no philosophical or ethical outlook can be programmatically excluded by a theology of conversion.

The theological presuppositions of the conversionist-motif are in line with the suggestion that this point of view may be held without prejudice against the possible objectivity of norms. By virtue of the conversionist's positive view of creation "he finds room for affirmative and ordered response on the part of created man to the creative, ordering work of God."[87] It is therefore not impossible that the knowledge of certain universally valid principles or hierarchy of being and value may be a part of man's "ordered response" to the ordering work of God. The conversionist puts special stress on the Incarnation of the Word who has entered into "a human culture that has never been without his ordering action."[88] It is therefore not impossible that in Christ the Redeemer of culture "the true light that enlightens every man was coming into the world" (John 1:9 RSV) for the conversion and redirection of the light already among men and in culture. While the conversionist asserts with the dualist a doctrine of the radical fall of man, he knows that "culture is all corrupted order" rather than ordered corruption: "The problem of culture is therefore the problem of its conversion, not of its *replacement* by a new creation."[89] In all these ways it should be clear that Niebuhr's fondness for relativism is not a necessary part of his theology of conversion, but rather a consequence of the influence of Troeltsch and others upon him and an aspect of his philosophical point of view, which itself, this chapter has suggested, needs to be interpreted —*perhaps* in part corrected—in the direction of relational objectivism.

St. Augustine was certainly a dynamic and thoroughgoing conversionist who—on Niebuhr's own accounting—did not believe that this position entailed relativism.

[85] Appendix I in Otto Gierke's *Natural Law and the Theory of Society 1500-1800* (trans. by Earnest Barker; Cambridge University Press, 1934), vol. I, pp. 201 ff.
[86] Cf. *Christ and Culture*, p. 145.
[87] *Ibid.*, p. 192.
[88] *Ibid.*, p. 193.
[89] *Ibid.*, p. 194 (italics mine).

[Augustine] the Neo-Platonist not only adds to his wisdom about spiritual reality the knowledge of the incarnation which no philosopher had taught him, but *this wisdom is humanized, given new depth and direction, made productive of new insights,* by the realization that the Word has become flesh and has borne the sins of the spirit. The Ciceronian moralist does not add to the classical virtues the new virtues of the gospel, nor substitute new law for natural and Roman legislation, but *transvalues and redirects in consequence of the experience of grace* the morality in which he had been trained and which he taught.[90]

In brief, "Christ is the transformer of culture for Augustine in the sense that he redirects, reinvigorates, and regenerates"[91] the whole life of man, including the life of moral reason and of the spirit, which is fundamentally good but misdirected. This approach enabled St. Augustine and the early medieval period—as two leading modern historians agree —"to overcome the radical deficiencies of the classical approach to experience" and "to heal the wounds inflicted by man on himself in classical times and, by transcending while still doing justice to the elements of truth contained in philosophic paganism, to revive and give direction to the expiring spiritual ideals of classical antiquity."[92] Christians of the present day need to take this same way of looking upon the best products of the human spirit in our own time, if there is any hope— not necessarily the hope, as Christians of the identifying and synthesist types desire, of averting the demise of Western democratic life any more than the transforming power of Augustinian Christianity saved Roman civilization—but if there is any hope of overcoming the deficiencies and wounds of the contemporary world and beyond probable tragedy reviving and giving redirection to the expiring spiritual ideals of modern democratic society.

[90] *Ibid.,* pp. 208-9 (italics mine).
[91] *Ibid.,* p. 209.
[92] Charles N. Cochrane: *Christianity and Classical Culture* (Oxford: Clarendon Press, 1940), p. 360. Cf. Herbert Butterfield: *Christianity in European History* (New York: The Macmillan Company, 1953), pp. 13-14.

6.

VALUE AND VALUATION

GEORGE SCHRADER

ONE of the characteristics which distinguishes the thought of H. Richard Niebuhr is the way in which he combines rigorous philosophical analysis with penetrating theological insight. He has a keen appreciation both of the philosophical implications of theology and of the theological implications of philosophy. Thus, his writings are as interesting and suggestive to the philosopher as to the theologian. Taking his stand within a tradition which is not noted for its philosophical interest or sophistication, Niebuhr looks on both sides of the fence and finds much that is significant in both directions. Although his ultimate commitment is to theology, he has a thorough grounding in the philosophical tradition and appropriates the insights and methods of the philosophers for his own inquiry. He has never looked with favor upon the attempt within liberal theology to effect a fusion of philosophy and theology; yet, he does not turn his back upon philosophy nor subscribe to the radical separation between faith and reason promulgated by Barth. The tension between reason and faith, philosophy and theology, was never more productive than in Niebuhr's thought.

For the most part Niebuhr does not choose to separate the two moments in his own thought. No one of his writings is without its philosophical overtones, even where the theme and method of treatment is most explicitly theological. The converse is no less true of his more explicitly philosophical writings, as for example in his exposition of the relational theory of value.[1] But in spite of his theological bent, Niebuhr commits himself to a philosophical theory of value and elects to argue it on philosophical terms. This essay, "The Center of Value," cannot be

[1] "The Center of Value" in *Moral Principles for Action* (ed. by Ruth Nanda Anshen); New York: Harper & Brothers, 1952.

173

fully appreciated, perhaps, apart from an understanding of his theological convictions. Yet, it is offered as a philosophical theory and must be judged accordingly. Niebuhr believes that other grounds may be offered for accepting such a theory, since he is convinced that of the various philosophical theories available it best accords with the fundamental tenets of Christian theology. Hence, a philosophical appraisal of the relational theory of value will not suffice to pronounce final judgment upon it, for this would be to accord to philosophical reason absolute and unconditioned authority—a concession which Niebuhr would not be inclined to make. But granted the larger context within which value-theory must be considered, Niebuhr's exposition of the relational theory constitutes an important contribution to the philosophical exploration of the problem of values and warrants a careful appraisal on philosophical grounds. I propose in the present chapter to undertake just such an appraisal.

1. THE RELATIONAL DEFINITION OF VALUE

One of the most heated controversies in recent philosophical discussion about value has centered on the question: Is goodness capable of being analyzed or defined? G. E. Moore, who regarded his *Principia Ethica* as comparable in its significance for ethics to the significance of Kant's *Prolegomena* for metaphysics, undertook to demonstrate that good is an unanalyzable quality. Although Moore's thesis that "good" cannot be defined in terms of other qualities or properties is sound, he errs, I think, in regarding "good" as a simple quality comparable to "yellow," "sweet," etc. "Yellow" is itself not so *simple* as Moore suggests, but even so it must be distinguished sharply from "good." The former is a concept, the latter a category. "Good" is ultimately indefinable not because it is *simple* but because it is a *categorical* principle governing a wide range of concepts. In putting "good" on the same level with such qualities as "yellow," Moore obliterates the important and necessary distinction between concept and category.[2]

All previous moralists had erred, so Moore believed, in thinking that "good" could be analyzed or defined. They had invariably confused goodness itself with some particular good and in analyzing the latter thought themselves to have analyzed goodness. Moore's thesis understandably provoked a great deal of discussion, for if his conclusion were true, much of the previous inquiry into the nature of goodness had been misguided and in vain. Not a few philosophers became persuaded of the truth of Moore's thesis and accepted the divorce between metaphysics and ethics which it implied. Some of those who accepted the thesis offered a different account of it than that furnished by Moore, namely, the emotive theory of value.

[2] Cf. *Principia Ethica*, pp. 9, 14 ff.

The movement from Moore's position to the emotive theory was natural and, perhaps, inevitable. But it was also somewhat paradoxical. For on Moore's view value is totally unrelated to anything actual or empirical, while on the emotive theory value is interpreted relationally. In the perspective from which one can now view this issue, the whole controversy appears somewhat foolish. Moore raised a number of significant questions about the nature and meaning of value and pointed out some genuine confusions in traditional value-theory. But it should not have been an innovation to suggest that "good" is ultimately unanalyzable and indefinable. If "good" is a category, as a great many of the previous moralists from Plato on had evidently believed, then it *cannot be defined precisely for the reason that it is a category.* Earlier philosophers did not always distinguish carefully enough between those objects or experiences of which goodness could be predicated and the predicate itself, but this does not mean that the distinction was not implicit in their thinking. If goodness is a category in the sense in which both Aristotle and Kant conceived of categories, then it is a necessary concept for the interpretation of human experience. We may be able to state in tentative fashion the conditions under which the category is to be applied, but this does not imply that we can define it or that we should be embarrassed by our failure to do so. In calling attention to the uniqueness of good as a predicate Moore does not demonstrate that it is an unanalyzable quality but only that it is a category. And this is surely no revolutionary proposal in the history of Western thought.

I have referred to the controversy over the definability of "good" because this is a question that must be raised with respect to Niebuhr's value-theory. Does he, we must inquire, propose to *define* value in terms of the relation of being to being? Or does he mean simply to state the conditions under which value occurs? If he intends to define value in terms of relations, this would imply that goodness or value is nothing unique and, hence, his theory would fall under Moore's ban. Although Niebuhr does not consider the question as to the definability of value, it seems evident to me that he does not attempt to *define* value in terms of relations. Appealing to his intentions may be precarious, for they can only be inferred from what is explicitly asserted. Hence, it may be advisable to make the more limited claim, namely, that he does not in fact define value in terms of relations. This saves him, I believe, from serious difficulties which would have been involved in the denial that value is a category. It is not the *meaning* of value with which Niebuhr is chiefly concerned, but the *ground* of value, the *conditions* under which it occurs and the justification for employing it as a predicate of any specific situation or experience.

In stating what he takes to be the fundamental tenet of relational value-theory, Niebuhr remarks: "Its fundamental observation is this:

that value is present wherever one existent being with capacities and potentialities confronts another existence that limits or completes or complements it."[3] This statement might well have contained a modifying phrase to indicate that value is present *only* under these conditions. His theory is as significant for what it denies as for what it affirms. Niebuhr does not claim that this is a definition of value or an analysis of the "meaning" of value. He contents himself with the far less ambitious assertion that these are the conditions under which value *appears*. To know this of value is to know something of the meaning of value and, hence, to have offered a partial analysis of it. Anything we say about the conditions under which value may or may not appear will reveal something of the meaning of the category. Such analysis is, in fact, the only avenue open to us in clarifying the meaning of categories. But this fact does not imply that value has been defined in the sense that the *definiens* could be substituted for the *definiendum*. Value, Niebuhr states, cannot be reduced to relations any more than it can be reduced to existent beings. "Value is not a relation but arises in the relations of being to being."[4] Value appears only because one being exists for another being or for itself. But being-for is not identical with being-good-for, and to state that value appears only where there is being-for is not to say that this is *the* meaning of value. The schematism of a category, to put it in Kant's terms, is actually a part of the meaning of a term. But the meaning of a concept or category always transcends its schema. Thus, we need not insist that Niebuhr contributes nothing to the analysis of the meaning of value predicates, though he does not offer an exhaustive definition of "good" or "evil."

So far as I know, Niebuhr never states that value is a category and, hence, never finds it necessary to consider the epistemological issues involved in the interpretation of categories. In suggesting above that value is actually regarded as a category by Niebuhr, I am in fact interpreting his analysis of the concept in the light of the context within which it is employed. Niebuhr has always been very much influenced by Kant. His early study of Troeltsch involved the consideration of the applicability of the general Kantian orientation and method to religious phenomena. Although Niebuhr by no means confines his interest to Kant, his thought bears the unmistakable imprint of the transcendental philosophy. This is especially true, I think, with respect to epistemology. Niebuhr's "objective relativism" goes beyond Kant and is more neo-Kantian than Kantian. But the fundamental commitment is to the Kantian rather than to the classical interpretation of knowledge. If this is the case, then it would be reasonable to expect Niebuhr to interpret value as a category and, further, to insist that value has no meaning

[3] "The Center of Value," p. 165.
[4] *Ibid*, p. 169.

apart from the situations to which it might be applied. Kant had said precisely the same thing about causality and the other categories, insisting that apart from experience they have no meaning or significance.

Niebuhr is, however, somewhat more realistic than Kant in stressing the objectivity of the value-situation. But we must remember that Niebuhr is writing about value from the perspective of the moral and the religious consciousness—what Kant would term the sphere of practical reason. In this context Kant himself was far more realistic than in dealing with causality and the realm of objective scientific cognition. When Kant discussed the moral subject, his freedom and responsibility, he was realistic and metaphysical. But he insisted upon the *practical* nature of reason engaged in this inquiry; he insisted upon the involvement of man as active moral subject. In Niebuhr's discussion of value more than anywhere else in his writings I seem to find traces of a realism and even a naturalism which seek to cast off the Kantian strictures. Thus, his analysis of value reflects the impact of Aristotle and Dewey as well as of Kant. Yet, in the final analysis it is Kant to whom he returns for support in insisting upon the relativity of value. If Niebuhr had been willing to renounce the Kantian standpoint completely and adopt the perspective of classical naturalism, he would have been unable to insist upon the ultimate relativity of value. It is this latter point which differentiates Niebuhr's theory radically from the naturalistic tradition and manifests his continuing indebtedness to Kant. But Niebuhr's theory is complex and subtle, and we must avoid any premature judgments as to its basic presuppositions.

It seems to me that Niebuhr's treatment of value results in employing it as a category for at least two reasons: (1) his repudiation of all views which regard value as an independently subsisting quality or property and (2) his insistence that value has meaning only with respect to beings and the relations between them. A further reason might be his stress upon value as a factor which is ingredient in the interpretation of experience from a particular situation or perspective. If value is a category and, further, if it has meaning only in relation to those situations of which it might be predicated—or rather where it is a necessary constitutive principle in the structuring of such situations—then it cannot be regarded as subsisting in some sort of transcendent and autonomous realm. Niebuhr wants to say that value is relevant not only to human existence but also to the life of animals and nature in general. But he cannot and does not deny that all valuation depends upon the interpretation of experience from the perspective of a valuing and, also, evaluated subject.

Niebuhr transcends the Kantian analysis of categories by taking into account the natural, cultural, and historical conditions involved in value-judgments. But even more important is his claim that human judgment, of whatever sort, is radically transcended in relation to the divine judgment. This raises an exceedingly interesting point, namely, how Niebuhr can actually account for the possibility of value and value-judgment from the perspective of both the human and the divine. He holds that in the encounter with God all human valuations are transformed, which adds still another dimension to value-relativity. But value remains a category for Niebuhr, I believe, even when the divine judgment is taken into account. For in all considerations of value, even from what is believed to be the perspective of God, human judgment and human categories enter into the picture. Revelation does not provide an escape from this situation. Man must still determine "the meaning of revelation" and is responsible for this interpretation. Here one encounters the limit of human judgment, a boundary which is never crossed nor obliterated.[5] Were Niebuhr not to acknowledge the inevitable fact of human judgment and the necessary horizon beyond which it cannot reach, he would be able to find no place for revelation, and his value-theory would become a surrogate for theology.

The upshot of this preliminary exploration of Niebuhr's exposition is that, although he does not discuss value in these terms, he actually considers it to be a category which has no meaning apart from the evaluative subject and the situation within which he judges. The category is relative not only to the situation, as Niebuhr makes unmistakably clear, but also to the subject—a point which is somewhat less explicit.[6] Value is not a property or quality which is predicated of a relational situation, but the actual structure of the situation which has been informed by the valuing of the subject. In other words, neither values nor valuing is detached, impersonal, disinterested. Value is a characteristic of the relations obtaining between existent beings, but ingredient in such relations is the valuing of the beings involved. Hence, there are "multiple centers of value" as well as multiple perspectives of valuing. Niebuhr is not attempting to define value as a category but to make explicit the meaning of value for human experience. He focuses more upon the value-situation than upon the evaluative process, but his objective relativism depends upon the consideration of both factors.

2. THE GROUND OF VALUE

There are values, Niebuhr maintains, only because there are beings and relations between beings. He does not hold that value depends exclusively upon the relation between two or more beings, for a being may be self-related. On his view a being may have value for itself or for another being. But no being has value simply in itself. Thus, Niebuhr

---

[5] Cf. "Value-Theory and Theology" in *The Nature of Religious Experience* (symposium in honor of D. C. Macintosh), New York: (Harper & Brothers), pp. 108 ff.
[6] *Ibid.*, p. 106.

denies flatly any theory which holds that life, personality, or any other phenomenon is a value in and of itself. This would be to regard value as some sort of transcendent quality or property by virtue of possessing which beings have worth. In rejecting this view of value Niebuhr seems to have two considerations in mind, one philosophical and the other theological. On philosophical grounds he is convinced that to regard value in this light is to subscribe to some sort of intuitionism and to relinquish any possibilities of providing a warrant for value-claims. On theological grounds he recognizes that such a view may result in a value-polytheism with a multiplicity of absolute centers of value. If values are dependent for their occurrence upon relations, one can avoid saying that any finite being has value in and of itself, and can also avoid any appeal to value-intuition. In taking this position Niebuhr joins forces with a considerable number of philosophers from Aristotle to Dewey and, at the same time, preserves the distinction so important to Christian theology between values and the ultimate source of all value. We must, I think, examine Niebuhr's value-theory with great care to see whether or not he can both avoid the acknowledgment of unique value predicates and maintain the relativity of all values.

So far as individual existents are concerned, Niebuhr grounds value in the relation between existence and essence. Beings are not yet what they ought to be—in that they have not yet achieved their internal possibilities. ". . . the state of realization, the essence which the being tends to realize in its existence, is its good."[7] Here Niebuhr appears to adopt a position very close to that of Aristotle, a fairly explicit theory of self-realization. An individual being has his good within himself in that he has possibilities which have not been realized. They are good-for him in that he needs and requires them for the fulfillment of his own being. They "ought to be realized," Niebuhr states, in that they signify a lack, a privation. The value appears to have its ground in the positive character of potentialities but, at the same time, to be grounded in a deficiency. Health, knowledge, physical and psychical maturity are good-for an individual because they constitute the realization of his potentialities.

In spite of his taking up a position apparently similar to that of Aristotle, Niebuhr departs from Aristotle on two important points. In the first place, he refuses to ground value in essences. In spite of Aristotle's own emphasis upon the intimate relation between actuality and potentiality and the grounding of actuality in the latter, he assigns to actuality or essence a preferential status which is refused by Niebuhr. There can be a good for the individual as such only because of potentiality which may be actualized. On this point both Aristotle and Niebuhr agree. But Niebuhr insists with greater force than Aristotle upon

[7] "The Center of Value," p. 166.

the importance of the relational situation for the goodness of essence. Aristotle implies that rationality, though an essence which may be achieved by man, is a good for him which may be realized and by virtue of which he becomes good. He emphasizes the relation obtaining between essence and actuality more than Plato is usually thought to have done but, like Plato, attaches a unique value-significance to the form or essence as such. This Niebuhr denies, for he takes potentiality and existence with far greater seriousness than had either Plato or Aristotle. In rejecting the essentialism of Aristotle, Niebuhr sides with the modern philosophers of process, such as Bergson and Dewey, and expresses the reverence for being which is characteristic of the Hebraic-Christian tradition. One recalls, in reading Niebuhr, Augustine's insistence that it is being itself which is good, not because of any form or attribute which it possesses or may come to possess, but because it is being. The ultimate source of this reverence for being is found in the doctrine of creation, in terms of which the finite universe is regarded as good simply because it is the handiwork of God. It is understandable that Niebuhr should find it necessary to make this correction of Aristotle in spite of his obvious affinity for certain features of Aristotle's thought.

It is beyond the province of this study to consider Niebuhr's subtle and intricate analysis of the self—though it is highly relevant for a complete examination of his value-theory.[8] We must content ourselves with the exploration of the more general principles which underlie his theory of existence. Within the specifically moral context Niebuhr takes account of man's self-alienation as well as his alienation from God and his neighbor. (The term "alienation" is my own term rather than Niebuhr's. Although the concept of alienation is implicit in Niebuhr's analysis of sin, I am considerably extending the metaphysical reference of the term.) Guilt and sin are rooted in this alienation and the assertion of will from which it stems. Niebuhr does not, so far as I know, extend the category of alienation to the general field of value, though he might well have done so. Good is possible for the individual, as we have seen, only because he has not yet realized his possibilities. The possibility which as essence has not been realized is good only in relation to the being which aspires toward it. But, we must inquire, what precisely is the nature of this relation which alone makes goodness possible? Quite evidently it is a situation in which a being is self-alienated, extended beyond itself, so that its essence is not identical with its existence. It has its good beyond it, but not in the sense of having some foreign property beyond it to which it may aspire—but rather as having its own being beyond it as future possibility. In having potentiality at all—and presumably all finite beings exhibit this characteristic—it does

[8] Cf. "The Ego-Alter Dialect and Conscience," *Journal of Philosophy* XLII, no. 13 (June 21, 1945).

not exist *simply*, but is distended and self-transcended. *Its goodness is its own being*, which it does *not* possess in actuality. It seeks to complete itself, to overcome the self-alienation, and thus, to realize the good for it. If this interpretation is correct, Niebuhr can consistently refuse to assign value to essence alone. By interpreting essence as an integral aspect of the being in question, he can regard the good of the self-related being as having its ground solely in the self-alienated character of that being.

In offering this interpretation of Niebuhr's view I am admittedly going beyond Niebuhr's own explicit theory. But if value is present only in a relational situation and if it springs from such a relation as that of potentiality and actuality, it seems to me that no other interpretation is available. On any other analysis of the value-character of essence Niebuhr would be forced to grant unique status to value. On the alternative I am suggesting it would be open to Niebuhr to claim that being alone is good and that the goodness of essential possibility is a special case of the goodness of being as such.

But this argument immediately poses a difficulty because it seems to result in the affirmation of the very thesis which Niebuhr intended to repudiate through his relational theory, namely, the attribution of value to being as such. To this I can only reply that Niebuhr may not be able to defend his relational theory without accepting this thesis. Moreover, the attribution of goodness to being as such does not involve the acceptance of any of the doctrines which Niebuhr seeks to avoid. Neither Plato nor Aristotle adopted any such view of being. Hegel embraced this view, as did a number of subsequent romanticist philosophers. One finds a reverence for being in Bergson and, to a lesser degree, in Dewey. But this affirmation of the primordial goodness of being is itself a reflection of the Hebraic-Christian insistence upon the goodness of the created world. Niebuhr finds much that is congenial in both Bergson and Dewey because of their stress on the ultimate fusion of being and goodness. He finds something of the same reverence in Royce but never, so far as I know, in Hegel—who is actually responsible to a large degree for the modern stress on the ultimate unity of being and value.

The place where Niebuhr must take issue with the romantics, idealists, and contemporary naturalists is where they deny the distinction between the created world and the creator, putting all being on the same level. Niebuhr actually refuses to attribute value priority to any finite being in relation to other finite beings. In acknowledging a radical ontological and valuational difference between God and all finite existence, he refuses to include the being of God within any all-inclusive monistic ordering of reality. A relational theory of value, such as that of Hegel or Dewey, which does not recognize the transcendence of

God, results in a value-monism. It is an important question whether Niebuhr's relational theory of value in itself provides a sufficient safeguard against such a monistic theory. It is not his *relational theory* as such which provides this safeguard, but rather Niebuhr's specific interpretation and application of the theory. It is the uniqueness of the special relation involved in man's encounter with God which makes it impossible to treat all values and all relations as fundamentally alike. The being of God and the value of God require special treatment, not because they necessarily involve an exception to his general theory, but, rather, because of the special character of the relation of God to man and to the natural world.

Thus far we have considered the *good-forness* of the essence but not the *ought-to-beness* intrinsic to the relational situation. In using the term "ought" Niebuhr clearly suggests that it is desirable that potentiality should be realized. "Beings are not yet what they ought to be— in that they have not yet achieved their internal possibilities."[9] But if the process of actualization does not have value solely because of the good which is realized—a view which Niebuhr denies—from whence does it derive its "oughtness"? It would appear that Niebuhr regards the process of actualization to be good in itself. But this again does not require any modification of what I take to be his general theory. If being is process, then the goodness of the specific process of actualizing possibilities would share in the common goodness of being in general. This is the position taken by a number of the "process philosophers" who regard becoming as good in itself. It is a view which is fully compatible with the biblical stress on the fundamental goodness of creation. It simply involves analyzing the being of the created world in process terms. We have, I think, actually come upon more than one connotation of the concept "good" as Niebuhr applies it to the situation of a self-related being. It refers to (1) the ideal possibilities, the good-forness of a being in relation to itself, and to (2) the process of actualization which ought to occur. It seems to me that these two meanings together imply still a third meaning, (3) the goodness of the existence which is related to itself through the essence.

Now, existence, essence, and the process of realizing essence are all constitutive moments of any dynamic being. In calling attention to self-relatedness Niebuhr delineates the relatedness of being to itself within the life of the individual existent. The goodness of the essence or possibility is the goodness of being viewed futuristically, and the goodness of existence as potentiality is the goodness of being viewed presently; the goodness of the process of actualizing possibility is the goodness of being as stretched between present and future. The being of the individual includes all three moments, existence in the past, present, and

[9] "The Center of Value," p. 166. Cf. "Value-Theory and Theology," p. 106.

the future. Niebuhr grounds the goodness of the individual in this self-relatedness, denying that the individual has value in himself as a being. But unless being itself is regarded as good, I do not see how either the good-forness of the essence or the goodness of the process of actualization can be accounted for. It seems to me that Niebuhr is ultimately driven to ground the goodness of essence and process in the goodness of existence, and the goodness of all three moments in the goodness of the being itself.

What I mean to suggest is that a being cannot be good for itself or in relation to itself unless its own being is fundamentally good. If it is good *to be*, and if whatever *is* is insofar good, then it is possible to develop a theory which will enable us to explicate the relational meaning of good-forness. It will be good for a being to realize its own potentialities, because in the process of actualization it achieves a fuller development and expression of its own being. Evil would, by the same token, be the negation of being as manifest in the failure to realize potentialities. The relational meaning of goodness would then be derivative and, further, the relational status of goodness would be a secondary and dependent status. In granting that goodness may be present to an individual because of his self-relatedness, Niebuhr in fact attributes intrinsic value to all beings characterized by potentiality. He thereby implies that they can have value only because they are self-related in terms of actuality-potentiality. But if my analysis is sound, Niebuhr must go further than this and grant that the being has value in itself as a being, for otherwise there is no way to account for the value which originates in self-relatedness. Goodness can appear in self-relatedness, I would argue, only because it was present in the being which is self-related. The self-relation, which actually takes the form of self-estrangement, the discrepancy between essence and existence, is a relation of being to itself. The derivative goodness which is made possible through this self-estrangement is a more significant goodness than would be possible for any *simple* being. But this should not divert our attention from the fact that such goodness is, nonetheless, a derivative form of value.

Niebuhr himself seeks to avoid this conclusion because he takes it to involve the attribution of a value predicate to finite beings and, possibly, the admission that finite beings may be unconditionally good. Indeed, it is precisely this consequence which he seeks to escape in putting the stress on relations. But he actually lets the camel's nose under the tent in granting that a being has intrinsic value by virtue of its self-relatedness. Niebuhr could afford to admit that any finite individual has value by virtue of the fact that he *is* and still deny that he has unconditioned value. All he needs to show is that the existence of finite individuals is conditioned and contingent. Niebuhr's theory of the self takes into account the mediated character of self-existence. Thus, he denies simple self-existence as well as the existence of an absolute self. He should, I think, maintain that the being of finite individuals is conditioned and mediated in a similar fashion. He could then hold that goodness has its ground in being and still deny that any particular finite being is unqualifiedly good. The mark of finitude is present in the self-related being which strives for the realization of potentiality. Its goodness is a limited and contingent goodness grounded in its finite and conditioned existence.

In considering the value which is ingredient in an individual existent, Niebuhr unguardedly slips into an Aristotelian frame of reference. He suggests that both existence and value may be, from one standpoint at least, unmediated. Had Niebuhr applied the insights of Royce, Dewey and Mead, which he so fully appreciates, to the analysis of self-existence, he would not, I think, have been content with an Aristotelian account of it. He would have noted that both the existence and essence of a finite being are mediated and, hence, involve relatedness with other beings. And he would have recognized that self-relatedness necessarily involves relatedness to other beings. This would have made evident the conditioned existence of the individual and, also, the qualified character of any value ingredient in finite existence.

3. RELATION BETWEEN BEINGS

I do not mean to suggest that Niebuhr is unaware of the significance of relatedness for the value intrinsic to an individual. He insists that every being is good-for other beings and, in turn, finds its own value in the existence of the other being. The difficulty I have been attempting to indicate above is that these two modes of value seem to be independent. Niebuhr seems to be saying that a being has value for itself as self-related *and* value for another and for itself because of its relation to other beings. The first premise involves a break in the relational structure of beings, a break which is seriously damaging to Niebuhr's general theory. It acknowledges multiple centers of value which are not dependent upon relations to other beings and, at the same time, attempts to ground value relativity in the relatedness between beings. The break is damaging, I think, because it permits both absolute and self-contained centers of value while insisting upon the relatedness between beings as the ground for most values. It combines, in short, value-absolutism with value-relativism, and the former threatens the ruination of the latter. If Niebuhr is to defend his objective relativism, so important for both his value-theory and his ethics, he must carry through his relational principle more radically and deny that any being has value simply in and of itself. He can do this easily enough by maintaining that self-existence is mediated and conditioned, reflecting relations with other beings, and, hence, that the intrinsic value of any individual is mediated and relational in the more comprehensive sense.

The most penetrating account of the nature of self-existence of which I know is that offered by Hegel in the *Phenomenology of Spirit*. In his analysis of self-consciousness Hegel inquires as to the necessary conditions of self-existence and argues with great power that self-existence is always mediated. Niebuhr would not be willing to accept this account as applying equally to God and man. For were he to accept Hegel's account, or that of any of Hegel's idealistic or naturalistic followers, he would inevitably end up with a monistic system of being and value which would leave no room for the distinction between creator and creature. But with the special consideration that must be given self-existence as it refers to God and all finite creatures, respectively, Niebuhr might well accept Hegel's thesis. He might accept it as applying to all finite existence and refuse to apply it without qualification to God. Hegel and Royce offer an account of self-existence which is radically different from that given by Aristotle. The Hegelian and Roycian metaphysics provide a far more adequate foundation for Niebuhr's value-theory than does the metaphysics of Aristotle. Nor will it do to combine Aristotle's theory of the individual with Hegel and Royce's analysis of the relatedness of all being. This leads to a rupture in metaphysics and value-theory of the sort which I have attempted to explicate.

As I have suggested above, Niebuhr's attribution of intrinsic value to the individual by virtue of his self-relatedness runs counter to his insistence upon value-relativity. The value which the individual has in himself is qualified by his relation to God, to nature, and to his neighbor. Man is a dependent being, a creature. He requires God even as he requires nature and society for the very possibility of existence. His existence is a mediated and conditioned existence in its very core and substance. Thus whatever value he has in and for himself is similarly mediated and conditioned. To admit that value is ultimately grounded in being and, derivatively, in the relatedness of being is not to admit that any finite being has absolute value. If Niebuhr is to make out his case that God is actually the absolute center of value he must make a distinction between the being of God and the being of life, nature, and man. He does make this distinction and does regard finite existence as dependent and conditioned. Unfortunately he does not take this metaphysical distinction into account in considering the ground of value in being. He might still have said that both man and God are good in themselves, good in that both are and have being and, secondarily, in that both are self-related, and yet have avoided the attribution of equal goodness to God and man. God is and can be the center of value only because he is the center of being, the one unconditioned and absolute being. It is the difference between the being of God and man that is crucial for the distinction between the value that is intrinsic to each.

At one point Niebuhr seems to carry through his relational theory with greater consistency than in the passages which we have been examining. Value depends unqualifiedly, he asserts, upon relations *between* beings. "For if anything exists in itself and by itself, even the universe, value would not be present. Value is the good-forness of being for being in their reciprocity, their animosity, and their mutual aid."[10] But this seems to me to be flatly contradictory to what he has said about the grounding of value in self-relatedness. For if any solitary being, including the universe, were to be self-related it would be capable of having value in itself. If Niebuhr is to be consistent he must qualify the statement quoted above by allowing self-relatedness to count as an instance of the relation of being to being. Clearly this is the way in which he thinks he has avoided the inconsistency. But I think this qualification will not suffice. It is difficult to see how the same characteristics of mutuality, reciprocity, and animosity obtaining *between* beings are to be found in self-relatedness. The relation of one being to another and the resulting value that they have for one another are signally different from the value of essential possibility in relation to a particular existent. Another independent being has its own potentiality and possibilities. It does not exist as a possibility for me to realize and, hence, its good-forness cannot consist in any such status. It is an actuality which confronts me, toward which I may be hostile or friendly, live with in strife or mutuality.

One might say, of course, that the value of other beings for the individual is instrumental to the realization of his own potentialities. But this would be to deny that there actually are other centers of value and, more important, that the value of the other being *for me* is a function of the independence and autonomy of the other being. The need I have for the other being is not simply as an instrument or means for the realization of my own potentialities—as Aristotle at times and Spinoza characteristically would suggest. I need to be recognized by the other being, to be loved by him, to be judged and forgiven by him. This is true not simply because my own essence lies in the other being but because my own existence is not self-sufficient and unconditioned. I require the existence of the other for my own existence as a self. I acknowledge him for the sake of being acknowledged, I value him for the sake of being valued. In becoming conscious of the meaning of my relation to the other being I discover that neither existence nor value is centered in myself alone but in the two of us and in all of the relations that obtain or may obtain between us.

He is good for me since he is himself a center of value and existence. Were he without value in himself he could at best be only of instru-

10 "The Center of Value," p. 169.

mental value to me, and I would become for myself the absolute center of value. Niebuhr overstates the case on both sides, I believe, in holding, on the one hand, that a being has its value without the mediation of other beings and, on the other hand, in maintaining that no being has value in itself. The truth of the matter lies between these two extremes and Niebuhr actually seems to put it there. No finite being, at least, has either value or existence immediately. Yet, it has being and exists and to this extent is a relative center both of being and of value.[11] The relativity of value must be grounded in the relativity of being. Relativity means primarily and fundamentally mediation. Thus, one may hold, as Niebuhr does, to both the relativity and the objectivity of values. Values are objective in that they are grounded in the actual existence and relation of beings; they are relative in that they are mediated, dependent always upon the relational structure of existence.

Niebuhr recognizes centers of value, but he seeks to interpret such value-centers as the result of the valuations of beings in relation to one another. Thus, the value of an entity is construed as having its ground in the valuing of another being. It has value because it may in some way serve, answer to, or fulfill a need in the other being. Thus, every being is a terminus and a value-center for any number of other beings and, in turn, the partial ground of the value of those same beings in relation to itself. Each being grounds the goodness of other beings. In this way each being is good-for-another, but no being is really good-in-itself. Niebuhr says that every good is both means and end, but it is difficult to see precisely what he means in saying this, unless he means to credit the intrinsic goodness of the being which is valued. It might be valued for its own sake by another being and even have respect for its own relative worth. Again, it might be valued by another as instrumental and even regard itself as of instrumental worth in relation to other beings. But how could this be possible if no being had intrinsic value in and of itself independently of its relations?

He does not mean to suggest that other beings are valued solely for their instrumental usefulness. He recognizes that this would by no means suffice as an analysis of the value put upon one person by another. The person is valued as a person, that is, as an autonomous subject. But Niebuhr wants to hold that the individual has this value only in relation to the other person who esteems him. He is not good, Niebuhr says, by virtue of the fact that he is a rational being, or has the attributes of personality, or is clever, intelligent, honest, etc. To accept such an explanation would be to revive value-predicates once more and give up the relational account of value. But what is it, we must inquire, that is

[11] Cf. "The Responsibility of the Church for Society" in *The Gospel, the Church and the World*, (ed. by Kenneth Scott Latourette. The Interseminary Series, vol. 3; New York: Harper & Brothers, 1946), pp. 116-17.

valued? If it is not any value-qualities in the other being, it must be the being himself. And to say this makes very good sense. It is fully compatible with the Christian reverence for all being and the Christian doctrine of love. In the love of God for man or the love of one man for another, in so far as it is modeled on the love of God for man, a being is accepted for what it is. Such a relation is existential and unmediated; it reaches to the heart and center of the other being. It is loved and in being loved is valued.

But Niebuhr wants to include under the rubric of valuation such relations as love, fear, hate, etc. He wishes to dispense with value-judgments as a species of unique appraisals made under the guidance of a special set of principles.[12] To value is to relate oneself to another being, to despise or cherish him, to trust or fear him. Trust, love, hope, fear, animosity, all are modes of valuation and, what is more significant, typical of all valuations. For valuation consists of precisely such concrete and active relations between beings. But the question is whether we always relate ourselves to other beings as we should and, further, whether the appropriateness of the relation is at all a function of the other being who is valued.

The fact that we hate another being does not make that being hateful, nor does the fact that we trust another being make that being *ipso facto* trustworthy. Our responses to other beings in our love and hate, our trust and fear, may be not at all appropriate to the nature of the other beings any more than they may be appropriate to our own nature. If all of our evaluations, namely, all of our existential relations to other beings, were what they should be, there would be no moral evil in the world and there would be no meaning to the term "ought." But Niebuhr is no less aware than other moralists of the tragedy of immoral relations obtaining between men. Hence, he must recognize that our responses are not always appropriate to other beings. But does this not mean that the value of the other being is not strictly a function of his relation to us? May we not be related to him in the wrong way, such that he has in fact negative value for us when he deserves to be valued positively? If so, it would appear that the value of the other being, even in relation to us, is grounded in his own existence as much as in our relation to him.

At this point I seem to find a rather serious inadequacy in Niebuhr's relational theory. So far as I can see, he must either regard all beings as of only instrumental value for other beings or else he must acknowledge that the value of individual beings has its ground in their own existence. They need not depend for all of their value upon their self-existence, for they may have value in-relation. Moreover, their value as self-existent beings may be thoroughly qualified by their relations

[12] Cf. "Value-Theory and Theology," p. 113.

with all other beings. But to say that their intrinsic value is *qualified* by such relations is not to say that it is *constituted* by the relations—and it is the latter which Niebuhr seems to affirm. For example, a woman has value as a mother in relation to her child and to society which she would not otherwise have. But unless she had intrinsic value in herself as an individual she could not have the value she does have as mother. In other words, the value she has as mother is mediated in at least two respects. It reflects her relation to the child and the dependence of the child upon her. But it also reflects and expresses her own intrinsic value as a self-existent individual. She is an instrumental value for the child in that she has conceived and given birth to it, sustained and nurtured it. But the child appreciates her or may appreciate her as an individual to whom certain responses, such as love and respect, are appropriate and fitting. The objective value which the mother has in relation to the child, her intrinsic value, is not a function of any need or desire on the part of the child. In his response the child acknowledges the being of the mother in its integral nature. We may admit that the mother as loved has a value which the mother would not have as not loved, but the mother still has the value of a being worthy of being loved. The mother is worthy of being loved not just as mother, although this is a special and highly significant ground for love, but as an integral being and ground for value. The mother does not have value just in herself, even her intrinsic value, but partially, at least, in the child and the relation obtaining between them. Without the child she could not be a mother or have the value which is possible only for a being having this particular relational property. But since her value as a mother is dependent upon her existence as an individual being, the latter is a presupposition and condition of the former value.

If we push this argument back to the consideration of the goodness of being itself, we must take into account the value of the world in relation to God. Is the world good because and only because God appreciates and enjoys it, or does he, in proclaiming its goodness, mean to acknowledge something about the world which he has created? It seems to me that, if the goodness of creation is a function solely of God's enjoyment of the world, then his creation is not really so significant. Only if God has brought into existence a reality which is worthy of praise, which has an integrity and existence of its own, is there anything marvelous or wonderful about God's handiwork. "And he saw that it was good." What is expressed in this succinct passage which sums up in a few words so much of the faith of the Hebrews? Is it not the glory and grandeur of the created world? Is it to be valued only because God values it or, rather, because God created it? It has been brought forth from nothingness and into being. Is it not the passage into being which is most significant about the creation? God has made a world, brought it into being and set it over against himself. He may then enjoy it, suffer and struggle with it, redeem and sustain it. But is its value only a reflection of his own majesty?

It is not open to us, on Niebuhr's theory, to regard the value of the world as a reflection of the glory of God, for God, too, has value only in relation to the world which he has created. "For if anything existed in itself and by itself, even the universe, value would not be present."[13] This situation seems to leave value in a curious situation, like a line stretched in the air but without being anchored at either end. Neither God nor the created world has value in itself, yet each achieves value through the other. God loves the world and is in turn loved by it; thus, both God and the world become valuationally significant. But can we really account for the valuing of either God or man in these terms? Is not the act of valuing essentially that of *acknowledging* something which exists and is relatively independent both of our own existence and of our evaluative act? The world is not independent of God so far as its original existence is concerned. But as existing is it dependent in the same way upon God for its value? Similarly, God is dependent upon man for praise and love, but does he have value only because of this dependence? In relating himself to God, does not man seek to acknowledge God's unconditioned existence as well as his unqualified goodness? Even if such love is possible only because of God's initiative in loving man, is it not the being of God toward which the man of faith reaches in his love and devotion? Is God not a center of value, the absolute center, the proper terminus of valuation? In God, as in man and all existents, value may not be separable from being, but we value a being because it *is* and for what it is, and these modes are at least relatively independent of our valuation.

What is actually needed for an adequate theory of value, and in this case as a correction or addition to Niebuhr's theory, is the recognition of the twofold status and ground of value. We have seen earlier that for a being to have value for itself as self-related it must have value in another dimension as a being which has become estranged from itself. The same thing must be true of God or any self-existent being. Niebuhr focuses upon value as it appears within a relational structure. He considers the value of a being within nature and society and in relation to God. He stresses the value and meaning of God as mediated through the complex of his relations to created nature. But he fails to recognize the value which God and finite creatures must have *in and of themselves* as the necessary ground for any value arising through relatedness.

But we must tread carefully here, for we are on precarious ground. I do not mean to commit myself to the view that being is ever simple and undifferentiated, without an internal relational structure. Hegel

[13] "The Center of Value," p. 169. Cf. "Value-Theory and Theology," p. 113.

struggled with this question and concluded that mediation is a necessary and essential component within being. We cannot avoid thinking of pure being, i.e., perfectly simple and undifferentiated being, but this may be only an abstraction—a moment of being rather than being itself. Hegel recognized, further, that truth and goodness are possible only because being is self-mediated. Only because being "others" and objectifies itself, becomes self-alienated and overcomes the alienation are truth and goodness possible. But truth and goodness must be acknowledged as having two important modes, namely, before and after the self-differentiation. God has a new and different value after the creation, but he has a prior value in the primordial character of his being. God may be fundamentally a self-differentiated and self-related being, but the ground which underlies the self-differentiation is the condition for a mode of goodness other than that which is relevant to his self-relatedness. God may be good-for-himself but only if he is good-in-himself. And the same thing must be said of any individual or "center of value."

It may be helpful at this point to shift our attention for a moment from value to existence and consider the nature of being and relations between beings. Without asserting the externality of all relations, it may be argued that a necessary condition of any relation between beings is the existence of those beings. A being must exist in itself before it can exist for another. The relation must have a ground, an anchor, and that can be provided only by the existence in which the relation terminates. Thus, a presupposition of a relation such as being-for-another is being-in-itself, which Hegel refers to as implicit being. To *be* is ontologically prior to *to-be for*. God's existence is prior to any relations he may have to other beings. The relations may alter his meaning and even his nature, but this, again, is possible only if he is self-existent. I should want to argue that the same thing must be said of value. Prior to any value-forness must be intrinsic value, the value which a being has as self-existent. It can have value for another, even as it has being for another, only in having value in and of itself.

4. VALUATION AS RELATIONAL

Actually, it is not so much value itself which is relational in character as it is valuation. Niebuhr quite properly rejects the respectable and well-entrenched but mistaken view of valuation which regards it as a special form of contemplative judgment. Closely related to his repudiation of special value properties is his rejection of special value-judgments. All valuation, he wishes to maintain, involves the active relation of one being to another. Without such relations and the possibility for them there could be no valuation. Thus, valuation has its ground in and is constituted by a rich variety of existential relations between beings. Beings can value each other only if they are involved with one another. All relations between beings have valuational significance. One can see why it is that Niebuhr denies that there is any radical difference between valuational experience and other modes of experience. Cognition is itself a form of valuation. At this point Niebuhr's view is fairly close to that of Whitehead, who regarded all relations as valuationally significant. Value-judgment, on this view, may be interpreted as the expression in propositional form of the quality of any specific relation of one being to another. Thus, to say that God is good is not to apply one or more special predicates to God, but rather to express the character of one's relation to God. This is not to suggest that the valuation is purely subjective or the mere utterance of a feeling. It is to say, however, that a value-judgment has its ground in a concrete and full-bodied relation between beings. The value-judgment in expressing the quality of the relation includes, also, the beings which are brought together in the relation. It expresses the being who is valued as well as the being who utters the judgment or initiates the relation.

Value-judgments may be correct or incorrect, not because they apply or fail to apply the proper predicates to a being, but rather because they express a relation which is either appropriate or inappropriate to the beings which are related. An incorrect value-judgment expresses an incorrect valuation—which is an improper relation. The relation may distort the character and existence of either the subject or the object. In viewing valuation in this fashion as relational it is possible to account for errors in valuation, for objectivity, and yet to deny that value-judgments are the result of disinterested and uninvolved appraisals. All valuation involves interestedness; it is a form of or expression of interest. It involves and presupposes self-interest as well as interest in other beings. It achieves objectivity not by escaping such interestedness but by including it and accepting it as the material component in all value-judgment.

A valuation may be false to the extent that it fails to express the nature of the subject or to acknowledge the character of the object. The relation then becomes dishonest, a relatedness which is unfaithful to either or both of the beings involved in the relation. A valuation which expresses contempt for another being may, for example, assert the unconditioned existence of the subject and the relative meaninglessness of the object. It may serve to falsify the nature both of the subject and of the object. All incorrect value-judgments are grounded in such dishonest and unfaithful valuations which fail to answer to the character of the beings which are related. It is the existence of the beings which makes possible the truth or goodness which may be expressed in any relations between them. Both goodness and truth are dependent upon relational situations for their realization, but there is a primordial good-ness and a primordial truth ingredient in existence which makes such determinate goodness and truth possible.

The relational analysis of valuation enables us to give a satisfactory account of judgments about justice, honesty, loyalty, etc., which would otherwise have to be regarded as based upon unique value-intuition. Although Niebuhr does not offer a relational account of valuation along the lines which I have suggested, it seems to me that it is both com-patible with and implied by his general exposition of value. To say that a state or a society is unjust, for example, is surely to express the unsatis-factoriness of one's relation to that state and, further, of the complex of relations within that state as one is inextricably involved in them. Plato described justice as a condition in which everything performs its proper function, where each entity receives its due. Injustice is a condition in which beings are improperly related to one another. Thus, injustice can be appraised only by an individual who is in some way actually related to the unjust society. The misfortune of such ill-relatedness focuses in his own situation, is expressed in his own existence. He can change the character of his judgment only by changing the condition of the state; as it improves, his situation will improve and be reflected in his altered judgment.

The ground of justice as a value is to be found in the existent beings which comprise the society. Injustice is not an abstract form or predicate but a concrete condition obtaining between beings. It is a condition of relatedness; it is a mode of valuation in which beings are not valued properly—which means simply that they are not related properly. A valuation of this sort is exceedingly complex in that it involves consid-erably more than a simple relation betwen two beings. In the case of an individual living within the state or any community whatever, he par-ticipates in a nexus of relations which is almost infinitely complex. He relates himself to other beings but, also, to the relatedness of other beings to one another and to himself. But the relations and their struc-ture are just as concrete as the beings related. Hence, in relating himself both to other beings and to the relational structure, the individual is actively involved in the life of the community. The judgments which he makes about the community, as to its justice or injustice, sickness or health, reflect the whole complex of relations in which he is involved. He shares or participates in the sickness or health of the community. Otherwise he could not judge it. Thus, value-judgments about the state may be accounted for in the same way in which we interpret value-judgments about individual beings. Both are relational and ultimately grounded in the actuality of the beings related.

If we take a typical value-judgment referring to an individual, on the other hand, we find the judgment expressing the nature of an actual relation obtaining between two individuals. If I say, for example, that someone is dishonest, I express a certain alienation between myself and the other person. In making this judgment I testify to the inadequacy of the relation actually obtaining between us. My own valuation is a concrete relation to the other, and an unfortunate one. I would like to correct it so that the alienation might in this particular regard be overcome. But the situation and the valuation are somewhat more complex than my remarks might suggest. Dishonesty is a relational attribute, a quality which no being could have as a simple, unmediated existent. Hence, in the judgment I express the relation as it terminates in me. But I also mean to express the other terminus of the relation and to take it into account in the judgment. I have related myself to the other negatively in regarding him as dishonest. The relation is unsatisfactory from my vantage point, and I express this deficiency. But the other person has also related himself to me, and his own initiative and subjectivity is as much involved in the valuation and the judgment as my own situation. It is a two-way relation, anchored in both termini. Hence, the value judgment expresses and must express the character of both parties to the relation.

5. THE FALLIBILITY OF VALUATIONS

Thus far we have been concerned with valuations where the relation has been correctly expressed or interpreted in the judgment which brings it to explicitness. But erroneous judgments also must be taken into account and explained. It is evident that valuations may be improper and that value-judgments may be incorrect. But in what way are they incorrect? We have seen already the way in which valuation itself may be mistaken. Any valuation is wrong when it is inappropriate to the nature of the beings which are existentially related in the valuation. The valuation may be basically false in misrepresenting the nature either of the subject or of the object. To be a true valuation it must represent and express the actual existence of the subject valuing and the real nature of the being valued. It may err in either direction, by falsifying the subject or the object, or in both directions. A value-judgment will be correct and true to the extent that it faithfully expresses in propositional form the valuative relation. The judgment itself is actually of secondary importance; it is the valuation on which it is based that is of greatest significance. The judgment proper may be taken as the rational form or structure of the evaluative relation and, hence, dependent for its truth or falsity upon the relation proper. Thus, to determine the truth or error of any value-judgment we must look to the situation which is expressed in it. We must determine whether the concrete relations constituting the valuation are themselves correct or incorrect.

We must take into account a situation where a mistake in valuation has occurred—for example, in a case where someone has been falsely judged to be dishonest. On the analysis that has been offered here, the false judgment is grounded in a false relation. We must then determine precisely the way in which valuative relations can be false. If this can be accomplished, we will have offered an adequate account of the possibility of error in value-judgments and, hence, a fuller explanation of the way in which they may be true. To judge that someone is dishonest is, as we have seen, to be concretely related to that individual in such a way as not to trust him. The judgment not only expresses mistrust but asserts something about the character of the individual who is being judged. Now, valuations would be incorrigible if they were always to be taken at face value as adequate expressions of the value-relations obtaining between persons. In that the judgment made in our example expresses a factual valuative relation it is necessarily true and no possibility of error enters the picture. This mode of truth is not trivial nor is the factuality of the valuational relation expressed in the judgment inconsequential. But we are concerned not only with the evaluative relation as such but also with its warrant or justification. Granted that someone is not trusted and thus is negatively valued, we must inquire whether or not he is worthy of trust. Is he honest or not? Although it expresses far more than this, the judgment has as an element in its content the presumed dishonesty of an individual. If the existence of the individual does not answer to this content, then the judgment and the valuation are false and mistaken.

Not all people are honest or trustworthy. This point hardly needs to be argued. What we must determine is the significance of untrustworthiness for a relational account of value and value-judgment. One thing is clear, namely, that untrustworthiness cannot be regarded simply as a function of the valuation. An attitude of trust or distrust cannot of itself make the object-individual trustworthy or untrustworthy. Our acknowledgment of him as trustworthy may prompt him to regard himself in this light and to respond to us in such a way as to justify our attitude toward him. But this does not always happen; he may betray our trust and force us to acknowledge the failure of our valuation. I have chosen a difficult example, for no empirical test may be adequate to the determination of trustworthiness. Nevertheless, our valuation imputes to the other being a dishonest character; and circumstances can be imagined where we would feel perfectly justified in concluding that we were right or wrong in our response to him. Now, admitting the important influence of attitudes such as trust and distrust in determining the character of other persons, we must, I think, recognize that the individual judged is assumed to have a character. It is his moral character that we are intending to take into account in our judgment and our valuation. We would readily admit, I believe, that we often do misjudge the character of others, on both the credit and the debit side. It is unfortunate that we must judge at all and we ought never to make unconditional judgments as to the character of other persons. But judge we must, and our life and the life and well-being of others depends to a great degree upon the wisdom of our judgments.

We are once again driven to recognize the value-ingredient in individuals in relative isolation from any and all relations. We regard them as "centers of value," to employ Niebuhr's terminology, and quite properly so. In various ways we judge them to be more or less good or evil. Our judgments about them, our valuative relations to them, may be fitting or unfitting, correct or mistaken, depending upon whether or not we have acknowledged their intrinsic valuational status. No man is or can be totally evil, nor can any being be totally evil. But men can be evil in and of themselves and must be judged accordingly. A correct evaluation will express the true character of the subject as well as of the object. This can be possible only if the good or evil of both subject and object is in some sense prior to the judgment or the valuation.

This does not mean that we must give up or even modify the relational account of valuation. Valuation remains a relation, and the correctness or incorrectness of it depends upon the fittingness or unfittingness of the relation. It is simply that the appropriateness of a relation cannot be determined apart from the value-character of the beings who are related in the valuation. To assume that the value of another being is wholly dependent upon our valuation of him would be tantamount to the denial that he is in any sense free or autonomous. Moreover, it would be to rule out one of the important conditions for the possibility of the correctness or incorrectness of valuations. Although we may alter or influence it, we do not *constitute* the disposition or moral character of another person by the way in which we relate ourselves to him. In failing to note this fact we would err in assuming either too much or too little responsibility for our action. Valuation is grounded in and expressed by a relational situation. But it is dependent for its warrant or justification upon the beings who are involved in the relation.

6. INTRINSIC AND INSTRUMENTAL VALUE

In attempting to account for values in relational terms, Niebuhr has been prompted to move too far in the direction of regarding all value as instrumental. In considering the value of a self-related being as well as in considering the terminus of valuations, we have found it necessary to acknowledge intrinsic value which is grounded in the being of individuals. But two important points remain to be examined. We must determine more precisely the way in which both intrinsic and extrinsic or instrumental value are possible. It is more satisfactory to begin with the latter mode of value and then to turn to the more difficult question as to the ultimate ground of value in being. In the final analysis we must see whether or not we can sustain the qualifications of the relational interpretation which has been offered and still come out with anything like a unified and systematic theory.

As we have noted, Niebuhr wants to maintain both the objectivity and the relativity of values. In order to sustain the objectivity of value he attempts to ground it in the need which beings have for materials which can be supplied only by other beings. Good is, on this analysis, to be interpreted as good-forness. Thus the value of food may be regarded as its capacity to satisfy the hunger of an animal, the value of a tool its usefulness for the technician. But there are other and more subtle values which may be analyzed in similar fashion. The value of a friend may be construed as his capacity to satisfy my own need for companionship. Niebuhr criticizes Aristotle for not having recognized adequately the importance of other beings in whose presence one realizes one's potentialities. "The Aristotelian form of relational value-theory seems to be inadequate at this point since it attaches greater value to the state of the being which realizes its potentialities than to the being in the presence of which such potentiality is realized.[14] Niebuhr hereby corrects an inadequacy in Aristotle's theory, but I wonder if his correction is really sufficient? It stresses the instrumental value of other persons as well as the value of one's own possibilities for self-realization. But does it not tend to regard the value of friendship as largely if not exclusively instrumental?

Niebuhr actually denies that any hard and fast line can be drawn between intrinsic and instrumental value. Here he sides with Dewey, insisting that all values are both means and ends. Thus, he might well object that I am introducing a distinction which is neither valid nor relevant. But before we can countenance this objection we must determine in what way Niebuhr actually provides for the possibility of values as *both* instrumental and intrinsic. It would appear that his relational theory allows only for instrumental value.

In saying that every good is an end, he seems to mean that it is the terminus of a valuation. Thus, essential possibilities are end-values for the being which needs to realize them. But every being constitutes a complementary good for every other being—is good-for other beings. Hence, all end-values may be instrumental values. But this account of end-values will not do! It seems to account for intrinsic goodness but does not actually do so. The goodness which essential possibilities have for an individual, namely, the fact that he needs to realize them, does not constitute his intrinsic value. The process of realizing possibilities must be good-in-itself or else it does not make sense to refer to any potential being as intrinsically good. The definition of value as the

[14] "The Center of Value," p. 167.

terminus of an end-directed process, a formulation which Niebuhr adopted from D. C. Macintosh, will not suffice for the explanation of the value of self-realization itself. It is well enough to say that value may function within an end-directed process as a terminus or end, but this by no means suffices as a definition of value. The process of realization of potentiality is good-in-itself, as Niebuhr admits in saying that it *ought* to transpire. Moreover, the being for whom the process takes place, whose existence is exhibited in the tension between actuality and possibility, is good-in-itself. Only if we analyze the value-ingredient in an individual in this fashion is it meaningful to say that the individual has intrinsic value. It is then not simply a matter of his having ends present to himself, but that he is himself an end, as Kant would put it "an end in himself." At this point Niebuhr's relational theory simply breaks down and must be revised. It carries us a long way and provides much illumination in our effort to understand the nature of value. But it fails to account for the sort of value which must be attributed to any being or object as intrinsic to its nature and existence. We must be able to say two things about individual beings which, so far as I can see, Niebuhr's theory does not permit. We must be able to assert that a being is good by virtue of the fact that it is and, secondly, that it is good by virtue of its character. I do not see how we can assert either of these if we must restrict ourselves to the value-forness of essential possibilities.

It is still possible to say, however, that every intrinsic good is also, and necessarily, an instrumental good for other beings. In so far as it satisfies any needs whatever in other beings it is good-for them and complements whatever value they may have as self-related. But the good-forness is also to be viewed as a value for the being who is capable of satisfying a need. The goodness of a plant as food is a mediated but intrinsic value for it. In this sense any value may be regarded as both intrinsic and instrumental. The plant does not have its value as food apart from the possibility of being eaten and consumed. But if we may recall the earlier analogy of the mother-child relation, the plant has a value as an existent which is not mediated through its relation to other beings.

Now, this value, too, may be instrumental, though in a somewhat different way. The intrinsic value of food as food is, as we saw, mediated; its instrumental value is actually prior to its intrinsic value. But a plant may be valued for its own sake, in which case it comes to have extrinsic value. But in the latter instance its intrinsic value is prior to its instrumental value. Its intrinsic value may be enhanced by being appreciated and enjoyed by other beings. Thus, it, too, may be mediated. Its existence may come to have a value for-itself through being valued by another being, which would not otherwise have been possible. It then has its own intrinsic value not merely implicitly but explicitly. The mediation made possible through valuation is essential to the realization of its intrinsic value. It is originally good-in-itself and secondarily good-for-another. But in the case we are now considering its goodness-for-another is conditioned by its prior intrinsic value. By virtue of the fact that it is good-for-another it becomes good-for-itself. And we may add—though with some hesitation lest we complicate the picture hopelessly—as good-for-itself it comes to have a new value for other beings. The tissue of relations between beings is infinitely rich. It would be impossible to delineate here the combinations and permutations which may obtain between them. The brief analysis of a simple case which has been given must suffice to suggest the importance both of immediacy and of mediation for valuation, as well as the significance of the distinction between intrinsic and extrinsic value.

The distinction between intrinsic and instrumental value is not absolute. Yet, it seems to be necessary to make a fairly firm distinction between those values which depend entirely upon relations for their appearance and those which have their sufficient ground in nonrelational existence. Existence may be self-related, but it is important to acknowledge the value of the self-related beings as such. The goodness of a friend does not consist simply in his capacity to satisfy needs of whatever sort in another being, nor in the potentialities which he may realize. As friend it is the individual himself who is valued and not merely his essential possibilities. The latter are important and constitutive for the inclusive value of the friend. But we value him for himself, for what he is, and not just for the ends toward which he strives. The need for friendship is a basic requirement of human nature. It is the need to be recognized, loved, esteemed, and aided by another person. But such a need can be met only by a being who is an end-in-himself.

The instrumental value which a friend has as friend is predicated upon his intrinsic value, the value which he has as a self-existent being. Thus, it does not seem to me that Niebuhr's correction of Aristotle goes far enough. It is necessary and important to recognize that self-realization takes place within a social context and that other individuals provide complementary goods for the process of self-realization. But we must note, also, the fact that the good-forness of such complementary values has its ground in the intrinsic goodness of other persons. The paradoxical fact which must not be overlooked is that *only a being which had value in and for itself*, in short, a person, *could satisfy the need for friendship*. No one can actually have a friend unless he acknowledges the integrity and equality of the other person. He knows implicitly, at least, that the friend can be good-for-him *as friend* only because the friend is good-in-himself. Niebuhr recognizes this fact and has more than adequately taken it into account in his examination of interpersonal relations. But his interpretation of value does not allow for its inclusion on philosophical grounds—which is an indication of the philosophical inadequacy of his theory.

7. VALUE AND EXISTENCE

We now come to the more difficult question as to the goodness of existence. I have found it necessary to maintain that value and valuation have their ultimate ground in the goodness of being. But it remains to be seen how value may be predicated of being within the limits of the principles which have been outlined. The goodness of self-relatedness has its ground in the being which is self-related. The self-relatedness involved in self-realization has been analyzed as a self-alienation, as the relation of a being to itself through the mediation of essence and possibility. A fuller exploration of this relation would require a detailed examination of essence and existence and, especially, of the involvement of finite beings in the matrix of time. But we can see, perhaps, that an individual existent may be characterized in terms of existence, essence, and process and that these are all moments within the being of that individual. Hence, it may be sufficiently clear how I have interpreted these moments as the self-relatedness of being. There are a number of important questions that might be raised as to the goodness of possibilities for self-realization and how they function normatively. These have been answered in principle, I believe, and the more detailed examination of their normative function lies beyond the province of the present study. It has been argued further that, although new values appear as a result of the relatedness of beings, they depend for their appearance, nevertheless, upon the intrinsic goodness of individual existents. Thus we are driven to consider directly the goodness of being itself.

On the view which has been offered, being *is* good and the ultimate ground and source of all value. All relational goodness must be regarded as the expression or affirmation of this primordial goodness of being. Self-realization is good because it is the expression and affirmation of being. Evil, by the same token, is the denial or positive negation of being. Finite beings have only finite existence. They are conditioned in goodness and conditioned in existence. If God is an unconditioned being, his goodness is unqualified. Thus, we are not committed to saying that all beings are good in the same way. Value-theory is ultimately dependent upon metaphysics; in fact, the two cannot be separated. It is impossible to deal with the question as to the ground of value apart from the inquiry into the nature of being and existence. Not only are finite beings conditioned as to value, but their existence and goodness are mediated by their relations to all other beings, including God. As creator, the being of God cannot be mediated in the same way as is the case for finite beings. Yet, he is related to the created world and this affects both his existence and his goodness. God, who originally existed only in himself comes, through the creation, to exist for himself through the mediation of the world. Similarly he comes to have value for himself through the same mediation—although he is the ultimate source and ground of value. It is impossible, on this view, to assign to man absolute value and ridiculous to assert the "infinite worth of human personality."

But what does it mean to say that being is good? Many modern philosophers would regard this statement as the sheerest nonsense. It is generally thought that goodness is a property only of actions or situations even as truth is a property only of propositions. Yet, there is a respectable tradition in philosophy which holds that both goodness and truth may be predicated of being itself. As I have suggested earlier, Augustine regarded being as good in itself. The problem involved here is serious, for we must not only explain the predication of goodness to being but, also, account for the fact that we say that being *is*. It is evident, I think, that is is quite different to predicate existence of a particular being than to say that being *is*. The former clearly involves the employment of a category and refers always to determinate existence. The same thing may be said for ordinary valuations. Usually we say that this being, this object, this situation or action is good, but not that *being* is good. Yet, if there is any warrant for our theory, we must be able to make this assertion, else all of our particular valuations are without foundation.

The reason why it seems absurd to say that being *is* is because being is thought of as that which is, as *isness* itself. Therefore, it seems like saying "that which is, is." Yet, we must be able to think and to assert that being *is* and *is good*. To be able to do this we must recognize the distinction involved in the predication of existence or value to being itself as contrasted with determinate beings. The distinction in predication is based upon a distinction between primordial being and derivative being, primordial goodness and derivative goodness. The former is implicit and simple, the latter explicit and differentiated. The latter can always be characterized in terms of structure and relation, whereas the former is devoid of both structure and relation.

There is a difference between being and existence, a radical difference, which Heidegger has characterized as the "ontological difference." Being is always transcendent to existence; yet it is the necessary ground and substance of existence. The being of a particular entity or individual transcends its existence; it is the ground and source of his existence. But the being of a finite individual is conditioned, for it is possible for him not to exist. He *is*, but not absolutely. Transcendent to his own being is the ultimate source and ground of all being, namely, God. Thus, the finite individual recognizes a twofold transcendence of being, the transcendence of his own being to his existence and the transcendence of God to his own being. Man participates with God both in being and in goodness; his being and his goodness have both a primordial and a derivative aspect as in the case of God. But his being and value remain qualified and conditioned even in their primordial character.

In all judgments about determinate existence and value, we employ categories. Existence and value are both categories, at once ethical and metaphysical. The categories themselves are differentiated to provide us with a rich conceptual framework for the interpretation of reality. These categories are not static forms but rather the actual rules or principles in terms of which we relate ourselves to ourselves and the world. All concrete relations, including valuations and cognitive judgments, exemplify and further differentiate the basic categories. It is significant to say that anything *is* or that it *is good*. But we seldom content ourselves with such judgments and in general would consider them to be empty or trivial. The reason is that we are not dealing with being or goodness as such but with determinate forms of being and goodness. Hence, it is important to specify the mode of being or goodness which is to be predicated of an entity or event. We specify goodness as moral good, aesthetic good, economic good, intellectual good, etc. In similar fashion we designate the various ways in which entities may be said to exist.

Now, underlying all of our judgments is our own existence and our certainty of that existence. Every judgment we make is an expression of our own existence and a relating of ourselves to the existence of others. But we are entitled not only to say "I exist" but also "I am." The former would be altogether too thin a statement to express what we know ourselves to be. We know that in ourselves we are related to being, that it is the proximate source and ground of our existence. We are noumenal as well as phenomenal, and our phenomenal existence is a manifestation of our noumenal being. Descartes did not recognize that the affirmation of one's own existence was mediated by the confrontation with the existence of other beings, that one had the world always with him. To know that I exist is to know that other beings exist. To know that I am is to know that other beings have a noumenal ground. Thus, the awareness of being is a presupposition of our every utterance and action. It makes sense to say that being *is*, for it is implicit in our statement that we exist.

Here, I think, we find the origin of the category. It originates in the self-expression and self-relatedness of being; it is the articulation of that self-relatedness. Being becomes a category in differentiating itself. The category informs our judgment but, more basically, it informs our existence. The predication of *isness* to being is understood prereflectively, prerationally. It is the understanding which we have by virtue of the fact that we are. It is dark and mysterious, neither understood nor capable of being understood. Yet it is the basic understanding which supports all knowledge and insight. I must know and understand what it means to be, to say that "I am" before I can understand what it means to say that "I am a man" or "I am a good man." The mystery depends upon the fact that the category is identical with that of which it is predicated. When I say that I am I recognize the unity of category and ground, that this is the most fundamental mode of predication or judgment. Though dark and mysterious, it provides the source of illumination for all predication and judgment, all knowledge. I must know what it is "to be" or I can know nothing whatever of existence.

If this is true, we do have a prereflective knowledge of being and understand what it means to say that being *is*. But do we have the same sort of understanding of what it means to say that being is good? I believe that we do, for in knowing that which primordially *is* we know that which primordially *is good*. This would generally be regarded as a synthetic proposition, the ground for which needs to be offered. And it is synthetic in that it relates two basic categories, being and value. But I would argue that it is, also, fundamentally analytic, for reasons which I shall attempt to make clear. In spite of the fact that our knowledge of being is presuppositional to all of our determinate knowledge, it is that of which we are often least aware and which we are least able to illumine. We come to the explicit consciousness of being only by way of the manifoldness of existence. Thus, it even seems strange to us to say that "being is" or to say simply "I am." In similar fashion we are least aware of the primordial character of value, since we come to it through the confusion of an infinite variety of determinate goods. We have no better explicit understanding of goodness itself than we have of being itself. Yet, every valuation presupposes the prereflective apprehension of goodness.

If it often seems to us that being is hopelessly divorced from value and at best joined only by virtue of our contingent judgments or valuations, this is because we begin with beings and values rather than with being and value. We despair of asserting either the unity or the necessary connection of the two because of our preoccupation with their seeming disparateness and the tenuousness of their connection in human experience. But being and value not only are related synthetically; *they are one*. Our fundamental cognition is at the same time a valuation. When I assert that "I am" I give expression to both being and value, or, more precisely, to the value of my being and the being of my value. I know that it is an ontological and an analytic unity, for I recognize that all of my judgments are valuations and all of my valuations are judgments. Every judgment and every valuation expresses and presupposes this unity which is originally a simple identity. Identity is a form of goodness even as goodness is a form of identity. If knowledge or valuation is to be possible, there must be a final convergence of all categories. They can and do converge only in the source from which they originate, namely, that unity of value and existence which is being itself.

The goodness of being is not a determinate character or quality of being; it is being. Hence, the knowledge of the goodness of being is as dark as the understanding of being in itself. Both are mysterious, constituting an unfathomable depth within which reason can cast only a faint glimmer of light. But that depth is still understood, and provides the illumination for all understanding. Plato misplaced the Good, I think, in putting it beyond being. This fails to understand the good and its original unity with being. It does make sense to say that being-is-good, though not the same sense as to say that "this flower is good." And we understand what it means to assert the more general statement. I do not pretend to have shed much light upon either the primordial character of being or goodness, or upon the unity of the two. If this point is to be made it must be made indirectly, namely, by exhibiting the necessity of accepting it if one is to make sense of human knowledge and valuation.

Although it is not possible to discuss in detail the implications of such an account of value for theology, it provides a promising vantage point for dealing with the question of the goodness of God. Niebuhr has rightly criticized those theologians and philosophers who ask the question: Is God good? and who then proceed to determine whether or not certain value-attributes are to be assigned to him. This seems to me just as absurd as Niebuhr has alleged and, hence, a procedure to be avoided at all costs. The absurdity of it consists in setting up an absolute standard of value and then asking whether or not God, who is taken to be the supreme being, conforms to it. This precludes the possibility that God should ever be credited with one of the necessary characteristics of deity, namely, to be supremely good. The religious believer who has had an encounter with God does not first come to know God and then discover that God is good. To him is disclosed at one and the same time the unity of being and goodness in God. He acknowledges that God is the supreme center both of being and of value. In recognizing God as the creator he recognizes him as judge, as worthy of both reverence and respect. He can never ultimately separate being and goodness in his consciousness of and response to God. He does not know fully what the determinate nature of God is with respect either to his existence or his goodness. Moreover, even as his own being is dark and mysterious, so too is the transcendence of God. He knows the "hidden God" as well as the "revealed God," and his awareness of the former is present in all apprehension of the latter. Transcendence, being, value, he encountered in himself. As he encounters them in God they appear in another dimension as unconditioned and unqualified. God is, for him, the absolute center of value because and only because he is the absolute center of existence.

7.

A THEOLOGICAL ANALYSIS
OF RACE RELATIONS

WALDO BEACH

1. BETWEEN THEOLOGY AND SOCIOLOGY

THIS essay may be regarded as an extended footnote to, or a full-length illustration of, H. Richard Niebuhr's theological approach to social ethics, in one of its most vexed and pressing forms: race relations. Other areas of application—economic, political, familial—might serve as well to illustrate the pertinence of Niebuhr's interpretation of Christian ethics. The "race" problem, more especially in its form of Negro-white relations, is here taken for examination, as a particular instance of perennial human problems which stand in need of continuing Christian reappraisal. Such an illustrative problem is bifocal in its perspective, looking to Christian theology for its categories of interpretation and to contemporary social science for empirical data about man's interracial behavior.

The approach here is intended to be "in the spirit of Richard Niebuhr," in two particular senses. For one, it begins and concludes with the faith that race relations can be understood most profoundly in terms of man's responses, false or true, to the activity of God as Creator, Judge and Redeemer. This presumes Niebuhr's Christian ethics of response: that what man ought to do in the realm of human decision should be done out of a trustful response to the manner in which God has acted and is acting, in his concurrent activities as Creator and Sustainer of all life, in his chastisement and correction of sin as the moral Governor of men, and in his grace as Healer and Redeemer. Secondly, it shares Niebuhr's ecumenical outlook—especially stressed by, though not of course unique with, him—that there can be, under the reign of an omnipotent God, no separation of "religious" from "secular" truth, as though religious truth were only one compartment of a many-sectioned body of knowledge. There are particular religious facts, to be sure, which are not the same as economic facts or biological facts. But the Christian *Weltanschauung* of radical monotheism must by definition include all of life in its purview and be ready to see truth from whatever source as of God. An attempt such as this to talk across the disciplines of theology and sociology, which are hardly on speaking terms today, may be highly vulnerable to the experts on both sides, but it is imperative in the name of the single Lord of all being.

This latter point has special pertinence for the issue of racial relations, which has been, at least in America, the special province of social science. Christian theologians have given relatively little attention to this problem, while sociologists have produced many detailed studies, in apparent independence of Christian inspiration. The spirit underlying the extensive literature by the students of interracial tension and co-operation, as with most social science, seems entirely quantitative, "scientific," naturalistic, positivistic. If theology was ever the queen of the sciences, for the major number of social scientists today she has long since been dethroned. Yet it may be—and this is one of the claims of this essay—that by whatever terminology, the sociologist is "thinking God's thoughts after Him" and retracing and confirming the authentic truths of the Christian faith about man's sin and God's grace. This fact may constitute a judgment upon the churches, especially on their sins of omission; but it is not the only time in history when God has manifested himself in unlikely, "secular" places, to rebuke the officially "religious" in their pretensions to monopolies on divine truth, or in their neglect of his appearance in common life outside of closed canons.

It is important to define even more carefully our standpoint midway between theology and sociology, or, as Niebuhr might put it, at the place of dialogue between theologian and sociologist. In its attempt to speak redemptively to man's racial tensions, Christian ethics is highly indebted to the descriptive factualism of the sociologist. The painstaking accumulation and analysis of the facts of racial configuration, of the manifold cultural factors affecting prejudice, of the types of discrimination, and the various studies in the reduction of prejudice, all provide data highly valuable for the Christian in his understanding of the permissive and constrictive conditions in which his actions have to be made as a human being of one race dealing with persons of other races. To know the full range of the empirical facts is to be corrected in too simple and sentimental diagnoses and prescriptions.

Yet, at the same time, the Christian must remind the sociologist that our racial behavior is not made over by the objective accumulation of data. The social scientist acknowledges the danger of sociologism with greater or less readiness. Nor is he in fact as detached as the creed of his discipline requires him to be. The very fact that social science in America has in the past quarter century been so preoccupied with the racial problem rather than with recreational mores, for example, or some other issue of comparable complexity, is sign that it is prompted by a deep moral compunction. Social science's interest in ethnic tensions as a form of social pathology is a mark of its concern for social health. Its assumption that the reduction of prejudice is desirable is not in any sense derived from the facts, but is an ethical dogma, taken for granted. Its objective analysis is sustained by the question: "What shall we do to be saved?"

The major studies of the race problem have quite boldly affirmed their moral bias and defended a departure from strict scientific neutrality as necessary and good. Gunnar Myrdal's *An American Dilemma*, the most exhaustive sociological treatise on race yet to appear, is informed throughout by a faith in the "American creed of equality and freedom" and finds the locus of the dilemma "in the heart of the American." Myrdal denies himself "the prerogative of pronouncing on *a priori* grounds which values are 'right' and which are 'wrong.' In fact, such judgments are out of the realm of social science, and will not be attempted in this inquiry."[1] Yet it is a working assumption of the whole study that the moral values of the American creed are of positive worth in ameliorating racial life.

Another competent student of the problem, Robert MacIver, would also regard himself as social scientist rather than theologian or moralist. Yet the approach of his book on race relations, *The More Perfect Union*, as the title implies, is in search of a social policy that can guide racial behavior toward more democratic community. He deplores the sociological assumption "that a more precise knowledge of the facts will itself provide the answer to our question. The unfortunate consequence is that generally the most scientific studies convey no message to the framers of social policy, while the mass of exhortatory or advisory literature has no sure foundation in scientific knowledge."[2]

It appears, then, that the sociologist of race is ready to acknowledge that he must be moralist despite himself, or at least that he has imported into his analysis moral allegiances which are in no sense to be derived

[1] Gunnar Myrdal, *An American Dilemma* (2 vols.; New York: Harper & Brothers, 1944), p. 1. Cf. Introduction, pp. xiv-xlix, and Appendix 1, pp. 1027-34.

[2] Robert MacIver: *The More Perfect Union*. (New York: The Macmillan Company, 1948), p. 18. See also Appendix 2, on *Social Science and Social Action*. Other recent extensive sociological and psychological studies of race relations might be used to illustrate an increased readiness of sociologists to acknowledge their *a priori* value-standpoints. Cf. G. E. Simpson and J. M. Yinger, *Racial and Cultural Minorities, An Analysis of Prejudice and Discrimination*. (New York: Harper & Brothers, 1953), p. 649; the UNESCO series on "The Race Question in Modern Science"; Brewton Berry, *Race Relations* (Boston: Houghton Mifflin Company, 1951), Chap. I; R. A. Schermerhorn, *These Our People* (Boston: D. C. Heath, 1949), pp. 516-18.

a posteriori from the facts. Whence these moral values, and what is their ground? Here the discipline of Christian ethics becomes pertinent. Throughout the literature on race there appears a wide disparity of persuasion as to the ground of the values of racial harmony. Among a few, a foundation in Christian doctrine is affirmed. Among many more, the religion of democracy, resting on its own bottom, is taken to be the justification of value. With others, "adjustment" of life to life and group to group becomes ultimate. At other points, science is taken as the basis of the moral ought. For the most part, these cluster about an inchoate kind of religion which has a constellation of human and this-worldly ends. Christian ethics must judge all these viewpoints as to their adequacy and ultimacy in the light of its faith in the character of God.

We have said that Christian ethics is indebted to the social scientist for his descriptive accuracy in factual data, and will concur with the judgment of the more astute sociologist that the problem of race is not really an outer or factual problem, but a moral issue or a problem of "conflicting valuations" (Myrdal).

Yet a closer look reveals that the problem must be analyzed at a third and still deeper level. Among both Christians and non-Christians, it is a common fallacy to ascribe racial prejudice and discrimination to the moral gap between "creed" and "deed," or between profession and practice. Ministers plead with church members to practice what they preach, and both are baffled to understand why they do not. The dilemma pointed up by Myrdal and others is the distance between the acknowledged American creed and the racial valuations that actually guide behavior. Their prescription presumably would be then to close this cultural lag.

One of the contributions of Richard Niebuhr to Protestant thinking has been in pointing up the inadequacy of such moralism. This lag view was in some ways as typical of the later social gospel proponents of Protestantism as it is of secular humanitarians. By the nature of its diagnosis it fails to provide the corrective dynamic for conversion from prejudiced to nonprejudiced behavior. If the issue were merely one of an acknowledged distance between an equality professed and an inequality practiced, then increased moral gumption should be sufficient to close the gap. But the Pauline contradiction of knowing better and doing worse is not so readily overcome. It is not just negative inertia and caution which lie behind racial discrimination, but the positive counter-faiths which produce them. The "conflicting valuations" turn out to be a warfare of the gods in the soul of man. Ultimately the racial problem is not one of hypocrisy but of idolatry, not of cultural lag but of conflicting faiths.

In sum, the problem of race is at its deepest level not a factual problem, nor a moral problem, but a theological problem. Its locus is not finally in man's cultural environment, nor in his inadequate knowledge of racial information, nor yet in his moral inertia. These are satellite powers to the final demonic iniquity, man's inner perversity of will, his worship of the finite. To make this claim in no wise invalidates the veracity of the factual or moral data supplied by social science. It only claims to set them in a frame where their deepest meaning can be seen. The theological and voluntaristic approach characteristic of Niebuhr's orientation in ethics appears to be completely remote from the contemporary science of society. This is all the more reason to attempt now, in profile, a theological analysis of American racial beliefs and practices, to assess how the findings of the students of society in fact do honor to the wisdom of Christian doctrine.

2. RACIAL LIFE IN CREATION

A theological analysis of racial life starts with the action of God the Creator. Despite the occasional pious distortions of a Protestant biblicism to support segregation and even white supremacy as being the Creator's intention, the clear consensus of Christian theology is to affirm the doctrine of the unity and equality of racial life in creation. The notion of God the Creator, needless to say, has primary reference for the Christian to the *present* dynamic action of God, only secondarily to the original creation or to a long-past source of mankind's present historical existence. In the present tense, God *is* creating a primal order of racial unity and equality amid diversity. Beneath the manifest empirical inequalities that appear "after the Fall" through man's corruption of the created order, there is a *given* order of equality-in-diversity. "All men are created equal" is the democratic dogma which coincides with the Christian dogma that "He hath created of one blood all men to dwell on the face of the earth." But the variety of the order of creation is as much a "given" as the unity. Hence, unity does not mean sameness, identity, but a *community* of diverse selves and diverse races who stand on the common ground of creatureliness.

The Oxford Conference Report phrases the matter thus:

The existence of black races, white races, yellow races, is to be accepted gladly and reverently as full of possibilities under God's purpose for the enrichment of human life. And there is no room for any differentiation between the races as to their intrinsic value. All share alike in the concern of God, being created by him to bring their unique and distinctive contribution to his service in the world.[3]

[3] J. H. Oldham (ed.), *The Official Report of the Oxford Conference* (New York: Willett, Clark Co., 1937), p. 60. Cf. *ibid.*, pp. 213-18. Many comparable statements might be cited from Christian sources. The Preliminary Report for the Second World Council of Churches Assembly at Evanston, *The Christian Hope and the Task of the Church* (New York: Harper & Brothers, 1954), restates the same doctrine. Mankind as "created and sustained by God" is "of one blood, possess-

Contemporary sociology plainly confirms the Christian doctrine of life in creation. Coming at the problem "empirically" rather than as apologists for any faith, the vast majority of cultural anthropologists and students of racial and ethnic varieties have affirmed the doctrine of equality-in-diversity. The Evanston Conference Report points to this coincidence, quoting the UNESCO series: "Most scientists today are agreed that there are no innate biological differences between races that justify an assumption of the superior moral or intellectual capacity by any race over another."[4]

There are, to be sure, manifest empirical inequalities of myriad kinds and degrees among ethnic groups. The patent differentials, however, are generally regarded by social scientists as cultural traits, "acquired" characteristics, which can in no fair sense be regarded as biologically inherent. The manner of the inheritance of these cultural traits—to what degree environmental and to what degree "inward," for example—of course continues to be a moot point among social theorists. What is significant, however, is the view so universally maintained that the equality is in some sense *prior* to the inequality. The actual empirical levels of superiority and inferiority which we meet in daily racial contacts are treated as deviation from a norm which is "given." How more aptly could the Christian doctrine of creation be expressed? Indeed, is not some such doctrine already implicit *a priori* in the empirical investigation guiding it to its *a posteriori* conclusion? If inequality is as quantitatively, statistically apparent as is equality, how is the priority of equality established, except by a kind of faith in an order of creation as ground for distinguishing the essential from the unessential?

This point is not made to accuse the social scientist of duplicity in procedure or of substituting propaganda for scientific objectivity. It is only to suggest that ontological preference operates secretly within scientific method, and that in the case of the most reputably scientific studies of race the faith standpoint is implicitly a Christian one.

Is the order of creation manifest in any empirical sense? In answer to

---

ing a fundamental unity in spite of secondary differences" (p. 26). Roman Catholic doctrine grounds the same equality in natural law. See, for example, John Lafarge, *The Race Question and the Negro, A Study of the Catholic Doctrine of Interracial Justice* (New York: Longmans, Green and Company, 1944).

[4] *Op. cit.*, p. 10. The UNESCO series is entitled "The Race Question in Modern Science." Cf. Myrdal, *op. cit.*, chap. 4; Ruth Benedict, *Race, Science and Politics* (New York: Viking Press, 1940); Ruth Benedict and Gene Weltfish, *The Races of Mankind* (New York: Public Affairs Committee, 1943); Otto Klineberg (ed.), *Characteristics of the American Negro* (New York: Harper & Brothers, 1944), and *Race Differences* (New York: Harper & Brothers, 1935); Clyde Kluckhohn, "The Myth of Race," in *Religion and our Racial Tensions* (ed. by W. L. Sperry; Cambridge, Mass.: Harvard University Press, 1945); M. F. Ashley-Montague, *Man's Most Dangerous Myth: The Fallacy of Race* (2nd ed.; New York: Columbia University Press, 1945).

this question, it again becomes of interest to watch the coincidence of sociology and theology. In one sense, it is evident that one can never say "Lo here" or "Lo there," since what is actually encountered is racially prejudiced behavior, and inequalities to greater or less degree. Yet the spontaneity and freedom with which children play in an inter-racial situation, oblivious of racial difference—or, if aware, unconcerned—is in a sense an image of the original community of creation. Watching children treat each other in this way, as persons rather than as cases of color, adults comment: "They're perfectly natural about it." Honor is here paid spontaneously to God the Creator. This should not mean, incidentally, any sort of romanticism, Christian or sociological, which sees children as purely innocent because not yet imprisoned by bad culture. To see prejudice as a cultural characteristic captivating the innocent spirit of man quite overlooks the many ways in which even children illustrate egocentric behavior, and the alacrity with which they shortly adopt from their elders racial discriminations as devices for achieving status.

3. RACIAL LIFE "IN THE FALL"

We have already hinted at the comparison of the Christian doctrine of sin with the sociological analysis of racial prejudice and discrimination. From the standpoint of classical Christian thought, of course, racial prejudice is not one of a catalogue of sins, but is a facet or expression of the single sin of "pride," the rejection of the Infinite Sovereign Source of life and the attempt to set up as final some substitute sovereignty derived from the finite. In so far as fallen, man tends to make of himself or some collective projection of himself the center of love and value. Racial pride within and discriminatory practices are one ready way among many to "exchange the truth of God for a lie" and to worship "the creature rather than the Creator." The result of racial pride is the distortion of value-judgments, whereby the neighbor is regarded not in the universal community of creation as a "Thou," but by reference to the partial principle of color, as a case of this color or that, as an "It." The community of persons is thus broken and divided.[5] The equality of primal community is perverted into the inequality consequent upon the spiritual habit of looking at the other not only as different but as inferior.

The judgment of God is visited upon this racial sin of pride, even to our children's children, in the form of inner guilt and frustration, in bad conscience, and in the outward hostilities and discriminations that pitch one group against another. One need not look to the apocalyptic event

[5] See H. Shelton Smith, "Christian Faith and Racial Valuation," *Theology Today*, II, no. 2 (July, 1945), for a suggestive theological analysis of racial prejudice.

to discern the days of the divine wrath. To the eye of the Christian faith the *dies irae* are as empirically real as is creation.

There are many points of analogy between a sociological view of racial prejudice and discrimination, with its social results, and the Christian doctrines of "the Fall," sin, and judgment. To be sure, the sociologist is constitutionally skittish about affirming any doctrine of man, let alone a doctrine of sin. He lays claim, he feels, only to certain specific conclusions about specific behavior of particular men or societies, and even about these he must remain tentative. Any such inclusive generalization as would speak of man as "sinner" strikes him as unscientific. He is especially chary of "original sin," because of the pietistic connotation he attaches to the phrase. Yet in point of fact generalizations of one sort or another, fluid and tentative though they must be, are the stock in trade of social science. And the terms are incidental. What is important are the points at which Christian teaching receives striking empirical confirmation; or, to turn it about, the aptness of Christian terminology to fit the sociological findings.

For one thing, as to the *locus* of racial sin, it is of importance to note a sharp turn in contemporary analysis from environmentalism toward an inner voluntarism in the descriptions of the sources and power of racial prejudice. By no means is the truth of environmental conditioning canceled, but there is a greater tendency than in earlier studies to look for the trouble as much in a bad will as in a bad culture. The contradiction between these two sources of prejudice should not be quite so sharply put: any respectable theory of social causation must include the truth of outer and inner factors. But ever since the publication of Myrdal's *An American Dilemma*, if not earlier, the marked interest in the psychology of racial prejudice has turned the social analyst to look within, at the heart of man, for the issues of racial life. The will-to-power which sustains racial prejudice is no mere reflection of cultural conditioning; it is itself dynamic, generating and protecting outward forms of discrimination. In his own search, then, the sociologist seems to be led to follow the Christian analysis of the "mystery of iniquity," tracing it back to its final lair in the will of man.[6]

Secondly, the whole Christian understanding of the *nature* of sin, as being the perversion of a created good rather than the demonic opposite of good, finds ample confirmation in a close look at the racially prejudiced mind. By its very nature, racial prejudice can more fitly be called per-

[6] The recent literature dealing with the psychology of racial prejudice is extensive. See Appendix B of Simpson and Yinger, *op. cit.*, for a full bibliography. The writing of Gordon Allport, especially *The Nature of Prejudice* (Cambridge: Addison-Wesley Publishing Co., 1954) represents well a voluntarism similar to Christian anthropology and characteristic of the newer trend. The Preliminary Report for the Evanston Assembly notes the confluence of scientific with Christian theories of the psychological sources of racial tension (*op. cit.*, p. 17).

versity of love than hatred. What one encounters in everyday racial practice, for example, in the complex contacts of Negro and white in the Southern states, is rarely the simple, brutal, outright animosity of the Ku Klux Klansman. The respectable white middle-class citizen, the pillar of the local Baptist or Methodist church, faithful denizen of a Men's Bible Class, be he textile millworker, store clerk, or lawyer, is of a much more mixed mind and heart. In his own estimation he loves the Negro and takes care of him. It is striking to note, amid the myriad encounters of Negro and white in a semisegregated culture, the vast amount of kindness and concern displayed by the white man for his Negro neighbor, and the return in kind. A solid proponent of segregation will call the wrath of all the gods of states' rights down upon the Supreme Court for its decision in favor of integration. But he will also drive far out of his way to get medical aid for the children of his Negro maid. The doctor in the "new" South will give hours of patient and compassionate time in a free clinic for Negroes, yet will oppose the admission of a Negro surgeon to the state medical society.

However bewildering and contradictory a moral phenomenon this seems to be, it is not so strange when illumined by the Christian understanding of sin. The respectable, cultured form of racial pride is exactly this paternalistic love, the concern of the superior for the inferior. The Negro neighbor is "loved," is cared for. Thus, in the eyes of the paternalist and churchman the law of Christ is fulfilled in his own behavior.[7] His very kindness is an aid to self-deceit. He is blinded to the corruption at the heart of paternalistic love: that the neighbor is loved, not by reference to God the Creator, but by reference to the sinful order of white superiority and Negro inferiority. The neighbor is loved only in so far as he understands the terms of the transaction and "keeps his place." Thus, the mutual love of the order of creation is poisoned at its font by self-love. The resultant paternalism is a disorder of God's basic order of created community.

Thirdly, the *voluntarism* implied above leads to a direct sociological confirmation of the Christian view of the relation of the will to the mind in racial behavior. A shorthand way of stating the Christian view of man's behavior is to say that man is and does as he loves in his will, rather than as he thinks in his mind. His will uses his mind to confirm its loves and to justify itself by devising a structure of rationalization. In the parlance of William James, this is "selective thinking." One needs to look no further than to the term "prejudice" (prejudge) for

---

[7] George Kelsey cites the results of a poll conducted by a national magazine, wherein 80 per cent of a cross section of the American population felt that they had fulfilled the law of love in their specific actions toward members of a different race. "Racial Patterns and the Churches," *Theology Today*, IX, No. 1 (April, 1952), p. 70.

warrant for this view of human nature. Testimony from all sorts of empirical studies supports the notion of Simpson and Yinger that "a strong prejudice can have an almost paralyzing effect on observation and rational judgment."[8] To cite one instance:

In a study of the rumor process, Allport and Postman described to various persons a picture containing a Negro and a white man with a razor in his hand. After the description, each person was asked to tell all he could about the picture to a third person, the third to a fourth, and the fourth to a fifth. In over half of the experiments, the razor was reported to be in the Negro's hand; and in several the Negro was threatening the white man with it.[9]

The detection of the subrational springs of prejudice by social analysis stands in confused relation to the rationalistic assumptions about man's nature which are taken for granted in much contemporary social science. A working premise of many academic sociologists is that information and education of the mind will vanquish the darkness of ethnic tension and racial discrimination. Yet an extended scrutiny of the diagnosis has pointed up the inadequacy of this rationalism. MacIver, for instance, concludes that "very disappointing results" follow from "the imparting of specific information calculated to refute prejudice, information about the groups who are its victims, information proving that the opinions of prejudiced people about these groups are contradicted by the evidence. . . . The primary assault is on attitudes, not on opinions."[10] Is this not a backhanded way of saying that the converted will is prior in importance to the informed mind?

Fourthly, the relation of the will to the mind in racial prejudice is most clearly illustrated by the use of a stereotype or "group image," employed by the inner self in its will to superiority. Control by stereotype is the habit of ascribing certain characteristics to a race as innate or "natural" and conforming all particular individuals to the type, whether in fact they really display these characterictics or not.[11] What MacIver calls "the distorting mirrors" operate in all intergroup relations. In most instances, the group image is unfavorable. The Jew is clannish, polemical, grasping. The Oriental is polite, feline, devious, hypocritical. The Negro is shiftless, improvident, superstitious, irresponsible, oversexed, odorous, etc. In the mind of the Southern white, poor or genteel, there is a fixed mental image of his Negro neighbor: he is a figure of happy-go-lucky disposition, whose diet consists of watermelon, fried chicken, and gin, who loves garish colors, loud clothes, and white-walled tires, a devotee of titles and long words, banter and hilarity,

[8] *Op cit.*, p. 669.
[9] *Idem.*
[10] MacIver, *op. cit.*, pp. 221 ff. Cf. Goodwin Watson, *Action for Unity* (New York: Harper & Brothers, 1947), chap. II.
[11] Cf. MacIver, *op. cit.*, chap. 8; Myrdal, *op. cit.*, chap. 4; Allport, *op. cit.*, chap. 12.

who is childishly innocent of sexual proprieties and elemental cleanliness. Stories about Negro preachers, the stock in trade of white ministers' conferences, provide jovial ways of confirming the stereotype. On the other side of the color line, the Negro maintains his image of the white man just as firmly: he is sharp, mercenary, hypocritical, friendly if if you are humble, curt if you stand up to him.

The power of the group image is strengthened by the way in which empirical evidence, in daily contact, seems to justify the image. Here a "vicious circle" increases the tension, and prejudice begets prejudice. The "vicious circle" is a kind of sociological parallel to the Christian view of sin as "original," i.e., as self-perpetuating.[12] When the white person sees the common slovenliness and the irresponsibility of the Negro—particularly at the distance required by segregation—his attitude will not be shaken one iota if he is told that these are "cultural" characteristics, in some instances protective colorations put on by the Negro to get on in a hostile situation, or, in short, that these are *human* characteristics which would be displayed as readily by the white man were he in like circumstances. Such corrective information may even be lodged in the head, but the perverse beliefs of the heart, at the springs of action, remain intact.

The group image, which so bedevils racial relations, illustrates the Christian view of sin in an especially clear way. For both self-love and self-righteousness find their ready food and expression in the treatment of the other by stereotype. "The easiest way to magnify ourselves . . . is to belittle others."[13] As one student of the matter puts it, "We misconceive group prejudice when we think of it as primarily a prejudice *against* some one or more particular groups. . . . It is at bottom a prejudice in favor of 'My Own Group', as against all others, '*pro us*' prejudice, eternal, live and waiting, ready to be focused and intensified against Any Other Group."[14] So the stereotype is perhaps the most powerful inner instrument of collective self-love. It has the further convenience of enabling its prisoner to justify himself in righteousness, for he can find plentiful evidence to lift his self-esteem by lowering his esteem of others, and wherewith to thank God that he is not as other men are. Among many "poor whites" who are actually on a lower cultural plane than their Negro neighbors control by stereotype becomes the last pathetic bastion of their pride.

The Christian doctrine of sin finds ample verification in racial life at a final point, in the sober claim of Christian theology to the *universal-*

---

[12] Myrdal calls this the "principle of cumulation." *Op. cit.*, pp. 75-78.
[13] MacIver, *op. cit.*, p. 196.
[14] Karl Llewellyn, "Group Prejudice and Social Education," in R. M. MacIver (ed.), *Civilization and Group Relationships* (New York: Harper & Brothers, 1945), p. 13.

ity of sin. It is perfectly evident that intergroup tension, whether based on ethnic or political or racial difference, is a world problem, appearing with baffling complexity and intensity wherever diverse peoples meet. It is not so evident to some, however, that moral responsibility for prejudice is in greater or less degree a responsibility shared by the aggressors and the victims. On the face of it the minority group is more sinned against than sinning. To many a militant liberal group, such as the N.A.A.C.P., the Negro is the victim of segregation, not himself its perpetrator. In one sense this is true enough, but in a more profound sense it overlooks indubitable evidence that the minority often mirrors and retaliates with prejudice the prejudice shown to them. The tight social stratification within the Negro community itself,[15] the dissembling unction of the "handkerchief heads," who "Uncle Tom" it in order to gain status, the tendency to suspect all gestures of courtesy from white people as hypocritical, the conservatism which maintains a vested interest in segregation, the deep-rooted resentment and bitterness—all these are not of course Negro traits, but human habits which make their appearance among those whom culture has disinherited and dispossessed.[16] The corruption of the heart is universal, and spiritual arrogance—as well as contrition and compassion—is not the special habit of one ethnic group. This Christian perspective on the matter is a corrective of all oversimple ways of locating the fault and a caution to all reforming groups which regard themselves as incarnations of the power of light against darkness.

4. THE JUDGMENT OF GOD

The sociologist who might concur in the analysis of prejudice thus far made would yet be reluctant to push further with the theologian to claim to discern a divine judgment at work in this pattern. His own categories of interpretation have no apparent space for such a bizarre and unempirical concept as the wrath of God. Such talk he would leave to the jackleg preacher or the deep-South novelist. Yet for the Christian the judgment of God is apparent *within* the empirical order, even though unapparent to a pure empiricism. The sovereignty of God is not

---

[15] Myrdal, *op. cit.*, chap. 32.

[16] George Kelsey supports the judgment of Reinhold Niebuhr that "there is an inequality of guilt between black and white people, but an equality of sin." Kelsey finds "the spiritual ingredients of the Negro's form of prejudice are resentment, bitterness, fear, and suspicion." He points out too that a myth of spiritual superiority has developed among many Negro Christians. "It is not uncommon to hear a Negro Christian say, 'I cannot trust the white man's religion.' The implication is that he can and does trust the Negro's religion." ("Racial Patterns and the Churches," *Theology Today* (April, 1952), p. 75.) Cf. an article by the same author in W. S. Nelson (ed.), *The Christian Way in Race Relations* (New York: Harper & Brothers, 1948), pp. 29-51. Also C. S. Johnson, *Patterns of Negro Segregation* (New York: Harper & Brothers, 1943), chap. 14.

escaped in racial sin. God confronts man as Accuser and as Troubler in the very intensity of the contradiction between creed and practice, in the desperation with which the self justifies itself in its racial pride, in the haste with which it covers its sin with pretensions to morality. The thrashings of the troubled conscience caught on the hook of God's judgment are nowhere more easily seen than in the clichés and phrases which are commonly made to justify segregation and the *status quo*.

"The Negroes are happier with their own people." "They prefer their own schools and churches." This is confidently pronounced by the opponent of integration in the name of the good of the minority group. The remark of the attorney general of Georgia, in response to the claim in the Supreme Court's decision that separation leads to a feeling of inferiority, was this: "Segregation does not present to the Negroes that we know in Georgia an inferiority complex. The Negroes in this state don't suffer that. I think perhaps they will suffer it more if they're forced to integrate with white children because complex and psychological factors will be a constant reminder that they are not up to par with the average white person."[17] In short, the good attorney general has the best interests of the Negro at heart.

Or the self-justification in the sight of God as Judge takes the form of the pietism of the Christian churchman, who will attempt to overcome the opposition between Christian morality and racial prejudice by a preoccupation with transcendent moral principles, avoiding all local application. "If men would only give their hearts to the Lord Jesus, all these social problems would be solved." The majority who bleat such pious sentiments accept segregation as of the order of common life, amoral, "our way of doing things." They simply cannot understand why some radical church groups call segregation "sinful." They manage to hide their sin from God, even from themselves, by an intense avowal of Christian devotion.

God's action as Judge is not alone to be found in the secret places of the prejudiced heart, in its confusion and troublement, in its often fierce self-righteousness, the more arrogant precisely because the more inwardly tender. It is also to be found in outer ways. God judges white pride through the Negro's response to that pride. Just as in international life the Christian sees God's hand in the power of communism as a judgment on the sins of capitalistic democracy, or colonial imperialism, so in modern racial life the Christian of sensitive and contrite spirit can acknowledge the divine chastisement upon his own sin and that of his people in the recent rise of aggressive Negro leadership, demanding equal rights and equal status.

The Christian will also be alert to the presence of divine judgment in the failure of the churches, at this point in their life, to be the con-

[17] AP News Release, May 24, 1954.

science of the community, to stand in clear Christian witness for the unity in Christ against the world's divisions which they have taken into their own life.[18] No denial of their Lord is more poignant than this, where the churches have become social clubs, complacent mixtures of pietism and Rotarianism. Out of comfort, fear, and blindness the churches have for the most part capitulated to the segregation and prejudice of the world, and have become salt without savor.

The inevitable judgment that follows from such worldliness is that the churches are "cast out and trodden under foot of man." Seeking their life in quantity, they lose their life in quality and only earn the scorn of men. No clearer illustration of this could be found than in the treatment of churches characteristic of the sociological literature on race. It is a dogma taken for granted by most sociologists that religion is a "function of culture." And in fact this is confirmed by the actual behavior of the churches which the sociologist encounters, for what he discovers is the "escapism" of Negro churches, with their practices compensatory for cultural frustrations,[19] and the inertia of the white churches. Simpson and Yinger conclude: "Although the Protestant churches stress (1) the dignity and worth of the individual and (2) the brotherhood of man, the racial behavior patterns of most church members have not been substantially affected by these principles."[20] No one of the major treatises on racial relations looks to the churches for any promise of leadership or guidance. "Few Christian churches have ever been, whether in America or elsewhere, the spearheads of reform."[21] Educational, legal, and political forces outside the Church are expected to succeed in bringing into concrete actuality the principles which the churches avow.

For the Christian who believes in the Church within the churches as a community with a common memory and hope in God in Christ there are grounds for certainty that this is not the whole of the story. The churches cannot be dispensed with merely as functions of culture. To the degree that the churches attend to a voice transcendent to that of culture, they escape the sociologist's generalization; they become

[18] One of the important twentieth century treatments of this failure of the churches is Richard Niebuhr's *Social Sources of Denominationalism* (New York: Henry Holt & Company, 1929). Chapter IX of this book, on "Denominationalism and the Color Line," is a sharp indictment of racism in the churches. Frank Loescher, *The Protestant Church and the Negro* (New York: Association Press, 1948), and Dwight Culver, *Negro Segregation in the Methodist Church* (New Haven: Yale University Press, 1953), are full documentations of Niebuhr's judgments. Cf. also Niebuhr's treatment of worldliness in the church in "The Disorder of Man in the Church of God." Amsterdam Assembly Series, vol. I, (New York: Harper & Brothers, 1948).

[19] Simpson and Yinger, *op. cit.*, p. 525. Cf. Myrdal, *op. cit.*, chap. 40.

[20] *Op. cit.*, p. 546.

[21] Myrdal, *op. cit.*, p. 877.

again "a city set on a hill," themselves instruments of judgment and redemption for culture. But to the great extent that they are indeed
worldly they deserve the scorn of the very society they seek to satisfy
and the casual dismissal they earn at the hands of the social scientists.
The Christian in the Church will accept this, in contrition and shame,
as the hand of God working through the affairs of men.

5. THE GRACE OF GOD IN RACIAL REDEMPTION

Racial sin and the judgment which is its inexorable consequent are
for the Christian neither final nor inevitable. They are to be seen as
within a process ultimately redemptive. For the final faith of the
Christian is that God judges in order to heal, that he casts down in order
to renew, that within history he is constantly restoring life out of
death and community out of disorder and warfare. Creation, Judgment,
and Redemption are not three discrete actions of God; but as God is
One Lord, they are simultaneous and concurrent. Redemption is to be
seen in Creation and healing felt, for the believer, even in the suffering
which attends a disordered world. In racial life, the redemptive process
is one wherein men are freed from the bondage of pride, from control
by stereotype, from the dividing sword of scorn, into spontaneous and
free relations, into an integrated community of mutual respect and
service like that originally intended in creation.

Though in the main unconsciously and with certain significant devia-
tions, sociological prescriptions about race relations confirm the redemptive faith of Christianity. Again, this is more true of the hidden
assumptions of social science than of its particular statements; but it is
these assumptions, after all, that are crucial.

The first point is so plain that it may readily be overlooked: the very
trust of the sociologist that improved race relations are possible, that a
segregated society can gradually become an integrated society, that
"intergroup" tensions can be reduced, displays a reliance on God
the Redeemer, in however attenuated and remote a form. For it is a
mark of a faith, derived extraneously from the facts, that there is an
order of universal community more valid than this present broken
and prejudiced one, whose validity the scientist counts on to "come
through" in time. Though, as will be seen shortly, this faith is also
unlike the Christian, it is at least like it in that it is sustained by a hope
for the restoration of true community.

Moreover, the Christian theologian can certainly concur with the
common assumption of most reputable social theorists: that integration
presents, among the viable options of racial relations, the morally
normative form.[22] As over against amalgamation, on the one hand,
which would absorb all differences into one "racial" type, or segregation

[22] Simpson and Yinger, *op. cit.*, p. 649.

(parallel cultures), on the other, which attempts to achieve equality in separation, integration would mean a relationship of equality and mutuality, where "every man, woman, and child shall be free to enter into, and contribute to, the welfare of all, without any restrictions or disabilities based on color caste."[23]

The long and troubled history of Negro-white relations in the Southern United States, with its movement from slavery through segregation to the present borderline situation between segregation and integration, is far too involved to traverse here, even briefly. The significant thing to the Christian in these chapters in the story of our life is how they verify the trust in God the Judge and Redeemer. History becomes "the laboratory of the abstract ideas of theology and ethics,"[24] where "the glory of the coming of the Lord" can be seen through the eyes of faith.

With the master-slave community smashed by the Civil War, the Reconstruction era saw the slow development of segregation in Southern custom and law. At its best, this legislation represented a feasible transitional arrangement, which, in theory at least, by substituting a wall for the ceiling of slavery, proposed to lift all restrictions upon Negro development and enable both Negro and white to achieve peace and concord by separation and mutual respect. Certainly under the aegis of this ideal, if not in fact because of it, there has been an astounding and rapid rate of growth to cultural maturity out of bewilderment and dependence on the part of the Negro minority. The ideal fostered, both in law and to a greater or less extent in public sentiment, the norm of equality. It is interesting to note that the Supreme Court decision of 1896 (*Plessy v. Ferguson*) which maintained the constitutionality of the separate-but-equal formula was at the time considerably ahead of much Southern sentiment which had no strong affection for racial equality even as a legal standard. In time, however, separate-but-equal has become the rallying point for racial conservatism.

By the process which corrupts even good custom and by the "idolization of an ephemeral institution," this segregation which was partially redemptive has now become the enemy of Christian community, the occasion for the sin of inhumanity of man to man, and the judgment of God. In common practice segregation is rarely, if ever, mutually administered or the fence lines determined by both sides. Segregation thus becomes a power instrument of white domination, and the wall becomes again a ceiling. Time and again separate-but-equal means separate and unequal, in public facilities, in education, in transportation, in eco-

---

[23] Buell Gallagher, *Color and Conscience* (New York: Harper & Brothers, 1946), p. 173. See *The Christian Hope and the Task of the Church*, pp. 22-24, for a similar arrangement of alternatives: integration, pluralism, segregation.

[24] Richard Niebuhr, *The Kingdom of God in America* (Chicago and New York: Willett, Clark and Co., 1937), p. viii.

nomic opportunity, not because of anything external in the laws but because of the perversity of human pride in taking practical exceptions to its own professed standard of value in order to serve its own interests. When the Supreme Court decision of 1954 found separate educational facilities to be "inherently" unequal, the moral premises for such a legal judgment can be seen to be implicitly Christian, by reference both to the Christian doctrine of sin and to the Christian norm of community. The decision itself is in effect an instrument of both judgment and redemption: of judgment in that it cuts down all the legal and pious self-justifications that support segregation, of redemption in that it points the way to a fresh beginning and a new life in more genuine community.

In still another way the moral preference of contemporary social science for integration confirms the Christian view of community under God. Integration is an occasion for redemption in that it involves an escape from the sin of control-by-stereotype which so easily besets those who live in a segregated way. Segregation always leads to the habit of treating the other race, at a distance, over there, with greater or less justice. The other person becomes "a case," an instance of a group. Integration, on the other hand, with all its opportunities for mutuality and intimacy, enables the white man and the Negro to know each other as persons, to thrust aside the stereotype, to move from "interracial" to "interpersonal" relations. This fulfills the radical individualism and universalism of the Christian ethic. Part of the joy in this salvation lies in a new-found freedom, which in Pauline terms is freedom from a will in bondage to the law of sin and death, the sin of stereotype and the death of persons. Such a freedom and such a respect for persons in community are the inherently Christian grounds sustaining the social theorist's case for integration.

On the other hand, there are points where Christian theology provides perspectives on the issues of racial relations profoundly different from those of current sociology, points where it finds the redemption there offered partial and inadequate. Such corrective as the theologian offers to the sociologist in no wise lessens his indebtedness for the scientist's service in explicating and documenting the human problem.

In the first instance, in so far as racial tension is seen with Myrdal to be an internal problem, a problem in the conscience, the gap between creed and deed is expected by him and many like-minded sociologists to be in itself redemptive. In effect, man saves himself racially by the progressive approximation in practice to the ideals of equality and mutual respect which he has himself posited. Man initiates, pursues, and completes his own racial salvation. In terms of its whole world view, Christian theology finds this two-dimensional picture quite too moralistic and flat. A third dimension of the process must be seen. It is the

Christian confession that we are redeemed racially, as in all other areas of life, by the grace of God, by an obedient and glad response to his forgiving and recovering work in human life. We are not the initiators, but first the recipients, then the reflectors of love. "We love, because he first loved us." We forgive as we are forgiven.

The norm of community where men regard each other as persons in mutual love, the integrated community, is not of human making, but is set there by a divine hand, both as a principle of judgment whereby men know their sin of prejudice and as a principle of grace and forgiveness whereby men are turned from their prejudice. To account adequately, in short, for the presence and power of the norm of human brotherhood in history, one must go beyond humanity and history and say that the norm is grounded in the revelation of God's grace. Theologically, of course, this is a primer point, but it is precisely where sociology must be "born again" in its premises in order to understand fully its own enterprise.

A close corollary is the claim of Christianity that, as "out of the heart are the issues of life," redemption in racial ways must be from within, in a changed heart expressing itself in outward nondiscriminatory behavior. The problem of inward *versus* environmental change is enormously intricate, and quite beyond the scope of the present study. It is curious to note, however, that, whereas in diagnosis social science has been increasingly "inward" and psychological, its prescriptions continue to be consistently "outward." It is through a more favorable outer context of human relationships that prejudice is to be overcome, it says. "I do not see any hope for control of the mass phenomenon by reconditioning the individual," one eminent sociologist put it, perhaps more extremely than would most.[25] MacIver concurs with Goodwin Watson in the judgment that "it is more important to attack segregation than it is to attack prejudice."[26]

The Christian should be quick to acknowledge that the environmentalism typical of sociological prescription is itself a rightful judgment on the failure of much moralism, especially that of the churches. The hearts changed by mass revivalism remain remarkably unchanged in racial affections. The Christian also is prepared to see the redemptive possibility of public law. Even where, as with the sequence of Supreme Court decisions outlawing segregation, the law of the land is ahead of private sentiment, it serves to create the outward circumstances conducive to changed attitudes within. Christian ethics cannot rest content with the easy generalization that "You can't legislate morality" any more than with its opposite, "There ought to be a law."

[25] John Dollard, "Acquisition of New Social Habits," in Ralph Linton (ed.), *The Science of Man* (New York: Columbia University Press, 1945), p. 463.
[26] MacIver, *op. cit.*, p. 90; cf. Goodwin Watson, *Action for Unity.*

What Christian ethics *is* prepared to say, however, is that a truly redeemed community of any sort, in political, economic, or racial dealings, must be freely and gladly willed from within. Law cannot run too far ahead of supporting sentiment and a community, however stringently integrated by law, could not be called redeemed if law encountered only surly conformity and private prejudice. The response, then, of the Christian is a double one: knowing as he does the recalcitrance and duplicity of the human heart in its sin, he will support those outward measures of legislation which check the evil of discrimination and which effect the outward conditions of mutual community. But knowing also the peril of "social engineering," a pitfall close to the road of sociological method, he will seek in every way at hand to hold open the inner sources of action, in himself and in his neighbors, to the corrective and forgiving power of God's grace.

Finally, Christian theology provides an important perspective on the practical strategies of amelioration of racial life in that it keeps a sense of the distance between the Kingdom of God and racial integration. These are by no means the same thing, and the awareness that they are not is a necessary corrective to a sociological messianism which speaks as if the elimination of segregation is the one more river to cross to enter the promised land. Just as segregation (or even racial prejudice) cannot be treated as the root of all evil but only as a noxious symptom of the deeper sin of self-sufficiency and pride, so conversely integration cannot be taken as the panacea of racial troubles. In the present borderline situation between segregation and integration certain liberal groups seek immediate integration and at all costs. Excessive zeal for this cause sometimes will sacrifice persons to its ends. Impatient for the new order, it neglects to offer the cup of cold water in the present one. There are parallels here to the Marxist fallacy of locating all evil in property, and redemption in its abolition. What follows for such misplaced fanaticism is the disillusionment of discovering that even the integrated society has its own stubborn problems, its own injustices not now forseen, its own occasions for human cruelty.

The Christian response is not trust in racial integration, or any other human arrangement as final, but a radical obedience to the God and Father of our Lord Jesus Christ, who gives and requires the love of the neighbor in and for himself. Walking the difficult borderline between segregation and integration, the response of obedience is a double one: (*a*) an ethic of *alleviation* within segregation and (*b*) the radical ethic of *reconstruction* which cuts through the lines that segregation draws. It is important that both of these be maintained. Even within a fallen and interim order of segregation, there is room for Christian action, for expressions of *agape*, for the unconventional tasks of tenderness which are to be done out of love, without waiting for the removal of segregation. Also, there is a Christian obligation to seek the greatest possible equality *within* the segregation that stubbornly prevails. One who would defy all segregation, and never compromise with it, has lost sight of the Christian insight that human beings are the ultimate units in question, whose needs must be served, despite and within a bad order. At the same time there is the revolutionary redemptive task of the overthrow of the system of segregation and the support of policies of integration. For it is through those outward arrangements created by integration that best can be realized the inner ethic of reconciliation, the recovery of interpersonal community—not the meeting of Negro and white groups, self-conscious of their racial equality, but a family reunion of individuals who are all the children of one Father.

8.

THE SITUATION OF
THE BELIEVER

JULIAN HARTT

PROFESSOR H. Richard Niebuhr has indicated in several ways how large the problem of religious relativity looms upon his theological horizons.[1] In *The Meaning of Revelation* he has pursued the problem in a richly suggestive way. I propose to deal with certain aspects of the situation of the Christian believer to which Niebuhr has not devoted a great deal of explicit attention. This venture is projected along lines independent of Niebuhr's views—as will be quickly and easily apparent —but lines which are suggested by his interpretation of Revelation.

In Niebuhr's view the situation of the religious man is embraced in an inclusive relativity, a relativity so inclusive that there seems but little to be gained in saying "the situation of the *religious* man," since these relativities are not at all constituted by one's faith but rather define one's whole being and thus one's religious life as well. Nonetheless, there is much to be gained by pursuing the point of religious relativity, since religious attitudes and beliefs are peculiarly susceptible to the great evil of absolutization. Of their religion more than of anything else people are likely to say, "This is the Lord's doing," and to derive from this claim all manner of preferential, prideful and wholly erroneous conclusions.

The dimensions of prime importance in the believer's situation are History, the Community, and God. In his treatment of each, Niebuhr builds an impressive case for its wholly relative character. In respect to history the believer stands at a particular point, from which he cannot reasonably hope or claim to comprehend the whole course and meaning

[1] Cf. *The Meaning of Revelation* (New York: The Macmillan Company, 1941), pp. vii, 16, *passim*.

of history. In respect to community, the Christian believer finds that his being-as-a-Christian is defined by a particular community which is finite and which is neither *the* pure church nor the all-inclusive community for *all* religious men. The community in which the believer finds himself is but one in a rich plurality of unique corporate expressions of religious experience and conviction. Finally, in respect to God, the believer is one finite spirit over against whom stands the absolute being, that One whom the finite cannot dream of comprehending in his richness and fullness. Ranging far into the past, and standing alongside the Christian believer, there is the whole company of finite spirits, of every conceivable religious persuasion, each with a mind of his own as to what God is and as to what God requires. Thus, at these three decisive points the believer finds his being defined by patterns of relationships, indeed, defined so comprehensively and exhaustively that, as Niebuhr seems to see the situation, the believer cannot properly and significantly conceive himself enjoying any being, value and power outside of these relations.

In each of these dimensions of relativity Niebuhr undertakes to show the presence and significance of objective, and so far independent, components; he contends that what the finite spirit sees or grasps is *there*, in its own right and with its own power. But our minds and imaginations impart to everything apprehended their own unique, time- and culture-conditioned qualities, concretely and practically inseparable from the objective realities. The objective realities are finally controlling; we do not succeed in making God and the world in accordance with our own images, however much we try. Our images are in the end conformed to being, not being to our images.

Granted Niebuhr's "critical" (Kantian) idealism, this power of correction implicit in Being could not be *clearly* exerted upon us in the realm of *cognition*, since *everything* there is patterned by the mind itself. We might say: *something* is being demanded by what is there, other or more than we are according it. But satisfactory determination of *what* is being demanded could only be inspired guesswork, unless we supposed that the *whole* demand was communicated, somewhere in the past, a supposition contrary to what Niebuhr takes to be the fact.

It is no part of my intention to argue that we ever do in fact find ourselves outside of relations. I propose rather to deal with the question whether the situation of the believer is apprehended by belief, or, on the other hand, whether there is a primary cognition or apprehension of this situation. Thus, we are committed to a kind of ontological analysis of the situation of the believer as recipient of and participant in Revelation. I shall argue that the "primitive" situation of the believer is not itself constituted by *belief*. For this purpose it is necessary first of all to distinguish *belief* from *apprehension* as a primary cognitive act. With this distinction in hand I shall try to show how the self-cognition of the believer is really an apprehension of a *finite terminal individual*.

How, then, is *belief* distinguished from *apprehension*? Belief is a disposition of the mind to accept an assertion or a proposal as true. In this disposition the power of mind called "will" is the prime mover and that power called "understanding" is a secondary mover. *Apprehension*, on the other hand, is a primary cognitive act, that is, an act by which an event is registered in the mind or by which a quality of an actual entity is grasped as such by the mind. To be "apprehensive" in ordinary language is to grasp a situation as alarming, formidable, or the like, as though the feelings of anxiety provoked by the situation were a definitive clue to its meaning. What is important in this common-sense understanding of *apprehension* is just the recognition of seizure, as it were, by the actualities.

As to *terminal individual*, I use the phrase to signify an actual entity which is not exhaustively constituted by its relations and which is therefore an irreducible "term," a "substantive," etc., in the *ordo essendi*.

The intent of the ontological analysis proposed here is to show, first, that the relativities do not exhaust the realities and, second, that analysis of the situation of the believer carries us necessarily into a realm other than belief.

1. THE ONTOLOGICAL SITUATION

The situation of the believer is not itself apprehended by belief. The situation of the believer is the content of a primary cognition. Here we must make a distinction in the meaning of "situation." The term suggests, on the one hand, the realities of one's place in history and culture and, on the other, one's mode of being *qua* being. It may be granted that what is here divided analytically is concretely indivisible; and furthermore, that *how* one is concerned about his mode of being *qua* being may reflect the mood of a cultural ethos and epoch. Nonetheless, "cultural situation" and "ontological situation"[2] are not purely substitutable for each other. What suffices as analysis and interpretation of one will not suffice for the other.

The ontological situation is grasped in a primary cognition or apprehension. A primary apprehension is one not mediated or otherwise determined by society and culture. It is a point of raw encounter of the self and being. If for the moment we may employ the terms of sensory perception, a primary apprehension yields (or relates the self to) a "brute fact-datum." To recognize and, even more, to name properly and acceptably what is so grasped involves reflective and expressive

---

[2] "Ontological" currently has a richer significance than "metaphysical," as well as a different one. It is permitted to take into the ontological situation more of the vividness and thickness of actual existence than survived in the generalities of classical metaphysics, e.g., Aristotle's.

activities upon which the social context exercises considerable influence. But the activities of recognition and of naming do not exhaust cognition, the primary element of which is apprehension or the grasping of what is.

What, then, is the ontological situation so apprehended? One knows that one exists, that one exists as a finite being, that one exists as a person. Let us express the ontological situation in this crude schematism:

(*a*) I know that I am (I exist).

(*b*) I know that I exist as a finite being.

(*c*) I know that I am a person.

The ontological situation is existence, finitude, personhood.

(*a*) "I know that I exist" means that there is something going on about which I cannot entertain the slightest serious doubt—that is, as to its going on. At the reflective level I may ask myself in which of two possible worlds this going-on is (or was) taking place: in a "dream world" or in the "real world." But the activity itself has itself to be grasped before such a question can be asked. When it is asked, for that matter, the question pertains much more obviously to the "object" of the activity than it does to the activity itself. For example, I may ask whether the hideous succubus which stalked me in the night is the substance of dream or of actuality, but the question cannot be put to the terror I felt. However baseless and base that feeling, *it purely was*. To which we must add: the I who had it (or which it had) was no afterthought conjured *ex nihilo* for the grammarian's satisfaction. The apprehended (felt) activity is an *occurrence* (as when we say, "It occurred to me"), not a mere event. It is immediately related to an agent or subject-being; it is grasped from *within*, not perceived as simply *there*. If Descartes supposed that this subject-being in and of an occurrence spontaneously (or upon inspection) erupted into the metaphysical structure of a "thinking substance," he was mistaken. He was correct if he meant only to call attention to the fact that this same subject endures in a considerable range of occurrent-activities (e.g., feeling, thinking, willing), and that its activities constitute the only forthcoming point in the whole world out of which and upon which community appears.

(*b*) "I know that I am finite" means that the activity of which I am the subject is transparently determinate, limited and bounded. Another activity takes its place, and this replacement is also wholly determinate, limited and bounded. "Determinate" means that the activity (so far as it is cognized at all) has a specific character and that it is in this way apprehended.[3] "Limited" means that any given activity endures so long

---

[3] There appear to be no generalized activities, no properly indeterminate ones; and the common-sense expression, "I do not know what I want but I want *something*," does not really point to an exception. We see no exception either in one way of reading the existentialistic concept of anxiety, viz., as a kind of indeterminate and generic situation. To feel anxiety, to be anxious, is to feel and to be one thing or one way rather than another.

and no longer; and this fact is apprehended in the activity itself, it is not a generalization read back into the activity. In the grip of a feeling one may wonder whether it will last forever (e.g., despair). This is hyperbolic wonderment and expression. "Bounded" means that no particular activity defines or includes so much of the world as is given in experience.[4]

Actually these conditions (determinate, limited, bounded) do not need to be established discursively or through conceptual analysis. At the reflective-expressive level one is well advised to choose carefully the words in which these aspects of existence are communicated; but the realities so designated are not the products of reflection and expression. They stand out in everything I do; and they are grist for the mill of metaphysical judgment and religious affirmation of the contingency of the self and the finitude of created individual substances. To be sure, primary cognition is not the sole component in such judgments and affirmations. Judgments concerning the ontological situation are the fruit of reflection. This reflection occurs in a social context from which the reflecting person obtains his food for thought—that is, the expressive form of his thought and his speech. In the Christian context the expressive form incorporates concepts such as guilt and sin, which to be efficacious (concretely significant) must be woven into the texture of individual feeling and volition. Accordingly, there is some warrant for treating the ontological situation of the believer as though sin and guilt were constitutive features of it in just the same way that finiteness is. Constitutive in some mode and sense they may be, but *not* as finiteness is. Considered as categories, guilt and sin serve to identify the believer with a believing community. Considered as categories they do not define the roots of the ontological situation. The believer may declare that sin goes to the roots of his being; but this does not mean that he apprehends sin as he apprehends the essential limitations of his being, in respect to the scope, power and perdurability of his actions.

(c) "I know that I am a person" means that I apprehend myself as one apprehending an other and as being apprehended by an other. This brings us closer to the full reality of subject-being; for so long as one is aware of oneself as simply involved in particular activities, that is, as

---

[4] The extreme cases here are mystical experience, especially ecstasy, and the unreality-systems of paranoidal personality. As to ecstasy we ask: Does it have any noetic quality or function as such at all? This is a very difficult question, surely. So long as one is in ecstasy (it may be supposed) one *attends* to nothing (no being). The powers of attention are short-circuited by an immense expansion of the powers of enjoyment (immediate participation). And when one is no longer in ecstasy one may assign to ecstasy a certain knowledge-value, perhaps on pragmatic grounds, for which there is in the nature of the case no direct confirmation. As to the unreality-systems of the paranoidal personality, his world-claiming, world-creating activities violate the real world, as they are also acts of self-violation; the world has to be coerced to take shape and place within the dominant activities of his ego.

being their "subject," one is not yet aware of the complexity of subject-being. To be a subject is to be apprehended by an other. This does not mean to be simply or primarily an *object* of another's activities.[5] It means to be involved in activity which embraces and qualifies two human beings *qua* human; activity which does not do something *to* one of these, but in which two people do something *with* each other. In this activity one may have the initiative; but the other does not *mechanically* respond; the response of the other modifies the situation as such; and thus, properly understood, initiative does not remain the prerogative and distinction of either to the exclusion of the other. Thus, it can be said with some propriety that to be as a person and to know oneself as person is to be grasped by activity which arises and is sustained beyond oneself but whose meaning and essential character come to light—are revealed—in oneself. There is something to be gained in so putting it; and this something is a clear gain over the atomizing tendencies of modern individualism. But there is also a danger in so putting it; and this danger is oblivion of the finite terminal individual. It appears to me that Niebuhr's view of the self and its relations sails perilously close to this reef. I may be mistaken in this. In any case I want to explore now the question whether there is an apprehension of a finite terminal individual in the self-cognition of the believer.

It seems to me that this question is to be answered in the affirmative. The situation of the believer is defined by apprehension of himself as a *terminal individual.* For certain purposes it may be supposed that experience is a nexus of relations. Does this imply that the person is a function of this nexus? Certainly this conclusion appears irresistible to many thinkers today: philosophers, theologians and social scientists. How far Niebuhr is prepared to go in this direction is not clear to me. But I believe that the "dialogic" view of Revelation and of the person—a view which he has developed very suggestively—requires something very different from the relational-nexus conception of the human situation. This I must now undertake to establish.

Let us say, first of all, that the aptest metaphor in Christian tradition for Revelation is speaking and listening: the utterance, reception and acknowledgment of the "word." This word is creative: it makes some-

[5] To be reduced to the status of being an object is, in point of fact, a double reduction: (*a*) a fall from the estate of being a subject, (*b*) a narrowing of the field of attention, *this activity* (*reduction itself*) *being participated in by both parties to the encounter.* (*a*) *is a consequence of* (*b*), *since one can fall decisively from subject-being only with and by one's own concurrence.* If another proposes to treat my body as though it were a *thing,* he is either stupidly ignorant of what this does to *me* or he does it to strike at me, to humiliate and to subjugate me. But even though he has absolute command of my body, he has command of my spirit only upon my abdication. He can kill me, but until I die or lose consciousness *I* shall see him and he has no power whatever over what *I* put into that look. (Cf. William Faulkner, *Light in August,* Joe Christmas' death scene.)

thing to be where there was nothing. The word is also re-creative: it revitalizes (resurrects) what was passive or moribund. But we are speaking metaphorically; and we have reason to suspect that metaphysics is sometimes a stowaway in the ship of metaphor. Specifically, the metaphor of the "word" would not ordinarily lead us to attribute to utterance the power to create *ex nihilo*. Such communicative rapport as the word may establish presupposes *integral existences* as the defining parties in that dialogue. The functions of the word are all consequent upon such existences (though we should take all reasonable precautions against stirring impiously the dust of the ancient quarrel: Which is first, person or word?).

There are of course facts and testimonies which cannot be conscientiously ignored in this context. For example, the inward testimony that our personhood comes into being only in the give-and-take of "dialogue." And there are the facts concerning "feral man"—the human animal becomes a person only when he hears and participates in human speech. But testimony and fact establish nothing ontologically. They only confirm when they are summoned by a prevenient metaphysical decision, viz., to equate "come into being" with "have a determinate manifest form" and "have meaning in and for a given and determinate society." This decision, while perhaps understandable as response to multiple pressures in our climate of opinion, seems to me to be wrong—wrong in itself and wrong as a metaphysical base upon which to erect a Christian view of Revelation.[6] Relative to the first claim, that the view is wrong which makes person a consequence of word, there are two general possibilities of argument: (*a*) an indirect and transcendental demonstration and (*b*) an appeal to evidence directly inspectable. These two lines of argument will be briefly examined.

(*a*) It may be said that an integral individual is a presupposition of intelligible discourse and thought (if the requirements of discourse are different from the requirements of thought). This argument appears to be identical with the argument for the persistence in and over time of a self-identical being; but perhaps the appearances are misleading, until at least we discover what being "integral" entails and presupposes. Suppose, for instance, "integral existence" means substantial being rather than modal being (which I think is the case). It would follow that in any given moment of time such a being would act as a source and center of power and not merely or simply as an attribute of another being

[6] This may seem an odd distinction. Surely if a view is wrong in itself, nothing more by way of defect or error need be added to it to make it wrong as a "metaphysical base, etc." Yet, since Christian theologians are in our time customarily little concerned with metaphysics, and since many of them reject the very notion of a metaphysical base for the doctrine of revelation, it is possibly useful to make a distinction not valid in itself.

or as an effect of another being. But it would not follow that such a being (substantial rather than modal) must enjoy "transcendence" over indefinite expanses of time, for in or at the end of any given moment this being might cease to exist. Now within the moment of its efficacy part of its power might be to seize its own image in the remembrance of its past. To do so would not be power over the past in the sense in which this substantial individual enjoys power in the present. (Whether there is such a thing as "power over the past" is a debatable question.) Nor would it be correct to say that the being of such an individual is partly in the past and partly in the present, if by "being" we happen to mean "efficacy of operation." A person is not this kind of "time-binding" individual. What is now, once was; but "once was" reveals both the fact of passage and the relinquishing of suzerainty over what has passed. At any given present moment only the shreds of suzerainty relative to what has passed remain; and the name for these shreds is Image.

Thus, it appears that at least one argument of classic vintage for the identity of the self through passage will not accomplish very much for the integral nature of the person. Where shall we find another argument? In a first cousin of the old argument: in the argument from the multiplicity and real differences in "phases" of action to a real, potent, unifying and organizing "center." What follows is a rough sketch of such an argument.

(i) Upon occasion and perhaps characteristically the things which persons resolve to do, and actually do, are constituted of parts. A part is not necessarily disjunctive in time from other parts. Objectively viewed a "part" or a phase is something done in the pursuit or furtherance of an aim broader and fuller than that particular action. For example, to rescue a child drowning in the middle of a lake one must first traverse the intervening watery distance. As we view the matter ordinarily, the program "rescuing the child" is one program and one action, and thus "traversing the intervening distance" is simply one of the things involved in "rescuing the child," as seizing the child in firm grip and moving off toward land with him is also. But this simply shows that the program comprehends various parts or phases.

(ii) But "parts" is an unhappy term simply because it suggests a kind of mechanical and external relationship. To the contrary, the end, the aim, lives in the phase, dominates and directs it, as it were, to its ful-fillment in a successive and consequent phase and so on until the end is achieved.

(iii) The end or aim is not confined to that one phase, and neither is it simply transmitted from one phase to its successor. A phase is what it is (i.e., it has a distinctive structure and movement or *nisus*) because of a president being in each such phase. This president being is an effi-cacious agent and as such is not democratically elected by or assembled out of the governed: it has a kind of monarchical grip upon its subjects.[7]

(iv) The agent is not the will or any abstract or isolate of the self but it is the person himself. Such a being is the presupposition of discourse and thought about human action, because it is the "one addressed" in human conversation and human reflection. It is presupposed of the one addressed that he recognizes phases of action and apprehends aims as being his own, and as being himself in the multiplicity of events and in the richness and confusion of concrete experience.

(b) An appeal may also be made to evidence directly inspectable. Indeed, the significance of the foregoing indirect and transcendental argument derives ultimately from (though logically it may not rest upon) directly inspectable evidence. This should be clear in the sketch of such an argument just given. To know what a "program" and its phases are an individual must have such things before him either as present *erleben* or as retrospective data. To know how multiple and multitudinous details are synthesized into an organic whole, he must be, or must have been, immediately involved in just this whole activity. We cannot claim that this direct testimony demands and accepts but one interpretation. In a strict sense direct evidence of experience demands nothing: minds alone make and acknowledge the demands of logic. Nevertheless, we may say that the conception of the integral agent is a well-grounded one when its empirical base consists of evidence of this sort.

A second claim now demands scrutiny, namely, that the conception of the integral agent is far more adequate as a metaphysical base for a Christian doctrine of Revelation than any view which makes the terminal individual either a function of relations or a nexus of relations to which conventionally we affix the name of self and person. Support for this claim is to be adduced from a view of God as Creator and Revealer.

For this purpose the decisively important aspect of the notion of God as Creator is that God is the ground and fulfillment of persons. It may be supposed that "Creation" names a wholly unique and wholly unimaginable activity by which something comes to be or is called into being. But what does it mean to call a person into being? At the very least it means to establish the conditions for "hearing" and "answering," that is, for participation in the give-and-take through which the human being emerges as person. These conditions are: (i) potency and efficacy of agency, in general; (ii) the powers of cognition; (iii) the powers of self-relation through feeling and imagination. Examination of these

[7] The social view of the self (I am thinking especially here of the views of Charles Hartshorne) encounters the problem of the president agent in a peculiarly vivid way. The "soul" does not rule the organism by resort to consensus; the "cells" do not elect the "soul." There is rule imposed downward from above. The subjects have of course to accept this or no work gets done; and if no work gets done, all die. To be sure, the molecules may go on; but the distinctive forms of that organic affair are dissolved. While life remains in that body, the presiding agent is monarch.

conditions reveals, in every instance, that their being "planted out" and their being brought to fruition cannot be conceived of in isolation from each other. Thus, the indivisibility of the doctrines of Creation and of Revelation becomes apparent as soon as we understand that revelation means an act of divine self-communication and self-disclosure. We must therefore proceed to an examination of the above-specified conditions for participation in the give-and-take of Creation and Revelation.

(i) The integral self exists only where there is both potency and efficacy in agency. An ontological maxim is involved with this dictum, namely, that whatever *exists, acts*. The judgment that something exists is a judgment that it acts in a specific way.[8] Now, if something acts, its act has a degree of efficacy, that is, something is effected or done in and by this act. In the case of the person (though not only there) we commonly distinguish immanent from transitive efficacy. An act, i.e., may be internal. Richard, Duke of Gloucester, resolves to destroy his brother Clarence at some future time. This resolution is more than a projected and postponed action: so to decide is itself an act. The face of the visible human world is not changed by it at that moment; outwardly it is as though nothing had happened; but the course of human events *is* changed at that precise moment; and, specifically, the future of England is thereby shaped. But the hour comes when Richard's act takes on transitive efficacy: nerve and muscle are moved to terrible deed as the decision becomes incarnate and manifest upon the stage of public events and large affairs. Yet, before it is incarnate it was first potential. So we are reminded that to be potential means more than simply to be a possibility. To be potential means to be grasped as possible by a potent agent, that is, by an agent endowed with the powers of actualization. Such an agent has potency therefore in the double sense of having power and of having this power in relation to possibility. At any given moment of its existence this power is actual, that is, is being expended in concretely irrecoverable decision; but at any such moment this power is also residual, that is, is being reserved for subsequent decision and act.

If, then, the person is recipient of Revelation, if he is drawn up into a process in which God the Creator is disclosed to him, *this first condition of integral selfhood must be at once established and illuminated by Revelation*. Revelation is not added to something that is already a going concern without it. The whole being of the finite agent must be given and must be put in motion by Revelation. If this is so, Revelation is anterior to any knowledge the finite person might have of it. I do not

---

[8] An existential judgment is a limited mode of ontological judgment, since we say of many things that they are when we certainly do not mean that they act. Merely subsisting entities and subsisting relations have being ("are," in this sense); but their functions are not actions, that is, they do not express agency.

and cannot remember how and when I came to be through the power and grace of God—not because memory does not range so far back but because before *I* come to be there is certainly nothing for me to remember or otherwise know. Thus, it would seem that if I am involved in the activity of Revelation as a "recipient" I must first be given before I can make a response to what I "hear." What I hear is God; but the instrument of hearing is the self itself. *If the self knows itself as addressed or spoken to, it is, and it knows itself as, integral and terminal.*

(ii) Power to know is also a condition of integral selfhood. A person responds as an efficacious being in and to a *situation*. A person does not respond to a mere *stimulus*. The difference between stimulus and situation is this: a stimulus is an excitation in and of the neurobiological system.[9] A situation is a state of affairs apprehended as having certain structural features. In the apprehension of a situation, stimuli are employed and interpreted; but no stimulus of itself apprises the person of a situation (except where the person uses, not always self-consciously, a stimulus as a symbol for the situation). This is because the structual features of a situation involve formal being, and formal being is grasped only by mind. A formal principle of being is involved wherever something is apprehended as acting or behaving *characteristically*. So, to identify something is to recognize it in a welter of occurrences as having a structure of its own, that is, an "essence" or formal nature.[10]

The situation in which we discover our humanity is itself personal. One is a person only in relation to persons and only where others are known as persons. *Known* first of all, rather than "presumed to be" or "acknowledged." Primary awareness of other persons is neither presumptive nor a concession to the arbitrary demands of morality.

What, then, is known in Revelation? A situation, not simply one Being who somehow produces that situation. God is the infinite and eternal in that situation; I am an integral self in that situation (and as such a genuine *other* to God), a self who is coming into existence through "hearing the word."

The power of knowing is given in Revelation, as a prime condition for the emergence of persons, and does not follow from Revelation as a temporally delayed effect. We do not first hear other things, other voices, and then the word of God and the voice of the Lord. We do

---

[9] Some say that a stimulus is the "cause" of the excitation. This is metaphysics, where it means anything at all beyond the plainest (!) testimony of the senses.

[10] Perhaps we should be reminded here that a visual field is an abstract or isolate of a concrete situation. A visual field seems not to be structured formally but materially only. But spatial configurations *are* formal, though of low-degree formality. This does not mean that they are "mental" in an idealistic sense of the term. The visual field is after all a field, an organization, a significant whole (significant as opposed to meaningless, chaotic, etc.). And even at first glance the field is ordered at least partly through its relation to the observer, the perceiving mind.

not move from a situation defined as interfinite into a situation defined as infinite-finite. The infinite-finite situation is absolute and is absolutely all-inclusive in respect to all other situations; it is *known* to be so, not merely presumed or acknowledged to be so, and it is not simply posited as such by the finite. A God merely posited by faith or presumed by hope to be would be creaturely at every decisive point, which is to say, no-God. No-God has many temples, many priests, and he is inspiration of many profits; but he is snare and delusion, and in his worship one must be ready to kiss eventually the feet of Abomination.

(iii) The third of the conditions of "hearing" and "answering" (that is, for being a party to Revelation and for emerging into personal existence) is possession and employment of the powers of self-relation. What does self-relation mean? It signifies those activities by which the self apprehends and reacts to a place and a function in a situation.[11] These activities are exhibited as *feeling* and *will*. In both, "subjective" and "situational" factors are present, although in the instance of feeling our culture has long been preoccupied with the subjective component to the virtual exclusion of the situational. What is thus falsely appropriated as "subjective" is really the spontaneity and immediacy of feeling as over against the mediate and deliberative character of intellection and ratiocination. "Feeling" is a spontaneous and immediate assessment and response to a situation, a response by which the person relates himself, disposes himself, in and to that situation. "Will" as self-relating activity incorporates deliberation and envisagement. It lacks the spontaneity and immediacy of feeling, except as impulse—which, relative to responsible selfhood, is pseudo will and an isolate of proper conation. On the other hand, "will" incorporates structual features of the situation as feeling does not. The will is the person (self) presiding in multiphasic activities; and it is the person pursuing the determinate good, the good in and of a particular situation.

"Self-relating" does not mean that the self or the situation is either totally plastic or totally rigid and predeterminate. The self "finds" itself, "comes to itself," in these activities; but what it relates is more than a deposit or residue of previous encounters. There is accrual of meaning—experience is a source and process of enrichment. But accrual and enrichment are not the whole story of Creation and Revelation. We have little doubt of this in interfinite and interpersonal affairs. There we judge unhesitatingly that a person who simply "plays back" what society has uttered is not a "real" or mature person at all. But how do we

[11] This does not mean that "place" and "function" are predetermined or pre-fabricated. To the contrary, in highly important ways these are mere possibilities before or apart from the self's own envisagement and potencies. This is clearly the case in the interfinite scheme. Whether it is the case in the infinite-finite scheme remains an active front in the theological wars.

judge the infinite-finite situation? There too the "possibility" is antecedent to the actuality of response to the divine will and word. God addresses *this one*; and this one is invested with all the powers and promise of individuality. These powers come into play most fully and most productively only in response to the Word: but without them Revelation reduces to the absurdity of a divine monologue, an absurdity precisely because we could say nothing whatever about this monologue unless we, or someone, overheard it, as it were, or could furnish strong presumptive evidence that it had occurred. But how, under the circumstances, would such a monologue be understood in the least degree?

The implication of the foregoing is that Revelation is essentially illumination of a situation and condition antecedent, in some sense, to the act of illumination. Granted that the light thereby shed abroad is unlike any other. The power and the glory are in the full being and act of God, not alone in the "light"; or, in other words, God's doing and God's making known what he has done, are not wholly the same, even though "making known" is one of his "doings." In more specific terms we are saying that the situation of the believer is one illuminated but not wholly defined by Revelation. Through Revelation the believer grasps the situation for what it really and fully is. He comes to see not only what he is but also what he has been and what he is to be. This past is not imaginary, though its significance is grasped in and through images; and this future is not wholly visionary because, so far as it is a real future, it concerns and is related to a given structure of real potencies and relevant possibilities.

Is this to deny to Revelation any constituting and reconstituting significance? Not at all. The human situation is not constituted all of a piece and all at once. It has real becoming and therefore real fluidity. And when, accordingly, light bursts upon it, great and far-reaching things happen. The field of relevant possibilities is illuminated, and a power is imparted for the unification and consolidation of the powers of the person. An imparted power, yes; but this is not the infusion of an alien substance. The power is the power to see deeply and courageously into oneself, even as we are seen by God; and it is the power to relate self to the relevant possibilities. By reason of infirmity or external circumstance this relating may lack efficacy. But the impact of Revelation is such as to charge the person with the will so to relate and express himself.

2. BELIEF

We have been dealing with what we may identify, in default of more adequate designation, as a kind of ontological analysis of the situation of the believer as recipient of and participant in Revelation. From here we proceed to the question of the relation of the belief-ful aspects of the situation of the believer, to the ontological-actual aspects of this situation. I have contended that the "primitive" situation of the believer is not constituted by belief. What, then, is the significance of belief, in that situation? Does belief simply "evaluate" a world determinate and stable without the factor of belief, or does belief significantly modify that situation? Does it, perchance, modify that situation by relating it to being that transcends the situation?

In order to come to terms with these and related questions we shall have to do two things: (1) attempt a nonontological analysis of situation; (2) inquire into the nature of belief.

(1) We can hardly do better than to follow Niebuhr in a psycho-sociological interpretation of the situation in which belief occurs. The situation is that in which a person sees or grasps a good and a truth which imparts meaning to his existence. This *perception* is manifestly the person's; the good and the truth are manifestations of an absolute and perfect good and truth (rather, of one who is absolutely good and true). Every person has these perceptions; and these perceptions always occur in a situation in which one is related to other persons who also apprehend absolute goodness and truth, necessarily each in his own way but each also in a determinate social context. Thus, there are as many manifestations of absolute being as there are persons apprehending the goodness and truth of being. So far it would seem that Revelation is a comprehensive name for a very large and very complex indefinitude of personal transactions with absolute being. Admittedly, the temptation is great to fly forthwith into the theological zone: why not simply say that Revelation is one, and once and for all, and that the "indefinitude" applies only to the acts of human response thereto? But there is surely something left to do in the realm of psychological and sociological analysis before we book one-way passage into theological discourse pure, if not simple. Therefore, let us state the matter of fact again: we have in Revelation a state of affairs in which there is a plurality of perceptions felt and claimed to be absolute. Actually, we seem to find the situation rather more decidedly complex than this: there is also a plurality, indeed a luxuriant manifoldness, of interpretations of these perceptions. Let us go even further: the plurality of interpretations has become a chaotic atomism. The gods are many, as numerous as the individual acts of perception and belief! It may be that powerful "pantheonic" (rather than monotheistic) forces are working, but their hope of real success is more than faintly tinged with the piety of desperation. In our world there are many, many voices. Do they utter a common language or bespeak the claims of One God? Certainly we believe the answer is Yes, but we have also to admit that this common language is largely implicit and covert. It is the language of the heart, it is the indestructible commonalty of humanity itself, expressing its constitutive and common

burden of fears and hopes, of love and hate, of fate and freedom, of intimations of things heavenly and divine, and of premonitions of things hellish and demonic. Is this not to say that the "luxuriant manifoldness of interpretation" itself attests to the inexpugnable drive in the person to relate himself to transcendent good and truth? The efficacy of traditional religion has been thrown off in our culture. The individual is no longer the creature of institutional forces obliging him to see his life under God. One may so see oneself, but to do so is, in our culture, a matter of choice rather than a necessity. Yet each takes unto himself a "god." Each honors and relates himself to that which is his surpassing good and his final truth; and each calls upon his god to justify him and defend him. This does not mean that everyone is consciously religious. It does mean that everyone has a "unifying image" of the world in relation to himself, which image he necessarily (as a practical necessity) regards as the truth and the good, or as the efficacious symbol thereof.

Niebuhr has also reminded us that the astounding plurality of interpretations of absolute being is a *social* phenomenon, not primarily an individual phenomenon. The individual person *finds* viable interpretation of life's meaning, he does not spin it out of his private resources. He commits himself to the good and the truth of a community which itself is but one among many, so far as manifest structure and content are concerned. But community itself is most creative when it defines its meaning relative to transcendent being and when therefore it confesses its participation in a community embracing all men and all time.

(2) What is belief? Relative to the foregoing, belief consists of two operations: (*a*) having a unifying image of the truth and goodness of being and (*b*) committing one's self to being thus apprehended.

(*a*) To have a "unifying image" is not to be confused with the process, say, of visual perception. The "image" involved in belief is much more clearly and certainly entertained as a symbol of an efficacious presence. To take an analogy from interpersonal relationships, when I say I believe in you (not simply when I say I believe that you exist) I have an image of you before me. This image is much more than an actual sensory representation. Around that representation conative and affective factors are densely woven, so that the "you" in whom I trust is partly actual and partly projective—partly given and partly prospicient and to-be. Analogously, for the Christian, the "face of Jesus Christ" is the image of Deity, not merely as a given representation but as a densely rich symbol inducing and inciting a personal response to One who is both "in" and "beyond" the image. When the Christian says, therefore, "I believe on the Lord Jesus Christ," Jesus Christ is double mediation: once as Jesus of Nazareth, twice as Eternal Son through whom alone we have access to God the Almighty Father.[12]

---

[12] "Once" and "twice" have nothing to do with temporal or chronological successiveness.

(*b*) The second operation to be distinguished in belief is commitment of self to being apprehended and unified through the image. It is proper to speak of this as a response elicited by God through the image; yet it is also proper and necessary to speak of self-resolution, for by lack of resolution the gospel may be nullified for and in the self. This is to say that belief is an act of the will. And the question is, then: to what is this act directed? We answer: to being apprehended under some image of truth and good. This act of the will is not directed to statements and propositions, since to accept a proposition "on faith" as true is, first of all, to resolve one's self in trust toward some concrete agency or power. Belief is therefore a relating of person to being, apprehended as pre-eminently trustworthy.

But now the situation of the Christian believer is such that he apprehends this being as transcendent and in itself absolute. The situation prompts these questions: is this apprehension a function of the image (or of Revelation)? Or is it an overplussage, an hyperbole, it might be said, of the will itself? These questions express interesting and important aspects of the contemporary situation of the Christian. For one thing, there is the fact that today many assume that the transcendent in belief is posited by belief itself. Man will have for himself a god; and for an assurance, an approval and a security above and beyond finite and human resources and dispositions, he posits a transcendent and superlative god. So runs the assumption.

This assumption has little illuminative power and less validity; and what little of either it has it derives from largely uncritical views of apprehension and cognition. A particular kind of perception is allowed to establish an hegemony over the whole complex terrain of *noesis*. And when it is discovered that this mode of perception does not itself yield the Transcendent, the conclusion is promptly drawn that the Transcendent is not actually apprehended at all but is merely posited—where in fact it is posited at all.

Let us look a bit further into this state of mind. Is the Transcendent, so posited, actual or is it illusory? Assume the latter. Then, to posit means to take something for and as actual which, *as it is taken*, is not actual at all, and which may not be actual in any event or for or in any perception of any conceivable existing noetic agent. (Since the last clause is the fruit of exuberance, we may ignore it, at least for the moment.) But does this mean that something, say an image, is by some psychical mechanism actually "put out in front of the mind," so that the mind grasps it (mistakenly, to be sure) as an actuality other than the mind or other than consciousness itself? Surely nothing is known of such a mechanism; and to speak of "projection" is not to lay bare or call up such a mechanism, but is only to direct attention to the presumptive effect of a presumptive mechanism.

There are other possibilities in the phrase "to posit." It might mean, for instance, to pretend that something is actual when in fact it is known *not* to be actual or is known to be nonactual. Unfortunately, this alternative does not move irresistibly in the direction of intelligibility. Certainly the "pretense" is often not a conscious ruse at all. Just as certainly it will not do to say that at any rate *other* persons know that transcendent being has no actuality, or that actuality comprises or comprehends no such being, for we are now examining the minds that do the positing, not the minds which fail to do the positing.

A further possibility engages us briefly. Let us suppose that to posit the Transcendent is simply to invest some aspect of the person or some contingent bit of experience with "infinite worth" and absolute existence. Even so, the problem remains whether this investiture is a conscious and deliberative operation or not. If not, then what to another seems to be "positing" may actually be an "apprehending." But if the operation is conscious and deliberative, it still does not clearly or necessarily mean that the positer is substituting a nonactuality for an actuality (an "illusion" for an "actuality"), or that he is trying to make up his world as he goes along. He may be doing something very different: he may be establishing or acknowledging certain symbols and images of transcendent being as binding and normative. And this leads us back to the first alternative, viz., that the Transcendent posited *is* actual, or has its own expression in actuality. It is not the *actuality* of the Transcendent that is posited. What is posited is the normative and binding character of certain of its images and symbols. And thereby we are back again upon the question whether the images and symbols are thrust upon us by God himself. Is this what we mean by saying of them that they are "normative and binding"?

Not necessarily. We may have in mind the historicultural norms and constraints. In the Christian Church certain symbols are normative, and their employment is constitutive of much of the Church's life. Thus, in the Church we say, "In these ways we express our apprehensions of Deity." But on second thought we are saying much more than this. We are also saying, "The life and power in these symbols is a *communicated* life and power, not a humanly projected or invested life and power—the images have chosen us, we have not chosen them!" If this is what we say or what we mean to say, then in effect we are saying that the images are integral elements in Revelation itself. The glass in which we see darkly is withal the glass of heavenly vision, heaven-sent and heaven-blessed.

It hardly follows that Revelation is a process of filling our minds with certain images. It would be far more appropriate to say actuality is flooded with the "signs and portents" of God. Belief is taking the "signs" to mean what they say, that the mysterious God is wholly good. Hence, the "signs and wonders" of New Testament faith. Who performs them? He who is the "word," the "image" of God. He points beyond himself but what he points to is also within him.[13] What the image does is a "sign"; but he is not a sign himself. He is Revelation. And that is why we say that Revelation is not God filling our minds with images. History is filled with the Image. Such representations as we may find ourselves stocked with cannot themselves in any literal or ordinary sense be said to be inspired, save in so far as they induce or constrain us to worship, love and obey God-in-Christ. This inducement and constraint, again, does not arise out of ourselves but it is "the indwelling presence and power of God."

3. THE TERMINAL INDIVIDUAL

How shall we bring the results of ontological and psychosociological analysis together? Shall we say that the "terminal individual" is himself an "image" of God the Transcendent? Shall we say that so far as finite beings apprehend the Infinite, they are constitutive and constituent parts of actuality? In Niebuhr's terms, if we say that the finite *has* a perspective upon the absolute, must we not also say that the finite *is not* a perspective of this ultimate being?

As I see it we must answer this latter question affirmatively. To *have* a perspective is not to *be* one. To apprehend Revelation, to be caught up in a dialogue with God, is to be a real terminal existent. What God "sees" when he beholds us, is not an appearance or "projection" of himself, but an other and an order of others. When he addresses one of these others, he addresses someone other than himself.

The foregoing ought not be displaced or denied by psychosociological observation and generalization; and it is also impervious to destruction at the hands of a dialectic of internal relations far more appropriately employed to prove that Reality is Absolute Mind. Psychosociological analysis does not reach into the ontological depths; and we may suppose that the word of Revelation is directed into these depths, as it arises out of the irreducibly mysterious depths of God.

What we learn from psychological and sociological analysis is that the "depths" of the finite are expressed in relatively stable character and social structure. It is reasonable to suppose that these structures are symbols and expressions of ontological structures and ontological relations. But the symbols may mislead us. Specifically we may forget that "structural relations" are the outworkings and deposits of the essential operations of terminal existents, as, for example, the structure of the family is "objective" relative to my conjugal and paternal sentiments. On the other hand, the "family" is not an ontic structure in itself and

---

[13] "He brightly reflects God's glory and is the exact representation of his being." Heb. 1:3 (Weymouth).

as such. The ontic structures here are terminal existents expressing themselves and being themselves in these expressions, relatively to one another. Here the "essential operations" are love, strife, affirmation, rejection, etc. These arise in the depths and assume public and expressive forms; but the public world is not the determining cause or ground of essential operations. The public world comes to be through the power of selves and persons to detach themselves from their operations or, more accurately, from the "effects" of these operations. To put the matter in the forms of temporality, the public world with its objective structures is the time (past) in which ostensibly each of us has his being. But there is also the "time" of personal encounter; and in this "time" we must try to pierce beneath and behind the expressive forms, the necessarily stylized social gestures of language and bodily movement, in order to apprehend the other in his decisive intentional activities relative to ourselves. Now, this time is the real "specious present," the present with elastic boundaries, because its presentness endures just so long as there is communication in and of the depths. Thus, this present is not at all a stationary point in a linear series. It is an affair of acute and intense activity; and in this sense it has indefinite and indeterminate temporal spread.

Indeed, this activity of communication is so demanding, so exhausting, that it is endurable only in flashes. So long as it endures, one snatches at any distraction to break it off and to hurry it along. But even if it were more continuously endurable—if, that is, our energies were much greater and our power of will incomparably firmer and steadier—the further problem would remain unchanged and unresolved: the encounter, the communion (if indeed conflict is moved in the direction of communion) seeks public expression, it clamors to go on record. And this is the beginning of the end. For then communion recedes into the past, the past claims it because the communicants have summoned the past. To be sure, the past is, or may be, thereby itself enriched, if only in the sense that lovers have splendid and stirring things to remember. Yet as actual and potent existents they cannot ever again meet in that memory, that past; and if the past is too tightly hugged, too dearly loved, the possibilities for present encounter and communion evaporate.

I digress. The central contention is that persons cannot be resolved or reduced into nexus of relations, for then the relations are left without ground and without meaning. I believe here at the end Niebuhr concurs, specifically in his striking notions concerning "social existentialism."[14] Relative to other finite persons each of us must acknowledge the pressure of the past of objective structures, and each of us must also acknowledge the present of personal encounter in

[14] Cf. *Christ and Culture* (New York: Harper & Brothers, 1951), pp. 241 ff.

which I resolve my being toward an other. Relative to God, the Infinite, each must—and in fact does—acknowledge the reality of history ("in diverse ways God has spoken to our fathers"). And each of us must, and does, acknowledge the present of personal encounter in which I must resolve my being toward and for the absolute other. For the "absolute other" there is no "public world," thus, no past, no stylized or conventionalized mode of expression. Therefore, there is no escape from Him, no evasion of encounter with Him: "If we live, we live unto the Lord, if we die, we die unto the Lord, living and dying we are the Lord's." Hence, the decision demanded of us is to believe on Him. We cannot, in truth, decide *to be*, in relation to Him; we can decide to find fullness of life, to find the sustaining promise of life-to-be in the power and glory of His Kingdom.

9.

THE REAL PRESENCE
OF THE HIDDEN GOD

CARL MICHALSON

THE doctrine that God is hidden is probably the most pertinent Christian witness about God for our time. It is true that the hiddenness of God has been affirmed in the Hebrew-Christian tradition since the giving of the second commandment and that it is reaffirmed in the major confessions of Catholicism and Protestantism. The truth is so basic that one can say, as Pascal did, "Every religion which does not affirm that God is hidden, is not true."[1] Yet, it seems to hold a special attraction for today. It is so obviously true that when one affirms it one can do so with every expectation of being on common ground with the majority point of view, an exhilarating experience for the Christian minority. Yet, the acclaim of honest common sense would lend no encouragement to the Christian were not the affirmation of God's hiddenness so fundamental to the very truth about God himself.

Not to understand that God is hidden might lead one to conclude from God's apparent absence that he is unreal. The nineteenth-century announcement of the death of God has been taken by many to signify the beginning of this age, an age in which it is no longer necessary or even possible to take God seriously. Hence, positivistic philosophies, which are the characteristic academic philosophies of the time, insist that what is not perceptible is not meaningful. Existential philosophies, the characteristic literary philosophies of the time, also avow atheism. They do not, however, say with positivism that the idea of God is meaningless. Rather, they build their philosophies upon the cruciality of God's absence. "The death of God" thus gives ground for an attack

[1] *Pensées*, No. 584.

upon the half-smiling indifference of believers to the seriousness of their faith as well as upon the pathetic caricature of a God to be found in the theistic formulations of modern Christendom from which "hiddenness" has been too much removed. Hence, when Sartre and Camus postulate God's nonexistence, they do so with the intensity with which a precocious son revolts against his parents. For permission is the largest ingredient in responsibility, they say; and only if God does not exist is everything allowed. Heidegger, seeing nothing in the world to validate the conjecture about God, grieves, and that not for God's death but for his absence. He then projects the question about God as one of the few major philosophical burdens of our time. Marcel and Jaspers deplore with Heidegger the "noumenal emptiness" of the world, but locate the source of life's profoundest meaning in a realm of being mysteriously beyond the world. Strangely, what is the least perceptible is for them most meaningful, so that hiddenness need not at all connote unreality.

Furthermore, not to understand that the fundamental reality of God is hidden could be the source of considerable social hostility and personal wretchedness. Social aggressiveness which is not brought under the consciousness of a reality transcending society is very apt to turn legitimate and creative human efforts into diabolically brutal devices. If there is a God "above" (and this is theology's mythological way of expressing God's hiddenness), then there can be no social peace in a system of things where men try to appear "as God" in the lives of others. It is just as true that a well-intentioned utopianism, uncontrolled by the realization that God cannot be made visible in the structure of society, may end in the moral and political exhaustion of disillusionment.

Nor is it an innocent thing for personal health if the hiddenness of God is overlooked. If the Lapland traveler refuses to wear colored glasses because he cannot see that all the primary colors are hidden in the vast whiteness of the snow, he will go blind (Herman Melville). It is one thing to dismiss from one's mind fortuitous matters on the grounds of their possible unreality. But when one dismisses the fundamental reality, then the God forgotten is not *ipso facto* gone. The effort to dismiss fundamental realities is more apt to result in the subtle interior bondage of repressiveness than in emancipation. The mind cannot conceive of God without worshiping him (Calvin). But if the mind dispenses with the God concept, it engages in whatever is the opposite of worship. The age of the so-called "death of God" is notably, therefore, also an age of the greatest social conflict and personal longing.

Not to understand that God is hidden is just as serious to those who accept his reality as to those who do not. To believe that God appears in some groups and not in others, and in some ways and not in others, fosters social exclusiveness and ecclesiastical divisiveness. Moreover, to believe that God appears to some individuals and not to others places some under suspicion either of hypocrisy or of semantic confusion—for God does *not* appear—and sets off in others a merciless marathon by which the human spirit extends itself infinitely—in search of what in fact does not appear.

Perhaps, then, the hiddenness of God may be considered as important for our time as, let us say, the unity of God was important for the eighth-century prophets. In an age of rival cultures, each endorsed by its own deity, and in the midst of a people with a theologically oriented history there was wisdom in the emphasis that wherever or whenever man deals with God he is dealing with the same reality. The prohibition of idolatry fits hand in hand with the affirmation of universalism if God is one, for either your God is my God or one of us is wrong about God.

Or possibly the concern over the hiddenness of God is for our time what the simplicity of God, his three-in-*oneness*, was for the early fathers. When the religion of revelation found itself being girdled by a politically oriented culture and infiltrated by culturally oriented religions, it was strategic to make one thing clear: notwithstanding God's advent in human history, the object of the Christian's devotion is neither politically nor culturally malleable, for he is God. This affirmation was accomplished with full justice to the mathematical singleness, the indivisibility, the historical reality, and the essential historical independence of deity. The theistic perspicacity of the early fathers may well have kept Christianity from dwindling into a legend, as Thomas Carlyle once observed. The trinitarian formulation of the simplicity of God at least prevented "the substance of paganism" from surviving under Christian forms.[2]

The Reformers, who are most responsible for the theological popularity of the reference to God as *absconditus*, gave greater prominence to the righteousness of God. The righteousness of God is the common denominator for Reformed confessions of divine sovereignty and Lutheran confessions of divine self-humiliation. That is, the relation of man to God is believed to be based upon what God does and not upon what God requires. This, it seems, performed a definitive service in a period in which the freedom of God was becoming increasingly bound to the ritual, moral, and even intellectual initiative of man—a period in which the divine refusal to yield to these human formulas was producing a painful conscience in the lives even of the saints.

The fourth significant moment in the elucidation of the Christian idea of God originated with Hegel. His contribution may not have been avowedly theological, but his dependence upon theology and his implications for theology are evident. The Hegelian dialectic in the nineteenth

---

[2] C. N. Cochrane, *Christianity and Classical Culture* (Oxford: Clarendon Press, 1944), p. 234.

century severed the venerable alliance between the Greek notions of static being and the Biblical idea of God by introducing becoming into the Godhead. In doing so, it provided intellectual grounds for theological equanimity in the presence of the new science. There is a divine history as truly as there is a natural history. The structure in the *relation* between God and nature may have been more adequately conceived by Kierkegaard than by Hegel; but when Hegel conceded development in God without surrendering His ultimacy, he artfully saved the relevance of major Biblical meanings for an age enamored of becoming.

The doctrine of the hiddenness of God may not be as theologically complete as these other doctrines. It is, however, in continuity with their method. The theologian is obliged to witness to the plethora of Christian belief concerning God, but he must organize his confession in the patterns most suggestive to his day. And today, even more so than when Pascal first affirmed it, the truth of the Christian belief about God appears to be tied up with the affirmation of his hiddenness.

But, while a religion is true only if it affirms God's hiddenness, a religion which does not explain why God is hidden "is not instructive." This also was Pascal's opinion. In order, then, to make the belief in the hidden God instructive, at least two fundamental issues should be discussed. The first will have to do with the reality of the hidden God, and the second with the meaning of his presence.

Through the singling out of these two factors it is intended that the reader be made aware of several emphases which have become characteristic of H. Richard Niebuhr's thought about God. The confession to the reality of God is "religious realism," an accent in American theology with which Niebuhr early identified himself. The presence of God is a subject treated by Niebuhr under the category of "objective relativism," a theme unique to him. These insights are correlative, however, for the God who is independently and objectively real is believed to come into relation with man—hence, the relativism—without prejudicing God's objectivity, and yet with the effect of relativizing man's position in nature and history.

The discussion here of the reality of God will appear to diverge from Richard Niebuhr's emphasis at the point of his doctrine of the Trinity. Niebuhr's strictly monarchian view of God tends to exclude a doctrine of the Trinity which adduces the grounds for theistic realism from Jesus of Nazareth as the real presence of God. The discussion of the presence of God takes its major clues from motifs which surround Niebuhr's "radical monotheism." However, Niebuhr tends to regard the ascription of deity to Jesus of Nazareth as a compromise of the unity of God. An alternative will be explored here. The case will be proposed that precisely *because* one maintains the unity of God one has not adequately expressed the redemptive aspect of God's action in history until he affirms that Jesus of Nazareth is the real presence of God undergoing a costly act for the reconciliation of man.

1. THE REALITY OF THE HIDDEN GOD

An emphasis upon the hiddenness of God infuses a new urgency into the question of God's existence. If God does not appear to exist, what reason has one to believe that he exists even in hiding? The proofs for God's existence, long the property more of philosophy than of theology, would seem now to carry a heavy theological weight. It is not immediately clear, however, that theology has any way of overcoming the old philosophical limitations.

The question of the possibility of God's existence is being subordinated in philosophy today to the question of the possibility of man's nonexistence. Since Kant, anthropology has had more status than metaphysics. But anthopology in its radical interrogation of the meaning of man—what he can know, what he should do, what he may hope—has led philosophy to the very edge of nihilism, to the affirmation of the possible nonexistence of man. The question, "Why am I something and not nothing?" though initially anthropological has been the gateway to a revised and fundamental ontology. The data of common human experience, of experience as it faces the situations of life which draw most drastically upon man's resources, have become the object of philosophical analysis. Radical theology inevitably becomes anthropology by denying the self-sufficiency of man, but radical anthropology moves just as well in the direction of theology by that same denial. The question of the possibility of God's existence, once subordinated, re-enters the philosophical dialogue under the chastened conditions of man's self-analysis. For when it is suspected that man does not have within himself the resources by which his continued existence is rendered meaningful, the question of the possibility of God's existence arises. God in this context is no longer, however, a theoretical possibility which one may affirm or deny. He is an existential requirement. The authenticity of man's life depends on God's reality. God is not a fact at the end of a line of reasoning, but a hope at the end of the rope of despair. We need God, as Unamuno has said, "not in order to think existence, but in order to live it."[3] Nihilistic conclusions about man do not, of course, lead of necessity to the affirmation of God's existence. The atheistic nihilists keep the spirit of God-denial alive and by that very token keep the affirmation of God at the level of wistfulness and hope, befitting the existence of a hidden God.

A by-product of this radical anthropology is that one no longer dares pronounce that God *exists*. "God does not exist," as Kierkegaard has

[3] *The Tragic Sense of Life* (trans. by J. E. Crawford Flitch; The Macmillan Company, 1921), p. 155.

said; "He is eternal."[4] The word "existence" has never enjoyed a closer alliance with the diminutive adjective "mere" than now. Existence means "to stand from"; it means radical contingency. But God traditionally conceived is *a se*, the one instance in all reality of independent being. God, then, cannot be said merely to exist.

This diminutive definition of existence, however, puts an unprecedented strain upon the traditional way of establishing the reality of God. Successful proofs for God must start from what one most assuredly knows. But all that man assuredly knows partakes of what he calls existence. Is God to be thought within the same category as hammers and typewriters, trees and flowers, or even persons? Is there anything which saves the conclusion that God exists as first cause or prime mover or supreme good from the charge of either idolatry or pantheism? A god whom we come upon by tracing back from anything within existence, as Karl Heim once said, may be either the first member in a series of which he is a part, which makes the worship of him idolatry; or he may be the whole series, which is pantheism. In the proofs for God's existence, does one ever get beyond the limitations inherent in "existence"?

Classical theists believe that the inference in this question is unfair. God is not the first in a linear series but the first in an ontological pyramid, and the gap between the apex and all other levels of reality is infinite. God is, as Aquinas believed, not *primus inter pares* but in a genus of which he is the sole member. He is in a class by himself.

But then the charge remains that the instant anyone begins to think about that God, he does so by analogy from and within the limited connotations of man's kind of existence. If the classical ontological pyramid keeps God beyond confusion with other existences, does the language it uses likewise escape that confusion? The classical theists believe so, and what they mean by analogy is a highly specialized way of protecting their view from the criticism that it is anthropomorphic. The ontological gap between God and existence is presupposed in analogical reasoning, not disregarded or dismissed. Predication by analogy is a less cautious form of predication than predication by negation, but it is nonetheless a species of the *via negativa*. It is a way of talking about God without either confusing what one says with what God is or separating what one says from what God is.

The God of the classical theists is a transcendent God who is not to be thought of as participating in the same order of reality as man. The reason he does not exist is that he is the Possibility of existence. Man exists but he is not possibility. Man *has* possibility. God is the Possible one. He is *the possibility of* all else. The phrase "the possibility

---

[4] *Concluding Unscientific Postscript* (trans. by David F. Swenson & Walter Lowrie; Princeton, New Jersey: Princeton University Press, 1944), p. 296.

of" is a syntactical symbol for the structure that relates God and man. Such a use of words is calculated. "Possible" is a term no Scholastic would apply to God because, ontologically, it connotes "potential," or the lack of actuality. Process philosophers today would use it on the very grounds for which Scholastics reject it. God's being, they believe, is in some sense in the process of actualizing itself. Both Scholastic and process philosophers would use the term "possible" epistemologically, for to say that God is possible means epistemologically that he is "conceivable" or that the God-concept is noncontradictory.

The use of the term "possible" in this present discussion, however, has neither of these meanings. It has the specialized character which the early church fathers believed they found in Greek philosophy and which it is being given in the philosophy of Martin Heidegger today. It is so specialized in meaning that Heidegger is obliged to employ for it another of his unusual words. There is a kind of being which is not properly defined until it is referred to as *das Mögliche*, the possible one. The meaning of this word seems similar to the meaning of the New Testament *dunatos*: "With God all things are *possible*."[5] Read the Magnificat, conserving the same translation of *dunatos*, and you will see what Heidegger means by *das Mögliche*: "He who is *possible* has done great things for me, and holy is his name."[6] This is the being which is the power of being. It is, as Heidegger says, *"stillen Kraft des Möglichen,"* "the secret power of the possible one."[7] The meaning conserved in this word seems to shift ontological concern from customary preoccupation with the intrinsic nature of being to its operations and to the consequent structure that exists in the relations of being. Furthermore, contrary to the usual epistemological inference, the structure suggested here implies a kind of relationship which resists the rational deduction of the nature of the transcendent member of the relationship.

Plato, the first great philosophical theist, hinted at this structure in his "idea of the good." Pythagoras had already seen it in his idea of the monad. What has the number one in common with all other number? Nothing. As *the possibility of* all number it is in a class by itself. So Plato's good, *the possibility of* all good, truth, and beauty, of all existence, is on the other side of essence and existence. It is transcendent.[8] Aristotle saw the same in his notion of *arche*. What has the source of motion in common with moving things? Nothing. It is *the possibility of* motion, but "not as an immanent part."[9] These are the

[5] Matt. 19:26.
[6] Luke 1:49.
[7] *Platons Lehre von der Wahrheit*, pp. 57, 58; cf. also *Sein und Zeit*, pp. 143, 144; *Vom Wesen des Grundes*, pp. 37 ff., and *Einführung in der Metaphysik*, pp. 150, 151.
[8] *Republic*, 509; *Phaedo*, 97c-99c.
[9] *Metaphysics*, 1013 a.

patterns of intellectual clarity in which the Christian theists cast their profound thoughts about the God of Abraham, Isaac, and Jacob and the God and Father of our Lord Jesus Christ.

The force of this pattern for Christian theology is not fully felt unless one knows that it was not the only pattern offered to primitive Christianity by the Greek mind. The *arche* thinking of Aristotle, Plato, and the pre-Socratics offered this concept of ontological transcendence to the Christians. At the same time, the Stoics, the Hellenists, and the Gnostics offered a principle of ontological immanence in their *logos* thinking. Everything has *logos* and is in that degree divine. So the Stoics claimed. There is a *logos* mediator between man and God which is neither man nor God but a third something, a principle of wisdom, which brings the two together as a Bethel ladder. So Philo claimed. There is a *logos* of God, a spiritual wisdom, a fragment of the fulness of the Godhead, which God slipped into the envelope of human flesh at man's creation by which to quicken man's return to God. So the Gnostics claimed. But, though the Christians referred to their God as *logos*, they defined this *logos* not as the Stoics, Hellenists, and Gnostics did, but in the *arche* terms of Aristotle, Plato, and the pre-Socratics, and thus believed they saved the meaning of the God of Israel and of the church.

Clement of Alexandria rejected the Stoic view: "We do not say as the Stoics do impiously that virtue in man and in God is the same,"[10] even though he was commenting on Jesus' injunction to be perfect "as your Father in heaven is perfect." Justin rejected Philo's analogy of the *logos* to God as rays to the sun.[11] Irenaeus rejected the Gnostic view: "God who sent forth the intellect is separate from it, and the intelligence separate from Him."[12]

The later fathers were well aware of what had been achieved by this theological decision for *arche* over *logos*, for transcendence over immanence. "What possible relation can exist between one who is eternal and another who at one time was non-existent and came into existence? . . . (They are) separated from each other and the gulf between them is unbridgeable." Theodore of Mopsuestia wrote that in his *Commentary on the Nicene Creed*. "So great is the interval between man and God as no language can at all express." Chrysostom wrote that in his treatise *On the Statues*.[13] "The Maker is in every way other than that which is made," Nestorius wrote in *The Bazaar of Heraclides*.

This much, then, is clear in classical Christian theism. God does not exist; he is the Possibility of existence. Through him all else exists and by his role as the possible one he is as singular as the Pythagorean

[10] *Miscellanies*, VII, xiv.
[11] *Dialogue with Trypho*, 128, 3.
[12] *Against Heresies*, II, xiii, 4.
[13] iii, 19.

Monad, or the Platonic supreme good, and as hidden. If God is one who holds existence from his hand, then man cannot describe him adequately in terms of what man holds in his own hands.

The most serious and accomplished refinement of classical theism today is to be found in the process philosophy which stems from the thought of A. N. Whitehead. Process theism finds the classically oriented Christian views to be defective on two counts: their God is static and too utterly transcendent. It is true that the same Greek ontology which gave to theology its notion of transcendence also gave it a notion of a static God. The refutation in process theism of the static character of God seems quite in keeping with the biblical view of a living, suffering God. The God of the Bible has a history of his own, but temporal connotations were completely excluded from the supreme being of Greek philosophy.

The process exponents, however, seem to have created a kind of philosophical package deal in which the notion of a transcendent God must be abandoned along with the notion of the static God. "Panentheism" is the result. Panentheism is a safeguard against the excessive immanence of Pantheism, which sees the all as God, for in panentheism the all can be in God without being God. But what seems unduly sacrificed is the notion of God's lordliness, his distinctiveness, his transcendence. In panentheism God remains transcendent in his "primordial" nature, but in his "consequent" nature God is transcended by man. God in one aspect of his nature is no longer the Possible one but a possibility alongside other possibilities. In panentheism man becomes in a sense the possibility of God. The modificaton of this depth dimension in reality appears to be too great a concession to make to the democratic prejudice in contemporary naturalism and to the existence-orientation in the language of contemporary scientific philosophies.

But, then, if God is allowed to be removed to so deep a level of reality that he is hidden from man's customary visual aids, how can one be at all assured that, when one aims at God with one's theistic demonstrations, one is hitting anything? Proofs for the existence of God which end in *ergo* and Q.E.D. seem to have one thing in common: the God they prove is not brought out of hiding by the proof. Kant's canny stricture still holds, for the intellectual necessity of God's reality does not thereby produce his reality. There is no radar device attached to the proofs for God which, when the proof is projected, reports back that the object of the proof has been engaged. If the question of the objective reality of God is unsatisfied by these customary proofs, one way remains. One may simply admit that the God being proved is a hidden God, and the proof will have the splendid advantage of being simultaneously incontestable and verifiable!

There is a valuable element in proofs for God's reality which is usually overlooked. Concern with striking a target ought not to be dissociated from the concern with which one takes aim. Nor ought the suspicion that the question of God's reality is so unanswerable distract one from the answer implicit in the fact that the question is so unavoidable. It is not simply a failure of philosophic nerve if one invokes Pascal's confession. The heart *has* reasons. No bifurcation of heart and head is known to the Bible. Hence, it may even be true that Anselm links Pascal with the Bible in his most theoretical proof for God's existence. The fool who said in his heart that God does not exist played the fool precisely because he denied in his heart what Anselm believed was undeniable in his head. Pascal made the head responsible to the heart, Anselm made the heart responsible to the head; but both insisted on the organic union of heart and head.

There is a tempting kinship between Pascal's "wager" and Pierce's so-called "neglected argument." Pascal believed that if you cannot know either that God exists or that he does not exist you are left with a gamble and ought to wager safely by betting on the existence of God. Pierce believed that the personal and social benefits from believing in God had not been taken seriously enough by philosophical theists. The sheer pragmatic value which belief in God's existence, notwithstanding his indemonstrability, has produced ought to throw more weight on the side of his possible reality than on the side of his possible unreality. The strong conviction that reality is not rounded out unless God be acknowledged is a type of argument which does not require *quod erat demonstrandum* or a punctured target, for it moves in an atmosphere of personal concern and sense of gratitude which bespeaks prevenient reality. It develops itself out of ingredients that seem, like Descartes's meditations—for that is what he calls his proof— to presuppose the truths they wish to demonstrate. Was it a breach in the total logic of his treatise that allowed Anselm to pray the prologue to his proof for God or Nicholas of Cusa to pray his entire theism? And is not the demonstration of a hidden God essentially confined to this tactic of circularity?

One who knows contemporary phenomenological philosophy will recognize familiar lines in the foregoing suggestions. A thoroughgoing phenomenologist, of course, would not concede them, for, as Husserl said, "God does not appear"; and hence a discipline that deals only with the facts themselves as they appear would not be found dealing with God. There is a significant structure in the phenomenological method, however, that is reminiscent of Anselm and Descartes and anyone else who, presupposing what he demonstrates, employs circularity in his thinking about God.

The phenomenologist believes that knowing takes place only when two conditions are operative. The knower reaches out toward the object and the object supplies the possibility of its being grasped. The knower "passionately loves" the object he would know, stretches out toward it with his consciousness. Confirmation of the reality of what is indicated is not entirely dependent on reaching it. There is theoretical validity and epistemological realism in the very stretching out. This thinking is the structure by which the existentialists safeguard their seriousness over human moods from the charge of mere subjectivism. Subjectivity can be truth if pointing to objects is given the validity which touching them formerly enjoyed.

Likewise, however, the object of knowledge has within itself the conditions by which the knower consummates his knowledge. In the nectar of a flower are the properties by which the acquisitive bee may construct wax bins for the storage of its honey. Reality bears a similar relation to the knowing mind.

Max Scheler, the philosopher of religion among phenomenologists, proposed within this context his "proof for the unprovability of God," at least if the God for whom the proof is probing is previously conceived to be a personal God.[14] The distinctive thing about a person is his ability to hide himself. No person is ever known apart from the voluntary unveiling of himself to the knower. If there be this kind of reality called personal, then, Scheler claimed, there is a kind of knowledge process which never consummates itself apart from the prior co-operation of the object known. And if the hidden God be of this personal nature, there is no proof for his existence which is consummated without the independent initiative of the object of one's proof.

If such be the case, there are two fools, and not simply one. There is the fool Anselm exposed who said, "There is no God," not knowing that, in the words of Max Picard, "he must continually tear the *no* away from the *is*, but again and again the *no* is brought back by the *is* and is swallowed up by it."[15] But there is also the fool who says "God is" and does not acknowledge that his predicate in some way is created in his mind and speech by his hidden subject, the "I am." The possibility for establishing God's reality from the first resides within the prevenient possibility beneath all reality. As Origen once said to Celsus, you cannot seek God and find him without help from God. God is the prevenient reality whose movement toward man is heard as invocation and toward whom man's rational movement takes on the aspect of a *sursum corda*.

The discussion thus far has come to this: whatever may be the importance of affirming that God is hidden, it carries a serious methodological disadvantage. What assurance has one that there really is a

---

[14] *Vom Ewigen im Menschen* (Leipzig, 1921), pp. 632 ff.
[15] *The Flight from God* (trans. M. Kuschitzky & J. M. Cameron; Regnery, 1951), p. 20.

God in the hiddenness? It has been pointed out, however, that the skepticism traditionally directed against God's reality has now been turned upon man himself and that the consequence of man's possible unreality has reopened with new seriousness the question about God as man's very possibility. Within these new conditions an old limitation perpetuates itself, namely, the problem of how to talk about God within the modes of expression available in man's own questionable existence. The Christian theists have attempted to circumvent this limitation by negative and analogical predication and by attributing to God a hiddenness beyond all attributes of "mere existence." It is believed that God transcends existence. But the initial problem crops up anew. Does one's indication of the *reality* of this hidden, transcendent God really encounter him anywhere? The intellectual image that results from this inquiry is the Christopher image of one who seeks for God until God finds him. Man's passionate concern for God moves within the context of God's prevenient reality.

One lingering question, however, can turn to dust and ashes the entire effort at establishing God's reality. A man may learn to say with confidence, "There is a God." Man may ask about God because he must, because the predicament of his existence requires it. One may protect one's language from sheer psychologism and projectionism by negative and analogical devices, and may concede that God exists beyond all the reality within man's reach. And one may even concede that all one says in one's intellectual movement toward God begins in God's own movement toward man. But is one yet beyond the crackling dryness of abstraction and the chambered echo of a human question? Can one say with any modicum of confidence, "There is a God"; can one remove suspicion from the claim that God, though hidden, *is*, without the ability somehow to say, *"There* God is?"

This candid requirement is the basis both for the critique of natural theology and for the vigorous renewal of Trinitarianism in theology today. It is a misunderstanding of the first order to charge that those who reject the surmise that God reveals himself in nature do not appreciate the value of the natural world for theological knowledge. No theologian is moving to eliminate psalmody from the Bible. The point is not whether one finds out something about God in nature but whether one finds *God there*. But surely, if God is the creator, his creative spirit is in nature—in a tree, or even in man's fabrication from a tree, such as a chair. No! God *is* in his creative spirit but he is not identical with what his creative spirit makes. He is present to it without being present in it. His presence is a hiddenness which is his absolute distinctiveness and transcendence. One must not perforate the line between the Possible one and existence. God is present to nature but nature is in no sense God. "The Divine power and light . . . is everywhere in Nature, yet Nature touches it not" (Jacob Boehme).

One may point to nature and say, "There *is* a God," but one cannot point to nature and say, "*There* God is." And if one says that you can know God from a tree or a chair, either one is committing the logical fallacy of composition by which the knowledge about God and the knowledge of God himself are lumped together indiscriminately; or one is committing the theological heresy of composition which holds that God's nature is such that he can parcel himself out and be at the same time a piece of nature and integrally himself. God *is* not in nature; he is the creator, the possibility of nature. His silence may be in nature; but not his speech. His hands and feet, perhaps, as Calvin said, but not his heart.

The Christian doctrine of the Trinity affirms, however, that there is a place in human existence to which one can point with the assurance of affirming, "*There* is God." That place is Jesus Christ. The meaning of the so-called special revelation is that the hidden God reveals *himself* in the world of men. At the point of the person of Jesus Christ, revealer and revelation are in some sense the same reality. The God of Christianity is not simply *Sein*. He is *Dasein*. His reality is not abstract, but concrete—a reality of which one can say, "It is *there*."

Not that Jesus Christ is the total revelation of God. He is rather the revelation of the total God. Where he is, God is. Not that the hidden God comes out of hiding, for that is not the meaning of the revelation. God does not appear even in Jesus Christ. He reveals himself in Jesus Christ, which is to say, in Christ God hides himself in human history. The revelation is the *act* of this divine self-hiding and not the removal of the veil from God. The witness to the revelation is not a claiming that the hidden God has been unveiled, but that the hidden God has revealed himself in human life—God at the breast of Mary, God on a cross, God in disguise, but *really* God—in Christ. The issue of the revelation of God in Christ and of its theological foundation in the doctrine of the Trinity is religious realism. In the witness to this revelation the Church believes there resides the divine possibility for resolving the agonized human surmise about the reality of the hidden God.

2. THE PRESENCE OF THE HIDDEN GOD

Even more crucial than the question of the reality of the hidden God is the question of his presence. So long as man exists he will keep alive the question of the possibility of a God. But the answer merely to that question will never satisfy the concerns out of which the question was originally raised. To know that there is a reality in the silent but suspected shadows can turn surmise to craven fear. The question about God will only begin to address itself to human need when it is known not simply whether there really is a God but whether the hidden God is really ever present and what the meaning of his presence is.

Furthermore, the question about God will only begin to do justice to what concerns Christianity most when it moves from the affirmation of his reality to the affirmation of his presence. For the question of the reality of God has been suggested to theology by doubts that have no original relation to Christian belief. To be sure, one must deal with these *bona fide* doubts, but not so earnestly as to neglect the prior Christian witness to the presence of the hidden God. According to the Christian faith, God is the "God with us." God is a God whose reality is not simply a being *there*; but, as a being there in Christ, he is a being there *for us*, a reality *pro nobis*. His reality is no longer simply an *ousia* but a *parousia*. And the Christian life is a life lived *coram deo*. As Roger Mehl has said, "The true propagators of atheism are . . . those who direct this doubt at the heart of the faithful: Is your god really interested in you, is your god really present?"[16]

The apparent absence of God does not bespeak his unreality, as has been seen. But, then, what is the nature of the presence of a God who is apparently absent?

The nature of God's presence is that God is so solely and completely God in his presence that he cannot but remain hidden. The universally admitted truth that God exists in hiding is not everywhere interpreted to mean the same thing. But in the Hebrew-Christian tradition the hiddenness of God refers to the way God has his being. To be sure, there is a sense in which God's hiddenness is an attribute of the myopic spiritual sight of man: our finite eyes strain after him and see nothing. Even truer than this, God's hiddenness is an attribute of the astigmatic vision of the erring man: we fail to see God because we are looking in a direction in which God does not dwell. But to attribute God's hiddenness to these factors alone makes of his hiddenness an accident of man's way of life and stops short of a profounder meaning.

The real truth of God's hiddenness is not appreciated until it is acknowledged that it is God's own way of life to be hidden. He is *ex officio* hidden. Hiddenness is intrinsic to his nature as God. God is not simply being; he is a very specialized kind of being such that one cannot even say of him, he is *a* being, for he is, as the pre-Socratic philosophers and the medieval mystics hinted, the possibility of being. As such, his way of being in relation to all other being implies a structure the recognition and appreciation of which is the presupposition for an understanding of the way of all other being. The hidden God is the God who transcends all being as the very possibility of being. He is the God whose relation to all other reality is of such importance that he is thereby confined to a class by himself. His hiddenness is the

[16] *La Condition du philosophe Chrétien* (Paris, 1947), p. 78.

aloneness of responsibility, the price of his greatness. Heraclitus put this truth aphoristically: "Invisible harmony better than visible." When this meaning is appropriated, philosophies of immanence and optical metaphors together will be rejected by Christian thought.

God occupies a place in reality that can be occupied by no other being. To know this is to realize that there is a structure in reality which is irreversible. The wretchedness of the human predicament is the consequence of this structure. For the structure is at the same time both a constant temptation to man to overthrow it and a boundary which is impervious to human striving to be as God. The first commandment, therefore, is not a moral dictum which man can choose either to keep or to violate. If it were, the law would have been no delight to the Psalmist and the Apostle. It is, rather, a benevolent announcement about reality. It is a guidepost for the *homo viator* to the effect that the way of man can be a way of satisfaction when that way is an open confession to the way of a God, who only can be God.

The doctrine of the hiddenness of God is an affirmation of the transcendence of God. It bespeaks God's way of being. It is not, therefore, a counsel of despair or a concession to human finitude but a positive description of God himself which performs a merciful service. It prevents man both from looking for God in the wrong place and from esteeming God's fundamental role in reality with less than ultimate seriousness. Just as the "religious realism" of the Christian faith will not settle for the identification of God as anything less than God himself, so the "radical monotheism" of the Christian faith will not tolerate the violation of the structure that puts God first.

The transcendence of God specifies the structure in the relation between God and man. The most obvious meaning in this structure is simply that God is different from man. "I am God and not a man" is a constant refrain in the prophetic literature of the Old Testament, notwithstanding the fact, or even because of the fact, that every time the prophet speaks of God he must invoke a language of analogy bordering on anthropomorphism. The transcendence of God is *qualitative*. Therefore, when one says of God something that can also be said of man, one means something that is different not only in degree but in kind. The holiness of God is an apt illustration of this. To say that God is holy could be a way of indicating that God is morally superior to any other instance in reality. But this would not begin to exhaust the meaning of the holiness of God in the presence of which one feels oneself over against God. God's holiness is a *mysterium tremendum* which, simultaneously repelling and attracting man, accentuates the difference between man and God. The holiness of God is not a moral characterization of his being, then, so much as it is an ontological specification of the gap that separates him from man. From a moral standpoint it is even conceivable that man could find himself superior to God, as Meister Eckhart did when he confessed with no sense of pride, "I am better than God is." For God is *exlex*, beyond the law. His holiness is his wholly otherness in the presence of which man feels not so much either a legal guilt or a moral self-satisfaction. He feels, rather, his role as creature. God is God and man is man, and between these two realities there is a gulf fixed.

It is even more definitive than fixing a great gulf between them to regard God as distinct from man as the spaces on a map or a checkerboard are distinct from each other. For God's transcendence is in an important sense *spatial*. He occupies a different space from man. Surely Josiah Royce is right in saying that "Chasms do not individuate." Yet, given individuation, do not chasms follow? When God is near to man, he is near to man as God and not as something which can in any way be confused with the human spirit. His omnipresence does not mean that he is present everywhere as a kind of divine fog which permeates the universe or the fragrance of a perfume which, emanating from a vial, merges indistinguishably with the olfactory nerves. His omnipresence means that he is wholly present in his presence. When God is in man, his space is in man's space, undistorted and uncompromised by man's space. When the Holy Spirit of God brings God near to the human spirit there is no merging of spirits, but rather a meeting of spirits. God is omnipresent by his Spirit, but he is first of all one God, which is to say, he does not parcel himself out. There is no composition in his being. He is integrally God and is always met as God and never as some diffuse extension of himself. To borrow a figure from Plato, God is in man more as a sailor in a boat than, to borrow a figure from Martin Buber, as air in the lungs. When God is in man, he is in man as God, which is to say he is in man neither as a fragment of God which God parcels out nor as a fragment of man which man assimilates from God. The proper role of man in relation to a spatially distinct God is the role of responsibility. He lives over against God, allowing God to remain present *as God*.

To say that God is different from and distinct from man is not thereby to say that God is not co-ordinable with man. God's transcendence is what Karl Heim has called a *dimensional* transcendence. Dimensional transcendence is a category which purports to protect the distinctness which the notion of spatial transcendence conserves. Yet it carries the analogy to the God-relation beyond figures drawn from juxtaposition. It attempts to do justice to the greater sense of intimacy in the Christian consciousness of the spiritual nature of the God-relation. In a flat universe, a two-dimensional universe, only two lines can intersect perpendicularly at a given point. In a depth universe, a universe of more than two dimensions, an infinite number of lines can intersect perpendicularly at the same point. Now, the force of this analogy is twofold. In one sense the God-dimension can be equally present to an infinite number of existences without jeopardy to the fullness of God's presence. In another sense, these intersecting lines are not mutually exclusive. The intersection can be intimate and all-embracing. The lines undergo genuine co-ordination, genuine overlap—without jeopardy to their distinctiveness as discrete lines. God's presence, dimensionally transcendent, can permeate the life of man without prejudice to the self-identity of either God or man.

The genuinely specifying element in the transcendence of God has not been dealt with, however, until one has referred to what might be called God's *functional* transcendence. God is man's beginning and his ending, his source and his destiny, his past and his future, the possibility of man. As has been said, God is different from man and distinct from man by what God is. And he is, notwithstanding these cleavages, co-ordinable with man. But he is co-ordinable with man in his presence in such a way as to enforce a structure which says that God remains irrevocably God, the possible one, the power of man's being.

This notion of transcendence has the value of minimizing the *purely* spatial connotations in hierarchial metaphors without dissolving the structural connotations. The boundary or frontier or limit in the God-man relation is less like the boundary between geographically defined limits and more like the boundary that defines the limit between supersonic speed and the speed of sound. You can know you are coming up against the boundary not simply by the objective marks at the frontier but by the tremor in your very being. It is like the boundary which marks off the stratosphere. You know you are up against it by the sense of suffocation in your spirit. For God is and does what man can never be and do. He maintains a role respecting man which man can never penetrate to share or overthrow. The God-man relation is what can be called an irreversible relation.

The language of logic refers to this type of relation as an asymmetric relation. It is the most definitive predication in all possible dyadic relations. It is likewise the most refined and accurate way, from a biblical standpoint, of characterizing God's life in relation to man's life. For one could simply say that God's presence means his nearness. And that would be true. For transcendence does not mean God is so far away that he is hidden but rather he is so near that he is hidden. But the relation of nearness is a symmetrical relation, like the relation of perpendicular lines. When God is near to man, man is likewise near to God.

Or, one can simply say that God loves man. Here one's language takes on a greater clarity and precision, not only for the reason that to proximity is added the connotation of affection, but for the reason that this relation, like the relation of friendship, is not in all instances reversible. To say that God loves man is not, *ipso facto*, to say that man loves God. The relation of love is a nonsymmetric relation which may or may not be reversed.

But to say that God is man's author and his finisher, his beginning and his end, his possibility, is to introduce the decisive factor into the God-man relation, a structure that dominates and defines all else that is said about that relation. For the relation "author of" or "possibility of" is an asymmetric relation which is strictly irreversible. The God whose role it is to hold man in his creative hand can never be manipulated by man. The God who is co-ordinable with man, however different and distinct from him, is so only within the terms and structure of a relation that cannot be upended. Everything man is and does presupposes the presence of a reality which must be taken into account but cannot be surmounted, which must be responded to but cannot be transcended. When God is near to man, man is near to God, but only as one who is held by God. When God is near to man in love, man is invoked and not coerced to respond within this nearness in love, but his love will fall within the structure of the relation characteristic of a creature's relation to a creator. The poet Hölderlin has caught this structure in the opening lines of his *Patmos*:

> Near is
> The God, and hard to grasp.

Here the vague symmetrical reference "nearness" is structured by the more definitive asymmetric reference "hard to grasp." Note also this line from Anslem's *Proslogion*[17]: "How far removed art thou from my vision, though I am so near to thine." Compare what Augustine says in his *Confessions*[18] about the Light which is God: "Nor was it above my soul as oil is above water nor yet as heaven above earth; but higher than my soul because it made me; and I below it, because I was made by it."

The transcendence of God is his way of being present to men. Hence, the popular or deistic connotation of transcendence as the remoteness of God misses the point as badly as notions of his immanence which regard him, on the contrary, as simply very near. It should be said that the more highly developed notion of the immanence of God in current process theology is more congenial to the biblical tradition in its understanding of immanence as the way in which God brings his perspectives to bear upon the developing situations of life without himself being identified with these situations.

God in his transcendence is neither very far removed from man nor mixed up with human nature. As Karl Jaspers has said, God is

[17] 16.
[18] X, 27, 38.

neither *jenseits* nor *diesseits*. He is *Grenze*.[19] He is the boundary, the limit, the frontier against which man bruises himself in his oversight of the structure of reality. He is the inescapable condition under which all life is lived. Wherever a man may flee, God is there. Not because man carries God around in himself, and not because God is indiscriminately everywhere, but because human life is set within the conditions of reality which make God the inescapably primal presupposition. The freedom of man to roam the distance between heaven and hell is a freedom which never really actualizes itself until it negates itself through the realization of the prior freedom of God. Man's freedom is nothing until and unless it is set within the structure in which God is free to be God. Is this not the purport of Richard Niebuhr's observation: "The fundamental over-againstness of self and that which it is up against, not the world but the ground of the world's being—this encounter . . . presents itself to many of us as *the* religious problem, the problem of ultimate concern"?[20]

Man's freedom to know God, for instance, is a freedom in vain until it is transcended by God's freedom to be present. For then the knowledge of God is never sought on the same conditions under which the knowledge of existence is sought. The God who is present as the hidden possibility of existence and our knowledge of existence cannot himself be pulled down into the sphere of customary cognition. He must be permitted to remain God even in the moment in which he would be known. God alone is the possibility of the knowledge of God. He cannot, therefore, be unfolded into man's perceptual or conceptual experience as one existence alongside others. He will be present to the knowledge of man as the hidden, the possible, the transcendent, the free one. Man's knowledge of God will reflect the structure which is in God's presence. That is to say, man will know God as a God who first knows man and holds all man's knowledge under the evaluation of his own prior and objective being. To know the hidden God is to allow God himself to become present to man *as God*.

Man's freedom to do God's will is a freedom in vain unless he realizes that God is a God who swears by nothing other than himself. Man's ethical creativity is carried on within conditions under which it is realized that there is only one creator, and that he knows no good but what he wills. The ethical life is the life that holds itself under the evaluating eyes of God, the life that refuses to tie God to the level of man's moral insight but resolves to keep man's sentiment for virtue under suspension to God's morally creative presence.

[19] *Philosophie* (Zweite, unveränderte Auflage; Berlin-Göttingen-Heidelberg, 1948), p. 685.
[20] Review of Tillich, *Systematic Theology*, vol. 1, in *Union Seminary Review* VII, No. 1 (November, 1951), p. 49.

Man's freedom to live in God's universe is a freedom in vain unless he realizes that the cosmos comes alive only when God speaks. Laws of nature are as tentative as laws of ethics, for God is not bound to his universe nor to the statistical averages in the probabilities which the natural sciences observe. If the daily rising of the sun takes on the character of predictable regularity, one ought to know it is because, as G. K. Chesterton was fond of saying, "Every morning God says to the sun, 'Get up.' "

Man's freedom to move through history is a freedom in vain unless he acknowledges that "the way of man is not in himself" (Jer. 10:23). God is not tied to man's past. If one does not know this one does not know the difference between Herodotus and Isaiah. The orderly and rational picture of human history as dug from the chronicle of past events is staggered by the ambiguities in man's emerging present. But man lives neither by his past nor by his present. He lives by God's hidden presence, by what God is doing, which is to man a future, a living largely in hope because established upon a God who is making history.

Again, as Richard Niebuhr said some time ago, "God, I believe, is always in history; he is the structure in things, the source of all becoming, the 'I am that I am,' that which is that it is. He is the rock against which we beat in vain, that which bruises and overwhelms us when we seek to impose our wishes, contrary to him, upon him."[21]

Man's freedom need not be in vain, however, because God's presence is not in vain. "Near is the God and hard to grasp," yes. But Hölderlin also knew, as he expressed it in his *Homecoming*, "That which thou seekest is near, and already coming to meet thee."

In Old Testament faith, God's presence is believed to be the appearance not of God but of his glory. And the glory of God is wherever God is not present in vain. At a certain moment in the life of Israel, however, the glory of God became synonymous with a hope projected upon the future. And when Jesus appeared as the Christ, he was himself proclaimed to be "the Lord of glory."[22] This designation bears a double significance for Christians. In the first place, Christ is himself the presence of God in glory, which is to say: in view of Christ, God is not present in vain. But, in the second place, the Church which lives from the glory of God's presence in Christ lives toward the full appearance of his glory in the last days. Meanwhile, then, the Christian's life is a life *in via*, a life "from glory to glory."[23] The Church lives by the sufficiency of Christ's glory as it participates in his presence through the Eucharist and as it experiences the intimacy of God's presence

[21] "A Communication," *The Christian Century*, April 6, 1932, p. 443.
[22] I Cor. 2:9; James 2:1.
[23] II Cor. 3:7 ff.

through the mediation of the Holy Spirit, whose role it is to make the glorified Christ present to the Church.

The presence of God in Christ is achieved through the overcoming of the limit of being which separates God and man. The great "new mystery" which the early fathers knew is that the structure which is irreversible from man's side has at one point been upended, from God's side. When the transcendent God crosses over into manhood in Christ, he does not abrogate this structure. He illustrates it. When John Calvin says that God was on earth without leaving heaven, he is not merely indulging himself in first-century mythology. He is elucidating the dialectical tension in the life of God which is God's cardinal redemptive act. The presence of God to the world in Christ, theologically speaking, is unique not simply for the reason that there are no other instances in which the faithfulness of God toward history is achieved by so ontologically traumatic a device. It is unique because there can be no other instances. He is the presence of the fullness of God, the *totus intra carnem*. This is the truth about God's seriousness with history which the early creeds meant to affirm when they located the son of God wholly on the Creator side of the Creator-creature structure without ceasing to refer to God as one and without ceasing to refer to the Christ as Jesus of Nazareth. In Christ the hidden God is present as he is present nowhere else.

And to what end? To the end that God, though hidden, is really present, and that his presence is not in vain but is a presence *pro nobis*. It is to the credit of the post-Christian gnostics that they saw this clearly. In culpable disregard of the boundary between God and man, mankind was found to be battering against that boundary in a futile effort to rise to heights belonging to God alone. The ill-conceived siege against the wall of heaven produced in the ontologically insensitive the psychologically intolerable moods of melancholy and dread, of fear and anxiety, clear symptoms that man was somehow living against his vocation. The Son of God, so the gnostics rightly believed, was sent across that boundary to reveal to man what it means to be a man, namely, to induce mankind to adopt for itself the boundaries which the structure of reality imposes upon human life. In abysmal irresponsibility toward the structure in reality which says God cannot come out of hiding, mankind was making itself wretched in its search for him. The gnostics believed the Son of God was sent across the boundary between invisibility and visibility to tutor mankind in just what is and what is not knowable. Not—as is often though mistakenly believed about such gnostics as the Valentinians—to teach the infinite details about God as if such knowledge about God were in itself redemptive, but to communicate this one redemptive bit of news—that God is not a God who can be held at the end of the human reach. When the understanding becomes satisfied that God is unknowable it is restored to health.[24] God became man in order that man might come to God on ontologically authentic terms.

Man hurts himself when he resists the conditions of reality in which there is one God. But the "new mystery" of the Christian faith is not that God is real, but that he is present and that his presence is not in vain. The "new mystery" is that God hurts himself in the act of overcoming the structure that necessarily separates him from man in order to dramatize the existence of the structure. In that act God loves the world. By that act God loves the world in such a way as to induce man's compliant, responsive, affectionate assumption of the human role.

The consequence of God's presence is what is decisive for man, for man's love of God is scarcely explicable simply on the basis of what God is. In the light of what God *is*, he is an object of competition, stirring up the marathon runner in man's soul and tempting him to overreach himself. Man will not be superseded, and the existence of one God, who alone is God, is the occasion of the deepest temptation in the human spirit. In the light of what God *is*, he is himself primarily a jealous God who will not brook the oversight of man. Jealousy in God, as the Epistle of James makes clear, is appropriate to God chiefly because it is so inappropriate to man. God has one unique prerogative that must be honored, namely, that he alone is first. When man reflects the existence of every other reality but God, God has no alternative but jealousy. Schleiermacher was quite wrong in refusing to attribute characteristics to God which one would find revolting in one's friends. Jealousy is incompatible with a human life in the same way that God-Almightyness is incompatible. It is appropriate to God alone.

But Luther was right: it is not religiously edifying to understand God outside of Christ, seeing in God the qualities which evoke only *Anfechtung* and feeling the rage of his jealous spirit. Nothing is more conducive to asperity in man than aseity in God. Seen in Christ, however, God is not simply *a se*. He is *pro nobis*. To understand God in Christ is to see that God is a God who hurts himself against the same barrier against which man is hurting himself, in order to reconcile man to his vocation as a man. He becomes a God who loves, whose suffering is a seal of his love, and whose suffering love provides the ground for the possibility of man's response of love. "This is the greatest proof of the goodness of God," said Clement of Alexandria. "Estranged by nature, yet he cares for us."[25] We love him because he first loved us. His act of love makes man's love possible. It is, therefore, ambiguous to say that God is good, or love, or faithful apart from this act by which

---

[24] Irenaeus, *Against Heresies*, II, xviii, 2.
[25] *Miscellanies*, II, xvi.

he incarnates himself in human existence in order to reconcile man to himself.

To say that God *is* love and thereby to mean that love is an attribute, or a perfection, or the very essence of God is to court real theological peril. God is *God*. Beyond the irreversible ontological structure involved in the sole deity of God, all predication takes on the tinge of a subjective valuing of God. But to evaluate God by identifying his being with love and goodness inverts the very structure that specifies his deity. The logic of "radical monotheism" is "objective relativism," to use Richard Niebuhr's phrases. The One God is not to be subjected to the human value sense. He is the objective origin of the values by which man's values stand revalued, or relativized. In his reality as God, he is the hidden valuer present to all human activity, setting the limits which mark out the contour and direction of the river bed in which the human stream may find its course. In his revelation in history God *acts* in love to invoke man's sensitivity to this ontological topography.

To say that God *is* love is to create an ontology out of the unreflective witness of Christian piety. The ontology is not as innocent as the witness. For when one says "God *is* love" the consequence of this predication is to say "God *must* love. It is his *nature* to love." But love that is natural or essential is necessary or obliged and therefore less than love. One ought not to infer from God's reconciling act in Christ a "redemptive principle" in God. Process theology makes this mistake in its most exaggerated form when it describes a structure of reality in which God does not need to incarnate himself in history because he is always and necessarily there, and in which mercy is not therefore optional to God.

There is only one thing God *must* be. He must be *God*. There is mystery enough in that: a mystery which, when unacknowledged, painfully thwarts the world. But when God in the freedom of his transcendent being plunges himself across the ontological barrier, stretches himself from heaven to earth in the lifetime of Jesus of Nazareth, to bring to man the gospel of God, he *loves* the world in a way that catches the world up short by its very newness. This is the *new* covenant, *kaine* and not *neos*, unique and not simply chronologically recent. This is the covenant *ephapax*, final, once-for-all, unrepeatable because inexhaustible. Not simply the being of God but his act in Christ gives to God the value of goodness and love and faithfulness. Not simply the reality of God as God but his will to be present to man in the faithfulness of a passionate act of reconciling concern. The hidden God who is really there in Christ is redemptively present there for us.

10.

THE KINGDOM OF GOD
IN AMERICA AND
THE TASK OF THE CHURCH

ROBERT S. MICHAELSEN

1. THE INTERPRETATION OF HISTORY

THE momentous events of recent years have forced many of us into a more thorough study of American history in an effort to discover who we are and where we are going. Involvement in two world wars, confrontation with the forces of German national socialism and Russian communism, development and use of weapons of tremendous power, our recent and rather dramatic ascension to an unparalleled position of world power—all these and other factors have compelled us to make a new effort to find out how we got this way, what guides we have lived by and will live by, what destiny belongs to us. In part we have been involved in a frantic effort to measure up to the crucial situation in which we find ourselves—to show a mature countenance to the almost overwhelming responsibilities which have been heaped upon us. We have hoped to impress the world—and especially those with a maturer and older culture than ours—that we have the depth, strength and maturity to play our role with competence and lasting success. In part we have intended to prove by citing our history and our ideals that we are indeed a superior people and that, if we but live by what has made us great, we need have no worries about weathering the present storm.

As we have turned with both anxiety and assurance to the study of our past, we have almost immediately become involved—consciously or unconsciously—in the question of what framework we will use to interpret our history, and to give meaning to our present and direction to our future. A few of the more scholarly investigators among us still cling to a purely "objective" study of history—hoping to allow history to speak for itself—but most of those who claim the badge of scholarship have more or less freely proceeded to write against the background of a particular interpretative framework, while the less scholarly or the unscholarly have made little or no pretense to objectivity. From the world of scholarship we have had an abundance of emphasis upon the determinative nature of economic factors in our history. We have been reminded that our classical documents and the ideology they set forth have been produced in large measure out of a conflict of class interest and an interaction between men and their environment (Beard, e.g.). We have been informed that our present world position has resulted largely from our unique situation in the Western Hemisphere, our relative sparseness or rarity of population, and our abundance of natural resources. Many who have begun with the premise of economic interpretation have concentrated upon the importance of the "frontier" in American history—stressing the role of this factor in the birth and growth of democratic theory and practice and in the development of our institutions and culture (the Turner school, e.g.). Those who have done this have not known just what approach to take in an America that is becoming more industrialized and urbanized. Now that the frontier—understood in traditional terms—is gone, what shall we look to as the stimulator of democracy?

On the other hand, there have been those in the world of scholarship who have turned more to ideological factors in their interpretation of our past and present. They have endeavored to find out what has gone into the making of the "American spirit" or the "American mind" —ferreting out such influences as those of Puritanism, the Enlightenment, "romanticism," "realism" (R. B. Perry, e.g.). They have striven to demonstrate that America is the product of a peculiar combination of ideas and ideals and not just the result of a certain concatenation of material or economic factors.

Outside the world of scholarship two interpretative frameworks especially have been employed in coming to some understanding of the meaning of American history and American destiny. One has been most popular outside of America, the other within this nation. The Communist has sought and found meaning in history from the standpoint of the Marxian interpretation. He presumes to see clearly the outlines of historical development and thus to know with certainty where we are going. He understands America as a bourgeois and imperialistic nation —as representative of a segment or element which is bound to be overcome with the triumph of the classless society. Knowing this, he can place himself squarely in line with developing historical forces— with the onward movement of the dialectic—and can, in a sense, determine the future. This future for America means either a destruction from without or a complete overturning from within.

On the other hand, the American patriot links the meaning of history with the fate of his nation. He regards the birth of his nation as a special act of providence or as that occurrence toward which the whole of historical development has been pointing. Confidently, he feels that the future of the world rests with the future of his nation, his political ideology, and his economic system. For him the study of American history takes the form of proving the superiority of his nation and upholding its "manifest destiny."

The interpreters of American religious history, or of the history of the Church in America, have also been involved in the necessity of writing their history from the standpoint of a particular interpretative framework. In many cases these interpreters have found the socioeconomic framework to be a very fruitful one. One of the most successful —and possibly most accurate—ways of understanding what has happened to religion in America has been that of pointing to the role of economic, class, national and racial factors in shaping American Christianity. And one of the most penetrating analyses based upon this framework is H. Richard Niebuhr's *The Social Sources of Denominationalism.* The appeal of this work is attested by the fact that it is still much in demand and widely used by the historians and sociologists who are concerned with religion in America, although it was first published over twenty-five year ago.

Other interpreters of religion in America have turned to the "frontier thesis" of F. J. Turner and have described American Christianity in terms of its reaction to the frontier—a reaction which has made it largely sectarian, individualistic, revivalistic, democratic and "unchurchly" in character (W. W. Sweet, e.g.). Still others have confined themselves to denominational developments and have attempted to apply European standards and techniques of church history to the writing of an "American church history."[1]

Our present situation in America has not only forced us to re-examine our history, it has also prompted us to call into question some of the ways in which we have approached that history in the past; or perhaps to accept them for their usefulness, and then to go beyond them in search of broader and more meaningful grounds of interpretation. For those of us concerned with American church history or American Christianity this has meant grasping for a framework which can account for or discover a unity in our religious diversity, an order in our apparent disorder and confusion. At the same time, we have hoped to find

[1] For a discussion of the various approaches to American church history see: L. J. Trinterud, "Some Notes on Recent Periodical Literature on Colonial American Church History," in *Church History,* XX (December, 1951), pp. 72-74; and "The Task of the American Church Historian," *Church History,* XXV (March, 1956), pp. 3-15.

grounds which will not only make evident to us a fuller meaning in our religious history but will also shed light upon the history and role of our nation in general. This turn from one framework in search for another and more satisfactory one is evident in Richard Niebuhr's study of American Christianity. Having produced an excellent study of American Christianity from the standpoint of a socioeconomic interpretation, he found that the picture he had painted was incomplete. He writes in the Preface to his second book on American Christianity:

> Though the sociological approach helped to explain why the religious stream flowed in these particular channels (*i.e.*, denominations) it did not account for the force of the stream itself; while it seemed relevant enough to the institutionalized churches it did not explain the Christian movement which produced these churches; while it accounted for the diversity in American religion it did not explain the unity which our faith possesses despite its variety; while it could deal with the religion which was dependent on culture it left unexplained the faith which is independent, which is aggressive rather than passive, and which molds culture instead of being molded by it.[2]

The new framework used by Niebuhr to interpret American Christianity is that of the idea of the kingdom of God. This is "the dominant idea in American Christianity." It has been understood mainly in terms of "sovereignty of God," "reign of Christ," and "kingdom on earth." These various interpretations have prevailed during different consecutive periods, but they also have been intimately related to each other in each period of American history. Within this framework it becomes evident that American Christianity cannot be understood apart from its dynamic aspects, apart from the fact that it has had a positive influence in shaping culture as well as the fact that it has been shaped by culture. Christianity, and particularly Protestantism, in America "must be understood as a movement rather than as an institution or series of institutions."[3] Use of this framework to interpret American Christianity also makes it evident that the Christian community has played its most vital role in relation to American society when it has been most faithful to its task of proclaiming the reality and relevance of the kingdom of God.

While this framework of the idea of the kingdom of God is primarily a way of interpreting the history of Christianity in America, it also offers insights into the meaning of American history itself. Those who have taken seriously the idea of the kingdom of God, who have striven to be citizens of that kingdom, and who at the same time have attempted to apply their insights to world or national history have frequently furnished us with most meaningful and helpful skeleton

---

[2] *The Kingdom of God in America*, (Chicago and New York: Willett, Clark & Company, 1937), pp. vii-viii.
[3] *Ibid.*, pp. xi-xii.

frameworks for the interpretation of history. This is true of the ancient Hebrew prophets, of St. Augustine, and of many others. It is also true of such thoughtful and God-centered Americans as Jonathan Edwards. Niebuhr wrote about the history of the *idea*, but this "leads on to the history of the kingdom of God" itself—a history which will see America in an ultimate theological frame of reference. He left us with the hope that his work might serve " 'even as a stepping stone' to the work of some American Augustine who will write a *City of God* that will trace the story of the eternal city in its relations to modern civilization instead of to ancient Rome, or of Jonathan Edwards *Redivivus* who will bring down to our own time the *History of the work of Redemption*." But even in his "preliminary" work Niebuhr underlined the conviction "that American Christianity and American culture cannot be understood at all save on the basis of faith in a sovereign, living, loving God."[4] And in his writing and teaching since the publication of that work he has helped us gain insights and understanding which may help us to see the meaning of the kingdom of God in and for America.

On the basis of these insights we shall attempt to write of the meaning of the kingdom of God to America's past, and especially to its present and future. What is attempted here is a constructive statement and not primarily an exposition of Niebuhr's analysis. The perceptive reader will understand, however, that what is really "constructive" in this essay is due almost entirely to Niebuhr's influence.

In times of crisis Christians have always turned to their past—to their "internal history"—to remind themselves of what has happened to them and of where they stand in their present, even as the Israelites in their times of distress constantly turned to the memory of their deliverance from bondage in Egypt, their wanderings in the wilderness and their Sinai, their confrontation and covenant with God. The Christian has learned once more to look upon history in terms of the acts of God—something which in more comfortable times he too frequently forgets to do. He has learned again that the kingdoms of this world have no ultimate meaning in and of themselves but can rightly be understood only in terms of the ultimate kingdom, the kingdom of God. Once more he has come to understand that his present and his destiny has significance only in the context of the purposes and actions of the almighty God.

Augustine, writing at the time of the collapse of Roman civilization, could find ultimate meaning in this event and all of history only in the light of the history of the city of God and its opposite, the city of earth. Calvin, standing at the edge of the modern era, could understand the religious, political, and social revolutions of his time only in terms of the designs of the divine sovereign. And Edwards, when he

[4] *Ibid.*, p. xiv.

endeavored to fathom the meaning of the "spiritual awakenings" which were occurring with such frequency and such violence in his time and to understand the significance of the separation of this "new world" of America from an older world of Europe, could do so only by tracing out the course of the One who is "Alpha and Omega." So the present-day Christian and the Christian community must speak of the kingdom of God in these critical times.

Anyone who attempts to write about the "acts of God" or the movement of the kingdom of God is constantly in danger of committing the gravest of errors—not only the error of inaccuracy but, what is worse, the error or even sin of pride or presumptuousness. We read, perhaps with mixed feelings, Edwards' arguments why "the latter-day glory is probably to begin in America,"[5] or Samuel Hopkins' detailed discussion of when the millennium will begin.[6] But we need not accuse them of being presumptuous, nor can we discard all of their work and their insights because they might have been wrong at points. We face a critical time, as they did, and we will do well indeed if we can bring to bear upon our age as much faith and wisdom as they brought to bear on theirs without committing error—let alone without succumbing to the temptation of pride. Despite just such dangers, we believe and hope that an attempt at a constructive statement of the present sort has some *raison d' être*, not only by virtue of the fact that the critical nature of our time demands a renewed attempt to find the meaning of our history, but also because each generation of Christians is faced with the task of attempting to come to an understanding of its time and its situation so that it can live with some responsibility and wisdom.

2. GOD IS SOVEREIGN

The kingdom of God means that God is sovereign. He is the ruler over the destinies of men and of nations, over history as well as nature. In fact the Hebrew prophets and most Christian theologians have been much more concerned with the God of history than with the God of nature—or more with God's acts in history than with God's acts in the world of nature.[7] This perspective differs from that common among the deists of the eighteenth century whose influence was so strong among America's founding fathers. They were well aware of "nature" and

---

[5] *The Works of President Edwards* (New York, 1830), vol. IV, pp. 128 ff.

[6] *Works* (Boston, 1854), vol. II, pp. 296 ff.

[7] "The God who brought his people out of the land of Egypt, out of the house of bondage, was to be celebrated in the Old Testament pre-eminently as the God of History. It seems to have been when the Children of Israel lapsed into idolatry—gave themselves over to the worship of Baal, for example—that they turned rather to the God of Nature, glorifying the forces of the physical universe and the fertility of the earth." Herbert Butterfield, *Christianity and History* (New York: Chas. Scribner's Sons, 1949), p. 1.

"nature's god" but their sense of God active in history was not as acute as that of their forefathers had been—or for that matter, as that of Abraham Lincoln three generations later. The point of view of many of these founding fathers of the eighteenth century gave birth to a common and highly important ideology in American history—an ideology which has stressed the role of the free man in determining his own destiny, in mastering his own fate. In this view the individual is given an impressive place in the founding and governing of the state and nation. He is sovereign. Ultimate power rests in the people. This, however, is not precisely the view expressed in the Bible and by Christian theologians through the ages. Ultimate power rests in God. He is sovereign.

There are many implications in the concept of God's sovereignty. One has been suggested already. Too optimistic a sense of man's power will be regarded as false by the one who takes God's sovereignty seriously. Furthermore, he will be compelled to warn his optimistic fellowman that he is doomed to be disillusioned. For just at that moment when men have been most secure in their sense of control over their destinies, their man-made structures have collapsed about them and they have found themselves the helpless victims of a wave of circumstance beyond their control. Just at that point, however, the one who begins with the sovereignty of God will want also to discourage a too-pessimistic view of man and his destiny. The temptation of the disillusioned optimist is to give over to despair and in that mood to leave himself at the mercy of the cynical demagogue.

God is sovereign over all. The Bible is "whole-istic" in its understanding of the sovereignty of God. He rules over all; no act or phase of history can be understood as being apart from his providence. We err if we think of his sovereignty solely in terms of what we regard as the "good" acts of man and nations or only in terms of the "good" which we experience. Just as in the world of nature "he makes his sun rise on the evil and on the good, and sends rain on the just and on the unjust," so in the world of history his sovereignty is evident in the acts of Israel and of Persia (or Cyrus) and his power is manifested in both the good and the evil that is done "in the city."[8]

The sovereignty of God is the guiding factor in understanding history. This does not mean, however, that one phase of history reveals his purpose as much as another or that his immediate purpose is clear even to the most astute and sensitive observers. He rules over all, but he also can and does select certain men and nations for special acts of providence or for a special role in the realization of his ultimate purpose. And, on the other hand, others may be rejected.

Beginning with the assertion that God is sovereign and the affirmation that he is the Lord of history, the sensitive Christian will endeavor

[8] Matt. 5:45; Is. 44:28; Am. 3:6.

to become a citizen of the kingdom of God, to give his allegiance to the sovereign, to live as best he can according to the sovereign's will, and to affirm his faith before others. We do not mean to imply that he has been or will be granted access to the secrets of the most high. He will need to judge the significance and meaning of each situation on the basis of what he knows from the past and upon the grounds of his faith that the sovereign Lord has revealed himself—his nature and above all his ultimate purpose for man—in Jesus Christ. Given this foundation, which is quite substantial indeed, the rest will have to be improvisation. We assume that the improvisation has meaning in terms of the purposes of the sovereign. Thus, we understand providence not as meaning that the whole thing is cut and dried from the beginning but simply that the sovereign is working out his purposes in a creative fashion and from moment to moment in interaction with factors and forces outside himself but not ultimately beyond his control.

The Protestant Reformers affirmed this sense of the sovereignty of God. They were vividly aware of God's acts in history, and they proclaimed his immediate and direct rule over the affairs of men. On this ground they stood in criticism of all men and institutions who tried to usurp sovereignty for themselves. With this conviction of God's sovereignty as a foundation, they attempted to erect a structure (religious, political, economic) which would witness to and remain true to the One beyond the many.[9] Their followers among the early settlers of this country carried on their attempt in terms of a Christian or biblical constitutionalism, in a church independent of culture but dependent on the kingdom of God, and in a recognition that all human power is temporal and limited.[10] Looking back upon the attempt of the settlers from another age with its different perspectives and values, we may well be inclined to pronounce it a miserable failure. And yet today we are not inclined to dismiss these early American Protestants as lightly as once we were. We recognize—grudgingly perhaps—that the early Puritans, Quakers, and others approached their tasks with bold designs and sincere efforts, that their lives—or their approaches to life—were characterized by a rare combination of realism and idealism, and that they found in their world a sense of unity and purpose which may even be instructive to us.

These early American Protestants wrote their history with constant reference to the providence of God. Patriarchs found abundant evidence of the mighty works of God in their own lives and in the communities in which they had lived and served.[11] Members of the second, third, and fourth generations looked back upon the societies established

[9] Niebuhr, *The Kingdom of God in America*, chap. I.
[10] *Ibid.*, chap. II.
[11] William Bradford, *Of Plymouth Plantation*; and John Winthrop, *Journal.*

by their fathers and recorded their convictions that God's mercies were especially evident in those societies.[12] We are skeptical of their certainty that God had withheld the discovery of America until the Protestant Reformation and scornful of their narrow identification of God's special providence with a Puritan commonwealth, with Boston, and with North Church.[13] But if we take seriously the idea of a sovereign God active in history we cannot totally discard their reading of history, although we may wish to relegate much of it to an irrelevant antiquity.

The fundamental conviction which these men shared with earlier theologians and writers of history, with the early Christians and with the prophets, was that God's acts, God's sovereignty, furnish the key to history. Without this understanding, all was confusion to them. This is perhaps best expressed in America by a late "Puritan," Jonathan Edwards. If we behold events in any other view than from the standpoint of the work of God, he wrote, "all will look like confusion, like the tossing of waves; things will look as though one confused revolution came to pass after another, merely by blind chance, without any regular or certain end." But considered under the sovereignty of God it all fits together. His providence is like "a large and long river, having innumerable branches, beginning in different regions, and at a great distance one from another, and all conspiring to one common issue." This "stream of divine providence" begins and ends in God. He "is the infinite ocean into which it empties itself." Or, "Providence is like a mighty wheel, whose circumference is so high that it is dreadful, with the glory of the God of Israel above upon it. . . ." We can see the revolution of this wheel, how it comes from God and returns to him. Or again, "All the events of divine providence are like the links of a chain; the first link is from God, and the last is to him. . . ." He is the Alpha and the Omega—"he *who is*, and *who was*, and *who is to come*."[14]

If one takes this view of the sovereignty of God seriously, one will endeavor to find meaning in America's beginnings, history, and destiny in terms of his providence and his sovereignty. One cannot stop with socioeconomic factors alone nor even with the movement of ideas and ideals—be they even religious ideas and ideals. In all humility and exercising utmost ability, one will want to search out the ways of God with this nation. Although satisfactory answers may be few, this much is certain: America did not create herself and she is not the sole master

[12] See Perry Miller and T. H. Johnson, *The Puritans* (New York: American Book Co., 1938), pp. 81 ff.

[13] Vernon Louis Parrington, *Main Currents in American Thought* (New York: Harcourt Brace and Co., 1927-1930), vol. I, p. 107; and Niebuhr, *The Kingdom of God in America*, p. 171.

[14] *Works*, vol. III, pp. 427 ff.

of her destiny. The hand of God has been laid upon this nation and she has a role to play in his providence; she has some relationship to his kingdom. A fuller analysis of the Christian understanding of the kingdom of God may provide a fuller basis for understanding that role and relationship.

3. GOD'S VISITATION IN JESUS CHRIST

The kingdom of God means the reign of Christ. Or, the kingdom of God means grace as well as sovereignty, or grace as an expression of sovereignty. It implies direct visitation by God—visitation pregnant with the reality both of judgment and of redemption. The Christian affirms that this visitation comes directly in Christ. In him God's purpose for man and nation becomes fully evident. In him God confronts man directly and decision becomes necessary. "The time is fulfilled, and the kingdom of God is at hand; repent, and believe in the gospel."[15] Before Christ men were in bondage to fear, sin, disorder, and were without hope. Through Christ comes redeeming grace, salvation, deliverance, liberty—the liberty of the children of God. These convictions are central in the New Testament. They were experienced anew among the early Protestants. As Richard Niebuhr says, their

common conviction was that whereas before the revolution of Jesus Christ men, with some exceptions, had to be kept in order and had to keep themselves in order by fear and restraint and were without hope, they now had experienced or could experience the "expulsive power of a new affection" which made a life of freedom possible. The new relation to God established by Jesus Christ meant that an order of liberty and love had been substituted for the order of regimentation and fear.[16]

The period of the Great Awakening in America was especially characterized by this sense of the reign of Christ. The leaders of that movement were overwhelmed by a feeling of urgency: God has spoken and speaks through Christ. All who do not hear or who turn away from Christ's kingdom are doomed. All who are made members of that kingdom have newness of life which cannot be compared with anything they have known before.[17] These leaders felt that God had chosen to pour out his grace in a special and bountiful fashion in their time. "The work of redemption in its effects," wrote Edwards,

has mainly been carried on by remarkable communications of the Spirit of God. Though there be a more constant influence of God's Spirit always in some degree attending his ordinances; yet the way in which the greatest

---

[15] Mark 1:15.
[16] *The Kingdom of God in America*, p. 90.
[17] See Edwards' description of the experience of his wife Sarah, *Works*, vol. IV, pp. 110-18.

things have been done towards carrying on his work, always have been by remarkable effusions, at special seasons of mercy. . . .[18]

Such a time was being experienced in the 1730's and 1740's, and that sense of God's visitation in and through Christ has continued to play a dominant role in American Christianity.

The leaders of the Great Awakening thought of God's visitation in Christ almost entirely in individualistic terms. Individuals are redeemed and become members of Christ's kingdom. Individuals find life and liberty in Christ. Individuals are called upon to live lives of "true virtue" characterized by "love of being in general" or "disinterested benevolence." But some of these leaders were also aware of God's visitation to a people or a nation, such as ancient Israel. They saw, though dimly, the concurrence of the Great Awakening with the stirrings toward political independence. They were aware that, in some sense, this was America's "national conversion."[19] or at least America's national visitation. Their message had significance for the nation about to be born as well as for the individuals who heard them. It is a message still to be taken very seriously by the Christian community concerned to live by its vocation.

Using the categories of sovereignty of God and reign of Christ and of providence and special visitation or grace, we might profitably look upon our national history. Parallels have been drawn between Israel and America. Can we speak of our deliverance from Egypt, our Sinai, our wilderness wanderings, and our entry into the promised land? Certainly many of our forefathers felt that they were escaping the bondage of Egypt when they came to these shores. Many of them also were certain that they were parties to a covenant with God. "Whether our nation interprets its spiritual heritage through Massachusetts or Virginia," writes Reinhold Niebuhr,

we came into existence with the sense of being a "separated" nation, which God was using to make a new beginning for mankind. We had renounced the evils of European feudalism. We had escaped from the evils of European religious bigotry. We had found broad spaces for the satisfaction of human desires in place of the crowded Europe. . . . We had been called out by God to create a new humanity. We were God's "American Israel."[20]

"The whole shaping of the fabric of our government is providential," wrote Bushnell. "God, God is in it everywhere. He is Founder before

[18] *Works*, vol. III, p. 184. Cf. p. 268.
[19] Niebuhr, *The Kingdom of God in America*, p. 126.
[20] *The Irony of American History* (New York: Chas. Scribner's Sons, 1952), p. 24. Unfortunately, and even tragically, many of the early settlers had such a sense of destiny as "new Israelites" that they could only regard the natives as "new Canaanites" to be treated with the same kind of zeal that the ancient Israelites used in subduing the "Promised Land."

the founders, training both them and us. . . . Our whole civil order is the ordinance of God. . . ."[21] If the hand of God was evident in the early settlements of this country, was it not even more evident in the birth of the nation? Just as we may speak of the birth of each nation in terms of God's visitation, so it was with America. Events conspired so that a new beginning became possible—a new beginning full of promise. Circumstances compelled a disparate people to become one. The land was there in all its abundance. There existed a remarkable amount of freedom from the bonds of existing and moribund structures and institutions. Many of the patterns of thought and of political and economic structure were such as to contribute to, rather than hinder, the founding of a new people. Men of vision met the opportunities of their time with courage and ability. The early national documents and the new political structure represent the efforts of these men to capitalize upon these opportunities and to establish a people and a nation. They are both gifts of God and response to God's gifts or God's visitation. In a sense they are the results of an American Sinai.

But we do not always regard them as such. Like the ancient Israelites, we are inclined to forget our deliverance from bondage or to credit this deliverance to our own efforts. We regard our freedom in terms of the right to assert ourselves and not as release from bondage to self. We are prone to disregard God's visitation in the time of our birth and to believe that we gave birth to ourselves unaided. We turn our backs upon our Sinai and violate the terms of the covenant. The "American creed" becomes a sacred document to be placed in the holy of holies and worshipped, but not to be followed. Or we constantly distort the creed until it becomes a means of self congratulation and self-adulation.

From the beginning the danger has existed that our response to God's visitation would be negative, that we would associate ourselves not with the city of God but with the city of earth. The citizens of this latter city receive the gifts of providence but do not acknowledge them or change their allegiance and their way of life. They are confident that they—and not God—manipulate the course of history. They feel that their destiny is irrevocably tied up with the race's welfare. They regard their prosperity as their own doing, and they attribute their adversity to their enemies. What ideals they have they pervert to their own selfish ends and for their own glorification. We assert that we are the masters of our fate. We regard our response as ideal and our well-being as indispensable to mankind's well-being.[22] We attribute our prosperity to our own virtue. ("Industry plus frugality equals wealth

[21] Horace Bushnell, "Popular Government by Divine Right," in *Building Eras in Religion* (New York, 1903), p. 310.
[22] See Reinhold Niebuhr, *The Irony of American History*, pp. 70 ff.

and virtue.")[23] And we dilute our high ideals with prudence and egoism.[24]

But the city of God flourishes and will flourish and the city of earth will perish.[25] The kingdom of God involves judgment, judgment upon those who turn their backs upon the reign of Christ or those who respond to God's sovereignty and visitation with an attempted denial.

What does judgment mean in the history of a nation? In part it means corruption within, challenge from without, and eventual dissolution. Self-exaltation is an acid which eats away at the foundations of life. Attempts to live as one's own sovereign gradually sever the roots which lie buried in the only true ground of sovereignty and power. The plant may grow and flourish for a time, but it cannot hope to live. Where shall it turn for nourishment? To itself? Then inevitably it will wither and die. Or, to use the Second Isaiah's figure,[26] pride is like a moth which consumes the garment bit by bit until all that remains is a tattered fragment. The nation which flaunts its own righteousness and self-sufficiency before God and the world slowly becomes corrupt within. It pretends to be its own guide and thus cannot be righteous. It creates its own morality and identifies right with its might. And so its statesmen, unless they stand on the true foundations of righteousness, will eventually betray it and its people, and it will betray the world.

Without strength within, how can the nation overcome pressure from without? For a time its might may prevail over the might of other cities of this world, but the corruption within will eventually so weaken it that it will crumble before superior force. Then where will its sovereignty be?

This story is told again and again in the Bible. Everything and every nation that asserts its self-sufficiency and that attempts to stand in the way of the work of redemption is destroyed. This is a major theme in the prophetic message. "And I will utter my judgments against them touching all their wickedness, in that they have forsaken me, and have burned incense unto other gods and worshipped the works of their own hands."[27] Our nation has today reached its highest

---

[23] *Poor Richard's Almanack.*

[24] "Everything in the Christian faith which points to ultimate and transcendent possibilities is changed into simple historical achievements." Reinhold Niebuhr, *The Irony of American History*, p. 12.

[25] "For the moth shall eat them up like a garment, and the worm shall eat them like wool: but my righteousness shall be for ever, and my salvation from generation to generation." (Is. 51:8). Edwards placed this verse at the beginning of his *History of the Work of Redemption.*

[26] Is. 51:8.

[27] Jer. 1:16. This applies specifically to Israel but elsewhere in Jeremiah, as in other prophets, it is applied to other nations. Cf. also, Edwards, *Works*, vol. III, p. 193.

point of power. But at the same time it faces its greatest challenge from without—and perhaps from within also. What, now, will be our response to this visitation? Are we too late?

"Once to every man and nation comes the moment to decide," writes Lowell. Perhaps there is a sense in which once a decision is made—by man or nation—it cannot be revoked. Once the back is turned, how difficult it is to turn about again! On the other hand, there is also a sense in which each new situation brings a new moment of decision and a new possibility. No situation is without hope. At least the prophets knew that where God is there hope is—that his redemption cannot be stayed, that his kingdom will come.

4. THE COMING KINGDOM

The kingdom of God means hope—hope for ultimate redemption and for the full manifestation of the sovereign. The reality of judgment, as seen in the crumbling of those things in which one puts one's personal hopes, and ultimately in the facing of death, but even more as experienced in the dissolution of national hopes and even of the nation itself, prepares one for the prayer, "Thy kingdom come, Thy will be done in earth, as it is in heaven."[28] The judgment of God is never an end in itself. Through judgment he seeks to heal and redeem, to bring men and nation to their true destiny. Judgment is an expression of grace.

The Scriptures abound in the hope for fulfillment. Prophet and apostle alike live in anticipation of the fullness of God's glory. The prophet, who has known God's sovereignty, has experienced his grace, and has seen his judgment upon his nation, can go on to proclaim comfort to his people because he knows that "the glory of the Lord shall be revealed, and all flesh shall see it together, for the mouth of the Lord has spoken."[29] The apostle, whose assurance rests on the solid rock of God's act in Jesus Christ, can assert that "the sufferings of this present time are not worth comparing with the glory that is to be revealed to us." He sees this future revelation and redemption as applying not only to us as individuals but to the "whole creation" as well. It too "waits with eager longing for the revealing of the sons of God. . . ." And, although (or because) it has been subjected to futility, it "will be set free from its bondage to decay and obtain the glorious liberty of the children of God." Thus the creation and we ourselves, also, wait—and groan in travail—for the future redemption. And by this hope we were (and are) saved.[30]

Hope in the coming kingdom has been asserted again and again in America. In the early period of American history this hope seems to have been almost entirely subordinate to the desire for individual

[28] Matt. 6:10.
[29] Is. 40:5.
[30] Rom. 8:18-24.

salvation or personal immortality. As a result, society was bypassed, being "conceived in rather static terms—as an affair of institutions and laws rather than as a common life with a grand destiny comparable to that of the human soul."[31] There were some exceptions among the early Puritans and particularly among the Quakers who were especially aware of divine judgment upon society. The real revival of Christian hope, however, began with the awakenings. As we have seen, the leaders of the Great Awakening were very sensitive to Christ's rule. They applied this rule to individuals and thus also thought of hope in terms of future personal well-being. But their intense awareness of God's sovereignty and God's righteousness produced an acute consciousness of judgment.[32] Again judgment was conceived mostly in individual terms, but the social aspects of judgment were not overlooked—especially as these men looked to a coming kingdom which impinged on this age and which stood over against present social patterns and actions.

This awareness of judgment was coupled with a proclamation of the good news. Those who had experienced God's grace in Jesus Christ could see in judgment light as well as darkness. Hope rested on this foundation—and apart from it, these men realized, there was no hope. Some of these leaders even dared to give voice to the hope that the awakening itself was but the beginning of the coming of God's kingdom in fullness. They felt that his sovereignty was about to break in full force upon America.[33] At any rate, it was a *coming* kingdom which "appeared not as a goal toward which men were travelling but as the end which was hastening toward them. . . ."[34] This coming kingdom would be a time of great social redemption initiated and carried out by God.[35]

The awakenings made the millenarian tendency "the common and vital possession of American Christians."[36] From the middle of the eighteenth century on, this hope in the coming kingdom was proclaimed again and again in America until it became one of the central elements in American Christianity. It served—in its less individualistic and less fantastic phases—as a basis of criticism upon society and as a means

---

[31] Niebuhr, *The Kingdom of God in America*, p. 130.

[32] See the titles of Jonathan Edwards' sermons listed by Niebuhr, *ibid.*, pp. 138-139.

[33] Edwards, *Works*, vol. IV, pp. 128 ff; and Hopkins, "A Treatise on the Millennium," *Works*, vol. II, pp. 225 ff. Cf. Niebuhr, *The Kingdom of God in America*, p. 141.

[34] Niebuhr, *The Kingdom of God in America*, p. 137.

[35] Edwards describes it as a time of great light and knowledge, of holiness, peace, love, temporal prosperity and joy. "It may be hoped, that then many of the Negroes and Indians will be divines. . . . Then shall all the world be united in one amiable society. All nations, in all parts of the world, on every side of the globe, shall then be knit together in sweet harmony." *Works*, vol. III, pp. 404 ff. Cf. Hopkins, *Works*, vol. II, pp. 261-87.

[36] Niebuhr, *The Kingdom of God in America*, p. 143.

of calling for social change. And it gave much impetus to those programs and schemes designed to root out social evils. The nineteenth century brought the fullest fruition of this hope in the evangelical revivals and what followed them, and in the Social Gospel movement. The social energies generated by this hope in the coming kingdom were especially evident in the antislavery movement and in the criticisms of American social and economic structure in the latter half of the nineteenth century.

The development from the awakenings through the Social Gospel movement is all of one piece, although vast changes occurred over a period of a century and a half. Most men in both movements looked for the coming kingdom of God, and their sense of the reality of this kingdom made them critics of existing structures and generated the spirit of reform. The earlier prophets thought more in eschatological and cataclysmic terms, while those in the Social Gospel movement expected an evolutionary development moving eventually to the full realization of the kingdom of God on earth. But in most cases the leaders of the Social Gospel movement placed their hope primarily in God, and this was the message proclaimed to the world. This hope was forgotten or perverted by some for a time in the early twentieth century, but it is being reasserted by the Christian community again today.

What does this hope mean for the nation? It is, first of all, a social hope, a hope for a new society. Thus, it speaks to men as members of groups and nations as well as to individuals. It is a hope best understood by those who also know the reality of judgment. We have spoken of judgment upon the nation involving corruption within, challenge from without, and the threat of eventual dissolution. If we read the history of nations even from a "this-worldly" or "secular" perspective, we know that corruption, challenge and threat are real whether they are attributed to divine judgment or not. Nations and civilizations are born, flourish, become corrupt, are challenged from without, and eventually pass away. From a "this-worldly" perspective history may appear to be only cyclical in character. The nations rise and fall, but we apparently can find no ultimate purpose in the cycle. The nation which understands itself in these terms—especially as it sees signs of entering on the downward slope of the cycle—can have no ultimate hope. But the perspective of the kingdom of God discloses light where there appears to be only darkness. From this perspective we know that the righteousness of God is forever, that his eternal purpose is being and will be accomplished, that his kingdom will come in fullness. This is evident in God's Word—in the Scriptures and in Jesus Christ.

Interpreters of the Word of God find grounds for hope first of all in the possibility of a positive response to God's confrontation—in the giving of allegiance to the sovereign and in righteous action. "In returning and rest you shall be saved," says Isaiah to Israel.[37] "Zion shall be redeemed by justice. . . ."[38] "Let justice roll down like waters and righteousness like an ever-flowing stream,"[39] urges Amos, and he does so with the suggestion that when this happens redemption will take place. John the Baptist and Jesus, following in this prophetic tradition, proclaim: The kingdom of God is at hand, therefore repent and be saved. And John, the seer, sees an angel proclaiming an eternal gospel "to those who dwell on earth, to every nation and tribe and tongue and people . . ." and saying: "Fear God and give him glory, for the hour of his judgment has come. . . ."[40]

The prophet constantly calls upon Israel to remember and renew her covenant, and the apostle urges the new Israel to hold fast to the promises made in Jesus Christ. If we are permitted to regard the birth of our nation in terms of a covenant relationship with God, then we can also urge her to return and to fulfill that covenant. That covenant speaks of all men as being created equal; it ensures each the right to life, liberty, and the pursuit of happiness; and it guarantees freedom of personal expression and profession. These terms of the covenant are not realized apart from responsibility—responsibility to the other party to the covenant, and the responsibility of the nation itself to labor for realization of the covenant terms for all.[41] We fail in this responsibility whenever a man is discriminated against because of his race, color, creed, class, or national origin; whenever a person is refused the right to say or write what he wants to if what he says or writes does not do injury to others or incite others to violence; and whenever we stand in the way of other peoples in their legitimate aspirations for self-fulfillment.

The modern interpreter of the Word of God needs to remind the "American Israel" of its birth under God and its covenant with him. A similar word was spoken by the ancient prophet each time Israel faced a new crisis and a new peril stemming from corruption within and threat from without. In such a situation the prophet saw God's confrontation of his people once more and his indication of the way to salvation. Repentance, turning about, renewal of covenant—these are the way to strength in time of weakness, to righteousness as against corruption, and to security in time of peril. Ultimate security cannot possibly be achieved solely through military might or through a bel-

[37] Is. 30:15.
[38] Is. 1:27.
[39] Am. 5:24.
[40] Rev. 14:6, 7.
[41] Responsibility involves both responsibility *to* someone and *for* something—to God as well as for the community. See H. Richard Niebuhr, "The Responsibility of the Church for Society," in *The Gospel, the Church and the World* (New York: Harper & Brothers, 1946), pp. 114-15.

ligerent and chauvinistic assertion of superiority over other peoples and nations. "Righteousness exalts a nation."[42] And that means righteousness achieved through obedience to the will of the sovereign Lord of history, through living up to the covenant with him, not self-righteousness.

But neither prophet nor apostle rested his sole confidence in the righteousness of his people or of the nations. Both knew this to be a weak reed. They had seen too much of the world, too much of man's turning away. Their solid hope was founded not on the righteousness of the world but on the righteousness of God. The point of Ezekiel's striking vision of the valley of dry bones, for example, is that out of death comes life, out of despair, hope, not because of any power inherent in the situation of Israel itself, but as a result of the outpouring of the Spirit of the Lord.[43] This is the ultimate hope of the prophet—that the Spirit of the Lord will come upon his people. We confess, from our perspective in the Christian community, that this hope is fulfilled in and through Jesus Christ, that in him we have experienced the first fruits of the outpouring of the Spirit of God with power, and we look forward to a full manifestation of the Spirit, the glory, and the power of God. Christian hope rests upon the sure foundation of God's sovereignty and his grace in Jesus Christ, but the structure has yet to be completed.

The kingdom of God, understood as hope, does not assure the well-being of any nation. It does, however, make clear the importance of a nation's attempt at righteous response to God's grace and it encourages men and nations to await with eager longing and with conviction the healing of the nations and the realization of the glorious liberty of the children of God.

5. THE CHURCH OF GOD

The concept or the reality of the kingdom of God is the ultimate framework from which those of us in the Christian community can (and must) interpret the events of history—especially our own history as individuals and as members of groups and nations. We understand and we confess that "the world of culture—man's achievements—exists within the world of grace—God's Kingdom."[44] Though we may owe much to the social historians in our understanding of American history, we cannot agree with their ultimate interpretations. Where they see men and movements in terms of economic forces and social loyalties we must add that some men and movements have been moved by forces and loyalties which transcend these. Richard Niebuhr says:

[42] Prov. 14:34.
[43] Ezek. 37:1-14.
[44] H. Richard Niebuhr, *Christ and Culture* (New York: Harper & Brothers, 1951), p. 256.

When we turn to the history of American Christianity . . . we are scarcely convinced by the arguments of social historians that a John Cotton, a Roger Williams, a Jonathan Edwards, a Channing and all the other reputed initiators of new movements were primarily representatives of social loyalties. For the kingdom of God to which these men and the movements they initiated were loyal was not simply American culture or political and economic interests exalted and idealized; it was rather a kingdom which was prior to America and to which this nation, in its politics and economics, was required to conform. . . . The prophetic or revolutionary strain demands rebirth rather than conservation; it announces divine judgment rather than divine protection; and it looks forward to God's salvation rather than to human victory.[45]

When the development of the nation is understood with reference only to geographic, political and economic factors we must point beyond to the role of that Sovereign in and through whom the ultimate destinies of men and nations are realized.

We have described the kingdom of God in terms of God's sovereignty and providence, his grace revealed in and through Jesus Christ, his judgment, and his promise of an ultimate fulfillment—a promise which constitutes our sole lasting hope. We do not mean necessarily to suggest a natural progression from sovereignty to grace and from judgment to hope. Either of these aspects or facets of the kingdom of God may be evident in any one moment. What we see and experience depends in part upon our own history and the direction of our vision. The nation in the throes of new birth may dimly be aware of providence and of visitation and grace in Jesus Christ. That nation which has exalted itself and debased and destroyed others only to be destroyed itself may come to see only judgment. And yet in its ruined state it may experience a rebirth of hope; it may hear as a faint whisper the promises of God in Jesus Christ.

The Church in America—as elsewhere—has had and continues to have an ambivalent relationship to the kingdom of God. The Church is not that kingdom. It is "the subjective pole of the objective rule of God." It is in and through the Church that his kingdom is apprehended and proclaimed.[46] However, this kingdom is a movement, not an ideal or an organization.[47] It is a movement rooted in the sovereignty of God, manifested in the reign of Christ, and pointing toward the ultimate triumph of God's righteousness. But the finite men who would be its citizens are constantly tempted to try to capture citizenship by force and to embody the kingdom in or identify it with their own institutions and creeds. Or they lose sight of the ultimate sovereign and attempt to find rest and security in the kingdom of this world. Two dangers beset

[45] *The Kingdom of God in America*, pp. 10-11.

[46] H. Richard Niebuhr, *The Purpose of the Church and Its Ministry* (New York: Harper & Brothers, 1956), p. 19.

[47] *The Kingdom of God in America*, p. 164.

the Church in its attempt to carry out its task relative to the kingdom of God: institutionalism and secularization.

Institutionalization represents a genuine effort to conserve something of value in a religious movement; it is necessary to the ongoing religious community. It becomes "institutionalism" when the forms and practices of the institution are regarded as the community or movement itself or as the essential elements in the life of the community.[48] Institutionalism is characterized by a looking to the past and a defensiveness about that past. Institutionalization is a genuine and necessary effort to adapt what was of value in the original movement to a new situation. Frequently, however, the institutionalized form of the movement will adjust more easily to the world than the original movement itself did. Secularization is the gradual surrender by a movement to the pressures of the culture in which it exists.[49]

In American history we can see institutionalism and secularization happening to the Christian community or the Church in almost every age, but they are more obvious in some periods than others. The original positive thrust of constructive Protestantism in the early Puritan and Quaker movements was followed by a period of distinctive decline. "Puritanism and Quakerism . . . poured white-hot convictions into the souls of men, only to have these cool off into crystallized codes, solidified institutions, petrified creeds."[50] Second- and third-generation Puritans attempted to maintain the high standards of the fathers by creedal formulations, by adoption of the halfway covenant, and by a glorification of the past in their writing of its history. Piety degenerated into moralism and legalism, and the covenant theology became a means of encouraging good works and the assurance of salvation. The kingdom of God came to be identified with the Puritan commonwealth. Industry and frugality were regarded as signs of God's favor, and the economic order was given direct divine sanction.

A similar modification was evident in the Quakerism of the early eighteenth century. Quakers met the challenge of new circumstances by reverting to their past and attempting to establish themselves as a "peculiar people." From a start as a people bent upon permeating the world they became a people dedicated to the formation of a "spiritual remnant" set apart to guard and preserve "the truth" amidst a crooked and perverse generation. "Quakerism" became an end in itself.[51] In an

[48] For a discussion of the Church as institution and as community, see Niebuhr, *The Purpose of the Church and Its Ministry*, pp. 27 ff.

[49] See H. Richard Niebuhr, "The Disorder of Man in the Church of God," in *Man's Disorder and God's Design* (New York: Harper & Brothers, 1949), vol. I, p. 85, for a contemporary description of the disorder of secularism in the Church.

[50] Niebuhr, *The Kingdom of God in America*, pp. 166-67.

[51] See Rufus Jones, *The Quakers in the American Colonies* (London: Macmillan and Co., Ltd., 1911), especially the Introduction; and *The Later Periods of Quakerism* (London: Macmillan and Co., Ltd., 1921), vol. I, chaps. II and III.

effort to maintain the heritage of the fathers among the children the Quakers adopted the principle of birthright membership—a principle with certain similarities to the Puritan halfway covenant. In the political realm the story of Quaker activity in the eighteenth century was one of gradual withdrawal—a turning of political activities over to the gentiles. And in the economic realm we find that much the same sort of thing went on as in later Puritanism, i.e., a sanctification of commercial activity.[52]

Again, in the institutionalization of the awakenings and the revivals we can see a similar decline. A quick and emotional conversion was substituted for regeneration. The revival became a technique to be manipulated rather than a spontaneous outburst under the influence of the Spirit of God. Moral activity became chained to single-purpose movements such as temperance. Out of the revivals came denominations which soon developed into rigid institutions bent upon their own survival. The period following the evangelical revivals saw an American Christianity which was becoming increasingly individualistic, denominational- or institution-minded, and less concerned for the unified witness of the Church of God or the redemption of society. (The rise of missions and reform movements in this period may appear to refute this claim, but on the whole missionary activity was individualistic, and the reform movements were not informed by much of a sense of the nature of the social order. They were mostly single-purpose movements.) The identification of American Christianity with American culture became increasingly evident in this period.

With the rise of liberalism and the social gospel we see some recovery of the sense of the Church's mission in proclaiming the kingdom of God in and to America. The leaders of the Social Gospel Movement were not—as some have maintained—the first to discover the social significance of the kingdom of God, but they did contribute much to our understanding of the gospel and of the nature of society. Once more, however, atrophy set in and the kingdom of God came to be identified with a social utopia or an American society not too far distant, and the activity of the divine sovereign in history was identified with human progress. Many again forgot that there is "no way toward the coming kingdom save the way taken by a sovereign God through the reign of Jesus Christ."[53]

6. THE TASK BEFORE US

This cursory description of American Christianity's entanglements in and surrenders to culture only serves to remind us that the Church has not always been faithful to its task, but that it has frequently failed

---

[52] See F. B. Tolles, *Meeting House and Counting House* (Chapel Hill: University of North Carolina Press, 1948.)

[53] Niebuhr, *The Kingdom of God in America*, p. 198.

in carrying out its primary responsibility to point beyond itself to the reality of God's kingdom. Nor has it adequately proclaimed to "the world," and specifically to the American people, the meaning of God's rule for men in varying times and circumstances. When Americans have searched about for an understanding of their nature and destiny as a people, they have not found a clear testimony and voice from the Christian community. When they have embraced inadequate views, they frequently have not heard a clear word of guidance for the people. Nevertheless, those who bear witness to God's manifestation of himself in Jesus Christ have a peculiar responsibility of testifying to the rule, righteousness, and grace of their everlasting Lord. No doubt God may find more profitable servants outside the Christian community than many inside that community. But we now address ourselves to those within that community and affirm what seems to us to be their especial responsibilities in this crucial period of American history.

What of now? What shall we do? As members of the Christian community we shall, first of all, confess and proclaim the gospel as we know it. "It is the Gospel, and that only, which has actually been the means of bringing the world to the knowledge of the true God."[54] Through the gospel we understand and profess that God is sovereign, that in Christ he has made his will and purpose known and has brought redemption to men and nations, and that his kingdom will come in fullness. We shall, first of all, then, strive to be faithful both as individual Christians and in the Church's proclamation of the gospel, realizing that the only source of our faithfulness is his steadfast love.

Secondly, we shall also call upon the Church in and through which we confess our faith to be faithful, to perform its true function as "the community which responds to God-in-Christ and Christ-in-God," as "a community which is always aware of and always responding to the redemptive principle in the world, to Christ-in-God, to the Redeemer."[55] The Church true to its function and responsibility is always a community which points beyond itself rather than to itself. It does not call itself the kingdom of God but must serve as a constant reminder of the past, present, and future reality of that kingdom. Its life is repeatedly nourished and refreshed from the blessed wellspring of grace which flows in and through its Lord, Jesus Christ. It is devoted to testifying to and serving as a channel of that grace. And its constant prayer is "not my will but thine be done." Such a community will be a dynamic movement ever responsive to God's ways and his acts, repenting for its failures and seeking anew to live as a chosen vessel. It cannot be a calcified institution claiming that its ways are his ways.

The Church true to its task will relate itself to the society of which it is a part and will speak to the needs of that society. The Church

[54] Edwards, *Works*, vol. III, p. 354.
[55] Niebuhr, "The Responsibility of the Church for Society," *op. cit.*, pp. 117-19.

points in two directions—to the kingdom of God and to the kingdom of this world—and its constant endeavor is to bring the cities of earth to an awareness of the reality and meaning of the city of God. Its chief goal is *"the increase among men of the love of God and neighbor."*[56] It is a channel of grace, always striving to facilitate the flow of God's blessing in Jesus Christ into the world. This channeling involves a continual attempt to speak a language meaningful to the world while not succumbing to the ways of the world. It involves an effort toward transforming and redeeming culture while not capitulating to the ways of culture.

Before it can move convincingly toward the redemption of society, however, the Church needs in itself to become a redeemed society. Before it can increase among men the love of God and neighbor, that love must be a reality within the Church. It is a reality because of God's gift of love and man's response in love to that gift. The gift means a Church that is a society in which the barriers of race, culture, caste, and class are dissolved in and through the love of God in Jesus Christ. It also means the Church's striving to become a social pioneer, to take a place at the forefront in the struggle for social justice by engaging in well thought-out and concerted programs and by sponsoring bold experimentation.

We are told that judgment begins with the household of God.[57] The people that claims for itself—as that chosen by God—a primary role in the proclamation of the good news that the kingdom of God is at hand will be the first to fall under condemnation if they fail. And how can this people witness to the kingdom of God if they accept and can condone the injustices of the society of which they are a part? Even more, where is the Church's witness if it has become so entangled with the ways of society that there is little or no difference between church and society? Just as judgment begins with the household of God, so also may and must redemption begin there. Only the redeemed society, or the society striving for redemption, can speak to the "world" about its redemption. Only the Christian community faithful, or striving to be faithful, to its covenant can speak to an American society about being true to its covenant.

Finally, we shall call upon the Church to be an eschatalogical community, a community or people which knows the limitations of man and nations, which expects judgment on all that is temporal, and which looks forward in hope to the full realization of the kingdom of God. This community or people can then speak to America about that present history and that future history which matters most.

[56] Niebuhr, *The Purpose of the Church and Its Ministry*, 31.
[57] I Pet. 4:17.

A BIBLIOGRAPHY OF
H. RICHARD NIEBUHR'S
WRITINGS

Compiled (1957) by Raymond P. Morris;
revised (1964) by Raymond P. Morris and Jane E. McFarland

BOOKS AND BROCHURES

Ernst Troeltsch's Philosophy of Religion. Yale University doctoral dissertation, 1924. (Available on University Microfilms, Ann Arbor, Mich.).

Moral Relativism and the Christian Ethic. New York [International Missionary Council, 1929?]. Pp. 11.
 Address given at a Conference of Theological Seminaries, meeting at Drew Theological Seminary, Madison, N.J., Nov. 29-Dec. 1, 1929, on Theological Education and the World Mission of Christianity.

The Social Sources of Denominationalism. New York: Henry Holt and Company, 1929. Pp. viii + 304. (Reprinted, with new preface, Hamden, Conn.: The Shoe String Press, 1954; New York: Meridian Books, 1957).

The Religious Situation, by Paul Tillich. Translated by H. Richard Niebuhr. New York: Henry Holt & Co. [1932]. Pp. 182. "Translator's preface," pp. vii-xxii.

The Church against the World, by H. R. Niebuhr, Wilhelm Pauck, and F. P. Miller. Chicago, New York: Willett, Clark & Co., 1935. Pp. 156.
 "The Question of the Church," pp. 1-13; "Toward the Independence of the Church," pp. 123-56.

The Kingdom of God in America. Chicago and New York: Willett, Clark and Company, 1937. Pp. xvii + 215. (Reprinted, with new preface, Hamden, Conn.: The Shoe String Press, 1956; New York: Harper Torchbooks, TB49, 1959).

In substance these chapters were given in the form of lectures in July, 1936, at the tercentenary summer session of the Harvard Divinity School, and in January, 1937, on the Alden-Tuthill Foundation lectureship at Chicago Theological Seminary. Translated as: *Der Gedanke des Gottesreichs im Amerikanischen Christentum.* Deutsche Ausgabe von R. M. Honig. New York: Church World Service, 1948. Pp. ix + 154.

The Meaning of Revelation. New York: The Macmillan Company, 1941. Pp. x + 196. Contains, with some additions and revisions, the Nathaniel W. Taylor lectures given in the Divinity School of Yale University in April, 1940.

The Gospel for a Time of Fears: Three Lectures: I. Our Eschatological Time. II. The Eternal Now. III. The Gospel of the Last Time. Washington, D.C.: Henderson Services, [1950]. Pp. 22.

The Washington Federation of Churches and The School of Religion, Howard University, Sixth Annual Lecture Series, 1950.

Christ and Culture. New York: Harper & Brothers, 1951. Pp. x + 259. (English edition: Faber and Faber Ltd., 1952. Pp. 256; New York: Harper Torchbooks, 1956).

Austin Presbyterian Theological Seminary Lectures, 1949.

The Churches and the Body of Christ. Philadelphia: The Young Friends Movement of the Philadelphia Yearly Meetings, 1953. Pp. 24.

The William Penn Lecture, 1953.

The Ministry in Historical Perspectives, ed. by H. Richard Niebuhr and Daniel Day Williams. New York: Harper, 1956. Pp. xi + 331.

The Purpose of the Church and Its Ministry, reflections on the aims of theological education, in collaboration with Daniel Day Williams and James M. Gustafson. New York: Harper, 1956. Pp. xvi + 134.

The Advancement of Theological Education, by H. Richard Niebuhr, Daniel Day Williams and James M. Gustafson. New York: Harper, 1957. Pp. xii + 239.

Bulletins issued by the Staff concerning the Inquiry into Theological Education in America. April, Sept., 1954; Jan., Sept., 1955; April, 1956. (mimeograph)

Radical Monotheism and Western Civilization. Lincoln: University of Nebraska, 1960. Pp. 101.

Montgomery lectureship on contemporary civilization, 1957. University of Nebraska.

Radical Monotheism and Western Culture, with supplementary essays. New York: Harper, [1960]. Pp. 144.

"Revised and expanded form [of] the Montgomery lectures on contemporary civilization . . . [given] at the University of Nebraska in 1957."

The Responsible Self; an Essay in Christian Moral Philosophy, with an

introduction by James M. Gustafson. New York: Harper & Row, [1963]. Pp. 183.
"Projected for future publication is a collection of previously published periodical articles and unpublished sermons, essays and articles."

ARTICLES APPEARING IN BOOKS

Encyclopaedia of the Social Sciences, ed. E. R. A. Seligman. New York: The Macmillan Company, 1931. Articles: "Dogma," vol. V, pp. 189-91; "Sectarian Education," vol. V, pp. 421-55; "Fundamentalism," vol. VI, pp. 526-27; "Higher Criticism," vol. VII, pp. 347-48; "Protestantism," vol. XII, pp. 571-75; "Reformation: Non-Lutheran," vol. XIII, pp. 190-93; "Religious Institutions, Christian: Protestant," vol. XIII, pp. 267-72; "Schaff, Philip," vol. XIII, p. 562; "Sects," vol. XIII, pp. 624-30.

Religious Realism in the Twentieth Century, in *Religious Realism*, ed. D. C. Macintosh. New York: The Macmillan Company, 1931, pp. 413-28.

Value Theory and Theology, in *The Nature of Religious Experience: Essays in Honor of Douglas Clyde Macintosh*, ed. com.: J. S. Bixler, R. L. Calhoun, H. R. Niebuhr. New York: Harper & Brothers, 1937, pp. 93-116.

The Religious Situation, in *Contemporary Religious Thought*, ed. T. S. Kepler. New York: Abingdon-Cokesbury, 1941, pp. 83-8.

An Encyclopedia of Religion, ed. V. Ferm. New York: The Philosophical Library, 1945. Articles: "Church: Conceptions of the Church in Historic Christianity," pp. 169-70; "Ethics: Christian Ethics," pp. 259-60; "Inspiration," p. 374; "Revelation," pp. 660-61; "Troeltsch, Ernst," pp. 795-96.

The Responsibility of the Church for Society, in *The Gospel, the Church and the World*, ed. K. S. Latourette. New York, London: Harper & Brothers, 1946, pp. 111-33.

Introduction to *Essence of Christianity*, by L. Feuerbach. New York, Harper, 1947, pp. vii-ix.

The Disorder of Man in the Church of God, in *Man's Disorder and God's Design*; vol. I: *The Universal Church in God's Design*. New York: Harper & Brothers, 1949, pp. 78-88.

Evangelical and Protestant Ethics, in *The Heritage of the Reformation: Essays Commemorating the Centennial of Eden Theological Seminary*, ed. E. J. F. Arndt. New York: Richard R. Smith, 1950, pp. 211-29.

The Center of Value, in *Moral Principles of Action: Man's Ethical Imperative*, ed. R. N. Anshen. New York: Harper & Brothers, 1952, pp. 162-75.

Who are the Unbelievers and What Do They Believe? Report submitted to Secretariat for Evangelism, World Council of Churches, Second Assembly, in *The Christian Hope and the Task of the Church*: Six Ecumenical Surveys and the Report of the Assembly prepared by the Advisory Commission on the Main Theme, 1954. New York: Harper & Brothers, 1954, pp. 35-7.

Christian Ethics: Sources of the Living Tradition. Edited with introductions by Waldo Beach and H. Richard Niebuhr. New York: Ronald Press Company, 1955. Pp. vii + 496. Chapters 1, 8, 9, and 13 by Niebuhr.

Sören Kierkegaard, in *Christianity and the Existentialists*, ed. by Carl Donald Michalson. New York, Scribner, 1956, pp. 23-42.

The Churches of the Middle Class, in *Religion, Society, and the Individual*; an Introduction to the Sociology of Religion, ed. John Milton Yinger. New York: Macmillan, [1957], pp. 453-58.

Modifications of Calvinism, in *Religion, Society, and the Individual*; an Introduction to the Sociology of Religion, ed. John Milton Yinger. New York: Macmillan, [1957], pp. 524-28.

Die Religion in Geschichte und Gegenwart. Dritte, völlig neu bearbeitete Auflage in Gemeinschaft mit Hans Frhr. v. Campenhausen, Erich Dinkler . . . 1958. Articles: "Emerson, Ralph Waldo (1803-82)," vol. II, pp. 454-55; "Individual- und Sozialethik," vol. III, pp. 715-19.

Foreword to *In His Likeness*, by G. McLeod Bryan. Richmond: John Knox Press, 1959, pp. 5-6.

Christ and the Kingdom of Caesar (from *Christ and Culture*), in *Dimensions of Faith; Contemporary Protestant Theology* by Karl Barth [and others], ed. William Kimmel and Geoffrey Clive. With a foreword by James Luther Adams. New York: Twayne [1960], pp. [341]-384.

Introduction to *The Social Teachings of the Christian Churches*, by Ernst Troeltsch. New York: Harper Torchbooks: The Cloister Library, TB71, 1960, pp. [7]-12.

H. Richard Niebuhr, in *How My Mind Has Changed* [by] John C. Bennett, H. Richard Niebuhr [and others], ed. and intro. by Harold E. Fey. Cleveland: Meridian Books, [1961], A Living Age Book, pp. 69-80.

   "The contributions . . . were first published as articles [in *Christian Century*] during the 1959-60 publishing year."

On the Nature of Faith, in *Religious Experience and Truth: a Symposium*, ed. Sidney Hook. [New York]: New York University Press, 1961, pp. 93-102.

   "Proceedings of the fourth annual New York University Institute of Philosophy . . . New York, October 21-22, 1960."

The Protestant Movement and Democracy in the United States, in

Religion in American Life, Vol. I: *The Shaping of American Religion*, ed. James Ward Smith and A. Leland Jamison. Princeton, N.J.: Princeton University Press, 1961, pp. 20-71.

The Grace of Doing Nothing, in *The Christian Century Reader*; representative articles, editorials and poems selected from more than fifty years of the *Christian Century*, ed. Harold E. Fey and Margaret Frakes. New York: Association Press, [1962], pp. 216-21.

The Story of Our Life, in *Interpreting Religion*, by Donald Walhout. Englewood Cliffs, N.J.: Prentice-Hall, 1963, pp. 305-14.

ARTICLES IN PERIODICALS

An Aspect of the Idea of God in Recent Thought, in *Theological Magazine of the Evangelical Synod of North America*, XLVIII (1920), 39-44.

The Alliance Between Labor and Religion, in *Theological Magazine of the Evangelical Synod of North America*, XLIX (1921), 197-203.

Christianity and the Social Problem, in *Theological Magazine of the Evangelical Synod of North America*, L (1922), 278-91.

Back to Benedict?, in *Christian Century*, XLII (1925), 860-61.

What Holds Churches Together?, in *Christian Century*, XLIII (1926), 346-48.

Theology and Psychology: A Sterile Union, in *Christian Century*, XLIV (1927), 47-8.

Jesus Christ Intercessor, in *International Journal of Religious Education*, III (1927), No. 4, 6-8.

Christianity and the Industrial Classes, in *Theological Magazine of the Evangelical Synod of North America*, LVII (1929), 12-8.

Churches That Might Unite, in *Christian Century*, XLVI (1929), 259-61.

Can German and American Christians Understand Each Other?, in *Christian Century*, XLVII (1930), 914-16.

The Irreligion of Communist and Capitalist, in *Christian Century*, XLVII (1930), 1306-307.

Religion and Ethics, in *World Tomorrow*, XIII (1930), 443-46.

The Grace of Doing Nothing, in *Christian Century*, XLIX (1932), 378-80. (See critique by Reinhold Niebuhr: Must We Do Nothing?, *ibid.*, 415-17. See also answer by H. R. Niebuhr: A Communication: The Only Way Into the Kingdom of God, *ibid.*, 447.)

Faith, Works, and Social Salvation, in *Religion in Life*, I (1932), 426-30.

Nationalism, Socialism and Christianity, in *World Tomorrow*, XVI (1933), 469-70.

What Then Must We Do?, in *Christian Century Pulpit*, V (1934), 145-47.

Inconsistency of the Majority, in *World Tomorrow*, XVII, 43-4. (Part of symposium: "Fellowship Reverberations.")

Man the Sinner, in *Journal of Religion*, XV (1935), 272-80.

Toward the Emancipation of the Church, in *Christendom*, I (1935-36), 133-45.

The Attack upon the Social Gospel, in *Religion in Life*, V (1936), 176-81.

Life is Worth Living, in *Intercollegian and Far Horizons*, LVII (1939), 3-4, 22.

The Christian Evangel and Social Culture, in *Religion in Life*, VIII (1939), 44-9.

Two Lenten Meditations ["Tired Christians" and "Preparation for Maladjustment"], in *Yale Divinity News* (March, 1939), 3-4.

The Christian Church and the World's Crisis, in *Christianity and Society*, VI (1941), 11-7.

War as the Judgment of God, in *Christian Century*, LIX (1942), 630-33.

Is God in the War?, in *Christian Century*, LIX (1942), 953-55.

War as Crucifixion, in *Christian Century*, LX (1943), 513-15.

The Nature and Existence of God: A Protestant's View, in *Motive*, IV (1943), 13-5, 43-6.

Towards a New Otherworldliness, in *Theology Today*, I (1944), 78-87.

The Ego-Alter Dialectic and the Conscience, in *Journal of Philosophy*, XLII (1945), 352-59.

The Hidden Church and the Churches in Sight, in *Religion in Life*, XV (1945-46), 106-17.

Unitarian Christianity, in *Christianity and Crisis*, VI (1946), 3-5.

The Norm of the Church, in *Journal of Religious Thought*, IV (1946-47), 5-15.

The Doctrine of the Trinity and the Unity of the Church, in *Theology Today*, III (1946), 371-84.

The Gift of the Catholic Vision, in *Theology Today*, IV (1948), 507-21.

The Churches and the Body of Christ, in *Friends Intelligencer*, CX (1953), 621-23.

   Reprint of the concluding section of "The Churches and the Body of Christ."

The Triad of Faith, in *Andover Newton Bulletin*, XLVII (1954), 3-12 (with leaf insert of explanation and errata).

   The Stephen Greene Lecture, 1954.

Why Restudy Theological Education?, in *Christian Century*, LXXI (1954), 516-17, 527.

The Idea of Covenant and American Democracy, in *Church History*, XXIII (1954), 126-35.

   Read before the American Studies section of the American Historical Association, at Chicago, Dec. 28, 1953.

Issues between Catholics and Protestants, in *Religion in Life*, XXIII
(1954), 199-205.
  Deals with "Protestants and Catholics in the Kingdom of God."
Theology—Not Queen but Servant, in *Journal of Religion*, XXXV
(1955), 1-5.
The Main Issues in Theological Education, in *Theology Today*, XI
(1955), 512-27. (With Daniel Day Williams and James M. Gustaf-
son).
Training a Preacher, in *Presbyterian Survey* (Sept., 1956), 24-5.
Reformation: Continuing Imperative, in *Christian Century*, LXXVII
(1960), 248-51.
  In the series "How My Mind Has Changed."
Science and Religion, in *Yale Divinity News* (January, 1960), 3-21.
  "A dialogue between scientists and theologians as it took place at a
recent [Yale] Divinity School Convocation . . . telescoped version."
Seminary in the Ecumenical Age (address delivered at the inauguration
of J. I. McCord, President, Princeton Theological Seminary), in
Princeton Seminary Bulletin, LIV (July, 1960), 38-45.
  Reprinted in *Theology Today*, XVII (1960), 300-10.
Die Wertmitte, in *Zeitschrift für Evangelische Ethik*, übersetzt von
Pastor E. Fischer, IV (1960), 148-59.
Reply to Professor Willem F. Zuurdeeg, in "Critic's Corner" in *Theology
Today*, XVIII (1961), 359-60.
  Zuurdeeg's response to Niebuhr in "Critic's Corner" in *Theology
Today*, XVIII (1961), 360-64.
Ex Libris, in *Christian Century*, LXXIX (1962), 754.
  A booklist submitted in response to the query: "What books did
most to shape your vocational attitude and your philosophy of life?"
The Illusions of Power, in *The Pulpit*, XXXIII (1962), 4(100)-7(103).
An Attempt at a Theological Analysis of Missionary Motivation, in *New
York (City) Missionary Research Library*. Occasional Bulletin. New
York, XIV (1963), [1]-6.

BOOK REVIEWS BY H. R. NIEBUHR

1931

Macintosh, *The Pilgrimage of Faith in the World of Modern Thought*;
Wieman, *The Issues of Life*; Miltner, *The Elements of Ethics*; Clark
and Smith, *Readings in Ethics*; Spaulding (ed.), *Twenty-four Views of
Marriage* (*Yale Divinity News*, XXVIII, No. 1, 3, 4).

1932

Schuetz, *Saekulaere Religion* (*Anglican Theological Review*, XIV, No.
4, 359-61); Whitley, *The Doctrine of Grace* (*Crozer Quarterly*, IX, No.
4, 475-76); Griffiths, *God in Idea and Experience or the Apriori Ele-*

ments of the Religious Consciousness. An Epistemological Study (*International Journal of Ethics,* XLIII, No. 1, 91-3); Pauck, *Karl Barth, Prophet of a New Christianity?*; McConnachie, *The Significance of Karl Barth* (*Yale Divinity News,* XXVIII, No. 2, 6); Troeltsch, *The Social Teaching of the Christian Churches;* Kirk, *The Vision of God;* Garvie, *The Christian Ideal for Human Society;* Green, *The Problem of Right Conduct;* Nixon, *The Moral Crisis in Christianity;* Russell, *The Church in the Modern World;* Jones, *The Christ of the Mount;* Temple, *Christian Faith and Life;* Lichtenberger, *Divorce: A Social Interpretation;* Harris, *Essays on Marriage;* Schmiedeler, *Readings on the Family* (*ibid.,* No. 3, 4, 5); Jones, *Contemporary Thought of Germany;* Sharp, *Ethics;* Driesch, *Ethical Principles in Theory and Practice; An Essay in Moral Philosophy,* trans. Johnston; Sidgwick, *Outlines of the History of Ethics for English Readers;* Everett, *The Education of Jeremy Bentham;* Kirby, *William Prynne: A Study in Puritanism;* Hall, *The Religious Background of American Culture* (*ibid.,* No. 4, 10); Hartshorne, *Character in Human Relations* (*ibid.,* XXIX, No. 1, 5).

1933

Dimnet, *What We Live By;* Dickinson, *After 2000 Years: A Dialogue between Plato and a Modern Young Man;* Flanders, *Taming Our Machines: The Attainment of Human Values in a Mechanized Society;* Spengler, *Man and Technics: A Contribution to a Philosophy of Life,* trans. Atkinson; Becker, *The Heavenly City of the Eighteenth Century Philosophers* (*Yale Divinity News,* XXIX, No. 2, 5); Lowrie, *Our Concern with the Theology of Crisis;* Keller, *Der Weg der dialektischen Theologie durch die kirchliche Welt;* Dewey, Tufts, *Ethics;* Brightman, *Moral Laws;* Winsor, *The Art of Behavior: A Study in Human Relations;* Barry, *Christianity and the New World;* McConnell, *The Christian Ideal and Social Control* (*ibid.,* XXIX, No. 3, 6); Morrison, *The Social Gospel and the Christian Cultus;* Ward, *In Place of Profit: Social Incentives in the Soviet Union;* Davis, (ed.), *The New Russia: Between the First and Second Five Year Plans;* Laski, *Politics;* Furnas, *America's Tomorrow: An Informal Excursion into the Era of the Two-Hour Working Day;* Ladd, *The Victorian Morality of Art: An Analysis of Ruskin's Esthetic;* Inge, *Things New and Old;* Fleming, *Ventures in Simpler Living;* Fiske, *A Study of Jesus' Own Religion;* Raven, *The Heart of Christ's Religion* (*ibid.,* No. 4, 4).

1934

Joyce, *Christian Marriage: An Historical and Doctrinal Study;* Jaspers, *Man in the Modern Age,* trans. Paul; Berdyaev, *The End of Our Time;* Alexander, *Beauty and Other Forms of Value* (*Yale Divinity News,* XXX, No. 2, 2, 3); McFarland, *The New Church and the New Ger-*

many: A Study of Church and State; Peck, The Social Implications of the Oxford Movement (ibid., XXX, No. 3, 3); Mencken, Treatise on Right and Wrong; Garvie, Can Christ Save Society?; Wagner (ed.), Social Reformers: Adam Smith to John Dewey; Burns, The Horizon of Experience: A Philosophy for the Modern Man; Rothschild, Reality and Illusion; Tufts, America's Social Morality; Newson, The New Morality; Rogers, Ethics and Moral Tolerance; Berdyaev, Christianity and Class War (ibid., XXX, No. 4, 5); Keller, Religion and Revolution; Flew, The Idea of Perfection in Christian Theology; Kirk, Conscience and Its Problems: An Introduction to Casuistry; Barth and Thurneysen, Come, Holy Spirit (ibid., XXXI, No. 1, 3-4).

1935

Brodrick, The Economic Morals of the Jesuits; Faulhaber, Judaism, Christianity and Germany, trans. Smith (Yale Divinity News, XXXI, No. 2, 4); Kirk (ed.), Personal Ethics (ibid., XXXI, No. 3, 3); Davis, Capitalism and Its Culture; Mathews, Christianity and Social Process; Saunders, The Ideals of East and West; Laski, The State in Theory and Practice; Carritt, Morals and Politics; Pinson, Pietism as a Factor in the Rise of German Nationalism (ibid., XXXI, No. 4, 1-3); Calhoun, God and the Common Life; Means, Things That Are Caesar's: The Genesis of the German Church Conflict (ibid., XXXIII, No. 1, 1, 4).

1936

Holt, The Search for a New Strategy in Protestantism (Christendom, I, No. 5, 877-78); Duncan, The Epistle of Paul to the Galatians (Religion in Life, V, No. 1, 1949); Keuren, Outfitting for Spiritual Marriage; Ward, Values and Reality; Berdyaev, Dostoievsky: An Interpretation; Davis, Moral and Pastoral Theology (Yale Divinity News, XXXII, No. 2, 4); Smith, Beyond Conscience (ibid., XXXII, No. 3, 3); Barry, The Relevance of the Church; Garvie, The Fatherly Rule of God; Simpson, The Fact of Christ; Simpson, The Fact of the Christian Church; Webb, The Kingdom Within; Allen, Kierkegaard: His Life and Thought; McConnell, Christian Materialism (ibid., XXXII, No. 4, 2-5).

1937

Homrighausen, Christianity in America: A Crisis (Christian Century, LIV, No. 1, 19-20); Dombrowski, The Early Days of Christian Socialism in America (Review of Religion, I, No. 3, 302-04); Henson, Christian Morality, Natural, Developing, and Final; Mossner, Bishop Butler and the Age of Reason: A Study in the History of Thought (Yale Divinity News, XXXIII, No. 2, 4); Van Dusen (ed.), Church and State in the Modern World (ibid., XXXIV, No. 1, 6).

1938

Brunner, *The Divine Imperative;* Kirk, *The Vision of God* (abbrev. ed.); Troeltsch, *The Social Teachings of the Christian Churches,* trans. Wyon; Niebuhr, *An Interpretation of Christian Ethics;* Taylor, *The Faith of a Moralist* (*Yale Divinity News,* XXXIV, No. 2, 2); Buber, *I and Thou;* Hall, *The Distinctive Elements in Christianity,* trans. Hope; Kierkegaard, *Philosophical Fragments or a Fragment of Philosophy;* Geismar, *Lectures on the Religious Thought of Sören Kierkegaard;* Haecker, *Sören Kierkegaard,* trans. Dru; Bain, *Sören Kierkegaard: His Life and Religious Teaching;* Allen, *Kierkegaard: His Life and Thought* (*ibid.,* XXXIV, No. 3, 6, 7); Berdyaev, *The Destiny of Man;* Plowright, *Rebel Religion: Christ, Community and Church;* Keller, *Five Minutes to Twelve;* Hendry, *God and Creator;* Association Press, *Hazen Books on Religion;* Stewart, *The Church;* Latourette, *Toward a World Christian Fellowship* (*ibid.,* XXXIV, No. 4, 4).

1941

Pratt, *Can We Keep The Faith?* (*Christendom,* VI, No. 4, 590-92); Morrison, *What is Christianity?* (*Journal of Religion,* XXI, No. 2, 189-92).

1943

Robinson, *Redemption and Revelation in the Actuality of History* (*Religion in Life,* XII, No. 3, 463-64); Cailliet, *The Clue to Pascal* (*Westminster Bookman,* III, No. 2, 9-10); Spencer, *Shakespeare and the Nature of Men* (*Yale Divinity News,* XXXIX, No. 2, 3).

1944

Case, *The Christian Philosophy of History* (*Journal of Religion,* XXIV, No. 2, 147-48; Smart, *What a Man Can Believe* (*Westminster Bookman,* III, No. 5, 17).

1945

Wach, *Sociology of Religion;* Sturzo, *True Life: Sociology of the Supernatural* (*Theology Today,* II, No. 3, 409-11); Quillian, *The Moral Theory of Evolutionary Naturalism* (*Yale Divinity News,* XLII, No. 1, 4).

1946

Clark, *The Cross and the Eternal Order, a Study of Atonement in its Cosmic Significance* (*Religion in Life,* XV, No. 2, 314-15); Dakin, *Calvinism* (*Westminster Bookman,* V, No. 5, 12-3); Baillie, *What is Christian Civilization* (*Yale Divinity News,* XLII, No. 2, 4).

1947

Brunner, *Revelation and Reason: The Christian Doctrine of Faith and Knowledge* (*Religion in Life*, XVI, No. 2, 314); Brunner, *Justice and the Social Order* (*Theology Today*, III, No. 4, 558-60); Brunner, *The Divine Imperative* (*Westminster Bookman*, VII, No. 1, 7-8).

1949

Tillich, *The Protestant Era* (*Religion in Life*, XVIII, No. 2, 291-92).

1950

Brunner, *Dogmatics*, vol. I: *The Christian Doctrine of God* (*Westminster Bookman*, IX, No. 5, 3-4).

1951

Fitch, *The Kingdom Without End: A Prophetic Interpretation of History and Civilization* (*Religion in Life*, XX, No. 2, 304-05); Tillich, *Systematic Theology* (*Union Seminary Quarterly Review*, VII, No. 1, 45-9).

1953

Tillich, *Systematic Theology* (*Theology*, LVI, No. 396, 225-28); Brunner, *The Misunderstanding of the Church* (*Westminster Bookman*, XII, No. 2, 11-3).

1959

Wingren, *Theology in Conflict* (*Westminster Bookman*, XVIII, No. 2, 2-4).

REVIEWS OF H. R. NIEBUHR'S BOOKS

The Social Sources of Denominationalism. Hightower, in *Crozer Quarterly*, VII (1930), No. 2, 250-51; Nagler, in *Garrett Tower*, V (1929), No. 13, 14; Sweet, *Journal of Religion*, XI (1931), No. 1, 131-33.

The Church Against the World. Holmes, in *Books* (*New York Herald Tribune*), VII (Dec. 8, 1935), 27; Hough, in *Drew Gateway*, VII (1935), No. 1, 7-8; I.M.C., in *Information Service*, XIV (1935), No. 33, 2; Macfarland, in *Reformed Church Messenger*, (Oct. 31, 1935), 2; Sperry, in *Christendom*, I (1935-36), No. 2, 367-70; Woodburne, in *Crozer Quarterly*, XIII (1936), No. 1, 52.

The Kingdom of God in America. Dillingham, in *Crozer Quarterly*, XV (1938), No. 1, 73-4; Haroutunian, in *Journal of Religion*, XVIII (1938), No. 3, 337-39; J.F.E., in *Information Service*, XVII (1938), No. 44, 2; Nagler, in *Garrett Tower*, XIII (1938), No. 2, 9-10; Scott, in

Christendom, III (1938), No. 2, 311-14; Weigle, in *Yale Divinity News*, XXXIV (1937), No. 1, 5.

The Meaning of Revelation. B.A.S., in *Christian Observer*, CXXIX (1941), No. 20, 9; Calhoun, in *Yale Divinity News*, XXXVII (1941), No. 3, 7; Caswell, in *Churchman*, CLV (1941), No. 6, 18; Davis, in *Crozer Quarterly*, XVIII (1941), No. 3, 262-64; Dieffenbach, in *Books (New York Herald Tribune)*, XVIII (1941), No. 6, 25; Ferré, in *Christendom*, VI (1941), No. 3, 439-41; Harkness, in *Garrett Tower*, XVI (1941), No. 3, 11-2; Haroutunian, in *Christianity and Society*, VI (1941), No. 3, 34-6; Hoyt, in *Christian Leader*, CXXIII (1941), No. 17, 378, 386; I.G.G., in *Church Management*, XVII (1941), No. 8, 504; Lawson, in *Library Journal*, LXVI (1941), No. 3, 139; Macfarland, in *Federal Council Bulletin*, XXIV (1941), No. 5, 18; Macfarland, in *The Messenger*, VI (1941), No. 9, 2, 23-4; McLaughlin, in *Daily Tribune* (Ames, Iowa), LXXIV (1941), No. 193, 3; Monsma, in *Review of Religion*, VI (1941-42), No. 1, 89-95; Morrison, in *Christian Century Pulpit*, XII (1941), No. 5, 119; *Pasadena Star News*, XXVI (1941), No. 25, 7; Pittenger, in *Living Church*, CIII (1941), No. 15, 19; Poling, in *Christian Herald*, LXIV (1941), No. 4, 54; Thomas, in *Journal of Religion*, XXI (1941), No. 4, 455-60; Tillich, in *Religion in Life*, X (1941), No. 3, 452-55; Tribble, in *Review and Expositor*, XXXVIII (1941), No. 2, 220-22; Wright, in *McCormick Theological Seminary Alumni Review*, XIX (1943), No. 1, 54.

Der Gedanke des Gottesreichs im Amerikanischen Christentum. Schrey, in *Theologische Literaturzeitung*, LXXXV (1950), No. 1, 47.

Christ and Culture. Bagby, in *Drew Gateway*, XXII (1951), No. 1, 41; Barnette, in *Review and Expositor*, XLIX, 457-59; Bennett, in *Christianity and Society*, XVII (1951-52), No. 1, 23-4; Bennett, in *Union Seminary Quarterly Review*, VII (1952), No. 2, 52-5; Burleigh, in *Scottish Journal of Theology*, VI (1953), 315-17; Butler, in *Downside*, LXX (1952), 423; Cavert, in *National Council Outlook*, I (1951), No. 6, 26; *Church Quarterly Review*, CLIII (1952), No. 309, 561; *Cleveland Open Shelf*, Nov. 26, 1951; C.R.S., Jr., in *Anglican Theological Review*, XXXVI (1954), No. 3, 244-45; Cully, in *Christian Century*, LXVIII (1951), No. 31, 895; Davis, in *Crozer Quarterly*, XXIX (1952), No. 1, 69-70; Dawson, in *Dublin Review*, CCXXVI (1952), No. 457, 64-8; Dawson, in *Religion in Life*, XXI (1952), No. 2, 298-301; Demant, in *Journal of Theological Studies*, n.s., IV (1953), Pt.1, 153-54; DeWolf, in *Zions Herald*, CXXIX (1951), No. 26, 614-15; E.A., in *Eden Theological Seminary Alumni Bulletin*, V (1951), No. 4, 2; *Expository Times*, LXIII (1952), No. 11, 325-26; Ferré, in *Westminster Bookman*, X (1951), No. 5, 1-2; Fletcher, in *Churchman*, CLXV (1951), No. 12, 15-6; Garrard, in *Modern Churchman*, n.s., I (October, 1957), 119-28.

Haroutunian, in *Interpretation* (1952), No. 6, 113-15; Hope, in *Princeton Seminary Bulletin*, XLV (1952), No. 4, 57; Hutchinson, in *New York Times*, July 1, 1951; J.N.D.K., in *Oxford Magazine*, LXXI (1953), No. 12, 199; *Kirkus*, XIX (June 1, 1951), 271; Kolbe, in *Garrett Tower*, XXVII (1951), No. 1, 14; L.H., in *Dublin Magazine*, n.s., XXVII (1952), No. 4, 51-2; Line, in *Theology Today*, X (1953), 270-71; Mairet, in *International Review of Missions*, XLI (1952), No. 164, 510-13; Micklem, in *Congregational Quarterly*, XXX (1952), No. 4, 362; Milhouse, in *Telescope-Messenger*, CXVII (1951), No. 34, 16; Miller, in *The Messenger*, XVI (1951), No. 18, 25; Minear, in *Journal of Bible and Religion*, XX (1952), 41-2; Mollegen, in *Yale Divinity News*, XLVII (November, 1951), 2; Morrison, in *Pulpit*, XXII (1951), No. 7, 30; O'Connell, in *Thought*, XXIX (1954), 311; *Pastor's Journal*, XXIII (1951), No. 5, 25; Read, in *The Listener*, XLVII (1952), No. 1213, 883; *Religious Book Club Bulletin*, XXIV (1951), No. 6, 1-2; Shinn, in *Christianity and Crisis*, XI (1951), No. 15, 117-20; *Theology*, LV (1952), No. 386, 281-82; *Times Literary Supplement* (1952), No. 2633, 473; *U.S. Quarterly Book Review*, VII (September, 1951), 252; Voss, in *Churchman*, CLXV (1951), No. 14, 17; Walsh, in *Living Church*, CXXIII (1951), No. 12, 21-2; Watkin, in *Church Quarterly Review*, CLV (1954), No. 1, 82-4; Whitley, in *Christian Evangelist*, LXXXIX (1951), No. 38, 912.

Christian Ethics. J.E.B., in *The Personalist*, XXXVII (1956), No. 3, 303-04; Fitch, in *Religion in Life*, XXV (1956), 143-44.

The Ministry in Historical Perspectives. Bebis, in *Greek Orthodox Theological Review*, IV (1958), No. 1, 82-6; *Booklist*, LIII (Feb. 1, 1957), 269; Burger, in *New York Times* (Jan. 13, 1957), 25; Handy, in *Union Seminary Quarterly Review*, XII (1957), No. 3, 88-90. Osborn, in *Encounter*, XVIII (1957), No. 2, 212-15; Shein, in *Journal of Bible and Religion*, XXV (1957), No. 3, 225-26; Van Dusen, in *Theology Today*, XIV (1958), No. 4, 546-49.

The Purpose of the Church and Its Ministry. Blizzard, in *Religious Education*, LII (1957), No. 1, 70; Editorial "Church and Ministry," in *Christian Century*, LXXIII (1956), 869-71; Fitzpatrick, in *The Chicago Theological Seminary Register*, XLVI (1956), No. 6, 24; Franklin, in *The Japan Christian Quarterly*, XXIII (1957), No. 2, 109-17; Graves, in *Review and Expositor*, LIII (1956), No. 4, 565-67; Handy, in *The Review of Religion*, XXI (1957), Nos. 3-4, 210-13; Livingstone, in *Union Seminary Quarterly Review*, XII (1956), No. 1, 67-9; Muelder, in *Journal of Bible and Religion*, XXIV (1956), No. 4, 281; R.E.O., in *Encounter*, XVII (1956), No. 4, 394-98; Pearson, in *The Pulpit*, XXVIII (1957), No. 1, 44-5; Van Dusen, in *Westminster Bookman*, XV (1956), No. 3, 18-9.

The Advancement of Theological Education. Come, in *Theology Today*, XIV (1958), No. 4, 549-51; Filson, in *Journal of Bible and Religion*, XXV (1957), No. 4, 324-25; Foelsch, in *Lutheran Quarterly*, X (1958), No. 3, 284-85; Jones, in *Interpretation*, XI (1957), No. 4, 484-86; McCormick, in *Thomist*, XXII (1959), No. 1, 120-24; "Seminary and Community," in *Christian Century*, LXXIV (1957), 509-11; Willand, in *Journal of Pastoral Care*, XII (1958), No. 1, 62-3.

Radical Monotheism and Western Culture. Ahlstrom, in *Saturday Review of Literature*, XLIV (March 4, 1961), 31; Allen, in *Church Quarterly Review*, CLXIII (1962), 351-52; Beach, in *Westminster Bookman*, XX (1961), No. 1, 12-4; Davies, in *Expository Times*, LXXIII (1962), No. 7, 204; Gaustad, in *Journal of Bible and Religion*, XXIX (1961), No. 3, 237-39; Hamilton, in *Journal of Religion*, XLI (1961), No. 4, 313; Kohl, in *Library Journal*, LXXXV (1960), No. 20, 4149; MacIntyre, in *Guardian* (Nov. 3, 1961), 7; Shinn, in *Interpretation*, XVI (1962), No. 2, 197-99; Thomas, in *International Review of Missions*, LII (1963), 471-74; Vahanian, in *Nation*, CXCII (1961), No. 13, 286-88; Williams, in *Union Seminary Quarterly Review*, XVII (1961), No. 1, 99-101; Zuurdeeg, in *Theology Today*, XVIII (1961), No. 2, 213-18; Zuurdeeg, in *Downside*, LXXX (April, 1962), 192.

The Responsible Self. Beach, in *Westminster Bookman*, XXIII (1964), No. 1, 33-4; Fitch, in *Christian Century*, LXXXI No. 9 (1964), 273; Kantonen, in *Religion in Life*, XXXIII (1964), No. 3, 467-68; Knight, in *Signs and Times of the Yale Divinity School*, IV (1963), No. 3, 2-11; Ramm, in *Christianity Today*, VIII (1964), No. 7, 24-5; Stotts, in *McCormick Quarterly*, XVII (1964), No. 4, 39-44.

CRITICISM OF H. R. NIEBUHR

Macintosh, D.C. Theology, Valuational or Existential?, in *Review of Religion*, VI (1939), 23-44.

Kuhn, Helmut. Conscience and Society, in *Journal of Religion*, XXVI (1946), 203-14.
    A criticism of "The Ego-Alter Dialectic and the Conscience."

Thelan, Mary Frances. *Man as Sinner in Contemporary American Realistic Theology.* New York: King's Crown Press, 1946. Especially pp. 148-63.

Loomer, Bernard H. Neo-Naturalism and Neo-Orthodoxy, in *Journal of Religion*, XXVIII (1948), 79-91.

Welch, Claude. *In This Name: The Doctrine of the Trinity in Contemporary Theology.* New York: Charles Scribner's Sons, 1952. Especially pp. 227-28.

Hartt, Julian. Theology of Culture, in *Review of Metaphysics*, VI (1953), 501-09.

Williams, Daniel Day. *What Present-Day Theologians Are Thinking*. New York: Harper & Brothers, 1952. Especially pp. 50, 64, 103.

Soper, David Wesley. *Major Voices in American Theology; Six Contemporary Leaders*. Philadelphia: Westminster Press, 1953. Especially pp. 153-90, "The Permanent Revolution; the Theology of Hope of H. Richard Niebuhr."

Rev. Dr. Niebuhr Sees American Church Emerging Despite Multiplicity of Protestant Denominations; Lists Cohesive Elements, in *New York Times*, Oct. 7, 1955, 23, col. 6.

Life, Dec. 26, 1955, 140. Contains portrait.

Cogley, J. The Enthusiasts, in *Commonweal*, LXVI (1957), 448.

Phibbs, R. C. Introductory Summary of the Basic Elements in the Thought of H. Richard Niebuhr, in *Brethren Life and Thought*, V (1960), 38-55.

Needed: New Symbols, in *Time*, LXXV (March 14, 1960), 48, 50. Portrait.

Beker, E. J. The Sovereignty of God in the Thought of H. Richard Niebuhr, in *Nederlands Theologisch Tijdschrift*, XV (1960), No. 2, 108-30.

Brinkerink, J. Richard Niebuhr, een te weinig bekend theoloog, in *Wendig*, XVI (1961), 470-82.

Williams, Daniel Day. Tradition and Experience in American Theology, in *Religion in American Life*, Vol. I: *The Shaping of American Religion*, ed. James Ward Smith and A. Leland Jamison. Princeton, N.J.: Princeton University Press, 1961. 468-71.

Cobb, John Boswell. *Living Options in Protestant Theology: A Survey of Methods*. Philadelphia: Westminster Press [1962]. Especially pp. 284-311.

Ramsey, Paul. *Nine Modern Moralists*. Englewood Cliffs, New Jersey: Prentice-Hall, [1962]. A Spectrum Book, S-36. Especially pp. 149-79.

Hamilton, K. M. Trinitarianism Disregarded; the Theological Orientation of H. Richard Niebuhr and Cyril C. Richardson, in *Encounter*, XXIII (1962), 343-52.

Culver, E. T. Earl Lectures: H. R. Niebuhr, in *Christian Century*, LXXIX (1962), 403, 405.

Berg, J. van den. Tussen Troeltsch en Barth, in *Gereformeerd Theologisch Tijdschrift*, LXIII (1963), 161-75.

H. Richard Niebuhr (1894-1962), in *Christianity and Crisis*, XXIII (Nov. 25, 1963).

    Contains: A Personal and Theological Memoir, by Daniel Day Williams, 209-13; H. Richard Niebuhr's Place in American Thought, by Sydney E. Ahlstrom, 213-17; A Decisive Influence on Protestant Ethics, by Joseph L. Allen, 217-19.

Macquarrie, John. *Twentieth-century Religious Thought; the Frontiers of Philosophy and Theology, 1900-1960.* New York: Harper & Row, 1963. Especially pp. 344-48.

Cauthen, Kenneth. An Introduction to the Theology of H. Richard Niebuhr, in *Canadian Journal of Theology,* X (1964), No. 1, 4-14.

DOCTORAL DISSERTATIONS

The Problem of Religious Knowledge in the Thought of Albrecht Ritschl, William James, and H. Richard Niebuhr, by Russell T. Blackwood, (Columbia University, 1957), Ann Arbor, Mich.: University Microfilms.

Methodology and Christology in H. Richard Niebuhr, by Lonnie Dean Kliever, (Duke University, 1963), Ann Arbor, Mich.: University Microfilms.

Social Norms and Protestant Ethics: The Ethical Views of Reinhold Niebuhr and H. Richard Niebuhr, by Donald Edward Damhorst, (St. Louis University, 1963), Ann Arbor, Mich.: University Microfilms.

UNPUBLISHED MASTER'S THESIS

The Doctrine of the Church in the Work of Nels Ferré and H. R. Niebuhr as a Theological Basis for Adult Education in the Church, by June Eileen Wenger, Columbia University, 1960.

DEATH OF H. R. NIEBUHR

H. R. Niebuhr Dies; Yale Theologian. *New Haven Register,* July 5, 1962, pp. 1-2.

Niebuhr, (Rev. Dr.) H. Richard. Dies, 67. *New York Times,* July 6, 1962, p. 25.

Remembered Mentor, in *Christian Century,* LXXIX (July 25, 1962), 905.

In Memoriam H. Richard Niebuhr (Selections from addresses by Charles Taylor and Charles Forman, October 3, 1962), in *Yale Divinity News,* LX (Nov., 1962), 8-13.

Obituary, by James Gustafson, in *American Sociological Review,* XXVIII (Feb., 1963), 135.

H. Richard Niebuhr—He Spoke as a Servant, by Sydney E. Ahlstrom, in *Dialog,* II (Winter, 1963), 8-9.

Memorial Minute for H. Richard Niebuhr, by James M. Gustafson, in *Program and Reports, 24th Biennial Meeting A.A.T.S.,* June 10-12, 1964. Southwestern Baptist Theological Seminary and Brite Divinity School, Fort Worth, Texas, pp. 17-8.

INDEX

(*References to the writings of H. Richard Niebuhr in this volume are listed by title under his name.*)

Abstract values (*see also* Value), 129-30, 152, 159
Absolutheit des Christentums und die Religionsgeschichte (Troeltsch), 57
Academic tradition in 19th c. theology, 10-12, 16-40
Action for Unity (Watson), 214 n., 222 n.
Actualism, 51, 52
Against Heresies (Irenaeus), 252 n., 266 n.
Agape and *Eros* (*see also* Love), 146-47
Agnosticism, 48, 54, 60, 154-55
Alienation, self-, 180-81, 200
Allport, Gordon, 212 n., 214, 214 n.
American: mind, 269; religious history, Niebuhr's interpretation of, 270-72
American Dilemma, An (Myrdal), 207, 207 n., 212
Analogy, 20, 51, 82, 83, 102, 250, 256
Analogia: fidei, 52, 86; *relationis*, 52
Anselm, St., 49, 254, 255, 262
Apologetics (*see also* Communication), 13
A priori, religious, 33, 54-55, 60
Aquinas, Thomas, 250
Arché and *logos*, 252
Aristotle, 175, 177, 179, 181, 184-86, 197, 199, 227 n., 251-252
Aseity, 50, 84, 102
Asymmetric relation of God to man, 261-62
Augustine, St., 6, 123 n., 167, 171 72, 180, 201, 262, 272
Aulén, Gustaf, 96, 96 n., 97
Awakening, Great, 277-78

Baillie, John, 44 n., 106
Balthasar, H. U. von, 40, 44 n.
Barth, Karl, xii, 10, 11 n., 78 n., 123 n., 149 n., 173; early works and viewpoint, 16, 29; and Schleiermacher, 39-40, 42-43, 78; revelation and theological method, 40-53; and Brunner, 43-44, 44 n., 49 n.; realism of, 46-47; doctrine of analogy of, 51; christocentrism of, 51, 51 n.; actualism of, 51-52; and Troeltsch, 53, 59-60, 64; Niebuhr and Troeltsch, 64; Niebuhr and Schleiermacher, 78; and Niebuhr, 86-87, 92, 101-3; and Niebuhr on Trinity, 101; on God's personhood, 102-3; Tillich and Niebuhr on God as person, 103; tendency to epistemological monophysitism, 106, 111.
Bazaar of Heraclides (Nestorius), 252
Beach, Waldo, v., xiii, 168 n., 205
Belief, 237-42; and apprehension, 226-27; and cognition, 226-27; and ontology, 237-38; nature of, 239-42; as unifying image, 239, 241, as commitment, act of will, 240; commitment and image, 241-42

Believer, situation of the, 225-244
Benedict, Ruth, 210 n.
Being: and value, 73, 76, 99, 141, 159, 161, 181, 183, 187-188, 200-1, 203; and goodness, 83, 201; as process, 182; order of, and order of knowledge, 71, 73, 76
Beings, relation between, 184-91
Bennett, John C., 124, 124 n., 130
Berry, Brewton, 207 n.
Bergson, Henri, 180, 181
Biblical: criticism, 23, 23 n., 24-25; exegesis and theology, 102; ethics, 140
Binitarian, 100 n.
Bonhoeffer, D., 137 n.
Boulding, Kenneth, 134 n.
Bradford, William, 275 n.
Brunner, Emil, 166 n.; and Barth, 43, 44, 44 n., 49 n.; ethics of creation, 168
Bultmann, Rudolf, xii, 51 n.; and Troeltsch, 62-64; his epistemological monophysitism, 106, 111; on Jesus' messianic consciousness, 110
Buber, Martin, 11, 14, 90, 260
Bushnell, Horace, 123, 278
Butterfield, Herbert, 172 n., 273 n.

Calvin, John, 123 n., 246, 272
Category, 174-78; Niebuhr interprets value as, 177-78; existence and value as, 202; origin of, in self-relatedness, 202-3
Catholic (*see* Roman Catholic)
Characteristics of the American Negro (ed. Klineberg), 210 n.
Christ (*see* Jesus Christ)
Christliche Dogmatik im Entwurf (Barth), 41 n., 45-47, 45 n., 46 n., 47 n., 53 n.
Christocentric: liberalism, 28, 31, 38, 51, 51 n., 63, 64, 78; theology, 38, 63; theology of Barth, 51, 51 n.; theology of Niebuhr, 77-78, 95-96
Christology, 104-16, 257; and Chalcedon, 104-5; and two natures, two histories, 104; of Schleiermacher and Ritschl, 112; inferential method in, 112-13; Niebuhr's moral approach to, 114-16
Christus Victor (Aulén), 96 n.
Christian Discourses (Kierkegaard), 167, 167 n.
Christian Doctrine of Creation and Redemption, The (Brunner), 168
Christian Faith, The (Schleiermacher), 37 n., 38 n.
Christian Hope and the Task of the Church (Evanston Assembly), 209 n., 212 n., 220 n.
Christian Social Ethics (Rasmussen), 125 n.
Christian Thought (Troeltsch), 57 n., 58 n., 59 n.
Christian Values and Economic Life (Bennett *et al*), 124 n.
Christian Way in Race Relations, The (ed. Nelson), 216 n.
Christianity: essence of, 26-28;

308

312

314

Revised October, 1965

hARPER ✦ CORChBOOKS

HUMANITIES AND SOCIAL SCIENCES

American Studies: General

THOMAS C. COCHRAN: The Inner Revolution: *Essays on the Social Sciences in History*   TB/1140

EDWARD S. CORWIN: American Constitutional History. *Essays edited by Alpheus T. Mason and Gerald Garvey*   TB/1136

A. HUNTER DUPREE: Science in the Federal Government: *A History of Policies and Activities to 1940*   TB/573

OSCAR HANDLIN, Ed.: This Was America: *As Recorded by European Travelers in the Eighteenth, Nineteenth and Twentieth Centuries. Illus.*   TB/1119

MARCUS LEE HANSEN: The Atlantic Migration: 1607-1860. *Edited by Arthur M. Schlesinger; Introduction by Oscar Handlin*   TB/1052

MARCUS LEE HANSEN: The Immigrant in American History. *Edited with a Foreword by Arthur M. Schlesinger*   TB/1120

JOHN HIGHAM, Ed.: The Reconstruction of American History   TB/1068

ROBERT H. JACKSON: The Supreme Court in the American System of Government   TB/1106

JOHN F. KENNEDY: A Nation of Immigrants. *Illus. Revised and Enlarged. Introduction by Robert F. Kennedy*   TB/1118

RALPH BARTON PERRY: Puritanism and Democracy   TB/1138

ARNOLD ROSE: The Negro in America: *The Condensed Version of Gunnar Myrdal's An American Dilemma*   TB/3048

MAURICE R. STEIN: The Eclipse of Community: *An Interpretation of American Studies*   TB/1128

W. LLOYD WARNER and Associates: Democracy in Jonesville: *A Study in Quality and Inequality* ‖   TB/1129

W. LLOYD WARNER: Social Class in America: *The Evaluation of Status*   TB/1013

American Studies: Colonial

BERNARD BAILYN, Ed.: The Apologia of Robert Keayne: *Self-Portrait of a Puritan Merchant*   TB/1201

BERNARD BAILYN: The New England Merchants in the Seventeenth Century   TB/1149

JOSEPH CHARLES: The Origins of the American Party System   TB/1049

LAWRENCE HENRY GIPSON: The Coming of the Revolution: 1763-1775. † *Illus.*   TB/3007

LEONARD W. LEVY: Freedom of Speech and Press in Early American History: *Legacy of Suppression*   TB/1109

PERRY MILLER: Errand Into the Wilderness   TB/1139

PERRY MILLER & T. H. JOHNSON, Eds.: The Puritans: *A Sourcebook of Their Writings*
Vol. I TB/1093; Vol. II TB/1094

KENNETH B. MURDOCK: Literature and Theology in Colonial New England   TB/99

WALLACE NOTESTEIN: The English People on the Eve of Colonization: 1603-1630. † *Illus.*   TB/3006

LOUIS B. WRIGHT: The Cultural Life of the American Colonies: 1607-1763. † *Illus.*   TB/3005

American Studies: From the Revolution to the Civil War

JOHN R. ALDEN: The American Revolution: 1775-1783. † *Illus.*   TB/3011

RAY A. BILLINGTON: The Far Western Frontier: 1830-1860. † *Illus.*   TB/3012

GEORGE DANGERFIELD: The Awakening of American Nationalism: 1815-1828. † *Illus.*   TB/3061

CLEMENT EATON: The Freedom-of-Thought Struggle in the Old South. *Revised and Enlarged. Illus.*   TB/1150

CLEMENT EATON: The Growth of Southern Civilization: 1790-1860. † *Illus.*   TB/3040

LOUIS FILLER: The Crusade Against Slavery: 1830-1860. † *Illus.*   TB/3029

DIXON RYAN FOX: The Decline of Aristocracy in the Politics of New York: 1801-1840. ‡ *Edited by Robert V. Remini*   TB/3064

FELIX GILBERT: The Beginnings of American Foreign Policy: *To the Farewell Address*   TB/1200

FRANCIS J. GRUND: Aristocracy in America: *Social Class in the Formative Years of the New Nation*   TB/1001

ALEXANDER HAMILTON: The Reports of Alexander Hamilton. ‡ *Edited by Jacob E. Cooke*   TB/3060

DANIEL R. HUNDLEY: Social Relations in Our Southern States. ‡ *Edited by William R. Taylor*   TB/3058

THOMAS JEFFERSON: Notes on the State of Virginia. ‡ *Edited by Thomas P. Abernethy*   TB/3052

BERNARD MAYO: Myths and Men: *Patrick Henry, George Washington, Thomas Jefferson*   TB/1108

JOHN C. MILLER: Alexander Hamilton and the Growth of the New Nation   TB/3057

RICHARD B. MORRIS, Ed.: The Era of the American Revolution   TB/1180

---

† The New American Nation Series, edited by Henry Steele Commager and Richard B. Morris.

‡ American Perspectives series, edited by Bernard Wishy and William E. Leuchtenburg.

* The Rise of Modern Europe series, edited by William L. Langer.

‖ Researches in the Social, Cultural, and Behavioral Sciences, edited by Benjamin Nelson.

§ The Library of Religion and Culture, edited by Benjamin Nelson.

Σ Harper Modern Science Series, edited by James R. Newman.

° Not for sale in Canada.

R. B. NYE: The Cultural Life of the New Nation: 1776–1801. † *Illus.* TB/3026

FRANK THISTLETHWAITE: America and the Atlantic Community: *Anglo-American Aspects, 1790–1850* TB/1107

A. F. TYLER: Freedom's Ferment: *Phases of American Social History from the Revolution to the Outbreak of the Civil War. 31 illus.* TB/1074

GLYNDON G. VAN DEUSEN: The Jacksonian Era: 1828–1848. † *Illus.* TB/3028

LOUIS B. WRIGHT: Culture on the Moving Frontier TB/1053

American Studies: Since the Civil War

RAY STANNARD BAKER: Following the Color Line: *American Negro Citizenship in Progressive Era. ‡ Illus. Edited by Dewey W. Grantham, Jr.* TB/3053

RANDOLPH S. BOURNE: War and the Intellectuals: *Collected Essays, 1915–1919. ‡ Edited by Carl Resek* TB/3043

A. RUSSELL BUCHANAN: The United States and World War II. † *Illus.* Vol. I TB/3044; Vol. II TB/3045

ABRAHAM CAHAN: The Rise of David Levinsky: *a documentary novel of social mobility in early twentieth century America. Intro. by John Higham* TB/1028

THOMAS C. COCHRAN: The American Business System: *A Historical Perspective, 1900–1955* TB/1080

THOMAS C. COCHRAN & WILLIAM MILLER: The Age of Enterprise: *A Social History of Industrial America* TB/1054

FOSTER RHEA DULLES: America's Rise to World Power: *1898–1954. † Illus.* TB/3021

W. A. DUNNING: Essays on the Civil War and Reconstruction. *Introduction by David Donald* TB/1181

W. A. DUNNING: Reconstruction, Political and Economic: *1865–1877* TB/1073

HAROLD U. FAULKNER: Politics, Reform and Expansion: *1890–1900. † Illus.* TB/3020

JOHN D. HICKS: Republican Ascendancy: 1921–1933. † *Illus.* TB/3041

ROBERT HUNTER: Poverty: *Social Conscience in the Progressive Era. ‡ Edited by Peter d'A. Jones* TB/3065

HELEN HUNT JACKSON: A Century of Dishonor: *The Early Crusade for Indian Reform. ‡ Edited by Andrew F. Rolle* TB/3063

ALBERT D. KIRWAN: Revolt of the Rednecks: *Mississippi Politics, 1876–1925* TB/1199

WILLIAM L. LANGER & S. EVERETT GLEASON: The Challenge to Isolation: *The World Crisis of 1937–1940 and American Foreign Policy* Vol. I TB/3054; Vol. II TB/3055

WILLIAM E. LEUCHTENBURG: Franklin D. Roosevelt and the New Deal: 1932–1940. † *Illus.* TB/3025

ARTHUR S. LINK: Woodrow Wilson and the Progressive Era: 1910–1917. † *Illus.* TB/3023

ROBERT GREEN MCCLOSKEY: American Conservatism in the Age of Enterprise: 1865–1910 TB/1137

GEORGE E. MOWRY: The Era of Theodore Roosevelt and the Birth of Modern America: 1900–1912. † *Illus.* TB/3022

RUSSEL B. NYE: Midwestern Progressive Politics: *A Historical Study of its Origins and Development, 1870–1958* TB/1202

WALTER RAUSCHENBUSCH: Christianity and the Social Crisis. ‡ *Edited by Robert D. Cross* TB/3059

WHITELAW REID: After the War: *A Tour of the Southern States, 1865–1866. ‡ Edited by C. Vann Woodward* TB/3066

CHARLES H. SHINN: Mining Camps: *A Study in American Frontier Government. ‡ Edited by Rodman W. Paul* TB/3062

TWELVE SOUTHERNERS: I'll Take My Stand: *The South and the Agrarian Tradition. Intro. by Louis D. Rubin, Jr.; Biographical Essays by Virginia Rock* TB/1072

WALTER E. WEYL: The New Democracy: *An Essay on Certain Political Tendencies in the United States. ‡ Edited by Charles B. Forcey* TB/3042

VERNON LANE WHARTON: The Negro in Mississippi: 1865–1890 TB/1178

Anthropology

JACQUES BARZUN: Race: *A Study in Superstition. Revised Edition* TB/1172

JOSEPH B. CASAGRANDE, Ed.: In the Company of Man: *Twenty Portraits of Anthropological Informants. Illus.* TB/3047

W. E. LE GROS CLARK: The Antecedents of Man: *An Introduction to the Evolution of the Primates.* ° *Illus.* TB/559

CORA DU BOIS: The People of Alor. *New Preface by the author. Illus.* Vol. I TB/1042; Vol. II TB/1043

RAYMOND FIRTH, Ed.: Man and Culture: *An Evaluation of the Work of Bronislaw Malinowski* ‖ ° TB/1133

L. S. B. LEAKEY: Adam's Ancestors: *The Evolution of Man and His Culture. Illus.* TB/1019

ROBERT H. LOWIE: Primitive Society. *Introduction by Fred Eggan* TB/1056

SIR EDWARD TYLOR: The Origins of Culture. *Part I of "Primitive Culture."* § *Introduction by Paul Radin* TB/33

SIR EDWARD TYLOR: Religion in Primitive Culture. *Part II of "Primitive Culture."* § *Introduction by Paul Radin* TB/34

W. LLOYD WARNER: A Black Civilization: *A Study of an Australian Tribe.* ‖ *Illus.* TB/3056

Art and Art History

WALTER LOWRIE: Art in the Early Church. *Revised Edition. 452 illus.* TB/124

EMILE MÂLE: The Gothic Image: *Religious Art in France of the Thirteenth Century.* § *190 illus.* TB/44

MILLARD MEISS: Painting in Florence and Siena after the Black Death: *The Arts, Religion and Society in the Mid-Fourteenth Century. 169 illus.* TB/1148

ERICH NEUMANN: The Archetypal World of Henry Moore. *107 illus.* TB/2020

DORA & ERWIN PANOFSKY: Pandora's Box: *The Changing Aspects of a Mythical Symbol. Revised Edition. Illus.* TB/2021

ERWIN PANOFSKY: Studies in Iconology: *Humanistic Themes in the Art of the Renaissance. 180 illustrations* TB/1077

ALEXANDRE PIANKOFF: The Shrines of Tut-Ankh-Amon. *Edited by N. Rambova. 117 illus.* TB/2011

JEAN SEZNEC: The Survival of the Pagan Gods: *The Mythological Tradition and Its Place in Renaissance Humanism and Art. 108 illustrations* TB/2004

OTTO VON SIMSON: The Gothic Cathedral: *Origins of Gothic Architecture and the Medieval Concept of Order. 58 illus.* TB/2018

HEINRICH ZIMMER: Myth and Symbols in Indian Art and Civilization. *70 illustrations* TB/2005

Business, Economics & Economic History

REINHARD BENDIX: Work and Authority in Industry: *Ideologies of Management in the Course of Industrialization* TB/3035

3

ERNST CASSIRER: The Individual and the Cosmos in Renaissance Philosophy. *Translated with an Introduction by Mario Domandi* TB/1097

FEDERICO CHABOD: Machiavelli and the Renaissance TB/1193

EDWARD P. CHEYNEY: The Dawn of a New Era, 1250-1453. * *Illus.* TB/3002

R. TREVOR DAVIES: The Golden Century of Spain, 1501-1621 ° TB/1194

DESIDERIUS ERASMUS: Christian Humanism and the Reformation: *Selected Writings. Edited and translated by John C. Olin* TB/1166

WALLACE K. FERGUSON et al.: Facets of the Renaissance TB/1098

WALLACE K. FERGUSON et al.: The Renaissance: *Six Essays. Illus.* TB/1084

JOHN NEVILLE FIGGIS: The Divine Right of Kings. *Introduction by G. R. Elton* TB/1191

JOHN NEVILLE FIGGIS: Political Thought from Gerson to Grotius: 1414-1625: *Seven Studies. Introduction by Garrett Mattingly* TB/1032

MYRON P. GILMORE: The World of Humanism, 1453-1517.* *Illus.* TB/3003

FRANCESCO GUICCIARDINI: Maxims and Reflections of a Renaissance Statesman *(Ricordi). Trans. by Mario Domandi. Intro. by Nicolai Rubinstein* TB/1160

J. H. HEXTER: More's Utopia: *The Biography of an Idea* TB/1195

JOHAN HUIZINGA: Erasmus and the Age of Reformation. *Illus.* TB/19

ULRICH VON HUTTEN et al.: On the Eve of the Reformation: *"Letters of Obscure Men." Introduction by Hajo Holborn* TB/1124

PAUL O. KRISTELLER: Renaissance Thought: *The Classic, Scholastic, and Humanist Strains* TB/1048

PAUL O. KRISTELLER: Renaissance Thought II: *Papers on Humanism and the Arts* TB/1163

NICCOLÒ MACHIAVELLI: History of Florence and of the Affairs of Italy: *from the earliest times to the death of Lorenzo the Magnificent. Introduction by Felix Gilbert* TB/1027

ALFRED VON MARTIN: Sociology of the Renaissance. *Introduction by Wallace K. Ferguson* TB/1099

GARRETT MATTINGLY et al.: Renaissance Profiles. *Edited by J. H. Plumb* TB/1162

MILLARD MEISS: Painting in Florence and Siena after the Black Death: *The Arts, Religion and Society in the Mid-Fourteenth Century. 169 illus.* TB/1148

J. E. NEALE: The Age of Catherine de Medici ° TB/1085

ERWIN PANOFSKY: Studies in Iconology: *Humanistic Themes in the Art of the Renaissance. 180 illustrations* TB/1077

J. H. PARRY: The Establishment of the European Hegemony: 1415-1715: *Trade and Exploration in the Age of the Renaissance* TB/1045

J. H. PLUMB: The Italian Renaissance: *A Concise Survey of Its History and Culture* TB/1161

CECIL ROTH: The Jews in the Renaissance. *Illus.* TB/834

GORDON RUPP: Luther's Progress to the Diet of Worms ° TB/120

FERDINAND SCHEVILL: The Medici. *Illus.* TB/1010

FERDINAND SCHEVILL: Medieval and Renaissance Florence. *Illus.* Volume I: *Medieval Florence* TB/1090 Volume II: *The Coming of Humanism and the Age of the Medici* TB/1091

G. M. TREVELYAN: England in the Age of Wycliffe, 1368-1520 ° TB/1112

VESPASIANO: Renaissance Princes, Popes, and Prelates: *The Vespasiano Memoirs: Lives of Illustrious Men of the XVth Century. Introduction by Myron P. Gilmore* TB/1111

History: Modern European

FREDERICK B. ARTZ: Reaction and Revolution, 1815-1832. * *Illus.* TB/3034

MAX BELOFF: The Age of Absolutism, 1660-1815 TB/1062

ROBERT C. BINKLEY: Realism and Nationalism, 1852-1871. * *Illus.* TB/3038

ASA BRIGGS: The Making of Modern England, 1784-1867: *The Age of Improvement* ° TB/1203

CRANE BRINTON: A Decade of Revolution, 1789-1799. * *Illus.* TB/3018

J. BRONOWSKI & BRUCE MAZLISH: The Western Intellectual Tradition: *From Leonardo to Hegel* TB/3001

GEOFFREY BRUUN: Europe and the French Imperium, 1799-1814. * *Illus.* TB/3033

ALAN BULLOCK: Hitler, A Study in Tyranny. ° *Illus.* TB/1123

E. H. CARR: The Twenty Years' Crisis, 1919-1939: *An Introduction to the Study of International Relations* ° TB/1122

GORDON A. CRAIG: From Bismarck to Adenauer: *Aspects of German Statecraft. Revised Edition* TB/1171

WALTER L. DORN: Competition for Empire, 1740-1763. * *Illus.* TB/3032

CARL J. FRIEDRICH: The Age of the Baroque, 1610-1660. * *Illus.* TB/3004

RENÉ FUELOEP-MILLER: The Mind and Face of Bolshevism: *An Examination of Cultural Life in Soviet Russia. New Epilogue by the Author* TB/1188

M. DOROTHY GEORGE: London Life in the Eighteenth Century TB/1182

LEO GERSHOY: From Despotism to Revolution, 1763-1789. * *Illus.* TB/3017

C. C. GILLISPIE: Genesis and Geology: *The Decades before Darwin* § TB/51

ALBERT GOODWIN: The French Revolution TB/1064

ALBERT GUERARD: France in the Classical Age: *The Life and Death of an Ideal* TB/1183

CARLTON J. H. HAYES: A Generation of Materialism, 1871-1900. * *Illus.* TB/3039

J. H. HEXTER: Reappraisals in History: *New Views on History and Society in Early Modern Europe* TB/1100

A. R. HUMPHREYS: The Augustan World: *Society, Thought, and Letters in Eighteenth Century England* TB/1105

ALDOUS HUXLEY: The Devils of Loudun: *A Study in the Psychology of Power Politics and Mystical Religion in the France of Cardinal Richelieu* § ° TB/60

DAN N. JACOBS, Ed.: The New Communist Manifesto and Related Documents. *Third edition, revised* TB/1078

HANS KOHN: The Mind of Germany: *The Education of a Nation* TB/1204

HANS KOHN, Ed.: The Mind of Modern Russia: *Historical and Political Thought of Russia's Great Age* TB/1065

KINGSLEY MARTIN: French Liberal Thought in the Eighteenth Century: *A Study of Political Ideas from Bayle to Condorcet* TB/1114

SIR LEWIS NAMIER: Personalities and Powers: *Selected Essays* TB/1186

SIR LEWIS NAMIER: Vanished Supremacies: *Essays on European History, 1812-1918* ° TB/1088

JOHN U. NEF: Western Civilization Since the Renaissance: *Peace, War, Industry, and the Arts* TB/1113

FREDERICK L. NUSSBAUM: The Triumph of Science and Reason, 1660-1685. * *Illus.* TB/3009

JOHN PLAMENATZ: German Marxism and Russian Communism. ° *New Preface by the Author* TB/1189

RAYMOND W. POSTGATE, Ed.: Revolution from 1789 to 1906: *Selected Documents*　TB/1063

PENFIELD ROBERTS: The Quest for Security, 1715-1740. * *Illus.*　TB/3016

PRISCILLA ROBERTSON: Revolutions of 1848: *A Social History*　TB/1025

ALBERT SOREL: Europe Under the Old Regime. *Translated by Francis H. Herrick*　TB/1121

N. N. SUKHANOV: The Russian Revolution, 1917: *Eyewitness Account. Edited by Joel Carmichael*
Vol. I　TB/1066;　Vol. II　TB/1067

A. J. P. TAYLOR: The Habsburg Monarch, 1809-1918: *A History of the Austrian Empire and Austria-Hungary* °　TB/1187

JOHN B. WOLF: The Emergence of the Great Powers, 1685-1715. * *Illus.*　TB/3010

JOHN B. WOLF: France: 1814-1919: *The Rise of a Liberal-Democratic Society*　TB/3019

Intellectual History

HERSCHEL BAKER: The Image of Man: *A Study of the Idea of Human Dignity in Classical Antiquity, the Middle Ages, and the Renaissance*　TB/1047

R. R. BOLGAR: The Classical Heritage and Its Beneficiaries: *From the Carolingian Age to the End of the Renaissance*　TB/1125

J. BRONOWSKI & BRUCE MAZLISH: The Western Intellectual Tradition: *From Leonardo to Hegel*　TB/3001

ERNST CASSIRER: The Individual and the Cosmos in Renaissance Philosophy. *Translated with an Introduction by Mario Domandi*　TB/1097

NORMAN COHN: The Pursuit of the Millennium: *Revolutionary Messianism in medieval and Reformation Europe and its bearing on modern Leftist and Rightist totalitarian movements*　TB/1037

G. RACHEL LEVY: Religious Conceptions of the Stone Age and Their Influence upon European Thought. *Illus. Introduction by Henri Frankfort*　TB/106

ARTHUR O. LOVEJOY: The Great Chain of Being: *A Study of the History of an Idea*　TB/1009

MILTON C. NAHM: Genius and Creativity: *An Essay in the History of Ideas*　TB/1196

ROBERT PAYNE: Hubris: *A Study of Pride. Foreword by Sir Herbert Read*　TB/1031

RALPH BARTON PERRY: The Thought and Character of William James: *Briefer Version*　TB/1156

BRUNO SNELL: The Discovery of the Mind: *The Greek Origins of European Thought*　TB/1018

PAGET TOYNBEE: Dante Alighieri: *His Life and Works. Introduction by Charles S. Singleton*　TB/1206

ERNEST LEE TUVESON: Millennium and Utopia: *A Study in the Background of the Idea of Progress.* | *New Preface by the Author*　TB/1134

PAUL VALÉRY: The Outlook for Intelligence　TB/2016

PHILIP P. WIENER: Evolution and the Founders of Pragmatism. *Foreword by John Dewey*　TB/1212

Literature, Poetry, The Novel & Criticism

JAMES BAIRD: Ishmael: *The Art of Melville in the Contexts of International Primitivism*　TB/1023

JACQUES BARZUN: The House of Intellect　TB/1051

W. J. BATE: From Classic to Romantic: *Premises of Taste in Eighteenth Century England*　TB/1036

RACHEL BESPALOFF: On the Iliad　TB/2006

R. P. BLACKMUR et al.: Lectures in Criticism. *Introduction by Huntington Cairns*　TB/2003

RANDOLPH S. BOURNE: War and the Intellectuals: *Collected Essays, 1915-1919. ‡ Edited by Carl Resek*　TB/3043

ABRAHAM CAHAN: The Rise of David Levinsky: *a documentary novel of social mobility in early twentieth century America. Introduction by John Higham*　TB/1028

ERNST R. CURTIUS: European Literature and the Latin Middle Ages　TB/2015

GEORGE ELIOT: Daniel Deronda: *a novel. Introduction by F. R. Leavis*　TB/1039

ETIENNE GILSON: Dante and Philosophy　TB/1089

ALFRED HARBAGE: As They Liked It: *A Study of Shakespeare's Moral Artistry*　TB/1035

STANLEY R. HOPPER, Ed.: Spiritual Problems in Contemporary Literature §　TB/21

A. R. HUMPHREYS: The Augustan World: *Society, Thought and Letters in Eighteenth Century England* °　TB/1105

ALDOUS HUXLEY: Antic Hay & The Gioconda Smile. ° *Introduction by Martin Green*　TB/3503

ALDOUS HUXLEY: Brave New World & Brave New World Revisited. ° *Introduction by Martin Green*　TB/3501

HENRY JAMES: Roderick Hudson: *a novel. Introduction by Leon Edel*　TB/1016

HENRY JAMES: The Tragic Muse: *a novel. Introduction by Leon Edel*　TB/1017

ARNOLD KETTLE: An Introduction to the English Novel.
Volume I: *Defoe to George Eliot*　TB/1011
Volume II: *Henry James to the Present*　TB/1012

ROGER SHERMAN LOOMIS: The Development of Arthurian Romance　TB/1167

JOHN STUART MILL: On Bentham and Coleridge. *Introduction by F. R. Leavis*　TB/1070

PERRY MILLER & T. H. JOHNSON, Editors: The Puritans: *A Sourcebook of Their Writings*
Vol. I　TB/1093;　Vol. II　TB/1094

KENNETH B. MURDOCK: Literature and Theology in Colonial New England　TB/99

SAMUEL PEPYS: The Diary of Samuel Pepys. ° *Edited by O. F. Morshead. Illus. by Ernest Shepard*　TB/1007

ST.-JOHN PERSE: Seamarks　TB/2002

GEORGE SANTAYANA: Interpretations of Poetry and Religion §　TB/9

C. P. SNOW: Time of Hope: *a novel*　TB/1040

HEINRICH STRAUMANN: American Literature in the Twentieth Century. *Third Edition, Revised*　TB/1168

PAGET TOYNBEE: Dante Alighieri: *His Life and Works. Introduction by Charles S. Singleton*　TB/1206

DOROTHY VAN GHENT: The English Novel: *Form and Function*　TB/1050

E. B. WHITE: One Man's Meat. *Introduction by Walter Blair*　TB/3505

MORTON DAUWEN ZABEL, Editor: Literary Opinion in America　Vol. I　TB/3013; Vol. II　TB/3014

Myth, Symbol & Folklore

JOSEPH CAMPBELL, Editor: Pagan and Christian Mysteries *Illus.*　TB/2013

MIRCEA ELIADE: Cosmos and History: *The Myth of the Eternal Return* §　TB/2050

C. G. JUNG & C. KERÉNYI: Essays on a Science of Mythology: *The Myths of the Divine Child and the Divine Maiden*　TB/2014

DORA & ERWIN PANOFSKY: Pandora's Box: *The Changing Aspects of a Mythical Symbol. Revised Edition. Illus.*　TB/2021

ERWIN PANOFSKY: Studies in Iconology: *Humanistic Themes in the Art of the Renaissance. 180 illustrations*　TB/1077

JEAN SEZNEC: The Survival of the Pagan Gods: *The Mythological Tradition and its Place in Renaissance Humanism and Art. 108 illustrations* TB/2004

HELLMUT WILHELM: Change: *Eight Lectures on the I Ching* TB/2019

HEINRICH ZIMMER: Myths and Symbols in Indian Art and Civilization. *70 illustrations* TB/2005

Philosophy

G. E. M. ANSCOMBE: An Introduction to Wittgenstein's Tractatus. *Second edition, Revised.* ° TB/1210

HENRI BERGSON: Time and Free Will: *An Essay on the Immediate Data of Consciousness* ° TB/1021

H. J. BLACKHAM: Six Existentialist Thinkers: *Kierkegaard, Nietzsche, Jaspers, Marcel, Heidegger, Sartre* ° TB/1002

CRANE BRINTON: Nietzsche. *New Preface and Epilogue by the Author* TB/1197

ERNST CASSIRER: The Individual and the Cosmos in Renaissance Philosophy. *Translated with an Introduction by Mario Domandi* TB/1097

ERNST CASSIRER: Rousseau, Kant and Goethe. *Introduction by Peter Gay* TB/1092

FREDERICK COPLESTON: Medieval Philosophy ° TB/376

F. M. CORNFORD: Principium Sapientiae: *A Study of the Origins of Greek Philosophical Thought. Edited by W. K. C. Guthrie* TB/1213

F. M. CORNFORD: From Religion to Philosophy: *A Study in the Origins of Western Speculation* § TB/20

WILFRID DESAN: The Tragic Finale: *An Essay on the Philosophy of Jean-Paul Sartre* TB/1030

PAUL FRIEDLÄNDER: Plato: *An Introduction* TB/2017

ÉTIENNE GILSON: Dante and Philosophy TB/1089

WILLIAM CHASE GREENE: Moira: *Fate, Good, and Evil in Greek Thought* TB/1104

W. K. C. GUTHRIE: The Greek Philosophers: *From Thales to Aristotle* ° TB/1008

F. H. HEINEMANN: Existentialism and the Modern Predicament TB/28

EDMUND HUSSERL: Phenomenology and the Crisis of Philosophy. *Translated with an Introduction by Quentin Lauer* TB/1170

IMMANUEL KANT: The Doctrine of Virtue, *being Part II of The Metaphysic of Morals. Translated with Notes and Introduction by Mary J. Gregor. Foreword by H. J. Paton* TB/110

IMMANUEL KANT: Groundwork of the Metaphysic of Morals. *Translated and analyzed by H. J. Paton* TB/1159

IMMANUEL KANT: Lectures on Ethics. § *Introduction by Lewis W. Beck* TB/105

QUENTIN LAUER: Phenomenology: *Its Genesis and Prospect* TB/1169

GABRIEL MARCEL: Being and Having. *Introduction by James Collins* TB/310

GEORGE A. MORGAN: What Nietzsche Means TB/1198

MICHAEL POLANYI: Personal Knowledge: *Towards a Post-Critical Philosophy* TB/1158

WILLARD VAN ORMAN QUINE: Elementary Logic. *Revised Edition* TB/577

WILLARD VAN ORMAN QUINE: From a Logical Point of View: *Logico-Philosophical Essays* TB/566

BERTRAND RUSSELL et al.: The Philosophy of Bertrand Russell. *Edited by Paul Arthur Schilpp*
Vol. I TB/1095; Vol. II TB/1096

L. S. STEBBING: A Modern Introduction to Logic TB/538

ALFRED NORTH WHITEHEAD: Process and Reality: *An Essay in Cosmology* TB/1033

PHILIP P. WIENER: Evolution and the Founders of Pragmatism. *Foreword by John Dewey* TB/1212

WILHELM WINDELBAND: A History of Philosophy
Vol. I: *Greek, Roman, Medieval* TB/38
Vol. II: *Renaissance, Enlightenment, Modern* TB/39

LUDWIG WITTGENSTEIN: The Blue and Brown Books ° TB/1211

Political Science & Government

JEREMY BENTHAM: The Handbook of Political Fallacies: *Introduction by Crane Brinton* TB/1069

KENNETH E. BOULDING: Conflict and Defense: *A General Theory* TB/3024

CRANE BRINTON: English Political Thought in the Nineteenth Century TB/1071

EDWARD S. CORWIN: American Constitutional History: *Essays edited by Alpheus T. Mason and Gerald Garvey* TB/1136

ROBERT DAHL & CHARLES E. LINDBLOM: Politics, Economics, and Welfare: *Planning and Politico-Economic Systems Resolved into Basic Social Processes* TB/3037

JOHN NEVILLE FIGGIS: The Divine Right of Kings. *Introduction by G. R. Elton* TB/1191

JOHN NEVILLE FIGGIS: Political Thought from Gerson to Grotius: 1414-1625: *Seven Studies. Introduction by Garrett Mattingly* TB/1032

F. L. GANSHOF: Feudalism TB/1058

G. P. GOOCH: English Democratic Ideas in Seventeenth Century TB/1006

J. H. HEXTER: More's Utopia: *The Biography of an Idea. New Epilogue by the Author* TB/1195

ROBERT H. JACKSON: The Supreme Court in the American System of Government TB/1106

DAN N. JACOBS, Ed.: The New Communist Manifesto *and Related Documents* TB/1078

DAN N. JACOBS & HANS BAERWALD, Eds.: Chinese Communism: *Selected Documents* TB/3031

ROBERT GREEN MCCLOSKEY: American Conservatism in the Age of Enterprise, 1865-1910 TB/1137

KINGSLEY MARTIN: French Liberal Thought in the Eighteenth Century: *Political Ideas from Bayle to Condorcet* TB/1114

JOHN STUART MILL: On Bentham and Coleridge. *Introduction by F. R. Leavis* TB/1070

JOHN B. MORRALL: Political Thought in Medieval Times TB/1076

JOHN PLAMENATZ: German Marxism and Russian Communism. ° *New Preface by the Author* TB/1189

KARL R. POPPER: The Open Society and Its Enemies
Vol. I: *The Spell of Plato* TB/1101
Vol. II: *The High Tide of Prophecy: Hegel, Marx, and the Aftermath* TB/1102

HENRI DE SAINT-SIMON: Social Organization, The Science of Man, and Other Writings. *Edited and Translated by Felix Markham* TB/1152

JOSEPH A. SCHUMPETER: Capitalism, Socialism and Democracy TB/3008

CHARLES H. SHINN: Mining Camps: *A Study in American Frontier Government.* ‡ *Edited by Rodman W. Paul* TB/3062

Psychology

ALFRED ADLER: The Individual Psychology of Alfred Adler. *Edited by Heinz L. and Rowena R. Ansbacher* TB/1154

ALFRED ADLER: Problems of Neurosis. *Introduction by Heinz L. Ansbacher* TB/1145

ANTON T. BOISEN: The Exploration of the Inner World: *A Study of Mental Disorder and Religious Experience* TB/87

G. P. FEDOTOV, Ed.: A Treasury of Russian Spirituality TB/303

DAVID KNOWLES: The English Mystical Tradition TB/302

GABRIEL MARCEL: Being and Having. *Introduction by James Collins* TB/310

GABRIEL MARCEL: Homo Viator: *Introduction to a Metaphysic of Hope* TB/397

GUSTAVE WEIGEL, S. J.: Catholic Theology in Dialogue TB/301

Oriental Religions: Far Eastern, Near Eastern

TOR ANDRAE: Mohammed: *The Man and His Faith* TB/62

EDWARD CONZE: Buddhism: *Its Essence and Development.* ° *Foreword by Arthur Waley* TB/58

EDWARD CONZE et al., Editors: Buddhist Texts Through the Ages TB/113

ANANDA COOMARASWAMY: Buddha and the Gospel of Buddhism. *Illus.* TB/119

H. G. CREEL: Confucius and the Chinese Way TB/63

FRANKLIN EDGERTON, Trans. & Ed.: The Bhagavad Gita TB/115

SWAMI NIKHILANANDA, Trans. & Ed.: The Upanishads: *A One-Volume Abridgment* TB/114

HELLMUT WILHELM: Change: *Eight Lectures on the I Ching* TB/2019

Philosophy of Religion

NICOLAS BERDYAEV: The Beginning and the End § TB/14

NICOLAS BERDYAEV: Christian Existentialism: *A Berdyaev Anthology. Ed. by Donald A. Lowrie* TB/130

NICOLAS BERDYAEV: The Destiny of Man TB/61

RUDOLF BULTMANN: History and Eschatology: *The Presence of Eternity* ° TB/91

RUDOLF BULTMANN AND FIVE CRITICS: Kerygma and Myth: *A Theological Debate* TB/80

RUDOLF BULTMANN and KARL KUNDSIN: Form Criticism: *Two Essays on New Testament Research. Translated by Frederick C. Grant* TB/96

MIRCEA ELIADE: The Sacred and the Profane TB/81

LUDWIG FEUERBACH: The Essence of Christianity. § *Introduction by Karl Barth. Foreword by H. Richard Niebuhr* TB/11

ADOLF HARNACK: What is Christianity? § *Introduction by Rudolf Bultmann* TB/17

FRIEDRICH HEGEL: On Christianity: *Early Theological Writings. Edited by Richard Kroner and T. M. Knox* TB/79

KARL HEIM: Christian Faith and Natural Science TB/16

IMMANUEL KANT: Religion Within the Limits of Reason Alone. § *Introduction by Theodore M. Greene and John Silber* TB/67

JOHN MACQUARRIE: An Existentialist Theology: *A Comparison of Heidegger and Bultmann.* ° *Preface by Rudolf Bultmann* TB/125

PAUL RAMSEY, Ed.: Faith and Ethics: *The Theology of H. Richard Niebuhr* TB/129

PIERRE TEILHARD DE CHARDIN: The Phenomenon of Man ° TB/83

Religion, Culture & Society

JOSEPH L. BLAU, Ed.: Cornerstones of Religious Freedom in America: *Selected Basic Documents, Court Decisions and Public Statements. Revised and Enlarged Edition* TB/118

C. C. GILLISPIE: Genesis and Geology: *The Decades before Darwin* § TB/51

KYLE HASELDEN: The Racial Problem in Christian Perspective TB/116

WALTER KAUFMANN, Ed.: Religion from Tolstoy to Camus: *Basic Writings on Religious Truth and Morals. Enlarged Edition* TB/123

JOHN T. MCNEILL: A History of the Cure of Souls TB/126

KENNETH B. MURDOCK: Literature and Theology in Colonial New England TB/99

H. RICHARD NIEBUHR: Christ and Culture TB/3

H. RICHARD NIEBUHR: The Kingdom of God in America TB/49

RALPH BARTON PERRY: Puritanism and Democracy TB/1138

PAUL PFUETZE: Self, Society, Existence: *Human Nature and Dialogue in the Thought of George Herbert Mead and Martin Buber* TB/1059

WALTER RAUSCHENBUSCH: Christianity and the Social Crisis. ‡ *Edited by Robert D. Cross* TB/3059

KURT SAMUELSSON: Religion and Economic Action: *A Critique of Max Weber's The Protestant Ethic and the Spirit of Capitalism.* ‖ ° *Trans. by E. G. French; Ed. with Intro. by D. C. Coleman* TB/1131

ERNST TROELTSCH: The Social Teaching of the Christian Churches ° Vol. I TB/71; Vol. II TB/72

NATURAL SCIENCES AND MATHEMATICS

Biological Sciences

CHARLOTTE AUERBACH: The Science of Genetics Σ TB/568

MARSTON BATES: The Natural History of Mosquitoes. *Illus.* TB/578

A. BELLAIRS: Reptiles: *Life History, Evolution, and Structure. Illus.* TB/520

LUDWIG VON BERTALANFFY: Modern Theories of Development: *An Introduction to Theoretical Biology* TB/554

LUDWIG VON BERTALANFFY: Problems of Life: *An Evaluation of Modern Biological and Scientific Thought* TB/521

HAROLD F. BLUM: Time's Arrow and Evolution TB/555

JOHN TYLER BONNER: The Ideas of Biology. Σ *Illus.* TB/570

A. J. CAIN: Animal Species and their Evolution. *Illus.* TB/519

WALTER B. CANNON: Bodily Changes in Pain, Hunger, Fear and Rage. *Illus.* TB/562

W. E. LE GROS CLARK: The Antecedents of Man: *An Introduction to the Evolution of the Primates.* ° *Illus.* TB/559

W. H. DOWDESWELL: Animal Ecology. *Illus.* TB/543

W. H. DOWDESWELL: The Mechanism of Evolution. *Illus.* TB/527

R. W. GERARD: Unresting Cells. *Illus.* TB/541

DAVID LACK: Darwin's Finches. *Illus.* TB/544

J. E. MORTON: Molluscs: *An Introduction to their Form and Functions. Illus.* TB/529

ADOLF PORTMANN: Animals as Social Beings. ° *Illus.* TB/572

O. W. RICHARDS: The Social Insects. *Illus.* TB/542

P. M. SHEPPARD: Natural Selection and Heredity. *Illus.* TB/528

EDMUND W. SINNOTT: Cell and Psyche: *The Biology of Purpose* TB/546

C. H. WADDINGTON: How Animals Develop. *Illus.* TB/553

Chemistry

J. R. PARTINGTON: A Short History of Chemistry. *Illus.* TB/522

J. READ: A Direct Entry to Organic Chemistry. *Illus.* TB/523

J. READ: Through Alchemy to Chemistry. *Illus.* TB/561

Communication Theory

J. R. PIERCE: Symbols, Signals and Noise: *The Nature and Process of Communication* TB/574

Geography

R. E. COKER: This Great and Wide Sea: *An Introduction to Oceanography and Marine Biology. Illus.* TB/551

F. K. HARE: The Restless Atmosphere TB/560

History of Science

W. DAMPIER, Ed.: Readings in the Literature of Science. *Illus.* TB/512

A. HUNTER DUPREE: Science in the Federal Government: *A History of Policies and Activities to 1940* TB/573

ALEXANDRE KOYRÉ: From the Closed World to the Infinite Universe: *Copernicus, Kepler, Galileo, Newton, etc.* TB/31

A. G. VAN MELSEN: From Atomos to Atom: *A History of the Concept Atom* TB/517

O. NEUGEBAUER: The Exact Sciences in Antiquity TB/552

H. T. PLEDGE: Science Since 1500: *A Short History of Mathematics, Physics, Chemistry and Biology. Illus.* TB/506

HANS THIRRING: Energy for Man: *From Windmills to Nuclear Power* TB/556

WILLIAM LAW WHYTE: Essay on Atomism: *From Democritus to 1960* TB/565

A. WOLF: A History of Science, Technology and Philosophy in the 16th and 17th Centuries. ° *Illus.* Vol. I TB/508; Vol. II TB/509

A. WOLF: A History of Science, Technology, and Philosophy in the Eighteenth Century. ° *Illus.* Vol. I TB/539; Vol. II TB/540

Mathematics

H. DAVENPORT: The Higher Arithmetic: *An Introduction to the Theory of Numbers* TB/526

H. G. FORDER: Geometry: *An Introduction* TB/548

GOTTLOB FREGE: The Foundations of Arithmetic: *A Logico-Mathematical Enquiry* TB/534

S. KÖRNER: The Philosophy of Mathematics: *An Introduction* TB/547

D. E. LITTLEWOOD: Skeleton Key of Mathematics: *A Simple Account of Complex Algebraic Problems* TB/525

GEORGE E. OWEN: Fundamentals of Scientific Mathematics TB/569

WILLARD VAN ORMAN QUINE: Mathematical Logic TB/558

O. G. SUTTON: Mathematics in Action. ° *Foreword by James R. Newman. Illus.* TB/518

FREDERICK WAISMANN: Introduction to Mathematical Thinking. *Foreword by Karl Menger* TB/511

Philosophy of Science

R. B. BRAITHWAITE: Scientific Explanation TB/515

J. BRONOWSKI: Science and Human Values. *Revised and Enlarged Edition* TB/505

ALBERT EINSTEIN et al.: Albert Einstein: Philosopher-Scientist. *Edited by Paul A. Schilpp* Vol. I TB/502 Vol. II TB/503

WERNER HEISENBERG: Physics and Philosophy: *The Revolution in Modern Science* TB/549

JOHN MAYNARD KEYNES: A Treatise on Probability. ° *Introduction by N. R. Hanson* TB/557

KARL R. POPPER: The Logic of Scientific Discovery TB/576

STEPHEN TOULMIN: Foresight and Understanding: *An Enquiry into the Aims of Science. Foreword by Jacques Barzun* TB/564

STEPHEN TOULMIN: The Philosophy of Science: *An Introduction* TB/513

G. J. WHITROW: The Natural Philosophy of Time ° TB/563

Physics and Cosmology

DAVID BOHM: Causality and Chance in Modern Physics. *Foreword by Louis de Broglie* TB/536

P. W. BRIDGMAN: The Nature of Thermodynamics TB/537

P. W. BRIDGMAN: A Sophisticate's Primer of Relativity TB/575

A. C. CROMBIE, Ed.: Turning Point in Physics TB/535

C. V. DURELL: Readable Relativity. *Foreword by Freeman J. Dyson* TB/530

ARTHUR EDDINGTON: Space, Time and Gravitation: *An outline of the General Relativity Theory* TB/510

GEORGE GAMOW: Biography of Physics Σ TB/567

MAX JAMMER: Concepts of Force: *A Study in the Foundation of Dynamics* TB/550

MAX JAMMER: Concepts of Mass *in Classical and Modern Physics* TB/571

MAX JAMMER: Concepts of Space: *The History of Theories of Space in Physics. Foreword by Albert Einstein* TB/533

STEPHEN TOULMIN & JUNE GOODFIELD: The Fabric of the Heavens: *The Development of Astronomy and Dynamics. Illus.* TB/579

EDMUND WHITTAKER: History of the Theories of Aether and Electricity
Volume I: *The Classical Theories* TB/531
Volume II: *The Modern Theories* TB/532

G. J. WHITROW: The Structure and Evolution of the Universe: *An Introduction to Cosmology. Illus.* TB/504

Code to Torchbook Libraries:

TB/1+	: The Cloister Library
TB/301+	: The Cathedral Library
TB/501+	: The Science Library
TB/801+	: The Temple Library
TB/1001+	: The Academy Library
TB/2001+	: The Bollingen Library
TB/3001+	: The University Library